NONPROFIT ENTERPRISE IN THE ARTS

YALE STUDIES ON NONPROFIT ORGANIZATIONS

Program on Non-Profit Organizations
Institution for Social and Policy Studies
Yale University

JOHN G. SIMON, CHAIRMAN
PAUL DiMAGGIO, DIRECTOR

DANIEL C. LEVY
Private Education: Studies in Choice and Public Policy

SUSAN ROSE-ACKERMAN
The Economics of Nonprofit Institutions: Studies in Structure and Policy

PAUL J. DiMAGGIO
Nonprofit Organizations in the Arts: Studies in Mission and Constraint

Other titles to be announced

Nonprofit Enterprise in the Arts

Studies in Mission and Constraint

PAUL J. DiMAGGIO

New York · Oxford
OXFORD UNIVERSITY PRESS
1986

Oxford University Press

Oxford New York Toronto
Delhi Bombay Calcutta Madras Karachi
Petaling Jaya Singapore Hong Kong Tokyo
Nairobi Dar es Salaam Cape Town
Melbourne Auckland

and associated companies in
Beirut Berlin Ibadan Nicosia

Published by Oxford University Press, Inc.,
200 Madison Avenue, New York, New York 10016

Oxford is a registered trademark of Oxford University Press

Library of Congress Cataloging-in-Publication Data
Nonprofit enterprise in the arts.
Includes index.
1. Arts—United States—Finance—Addresses, essays, lectures.
2. Corporations, Nonprofit—United States—Finance—Addresses, essays, lectures.
3. Art patronage—United States—Addresses, essays, lectures.
I. DiMaggio, Paul.
NX711.U5N66 1986 700'.68'1 86-670
ISBN 0-19-504063-5

Printing (last digit): 9 8 7 6 5 4 3 2 1
Printed in the United States of America
on acid-free paper

Series Foreword

This volume and its siblings, comprising the Yale Studies on Nonprofit Organizations, were produced by an interdisciplinary research enterprise, the Program on Non-Profit Organizations, located within Yale University's Institution for Social and Policy Studies.[1] The Program had its origins in a series of discussions initiated by the present author in the mid-1970s while serving as president of Yale. These discussions began with a number of Yale colleagues, especially Professor Charles E. Lindblom, Director of the Institution, and Professor John G. Simon of the Law School faculty. We later enlisted a number of other helpful counselors in and out of academic life.

These conversations reflected widespread agreement that there was a serious and somewhat surprising gap in American scholarship. The United States relies more heavily than any other country on the voluntary nonprofit sector to conduct the nation's social, cultural, and economic business—to bring us into the world, to educate and entertain us, even to bury us. Indeed, the United States can be distinguished from all other societies by virtue of the work load it assigns to its "third sector," as compared to business firms or government agencies. Yet this nonprofit universe had been the least well studied, the least well understood aspect of our national life. And the nonprofit institutions themselves were lacking any connective theory of their governance and function. As just one result, public and private bodies were forced to make policy and management decisions, large and small, affecting the nonprofit sector from a position of relative ignorance.

To redress this startling imbalance, and with the initial assistance of the late John D. Rockefeller III (soon joined by a few foundation donors), the Program on Non-Profit Organizations was launched in 1977. It seeks to achieve three principal goals:

[1] The sharp-eyed editors at Oxford University Press requested that we explain the presence of an intrusive hyphen in the word "Non-Profit" in the Program's title, and suggested that the explanation might be of interest to this volume's readers. The explanation is simple: At the Program's inception, it adopted the convention, in wider currency than it is today but even at that time incorrect, of hyphenating "non-profit." Since then the Program has mended its ways wherever the term "nonprofit" is not used as part of the Program's title. But in the Program's title, for reasons both sentimental and pragmatic, the hyphen remains, as a kind of trademark.

1. to build a substantial body of information, analysis, and theory relating to nonprofit organizations;
2. to enlist the energies and enthusiasms of the scholarly community in research and teaching related to the world of nonprofit organizations; and
3. to assist decision makers, in and out of the voluntary sector, to address major policy and management dilemmas confronting the sector.

Toward the first and second of these goals the Program has employed a range of strategies: research grants to senior and junior scholars at Yale and at forty-one other institutions; provision of space and amenities to visiting scholars pursuing their research in the Program's offices; supervision of graduate and professional students working on topics germane to the Program's mission; and a summer graduate fellowship program for students from universities around the country.

The Program's participants represent a wide spectrum of academic disciplines—the social sciences, the humanities, law, medicine, and management. Moreover, they have used a variety of research strategies, ranging from theoretical economic modeling to field studies in African villages. These efforts, supported by fifty foundation, corporate, government, and individual donors to the Program, have gradually generated a mountain of research on virtually every nonprofit species—for example, day-care centers and private foundations, symphony orchestras and wildlife advocacy groups—and on voluntary institutions in twenty other countries. At this writing the Program has published 100 working papers and has sponsored, in whole or in part, research resulting in no fewer than 175 journal articles and book chapters. Thirty-two books have been either published or accepted for publication. Moreover, as the work has progressed and as Program-affiliated scholars (of whom, by now, there have been approximately 150) establish links to one another and to students of the nonprofit sector not associated with the Program, previously isolated researchers are forging themselves into an impressive and lively international network.

The Program has approached the third goal, that of assisting those who confront policy and management dilemmas, in many ways. Researchers have tried to design their projects in a way that would bring these dilemmas to the fore. Program participants have met with literally hundreds of nonprofit organizations, either individually or at conferences, to present and discuss the implications of research being conducted by the Program. Data and analyses have been presented to federal, state, and local legislative and executive branch officials and to journalists from print and electronic media throughout the United States to assist them in their efforts to learn more about the third sector and the problems it faces.

Crucial to the accomplishment of all three goals is the wide sharing of the Program's intellectual output not only with academicians but also with nonprofit practitioners and policy makers. This dissemination task has been an increasing preoccupation of the Program in recent years. More vigorous promotion of its working paper series, cooperation with a variety of nonacademic organizations, the forthcoming publication of a handbook of research on nonprofit organizations, and the establishment of a newsletter (published with increasing regularity for a broad and predominantly non-academic list of subscribers) have all helped to disseminate the Program's research results.

These efforts, however, needed supplementation. Thus, the program's working papers, although circulated relatively widely, have been for the most part drafts rather than finished papers, produced in a humble format that renders them unsuitable for the relative immortality of library shelves. Moreover, many of the publications resulting from the Program's work have never found their way into working paper form. Indeed, the multidisciplinary products of Program-sponsored research have displayed a disconcerting tendency upon publication to fly off to separate disciplinary corners of the scholarly globe, unlikely to be reassembled by any but the most dogged, diligent denizens of the most comprehensive of university libraries.

Sensitive to these problems, the Lilly Endowment made a generous grant to the Program to enable it to overcome this tendency toward centrifugality. The Yale Studies on Nonprofit Organizations represent a particularly important part of this endeavor. Each book features the work of scholars from several disciplines. Each contains a variety of papers, many unpublished, others available only in small-circulation specialized periodicals, on a theme of general interest to readers in many regions of the nonprofit universe. Most of these papers are products of Program-sponsored research, although each volume contains a few other contributions selected in the interest of thematic consistency and breadth.

Thus, the present volume, edited by Paul J. DiMaggio, Associate Professor in the Yale Department of Sociology and School of Organization and Management, and the Executive Director of the Program on Non-Profit Organizations, deals with the arts—with the role, behavior, management, and financing of private nonprofit cultural institutions, in comparison with government and for-profit organizations.

As the reader will already have observed, I do not write this foreword as a stranger. I am very much a member of the family, someone who was present at the creation of the Program of Non-Profit Organizations and continues to chair its Advisory Committee, and who also serves Oxford as Master of University College. What this extended family is doing to advance knowledge about the third sector is a source of considerable satisfaction. From its birth at a luncheon chat more than a decade ago, the Program on Non-Profit Organizations has occupied an increasingly important role as the leading academic center for research on voluntary institutions both in America and abroad. And now the publication by Oxford University Press of this volume and the other Yale Studies on Nonprofit Organizations enlarges the reach of the Yale Program by making its research more widely available within the scholarly community and to the larger world beyond.

London
October 1985

Kingman Brewster

Preface

The primary purpose of this volume is to initiate a process of inquiry into the production and distribution of art in the United States. This effort requires that we raise questions about something that most Americans take for granted: the performance or display of "high culture" (painting, sculpture, symphonic and chamber music, serious theatre, opera, and the dance) under the auspices of nonprofit firms, as opposed to proprietary firms (which dominate other kinds of cultural production in the United States) or government agencies (which sponsor serious artistic activities in much of the rest of the world).

Given the crucial role that nonprofit organizations play in the artistic life of the United States, it is essential that we begin to to understand more thoroughly the implications of their predominance. The articles in this book examine the ways in which it may matter that certain artistic enterprises are organized as nonprofit firms rather than as for-profits or public agencies. They also cast light on some of the special tensions that beset arts management and policy, the ways cultural institutions are changing, or are likely to change, and the policy alternatives that we all face.

A second purpose of this book is the same as that of the series of which it is a part: to make more widely available the products of research sponsored over the past decade by Yale University's Program on Non-Profit Organizations. Eleven of this volume's 15 contributions represent such products, and the research reported on in 2 others was presented in preliminary form at the Program's seminars. Almost half of the papers are published here for the first time; the others have appeared in divers special-interest publications, for the most part of narrow circulation. Few of the papers are likely to be familiar to any but the most dedicated specialists. Because they are all of substantial interest both to students of the arts and to practitioners concerned with the welfare of contemporary cultural institutions, their appearance together provides a new resource for scholars, managers, and policy makers alike.

AKNOWLEDGMENTS

I am indebted to the Lilly Endowment, Inc. for a grant to the Program on Non-Profit Organizations in support of the production of this volume. The

Andrew W. Mellon Foundation contributed greatly to the work, first with a grant to the Program on Non-Profit Organizations in support of my research on the social organization of the arts, and second, with a grant to the Center for Advanced Study in the Behavioral Sciences in partial support of a fellowship year during which much of the manuscript was readied for publication. Sabbatical support from Yale University and institutional support from the Program on Non-Profit Organizations and the Center for Adavnced Study is gratefully acknowledged, as is the administrative aid of Ella Sandor of the Program and the clerical assistance of Leslie Lindsey of the Center. I have been extremely fortunate in colleagues, and whatever virtues this volume possesses undoubtedly reflect the influence of my colleagues at the Yale Program on Non-Profit Organizations and Institution for Social and Policy Studies. Of these three—Daniel Levy, Walter W. Powell, and John G. Simon—deserve special mention for their unstinting intellectual generosity and for all they have taught me about the matters that this volume addresses. (John Simon deserves additional thanks for applying his unparalleled editorial skills to the introduction and to Chapter 4.) More specific debts, of which there are many, are acknowledged in the notes to specific chapters or, alas, are not adequately acknowledged at all.

New Haven, Connecticut P.J.D.
June 1986

Contents

Contributors

Elizabeth A. Cavendish graduated *summa cum laude* from Yale University in 1982, with a major in American Studies, and is currently enrolled in the Yale Law School.

Paul J. DiMaggio is Associate Professor at Yale University in the Institution for Social and Policy Studies, Department of Sociology, School of Organization and Management, and is executive Director of Yale's Program on Non-Profit Organizations. He has written widely on cultural policy and the social organization of the arts in the United States.

Marc R. Freedman is Program Officer at Public/Private Ventures, a Philadelphia nonprofit research and development organization focusing on education and job-training programs for disadvantaged youths. A graduate of the Yale School of Organization and Management, he has been Managing Director of the South Street Dance Company and a consultant in arts administration to the Cleveland Foundation. He is currently at work on a study of mergers in the nonprofit sector.

Rebecca Jo Friedkin is a doctoral candidate in sociology at Yale University. Her research areas include the study of complex organizations and social stratification.

Henry Hansmann is Professor of Law at Yale, where he also undertook his graduate training, receiving both a law degree and a doctorate in economics. He taught Law, Economics, and Public Policy at the University of Pennsylvania from 1975 until 1983, when he returned to Yale to join its law faculty. He is the author of a number of articles on the law and economics of nonprofit and cooperative organizations and is interested in the economic analysis of legal rules and institutions.

Christopher Jencks is Professor of Sociology and Urban Affairs at Northwestern University. He has been investigating recent social trends for some years, with special emphasis on changes in the form and level of individuals' concern for others, and has written widely on social policy.

Stephen I. Kutner is an economist in the Deaprtment of Finance and Economics, School of Management at Boston University. He has prepared research studies on education and arts policy for public and private agencies, including the Museum of Contemporary Art in Los Angeles, the National Institute of Education, and the Ford Foundation. He is currently conducting research on designing voluntary early retirement programs for college and university faculty.

John Michael Montias is Professor of Economics in the Department of Economics and in the Institution for Social and Policy Studies at Yale University. He combines specialization in comparative economics with a strong interest in the economics of the arts, both in contemporary and historical perspective. He is presently engaged in a study of trade in artworks in the seventeenth century in the Netherlands.

Richard A. Peterson is Chair of the Department of Sociology and Anthropology at Vanderbilt University, on leave in 1985–86 as Director of the Vanderbilt-in-England program at Leeds University. Peterson has written widely on the music industry, the arts, and the production of culture. He is currently completing a monograph on the commercialization and commodification of folk culture, focusing on country music.

Walter W. Powell is Associate Professor of Organization and Management and Sociology at Yale University. His most recent book is *Getting Into Print: The Decision Making Process in Scholarly Publishing,* published by the University of Chicago Press along with the paperback edition of *Books: The Culture and Commerce of Publishing* (written with Lewis Coser and Charles Kadushin).

J. Mark Davidson Schuster is Assistant Professor and Assistant Department Head in the Department of Urban Studies and Planning, Massachusetts Institute of Technology. His research has been focused on the analysis of tax incentives and other forms of indirect aid to the arts. He has served as a postdoctoral research fellow in the Research Division of the French Ministry of Culture and is coauthor of *Patrons Despite Themselves: Taxpayers and Arts Policy,* a Twentieth Century Fund Report. Recently, he completed *Supporting the Arts: An International Comparative Study,* which looks at the arts funding policies of eight countries, for the National Endowment for the Arts.

Nancy L. Thompson is an attorney and has been associated with the New York office of LeBoeuf, Lamb, Leiby & MacRae since October 1984. She graduated from Yale Law School in 1983 and subsequently served as a law clerk to the Hon. Herbert J. Stern of the U.S. District Court in New Jersey. Ms. Thompson has had a life-long interest in art and its related policy concerns. She minored in art history at Oberlin College and spent a summer working as a student intern at Oberlin's Allen Memorial Art Museum.

Michael Useem is Director of the Center for Applied Social Science and Associate Dean of the College of Liberal Arts at Boston University. His recent research has focused on the social and political activities of corporations and their managers, and his articles have appeared in *Administrative Science Quarterly, American Sociological Review,* and *Sloan Management Review.* He is the coauthor, with Paul J. DiMaggio, of a report on arts audiences in the United States, published by the National Endowment for the Arts, and he is the author of *The Inner Circle: Large Corporations and the Rise of Business Political Activity in the U.S. and U.K.* (Oxford University Press, 1984).

Vera L. Zolberg is Senior Lecturer in Sociology in the Masters of Arts in Liberal Studies Program of the New School for Social Research Graduate Faculty. She did her doctoral work at the University of Chicago in the sociology of culture and the arts and the sociology of education. She has written and published on the sociology of the avant-garde, bohemianism, cultural institutions, and cultural policy. She is currently writing a book on the rise of the turn-of-the-century avant-garde art movements, as well as doing research on the interactions of markets and the state in cultural policy in the United States and France.

NONPROFIT ENTERPRISE IN THE ARTS

Introduction

PAUL J. DiMAGGIO

I must confess that when I agreed to edit this volume, I feared that its two objectives—addressing a specific set of substantive concerns and increasing the availability of work sponsored by a specific research program (The Yale Program on Non-Profit Organizations)—might at some point collide. If the purpose of a collection of this kind is, to borrow the official language of the National Endowment for the Arts during the Carter years, to increase "access to the best," is it not provincial to rely so heavily on work generated in and around one academic institution?

As plans for the volume developed, my anxieties on this score subsided, for several reasons. First, it became clear that the volume would fill a special niche that reflects the focus of the Program on Non-Profit Organizations and of the Yale environment of which the Program is a part, on the relationship between industrial organization and social purpose. Students of the arts have spent relatively little time addressing this concern; to some extent, therefore, the Program possessed a commanding position in a small oligopolistic market. Second, the volume is intentionally interdisciplinary, including papers by seven sociologists, three economists, two students of management, and two lawyers. This catholicity of approach also reflects one of the special assets of the Yale Program, which is still the only multidisciplinary center for the study of the nonprofit sector. Third, it has been the program's good fortune to be associated with some of the best work in the economics and sociology of cultural organizations. Finally, where a narrow construction of the volume's second purpose would have led to significant omissions or provincialism, I have exercised my editorial prerogative to recruit papers from outside the Program's orbit and to write one entirely new one myself.

This volume, then, is not a study in the sociology of art (although it is certainly influenced by the "production-of-culture" approach developed by Richard Peterson and his colleagues); it is not a reader in cultural economics (although it includes three exceptional expressions of this subdiscipline); nor is it a handbook on arts management (although several of the contributions deal explicitly with management issues and all are relevant to policy and management). Rather it is an effort to bring together some of the best work from several disciplines that focuses on the significance of the nonprofit form for our cultural industries, the ways in which nonprofit cultural enterprise is financed, and the constraints that patterns of funding place on the missions that artists and trustees may wish to pursue.

It is no accident that interest in the industrial organization of the arts has emerged at this point in our history. The past 30 years have been a period of dramatic flux in the organization of U.S. art, music, drama, and dance, as well as in the way we think about them.

For one thing, the postwar years have been marked by growth in the number and scale of high-cultural institutions. Whereas in 1955 the dance and the professional stage were dominated by a few for-profit institutions, opera was monopolized by an even smaller number of nonprofit companies, and community and neighborhood arts organizations barely existed, today each represents a national nonprofit industry consisting of hundreds of firms. The established nonprofit cultural agencies—the art museums and the symphony orchestras—have grown mightily as well. The past 30 years have also witnessed a more modest increase in high-cultural consumption by middle-class Americans, propelled by the supply-side revolution, by heightened levels of higher education, and by the pump-priming activities of private foundations, corporations, and, especially, federal and state government.

These institutional ventures in patronage constitute an important transformation in the sources of arts organizations' revenues since the mid-1950s. This transformation was effected, first, by the Ford Foundation's massive efforts in the performing arts during the late 1950s and the 1960s, then by the creation of the National Endowment for the Arts in 1965 and the state arts agencies shortly before and after 1965, and, more recently, by the increase in corporate arts philanthropy. None of these institutions—the private foundations, governments, or the corporations—played an important aggregate role in nurturing the nonprofit arts before 1955. Now they represent an institutional tripod on which our nation's artistic enterprises rest.

The growth of the nonprofit arts sector and the substitution, to a great extent, of large institutions for private patrons as the source of its contributed revenues, have also changed the way in which arts organizations are administered, the balance of interests within them, and the goals that they pursue. In earlier years, our established nonprofit arts, the symphonies and art museums, were run (the word "managed" may imply more systematic procedures than were often applied) by coalitions of wealthy trustees, artists or (in the case of museums) art historians, and poorly paid administrators. Of this triumvirate, the trustees were ordinarily the dominant partner, at least so long as they could pay the bills. (When financial crisis struck, as it did with special force during the 1930s, and the patrons could no longer meet deficits, our museums and symphonies frequently lurched towards local government funding with outreach or education programs. But their hopeful advances towards the public purse were usually repelled and the shift in mission short-lived.)

In the symphony orchestras, trustees favored decorum and exclusivity, with enough catering to middle-class taste (which they shared) to maintain satisfactory levels of earned income. And despite the foothold of scholarship in the leading museums and the significant educational reforms of such progressive popularizers as John Cotton Dana, most art-museum trustees enjoyed the exclusive character of museums, upon whose staff they relied for advice in building and disposing of their own collections. By contrast, the emerging nonprofit arts, then a few nonprofit theatres and dance companies, lacking powerful boards, usually reflected the intensely held artistic visions of their artist-founders. In any case, what the established and emerging nonprofit arts organizations had in common was that they were casually administered and usually content, in practice, to serve a limited and exclusive public (the former because their trustees preferred it, the latter because their artistic directors had little time to devote to expanding audiences).

The advent of institutional funding has tended to change all that. For obvious reasons, large foundations and public agencies have wanted arts organizations to be able to account for the money they are granted and, increasingly, have required evidence of sound fiscal management in advance of making a grant. Moreover, the major national foundations and the public agencies, believing that art is a good thing and that it should be spread around, have encouraged cultural institutions to evince some interest in expanding their publics and serving their communities. These two imperatives, administrative efficiency and concern for expansion, are united in the preference of institutional funders for supporting cultural organizations that can boast high levels of earned income, as evidence both that they enjoy community support and that they will not become embarrassingly dependent upon their patrons for their survival. Nonprofit arts organizations have responded to such demands with a proliferation of administrative staff in such areas as finance and marketing and with a gradual shift in the balance of internal power from trustees or artists to professional managers.

The ascendancy of the managers, both in the agencies that fund the arts and in cultural organizations themselves, has marked a change in rhetoric, perhaps more marked than changes in practice, from the romantic oratory of the nineteenth century to the rational, businesslike cadence of contemporary arts administration and policy. The creation of our first museums and symphony orchestras represented an antimarket social movement by wealthy entrepreneurs attempting to seal off their own adoptive culture (and with it their own status group) from the ravages of the national market economy that they were themselves instrumental in constructing. The aversion of the romantic artist, and sometimes even the arts manager, to the language of efficiency and the marketplace, and the absence of management courses in most fine-arts, music, and drama schools (at least until the 1960s), reflected the patrons' antimarket ethos as much as it mirrored the ideology of the artists themselves. Indeed, the notion of "the arts" as an institutional entity (as opposed to an abstract realm of spirit) was remote from the experience of most musicians, actors, or curators until well into this century. It only became established once the rise of public funding welded the disparate nonprofit cultural enterprises into a single, increasingly unified constituency.

And if it might seem odd to speak of "the arts" as an economic sector, the notion that they constitute an "industry" would have positively repelled most cultural leaders before the 1960s. With the advent of public funding, however, advocates of government aid lost no time in gathering industry statistics useful for constructing reports on the "economic impact of the arts" and other instruments of political suasion. If many in the established arts still find distasteful the notion of "the arts-service-delivery-system," which attained some currency in government circles during the 1970s, the concept of arts as "industry" now seems increasingly natural and suggestive of an almost corporate gravity of purpose.

The publication of this volume, which treats the "arts industry" as a whole, thus both reflects a gradual transformation in the social conception of cultural enterprise and provides an opportunity to increase our understanding of the trends that it reflects. The links between organizational form and financial sustenance, and between revenues and mission, dominate the first three parts of this volume. In parts IV and V, we return to these questions from different perspectives that focus, first, on nonprofit enterprises in cultural industries that are by-and-large commercial and then on systems of arts support that prevail in Europe.

Part I consists of two papers that set out in stark contrast very different ways of addressing the question, "Why is so much of our artistic production and distribution organized into nonprofit organizations?" Henry Hansmann, who is an economist as well as a legal scholar, approaches this question inductively, arguing that the nonprofit form offers a natural solution to the technical and financial problems of the live performing arts. He begins with Baumol and Bowen's contentions that, because performing-arts organizations cannot boost productivity sufficiently to meet inflationary pressures, they require subsidy to survive. Hansmann demonstrates that, given this imperative, the nonprofit form enables cultural enterprises to maximize a combination of earned and contributed income. His argument is compelling and suggests that if the nonprofit form had not already existed, performing-arts organizations would have had to invent it.[1]

By contrast, my own contribution takes an historical tack, asking what groups were involved in and what interests were served by the creation of the United States' first modern nonprofit art museums and orchestras in the late nineteenth century. If Hansmann's theory is notable for its elegance as an effort to account for a great many phenomena with just a few theoretical propositions, my paper has the virtue, such as it is, of muddying the theoretical waters by treating the social definition of "art," or at least of serious culture, as problematic, historically changing, and a matter over which social groups have contended. Based on a study of nineteenth-century Boston, I argue that the difference between "culture" and mass entertainment was poorly understood until nonprofit cultural organizations were created to clarify and embody that distinction, and that the incorporation of certain kinds of art into these organizations, far from reflecting the working of the marketplace, represented a concerted effort by the champions of such art to avoid the marketplace and its laws.

The difference between these two methods of explaining the prevalence of nonprofit enterprise in the production and distribution of certain kinds of art reflects a common divergence in explanatory style between economists and sociologists. The former tend to regard market efficiency (or the absence thereof) as the driving force in the choice of organizational form, and the latter, especially in their treatment of nonprofit organizations, emphasize institutional patterns and the sometimes noneconomic interests of social collectivities.

The difference also reflects a persistent tension in the arts themselves, however. From the beginning, the governors of our nonprofit cultural institutions have subscribed to purposes—whether popular betterment, the cultivation of the finest expressions of certain forms of art, or the maintenance of social boundaries—that could not be advanced by proprietary entrepreneurs whose gaze focused on the bottom line. Yet, at the same time, U.S. performing-arts organizations have always been enmeshed to some degree in the market, dependent upon admissions or ticket sales for their survival. In the early years, the private patrons who supported the arts traded exclusivity for middle-class dollars in order to keep the orchestras afloat. Throughout our history, artist-entrepreneurs have been forced to compromise their aesthetic convictions or face penury, insolvency, or both. More recently, the preference of institutional funders for an expansion of the audience's social base has run up against the need for earned income, which can best be obtained by subscription sales to conventional arts attenders.

The aesthetic goals of many artists and curators, the status concerns of many trustees, the educational visions of institutional funders, and the realities of the economic marketplace, from which nonprofit arts organizations are buffered but not exempt, frequently clash. The resulting tensions have shaped the development of cultural institutions in the United States to a greater extent than in other countries, where the public sector has played a larger role. In Part II, we consider the financial context within which struggles over mission take place: the sources of nonprofit cultural organizations revenues, the purposes that motivate the arts' various patrons, and the constraints that the search for revenues imposes.

The first chapter in this section, which I have revised and updated to reflect the state of events as this book goes to press, describes the range of players—foundations, government, corporations, and private patrons and the market—in the pluralistic U.S. system of cultural support.[2] The virtues of a system that gives privately governed arts organizations many doors on which to knock are considerable. Yet, at the same time, we see that there are some kinds of organizations, purposes, and definitions of art for which few, if any, doors will open, and for which the marketplace holds no promise. If there is one moral to this brief overview, it is that revenue sources are not fungible and that shifts, for example, from public to private grants, are likely to sacrifice some organizations or purposes in favor of others.

The subsequent chapters in this section focus in more detail on three important forms of financing the arts: corporate philanthropy, grants from private foundations, and direct provision by agencies of government. Michael Useem and Stephen Kutner emphasize two results of their own survey of Massachusetts corporations. The first is that, although many firms, especially larger ones, have "professionalized" their giving operations with clear statements of purpose, the addition of professional staff, and, in some cases, the creation of company foundations, nevertheless chief executive officers still set the tone for even the most professional corporate philanthropies, in many cases maintaining close oversight even over specific grants. Moreover, and in contrast to the pronouncements of government agencies that public grants represent the most significant "seals of approval," corporate philanthropists report that they are much more influenced by the policies of companies like their own than by the gifts of federal or state agencies. In short, company foundations appear to operate in much the same way as private patronage, through networks of CEOs and giving professionals who rally one another to support the arts in general and specific causes in particular.

The next chapter, which I wrote for this volume, deals with the private foundation, a source of contributed income that has, in recent years, received less attention than companies and government, despite the fact that foundations give roughly as much to the arts as corporations or the public sector. One purpose of the chapter is simply to document trends in foundation support for the arts over the past 50 years. A second is to explore a paradox. Private foundations are relatively unconstrained by law or external dependence (for example, they have no stockholders, customers, public donors, or political constituents). Nonetheless, as a group (and admitting some important exceptions) they have been both conservative and rather uniform in their patterns of giving. Although a few of the better known foundations have launched innovative and groundbreaking programs of philanthropy, the vast bulk of foundation arts support goes quietly to established local institutions, often for building or endowment campaigns. The explanation, I suggest, may be found in the social pressures to which trustees of locally oriented foundations are subject and, more generally, in the uncertainty and high cost of information attendant upon cultural philanthropy.

Finally, Elizabeth Cavendish's chapter describes part of this country's one great experiment with direct government cultural provision, the WPA arts projects of the New Deal. Focusing on the Federal Theatre Project in Connecticut, Cavendish reveals a saga that may disappoint both enthusiasts and detractors of public cultural enterprises. In contrast to the better known New York project, the Connecticut Federal Theatre was anything but a hive of subversion; nor was its administration particularly autocratic, wasteful, or inept. Rather the agency was so dependent on popular favor, so vulnerable to politically motivated attacks by conservatives in the press, and so reliant upon the support of community notables that it quickly abandoned much of the social and artistic mission that distinguished it from the popular stage. Although the achievements of the Connecticut Project in children's theatre and in the provision of opportunities for minority actors were substantial, Cavendish's account reminds us that even public enterprises are not exempt from the market's demands when they are embedded in a market society.

The combination of tensions and constraints peculiar to our mixed system of public subsidy, private patronage, and earned income and the impact of these factors on the missions of arts organizations is the topic of Part III. It is never easy to determine what an organization's mission is, especially when, as in the case of nonprofit cultural institutions, there are several legitimate purposes, each of which has its own sets of internal and external constituents. Indeed, nothing is more dangerous than personalizing the arts organization and attributing to it the motives of innovation and artistic virtuosity long associated with romantic notions of art. For one thing, the extent to which the artists (or curators) who work in our nonprofit orchestras, museums, opera companies, or theatres hold to such values is an empirical question. More important, artists are rarely the most powerful or influential participants in cultural organizations, so their own values are rarely the ones that the nonprofit firms attempt to maximize. Be that as it may, the leaders of most cultural organizations do espouse certain aims of an aesthetic and educational character, and most of them are relatively sincere. From the standpoint of policy and practice, then, it is important to consider to what extent the organization's fiscal environment enables it to pursue its core artistic or educational missions and to assess the constraints that the environment imposes.

Richard Peterson's chapter traces the change in the character of management of the more prominent arts organizations from the nineteenth century to the present. The early managers were often flamboyant impresarios who, in many cases, used their positions as the hubs of larger financial empires. Although they often mastered a great many technical details (in touring orchestras, managers literally had to make the trains run on time), their most important skills were social, enabling them to maintain close informal relationships with patrons, trustees, and leading artists. Since the 1960s, writes Peterson, the impresario has been replaced by the professional administrator, versed in financial management, personnel relations, and labor law, less entrepreneurial and more formal in administrative orientation. The rise of the administrator, he argues, is less a product of the growth or increased complexity of the arts organization itself than of the rationalization of the environment in which arts organizations operate—the emergence, to which I have already alluded, of institutional patrons such as corporations and government agencies, which require of grant recipients a degree of bureaucratization and administrative rationality similar to their own. As Peterson points out, the trend towards administrative professionalism has been more marked in the larger and more stable cultural institutions; and even here the extent to and precise ways in which it represents a substantive change, as opposed to an alteration of style or rhetoric, remains to be seen.

Although the trend towards managerial professionalism spans all the arts, the tension between the aesthetic and educational mission has always been especially acute in the art museum. In a paper based on her detailed historical study of the Chicago Art Institute, Vera Zolberg details the conflict between these aims, demonstrating that for all the rhetorical attention education has received in public accounts of museum objectives, it has traditionally garnered fewer resources and received a lower priority than many of the museum's less publicized concerns.

If the traditional museum or symphony orchestra was insular in perspective, with authority closely guarded by trustees and staff, one sign of the increasing rationalization of the environment of nonprofit cultural organizations is the vogue (especially on the part of public and private institutional patrons) for administrative coordination, which requires that arts organizations begin to surrender some of their autonomy. Marc Freedman reports on one of the most widespread instruments of coordination, the performing-arts center, which integrates business functions for a community's primary theatre, music, and dance organizations. As Freedman demonstrates, the rationale for administrative coordination as a means of enhancing efficiency is unassailable. Yet, in practice, coordination rarely if ever works out the way it is planned. The programs of the performing-arts centers he studied in most cases reflected the aspirations of corporate patrons rather than of the members themselves, and they were endemically bogged down in controversy among their constituents, who cooperated reluctantly if at all. Freedman is not prepared to give up on administrative coordination, instead noting the special conditions under which it is likely to succeed. But his study points to the chimerical quality of efficiency as a policy goal in the nonprofit cultural arena, to the inevitable intrusion of politics into administrative matters, and to the danger of importing into the arts models from other sectors (for example, from the social services, where cooperation and coordination have been bywords for at least two decades).

Finally, Nancy Thompson's chapter highlights the legal problems facing museums (and other nonprofit cultural organizations) that attempt explicitly to change their missions. Her comprehensive overview of the statutory and court-made law that bears on the power of trustees to change direction, including the doctrines of *cy pres* and deviation, points both to jurisprudential anomalies and to suggestions for the law's reform.

To this point, we have taken for granted the conventional definition of "the arts" and emphasized organizations—orchestras, theatre companies, art museums—in fields that are predominantly nonprofit in charter. Yet the problems of the traditional nonprofit cultural sectors may be illuminated by investigating the nonprofit regions of predominantly proprietary cultural industries. Organizations that do not hew to the organizational form prevalent in the industry to which they belong are often institutionally invisible. There is a dearth of research on nonprofit fiction presses, nonprofit record companies, or nonprofit magazines (or on proprietary museums or orchestras). Yet such organizations do exist and, by virtue of their very deviance, may tell us much about the limits and possibilities of the nonprofit form.

Part IV addresses nonprofit enterprise in for-profit cultural industries. It begins with a chapter by Walter Powell and Rebecca Jo Friedkin on public television stations, based on case studies of New York's WNET and the Connecticut public television network. The problems of acquiring resources and charting a coherent course that Powell and Friedkin document will be familiar to students of the more conventional nonprofit arts organizations. But in television they are made more complex by the need of public stations to establish that they are different from their commercial counterparts. Ironically, the broad audiences and community support demanded by funders of public stations can be gained most easily if stations offer schedules that resemble those of commercial television. In appealing to viewer preferences, however, public stations run the risk of eliminating the rationale for their very existence.

Similarly, Powell's chapter on the nonprofit university press portrays an island of nonprofit activity in a proprietary sea. Driven by tight university budgets to compete with commercial publishing houses, the university presses must maintain a role that is distinctive enough to justify continuation of subsidies and tax advantages and, at the same time, earn enough money to survive.

Christopher Jencks' essay questions whether the profit motive is consistent with the obligations of the press in a democratic society and offers a modest proposal: Government, he argues, should purchase the newspapers and turn them over to local private nonprofit corporations. Although the particulars of his proposal are ingenious, it is unlikely to set our representatives to penning legislation. Yet it raises important questions about the distribution of the nonprofit form across our cultural landscape, all the more so because, since Jencks wrote his essay, a number of leading magazines of opinion, from the *National Review* to *Harper's* to the *Nation*, have switched from the proprietary to the nonprofit form.

The final part of this volume offers a different kind of comparison, with papers by John Michael Montias and J. Mark Davidson Schuster on, respectively, direct and indirect public support for the arts in Europe. Based on a fastidious mining of often obscure reports and government documents, these papers permit us to assess the degree of U.S. exceptionalism in cultural policy. Montias' study indicates that, with respect to direct aid, it is substantial: No European government gives so little to the arts as does our own. Schuster's chapter indicates that, with respect to indirect support, the United States is less exceptional than we like to think: European governments have a wide array of tax mechanisms, including the charitable deduction, that assist public and nonprofit arts organizations (and in the case of special value added tax rates, some for-profit cultural industries, as well).

Taken together, the contributions to this volume require a reassessment of the role of nonprofit cultural enterprise that has implications for practice and policy as well as for theory. They demonstrate that the lines between nonprofit and proprietary cultural enterprise are neither so rigid as is often supposed nor so natural as we often assume. Many of the kinds of organizations that are now nonprofit (e.g., theatres, orchestras, and art museums) were once proprietary, and many of the industries that are still predominantly proprietary (small presses, magazines of opinion, jazz ensembles) may become increasingly nonprofit. Many legally nonprofit enterprises operate in a manner calculated to optimize revenues or are at least pressed to do so by significant parts of their business environments.

If the boundary between high culture and mass culture is growing less sacrosanct—as a variety of aesthetic developments such as pop art and performance art suggest—so our assumptions about the boundary between proprietary and nonprofit cultural enterprise are also being called into question by the developments in the economic and political realms that the contributions to this volume describe. These latter developments require that nonprofit arts organizations take stock of their missions, decide what business they want to be in, and consider whether their legal charters still match their aspirations. They also suggest that a nonprofit charter, by itself, provides little protection from the rigors of the competitive marketplace. If nonprofit cultural organizations are to continue to provide alternatives to mass media in the face of economic constraint, cultural policy makers must nurture fiscal environments that enable such organizations to pursue missions that are distinctive in substance as well as in rhetoric. Finally, such changes pose the possibility that the ends of cultural policy might be pursued in predominantly for-profit as well as nonprofit cultural industries, either through subsidy of nonprofit oases within those industries or through tax incentives to risk-taking proprietary firms.

Such notions take us beyond the descriptive and analytical intent of the contributions that follow and toward the considerations of value that inevitably inform discussions of policy and mission. If the reader is encouraged to confront such discussions with an awareness that the range of options may be broader than it often appears, this volume will have achieved its purpose.

NOTES

1. I place Hansmann's paper, which is the most technical in this volume, at the fore despite some concern that a casual perusal might frighten off the less technically oriented. Such readers should take heart, first, in the fact that of all the contributions, only two—Hansmann's and Montias's—contain so much as an equation; and, second, in the recognition that both Hansmann and Montias write so clearly as to make their arguments thoroughly accessible to even the most mathematiphobic reader.

2. Lest the reader fear that this volume is dominated by the editor's handiwork, I should point out that my own contributions are restricted to Parts I and II.

1

WHY ARE SO MANY ARTS ORGANIZATIONS NONPROFIT?

1

Nonprofit Enterprise in the Performing Arts

HENRY HANSMANN

The live performing arts—including orchestral music, opera, theatre, and ballet—are today in large part the product of nonprofit institutions. At the same time, there remain some segments of the performing arts, such as Broadway theatre, that are vigorously for-profit (and profitable[1]). Moreover, in the past profit-seeking institutions were apparently the rule rather than the exception in the performing arts; not only serious theatre but even symphony orchestras were commonly proprietary. The dominance of nonprofit institutions in this industry is largely the product of recent decades and is still far from complete.[2]

The existing literature offers no satisfying analysis of the factors that have caused this industry to become so heavily nonprofit, nor does it offer much in the way of a positive or normative perspective on the behavior of the nonprofit firms involved. Perhaps as a consequence, there also exists no well-articulated rationale for public subsidies to the performing arts, much less a coherent set of criteria by which to determine the appropriate amount and structure of such subsidies. This chapter addresses each of these issues.

WHY ARE THE PERFORMING ARTS NONPROFIT?

Donative funding

Nearly all nonprofit performing arts groups depend upon donations for a substantial fraction—commonly between one-third and one-half—of their

From *Bell Journal of Economics* 12, 2: 341–361, copyright © 1981. Reprinted by permission of *The Rand Journal of Economics*. The author acknowledges particular debts to Alvin Klevorick, Richard Nelson, Oliver Williamson, Sidney Winter, and the referees of the *Bell Journal* for helpful comments. Preparation of this paper was supported by a grant from the Program on Non-Profit Organizations at the Institution for Social and Policy Studies, Yale University.

income.[3] Because, for reasons that I shall return to below, an organization that is dependent upon donations must generally be organized as a nonprofit, this pattern of financing provides a preliminary explanation for the predominance of the nonprofit form in this industry. But why are the performing arts so heavily financed by donations?

In other sectors such donative financing for nonprofits sometimes serves as a means for supporting the private production of public goods.[4] Consistent with this notion, it has frequently been argued that the performing arts exhibit substantial beneficial externalities, and that this in turn provides a rationale for both public and private subsidies.[5] For example, prominent cultural institutions bring prestige and tourism to both the city and the nation. Likewise, such institutions may, through indirect processes of cultural stimulus and transmission, ultimately contribute to the cultural experience even of people who do not attend their performances. But the ratio of such external benefits to the private benefits (that is, those enjoyed by members of the audience) for any performance is doubtless rather small—much smaller than the ratio of contributions to ticket receipts for the organizations involved.[6] In any case, it does not appear that such external benefits are a major stimulus for the donations received by performing arts groups. Indeed, the evidence is strongly to the contrary, for it appears that the great bulk of the donations received by performing arts groups comes from people who actually attend the groups' performances, and not from the other members of the public who partake only of the prestige and other external benefits that the performances confer upon them.[7]

Another explanation commonly encountered is that donations are a private subsidy that enables ticket prices to be kept down to levels at which they can be purchased by people who could not otherwise afford them. Undoubtedly this is part of the motivation of at least some who contribute. Yet the vast majority of people who attend the performing arts are quite well-heeled.[8] Surely it is doubtful that the performing arts are organized on a nonprofit basis primarily to provide a vehicle whereby the rich can subsidize the merely prosperous.

The situation, then, is at first appearance rather paradoxical. Here we have a service, essentially private in character, financed partly by donations and partly by revenue from ticket sales. Yet the people who donate are also the people who attend the performances—that is, who buy tickets. Moreover, it appears that performing arts organizations commonly price their tickets so low that they operate well within the inelastic portion of their demand curve, thus failing to maximize receipts from ticket sales.[9] Why do these organizations seek to extract part of their revenues from the audience through donations, rather than simply by raising their ticket prices?

Price Discrimination

These phenomena all become understandable if we simply recognize contributions in the performing arts as a form of voluntary price discrimination.[10]

The considerable costs of organizing, directing, rehearsing, and providing scenery and costumes for a performing arts production are essentially fixed costs, unrelated to audience size. Marginal costs are correspondingly low: once one performance has been staged, the cost of an additional performance is relatively small, and, as long as the theatre is unfilled, the cost of admitting another individual to a given performance is close to zero. At the same time, the potential audience for high-culture live entertainment is limited even in large cities; consequently, for any given production there are typically only a few performances over which to spread the fixed costs—often three or fewer for an orchestral program and only several times that for opera, ballet, and many theatrical productions. Thus, fixed costs represent a large fraction of total costs for each production.[11]

The result is that if ticket prices are set close to marginal cost, admissions receipts will fail to cover total costs. Indeed, it appears likely that for most productions staged by nonprofit performing arts groups the demand curve lies below the average cost curve at all points, so that there exists *no* ticket price at which total admission receipts will cover total costs.

If the organizations involved could engage in price discrimination, they might be able to capture enough of the potential consumer surplus to enable them to cover their costs.[12] In the performing arts, however, the effectiveness of discriminatory ticket pricing is limited by the difficulty of identifying individuals or groups with unusually inelastic demand, and by the difficulty of making admission tickets nontransferable. To be sure, a degree of price discrimination can be, and often is, effected by charging higher prices for more desirable seats: if those patrons whose demand for a given performance is most inelastic also have the strongest relative preference for good seats over bad seats, then it may well be possible to establish a price schedule that will channel those with inelastic demand into the good seats at high prices, and those with more elastic demand into the inferior seats at lower prices.[13] This device is limited, however, by the strength of the preference for good seats over bad that is exhibited by patrons whose demand for performing arts productions is relatively inelastic.[14]

Yet, even if it is difficult to establish effective price discrimination via ticket pricing, it is still possible to ask individuals simply to *volunteer* to pay an additional amount if the value they place upon attendance exceeds the price charged for admission. And this, in effect, is the approach taken by nonprofit organizations in the performing arts.

Of course, the services paid for by a voluntary contribution to a performing arts group are public goods for all individuals who attend the group's performances,[15] and there is a clear incentive to be a free rider. As a consequence, many people contribute nothing, and presumably most of those who do contribute give something less than their full potential consumer surplus. Nevertheless, many individuals *do* contribute when confronted with solicitations pointing out that, in the absence of contributions, the organizations on which they depend for entertainment may disappear. Indeed, it appears that roughly 40 percent of those who attend the live performing arts contribute at least occasionally.[16]

The fact that contributions to nonprofit performing arts groups are deductible under the federal income tax is undoubtedly important in reducing the incentive to be a free rider (discussed later). Donors' committees and other organizational strategies are also presumably important in creating incentives and social pressure to help overcome free-rider behavior[17] though here, as in the case of many other private nonprofits providing public goods (such as those devoted to political causes, environmental protection, and medical research), a surprisingly large number of individuals seem willing to respond even to impersonal solicitations received by mail.

Those areas of the performing arts that are organized on a profit-seeking basis typically differ from the areas that are nonprofit in having a much larger audience over which to spread the fixed costs of a production, so that the ratio of fixed to variable costs is relatively small, and there is consequently little difference between marginal and average cost. Broadway shows, for example, typically run for several hundred performances.[18] Similarly, although the cost of producing a movie commonly runs into many millions of dollars, the audience over which that cost can be spread is enormous; consequently, only about 15 percent of movie theatre receipts is devoted to covering production costs.[19] Therefore, substantial price discrimination—and, in particular, voluntary price discrimination—is not necessary for survival, and thus the nonprofit form loses its special comparative advantage. Since, in the absence of such a comparative advantage, nonprofit firms seem, for a number of reasons, to be less efficient producers than for-profit firms,[20] it is to be expected that competition should favor for-profit firms in these areas.

Note that this analysis also suggests an explanation for the observed tendency, noted above, of nonprofit performing arts organizations to price their tickets below the level that maximizes total admissions receipts—much less the level that maximizes receipts in excess of variable costs. It seems likely that an increase in ticket prices will generally lead to a decrease in donations, since the total reservoir of consumer surplus from which those donations derive will decrease.[21] Consequently, total revenue—which includes both ticket sales receipts and donations—will be maximized at a lower ticket price than that which maximizes admissions receipts alone.

Some Historical Evidence

The analysis offered here may also help to explain why nonprofit organizations have become increasingly prominent in the performing arts through the years. Because productivity in the live performing arts has not grown at the same pace as in the economy at large, the cost of performing arts productions has increased disproportionately to that of most other goods.[22] As a consequence—and also, undoubtedly, because of competition from new entertainment media such as movies, radio, and television—demand for the live performing arts has remained small, and even, by some measures, declined.[23] Beyond this, however, it appears that fixed costs have consistently risen at a faster rate than have variable costs and thus have come to represent an increasingly large share of total costs.[24] These developments have presumably given nonprofit organizations, with their access to the form of price discrimination described above, an increasing advantage over their profit-seeking counterparts, which are dependent upon ticket sales alone to cover both fixed and variable costs.

The Nonprofit Form

Thus far I have been assuming that even if an individual is willing to donate money to a performing arts group above and beyond the amount he must pay for a ticket, he will do so only if the organization involved is nonprofit, and not if it is profit-seeking. That is, only nonprofits will have access to the form of voluntary price discrimination I have been describing. Although the reason that this is so may seem obvious, it is perhaps worth being somewhat more explicit.[25]

When a contributor gives money to, say, an opera company, he is actually trying to "buy" something—namely more and better opera. Such contributions differ from ordinary prices paid for goods and services in that the latter are clearly and directly conditioned upon specific, identifiable activity on the part of the person to whom the price is paid, such as delivering certain goods to the purchaser or permitting him to occupy a given seat at a given performance in a given theatre. That is, when one pays what we usually term a "price," one commonly knows whether the services offered in exchange were performed satisfactorily and can seek redress if they were not. But with those payments that we term "donations," things are more difficult.

Suppose that an opera company solicits donations and asserts that it will devote all funds received to the production of opera. And suppose that an individual, in reliance on that representation, contributes. How does he know that his money was in fact devoted to opera productions? His only meaningful assurance lies in the opera company's nonprofit form of organization. For a nonprofit organization is in essence an organization that is barred by law from distributing net earnings—that is, anything beyond reasonable remuneration—to persons who exercise control over it, such as its directors, officers, or members. Consequently, one can make contributions to such an organization with some assurance that they will be devoted to production of the organization's services. With a profit-seeking organization it is difficult to obtain such assurance where, as with the performing arts, the connection between an individual contribution and increased production of services is not directly observable.

Summary

In sum, it appears that nonprofit firms in the performing arts, like their for-profit counterparts, serve primarily to sell entertainment to an audience. The difference between the two types of firms lies simply in the way in which payment is received. But the difference has significant consequences. The nonprofit firm, through its access to voluntary price discrimination, is viable in segments of the performing arts market where for-profit firms cannot survive.[26]

THE ECONOMIC BEHAVIOR OF PERFORMING ARTS ORGANIZATIONS

The Firm's Objectives

Presumably profit maximization is excluded as an objective for any legitimate nonprofit; consequently, the organization must select other goals. This choice of goals may be in the hands of any one or more of several individuals or groups, including performers, directors, producers, professional managers, substantial donors, and donors' committees.

One likely possibility—particularly if control over the organization lies with professionals who have devoted their careers to a particular art form—is that the organization will place special emphasis upon the quality of its performances. Such a pursuit of quality might take either of two forms. First, the organization could seek to make its production of any given work as impressive as possible, for example by hiring exceptionally skilled performers, constructing lavish stage sets, and so forth. Second, the organization could choose to produce works that appeal only to the most refined tastes, avoiding the more popular items in the repertoire.

Alternatively, a performing arts group might feel a mission to spread culture to as broad a segment of the populace as possible, and consequently seek to maximize attendance for any given production. Or, as yet another possibility, control might lie in the hands of managers who are organizational empire-builders, and who seek simply to maximize the total budget they administer.

In what follows I shall develop a simple model of a performing arts organization, based on my earlier analysis of why the performing arts are nonprofit, that permits exploration of the consequences of pursuing each of the alternative objectives just described. The exercise is of interest not just as a matter of positive theory but for normative purposes as well. At present there is considerable debate concerning the way in which the management of performing arts organizations should exercise the substantial degree of discretion they enjoy. A recurrent theme in this debate is the choice between quality of production and refinement of taste on the one hand, and outreach to broader audiences—via lower prices and appeal to more popular tastes—on the other.[27]

In the discussion of the model the term "quality" will generally be used in the first of the two senses described here (lavishness of production). As noted below, however, the model can be interpreted in terms of the second form of quality (appeal to refined tastes) as well.

The Basic Model of the Firm

The size of the audience that the organization attracts for all performances of a given production (or, alternatively, for all of its productions combined) will be denoted by n,[28] while q represents the quality of the work(s) performed. The ticket price P charged for admission to a performance is expressed by the inverse demand function $P=P(n, q)$, $P_n<0$, $P_q>0$. Total donations received by the firm are taken to be inversely related to P and directly related to q, $D=D(P, q)$, $D_p<0$, $D_q>0$. Expressed in terms of n and q, $D=D[P(n, q), q]=D(n, q)$, $D_n>0$, $D_q \gtreqless 0$. A special case is

$$D=\delta\left\{\int_0^n P(v, q)dv - nP(n, q)\right\}. \tag{1}$$

This is the donation function that would result if all donations were to come from individuals who attend performances, and if such individuals were to donate, on average, a given fraction, δ, of the consumer surplus that they would otherwise enjoy at price P and quantity q.[29]

Total costs are given by $C=C(n, q)$, $C_n>0$, $C_q>0$. Since the firm is nonprofit, net revenue, NR, is constrained to be zero:

$$NR \equiv nP(n, q)+D(n, q)-C(n, q)=0. \tag{2}$$

The firm's objective function is given by $U=U(n, q)$, $U_n \geq 0$, $U_q \geq 0$, $U_{nn} \leq 0$, $U_{qq} \leq 0$. For the pure quality maximizer $U(n, q)=q$; for the pure audience maximizer $U(n, q)=n$; and for the budget maximizer $U(n, q)=C(n, q)$.

The firm maximizes $U(n, q)$ subject to (2).[30] The Lagrangian is

$$\phi=U(n, q)+\lambda[nP(n, q)+D(n, q)-C(n, q)]. \tag{3}$$

Assuming an interior solution,[31] the first-order conditions are (2) and

$$NR_q \equiv nP_q+D_q-C_q=-\frac{U_q}{\lambda} \tag{4}$$

$$NR_n \equiv P+nP_n+D_n-C_n=-\frac{U_n}{\lambda}, \tag{5}$$

where $NR_q \equiv \partial NR/\partial q$, etc., and λ is a Lagrange multiplier.

The slope of the nonprofit constraint (2) at the point at which the firm operates is, from (4) and (5):

$$\left.\frac{dq}{dn}\right|_{NR=0}=-\frac{NR_n}{NR_q}=-\frac{U_n}{U_q}. \tag{6}$$

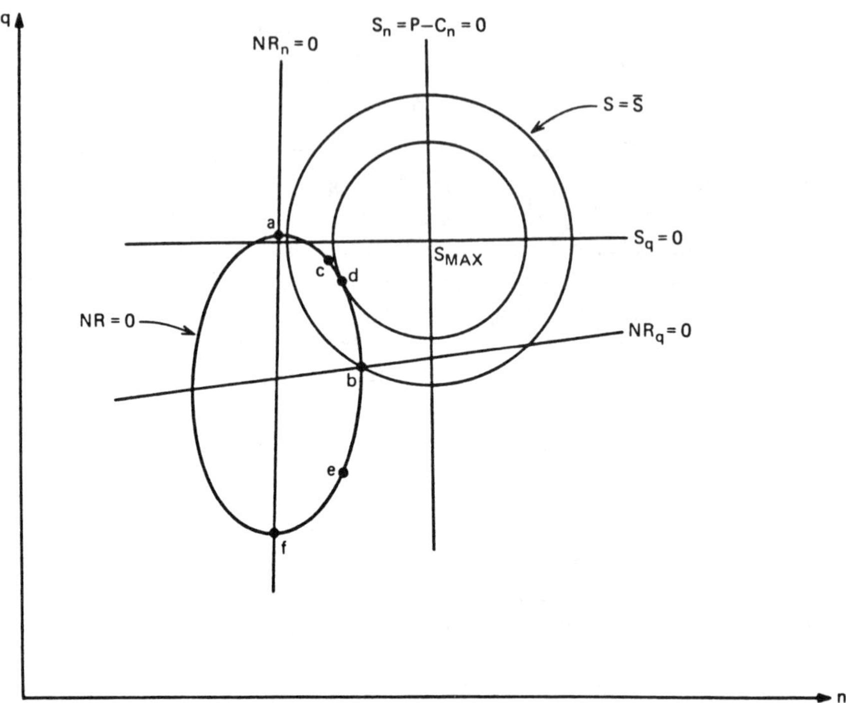

Figure 1.1 Firm Behavior and Welfare Optimization

For the quality maximizer, for which $U_n = 0$ and $U_q = 1$, this slope is zero; for the audience maximizer, for which $U_n = 1$ and $U_q = 0$, the slope is $-\infty$. These points are shown, respectively, as *a* and *b* in Figure 1.1. If the firm values both quality and audience size, so that $U_n > 0$ and $U_q > 0$, then the firm will operate at a point such as point *c* on the arc between points *a* and *b*.

Consumer surplus, which I shall denote by *S*, and which I shall use as a measure of welfare, is given by

$$S = \int_0^n P(v, q)dv - C(n, q). \tag{7}$$

This expression is at a maximum with respect to *q* and *n* when

$$S_n = P - C_n = 0 \tag{8}$$

$$S_q = \int_0^n P_q(v, q)dv - C_q = 0. \tag{9}$$

Condition (8) says simply that price should be set equal to marginal cost. Condition (9) says that quality should be at a level at which the marginal cost of greater quality just equals the marginal valuation put upon quality by the audience as a whole. There is no reason to believe, however, that these marginal conditions are consistent with the financial constraints under which the nonprofit firm must operate. Thus, for example, price can be set as low as marginal cost only if donations are sufficiently large to cover fixed costs.

More relevant to evaluating the performance of the nonprofit firm is the constrained social optimum determined by maximizing (7) subject to the nonprofit constraint (2). The resulting Lagrangian is $\theta = S + yNR$, where y is a Lagrange multiplier. The first-order conditions are

$$\frac{\partial\theta}{\partial n} = S_n + yNR_n = P - C_n + yNR_n = 0 \tag{10}$$

$$\frac{\partial\theta}{\partial q} = S_q + yNR_q = \int_0^n P_q(v, q)dv - C_q + yNR_q = 0. \tag{11}$$

The slope of the constraint, $NR = 0$, at the constrained social optimum, shown as d in Figure 1, is therefore

$$\frac{NR_n}{NR_q} = \frac{P - C_n}{\int_0^n P_q(v, q)dv - C_q}. \tag{12}$$

The nonprofit firm will be operating at the social optimum, given its financing constraints, only if the slope given in (12) is equal to that in (6), i.e., only if, at the (n, q) combination chosen by the firm,

$$\frac{U_n}{U_q} = \frac{P - C_n}{\int_0^n P_q(v, q)dv - C_q}. \tag{13}$$

Whether or not this condition is satisfied will depend upon the firm's objective function as well as upon the cost and demand functions that the firm faces, as the following discussion shows.

The Quality-Maximizing Firm

For the quality-maximizing firm, for which $U_q = 1$ and $U_n = 0$, condition (13) will hold, and the firm will be operating at the constrained optimum, only if $P = C_n$. From condition (5), however, it follows that for the quality maximizer

$$NR_n \equiv P + nP_n + D_n - C_n = 0. \tag{14}$$

That is, for any given quality level, q, the quality maximizer will choose the audience size, n, that maximizes its net revenue, which it can in turn use to purchase more quality. This is consistent with the condition that $P = C_n$ only if $D_n = -nP_n$, which is to say that, at the margin, when audience size increases (because of a decrease in ticket price) members of the audience increase their donations by precisely as much as their ticket prices decrease.[32] In terms of the donation function (1), for example, this will be the case only if $\delta = 1$—that is, only if audience members donate 100% of their consumer surplus to the firm. In the face of less generous—but more plausible—contribution levels, the firm will sacrifice audience size too heavily for the sake of quality.

The Audience-Maximizing Firm

For the audience maximizer $U_q = 0$; it therefore follows from (4) that

$$NR_q = nP_q + D_q - C_q = 0. \tag{15}$$

That is, for any given audience size, the audience maximizer will choose that level of quality that maximizes net revenues, since those revenues can be used to reduce ticket prices, which will in turn attract a larger audience.

From (13), we see that the audience maximizer will operate at the constrained optimum only if $S_q = 0$ so that condition (9) holds. For (9) to obtain when the firm is an audience maximizer—and hence (15) holds—we must have:

$$\frac{1}{n}\int_0^n P_q(v, q)dv - P_q = \frac{D_q}{n}. \tag{16}$$

If $D_q = 0$, then (16) is equivalent to the condition shown by Spence and Sheshinski[33] to be necessary for a profit-maximizing monopolist to select the socially optimal level of quality for its product: the valuation put upon increases in quality by the average member of the audience must equal the valuation put upon such increases by marginal members of the audience.

The interesting fact established by (16), however, is that the responsiveness of donations to changes in quality, D_q, can serve to reduce the incentive for the firm to choose a nonoptimal level of q in those cases where the average and marginal audience members value quality differently, because donations presumably reflect primarily the preferences of inframarginal—and hence more typical—audience members. This point appears clearly if we rewrite condition (16) using the donation function (1):

$$(1-\delta)\left[\frac{1}{n}\int_0^n P_q(v, q)dv - P_q\right] = 0. \tag{17}$$

Here we see that the firm's choice of quality moves closer to the optimum, not only as marginal and average consumer valuations of quality converge, but also as $\delta \to 1$.

If donations respond as in (1), and if $\delta < 1$, it is easy to show that, as with the profit-maximizing monopolists considered by Spence and Sheshinski, when marginal consumers value quality increases less than does the average consumer—i.e., when $P_{qn} < 0$—the audience maximizer will choose a level of q below that which represents the constrained social optimum, while the reverse is true if $P_{qn} > 0$. (In diagrammatic terms, if $P_{qn} < 0$, the locus $S_q = 0$ lies above the locus $NR_q = 0$, as in Figure 1.1, while the reverse is true if $P_{qn} > 0$, as in Figure 1.2; the two loci coincide if $P_{qn} = 0$.)

The Budget Maximizing Firm

For the budget maximizer $U(n, q) = C(n, q)$ and, as noted earlier, such a firm will operate at a level of (n, q) such as that indicated by point c in Figure 1.1, intermediate between the points chosen by the quality maximizer and the audience maximizer. From the preceding analysis of the audience maximizer, it follows that generally the budget maximizer will operate at or near the constrained social optimum only if consumer preferences for quality are such that $P_{qn} < 0$.

Some Comparisons

Of the three types of firms analyzed above, which is likely to perform most in accord with maximal social welfare? There is, interestingly, no simple response—the answer evidently depends heavily upon the nature of consumer demand and donative behavior.

If $P_{qn} \geq 0$, the audience maximizer will unambiguously turn in the best performance—at least if donations respond as modeled in (1). In the intuitively more plausible case where $P_{qn} < 0$, however, the budget maximizer or the quality maximizer might perform better; their higher emphasis on quality compensates for the atypically low taste for quality that characterizes the marginal consumer, whose tastes dictate the prices at which tickets can be sold.

Quality as Refinement of Taste

The discussion so far has proceeded largely on the assumption that the variable q represents the first type of quality discussed earlier, namely the lavishness with which any given work is produced. The model as developed above can, however, alternatively be interpreted with q representing the degree to which the firm's productions appeal to highly refined tastes. Viewing the model in these terms, one might assume that the amount to be spent on performers, sets, costumes, the director's fee, etc., are fixed, leaving the firm free to choose only among works that can be staged with these given resources. A quality-maximizing firm would then be one that chooses works that appeal to a highly cultured, but also small, audience.[34] In terms of the model, this means that $C_q = 0$ and, beyond a certain minimal level of q, $P_q < 0$.[35]

The preceding analysis and conclusions remain valid for this alternative interpretation of q and the accompanying change of values for C_q and P_q.

Note, however, that with $C_q = 0$ the budget maximizer and the audience maximizer are identical.

THE RATIONALE FOR SUBSIDIES

If the analysis offered earlier of why the performing arts are nonprofit is correct, then the most compelling rationale for providing subsidies to performing arts organizations is not that they produce external benefits or serve as a vehicle for redistribution of income—which are the rationales that have been the primary focus of discussion to date[36]—but rather that the high fixed costs that such firms face will, in the absence of a subsidy, force them to set prices too high to satisfy marginal criteria for efficiency, and may well make them unviable.[37]

As in the case of all such subsidies, there is a substantial conflict between equity and efficiency. Although the subsidy may help establish efficient pricing, the individuals who consume the services financed by the subsidies are likely to constitute only a small fraction of the people who pay for them—at least if the source of the subsidy is the public fisc. Indeed, given that the class of people who attend the performing arts is not only small but unusually prosperous and geographically concentrated, the problem of equity raised by subsidies is particularly acute.

WHEN IS A SUBSIDY EFFICIENT?

If a performing arts organization, in the absence of a subsidy, is setting its ticket prices well above marginal cost to cover the fixed costs associated with its productions, then it is possible that a subsidy will lead to more efficient levels for price and output. But this need not be the case. As the following discussion shows, a subsidy can in some cases lead to even greater inefficiency, quite apart from its likely adverse distributional consequences.

The General Model

For the moment I shall confine the analysis to a lump-sum subsidy. Similar results for other kinds of subsidies follow directly from the analysis in later sections.

Consider the same firm modeled above, except that its revenue now includes a lump-sum subsidy, L. Thus the firm now seeks to maximize $U(n, q)$ subject to

$$NR = nP(n, q) + D(n, q) + L - C(n, q) = 0. \tag{18}$$

Assuming an interior solution, the first order conditions for a constrained maximum with respect to n and q are unchanged from (4) and (5) above;

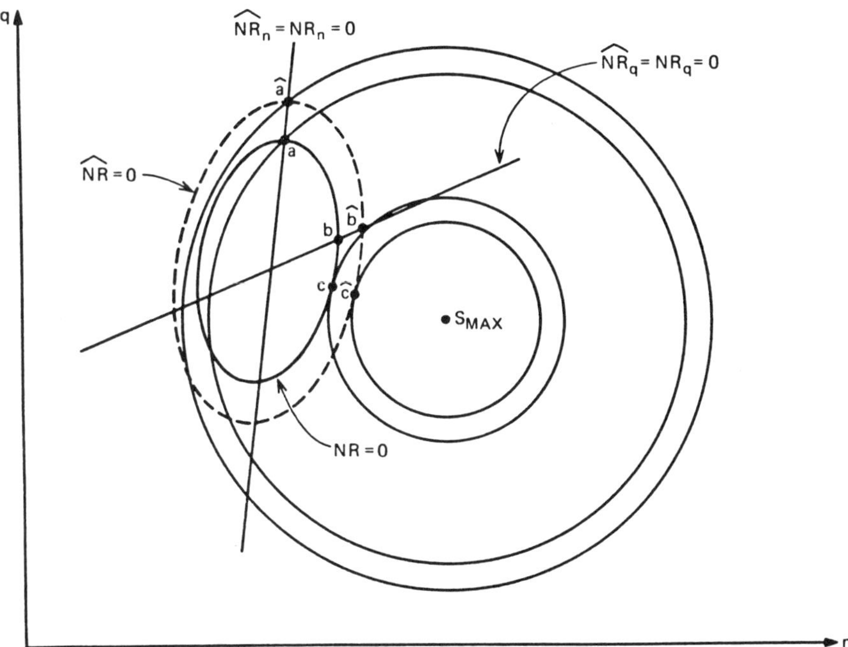

Figure 1.2 The Effect of a Lump-Sum Subsidy

the constraint (18) becomes the third condition. In diagrammatic terms, the consequence of increasing the subsidy, L, is to enlarge the closed curve representing the nonprofit constraint, as shown in Figure 1.2. The loci $NR_n=0$ and $NR_q=0$ remain unchanged. The quality maximizer, which operated at point a without the subsidy, will operate with the subsidy at point $\hat{a}$, while the audience maximizer will shift from b to $\hat{b}$.

To determine whether such shifts will lead to an increase in social welfare, we can differentiate (7) with respect to L,

$$\frac{dS}{dL} = S_q \frac{dq}{dL} + S_n \frac{dn}{dL} = \left[\int_0^n P_q(v, q)dv - C_q \right] \frac{dq}{dL} + [P - C_n] \frac{dn}{dL}, \qquad (19)$$

and then evaluate (19) by using simple comparative statics to determine dq/dL and dn/dL for the firm.

For simplicity, I shall confine the analysis to the polar cases of the audience-maximizing firm and the quality-maximizing firm.

The Quality Maximizer

Consider first the quality maximizer. Setting $U_q=1$ and $U_n=0$ in (4) and (5), and totally differentiating (4), (5), and (18) with respect to L yield:

$$\frac{dn}{dL}=\frac{NR_{qn}}{NR_q NR_{nn}} \tag{20}$$

$$\frac{dq}{dL}=\frac{-1}{NR_q}\,. \tag{21}$$

Since the quality maximizer operates where $NR_q<0$, it follows from (21) that $dq/dL>0$: increasing the subsidy, L, will, as expected, cause the quality maximizer to raise its quality level.

Whether an increase in the subsidy will also generally lead to an increase in the size n of the audience that sees a given production is less certain. Since $NR_q<0$, and since, if the second-order condition holds, $NR_{nn}<0$, the sign of dn/dL is the same as that of NR_{qn}, which equals $P_q-C_{qn}+(1-\delta)nP_{qn}$ when the donation function is given by (1). Given that $P_q>0$, $C_{qn}>0$ (if we are again speaking of quality in terms of lavishness of production[38]) and $P_{qn}\lesseqgtr 0$, it follows that NR_{qn}, and thus dn/dL, are indeterminate in sign. Conditions favorable to an audience increase are: (1) a low value of C_{qn} (increasing the audience does not much increase the cost of quality), and (2) $P_{qn}>0$ (the new [marginal] audience members admitted have an unusually strong taste for quality).

Turning to the welfare implications of such behavior, we have $S_n=P-C_n$, and as discussed above this will always be nonnegative for the quality maximizer. Thus, increases in audience size are unambiguously desirable for the quality maximizer. On the other hand, the desirability of an increase in quality is less clear; using (1), we have

$$S_q=\int_0^n P_q(v,\,q)dv-C_q=(1-\delta)\left[\int_0^n P_q(v,\,q)dv-nP_q\right]-\frac{1}{\lambda}\,. \tag{22}$$

Since $\lambda>0$, this expression will be unambiguously negative whenever $P_{qn}>0$. Only where $P_{qn}<0$ can S_q be positive.

The overall effect on welfare of increasing the subsidy, L, is therefore indeterminate. The condition required for the first term in (19), $S_q[dq/dL]$, to be positive, $P_{qn}<0$, is simultaneously conducive to a low, and possibly negative, value for the second term, $S_n[dn/dL]$. It is easy, however, to construct examples in which increasing L decreases welfare, even though the quality maximizer's ticket price in the absence of a subsidy is well above marginal cost.[39] Such a case is illustrated in Figure 1.2 (which is drawn so that $P_{qn}>0$), where $\hat{a}$ lies on a lower iso-social-welfare curve than does a.

The Audience Maximizer

Turning to the audience maximizer we have

$$\frac{dn}{dL}=\frac{-1}{NR_n} \tag{23}$$

$$\frac{dq}{dL}=\frac{NR_{qn}}{NR_n NR_{qq}}\,. \tag{24}$$

By logic parallel to that employed in analyzing the quality maximizer, it follows that $dn/dL > 0$, while the sign of dq/dL is the same as that of NR_{qn}, and therefore ambiguous.

From (19), an increase in n will be desirable as long as $P > C_n$. Using (1), the S_q term in (19) becomes

$$S_q = (1-\delta)\left[\int_0^n P_q(v, q)dv - nP_q\right]. \tag{25}$$

Thus sgn $S_q = -\text{sgn}P_{qn}$. If follows that $S_q[dq/dL]$, and hence (19), are ambiguous in sign: it is possible that a lump-sum grant to an audience-maximizing firm, as to a quality maximizer, can lead to a reduction in welfare, even when, in the absence of a subsidy, the firm is operating where $P > C_n$.[40] (Figure 1.2 illustrates a case where $dS/dL > 0$.)

DONATION SUBSIDIES

In fact, subsidies to the performing arts are frequently not lump-sum in nature, but rather take the form of matching grants for donations—that is, μ dollars of subsidy are given for every dollar in individual donations received by the organization. This is true, for example, of a substantial portion of the performing arts grants provided by the National Endowment for the Arts (NEA), and of some foundation and corporate grants as well. It is also the approach that characterizes what is by far the largest public performing arts subsidy program of all, namely, the deductibility of contributions under the federal personal income tax.[41] Are such donation subsidies superior to lump-sum subsidies?

The General Model

In making the comparison I shall assume, as seems empirically the case,[42] that donations respond positively, if at all, to a matching subsidy. Thus, if μ is the rate at which donations are matched, then $D = D(n, q, \mu)$, $\partial D/\partial\mu > 0$. In particular, I shall sometimes assume (as a special case of (1)) that

$$D(n, q, \mu) = \delta(\mu)\left[\int_0^n P(v, q)dv - nP(n, q)\right], \tag{26}$$

where $\delta'(\mu) > 0$.

With a donation subsidy at a rate μ, the firm's nonprofit constraint becomes

$$NR = nP(n, q) + (1+\mu)D(n, q, \mu) - C(n, q) = 0. \tag{27}$$

If the firm maximizes $U(n, q)$ subject to this constraint, the first-order conditions are, in addition to (27),

$$P+nP_n+(1+\mu)D_n-C_n=-\frac{U_n}{\lambda} \tag{28}$$

$$nP_q+(1+\mu)D_q-C_q=-\frac{U_q}{\lambda}, \tag{29}$$

where λ is a Lagrange multiplier.

Proceeding as in the case of the lump-sum subsidy, we can evaluate the effect of an increase in the subsidy rate μ on n, q, and S by differentiating (27)–(29) with respect to μ, solving for $dn/d\mu$ and $dq/d\mu$, and then determining $dS/d\mu$ by means of

$$\frac{dS}{d\mu}=S_q\frac{dq}{d\mu}+S_n\frac{dn}{d\mu}=\left[\int_0^n P_q(v,\,q)dv-C_q\right]\frac{dq}{d\mu}+[P-C_n]\,\frac{dn}{d\mu}. \tag{30}$$

The Quality Maximizer

For the quality maximizer we have

$$\frac{dq}{d\mu}=\frac{dq}{dL}[D+\mu D_\mu]+\frac{dq}{dL}\,D_\mu \tag{31}$$

$$\frac{dn}{d\mu}=\frac{dn}{dL}\,[D+\mu D_\mu]+\frac{dn}{dL}\,D_\mu-\frac{1}{NR_{nn}}\,[D_n+(1+\mu)D_{n\mu}] \tag{32}$$

$$\frac{dS}{d\mu}=\frac{dS}{dL}\,[D+\mu D_\mu]+\frac{dS}{dL}\,d_\mu-\frac{(P-C_n)}{NR_{nn}}\,[D_n+(1+\mu)D_{n\mu}], \tag{33}$$

where dq/dL, dn/dL, and dS/dL are the effects upon q, n, and S of a one-dollar lump-sum subsidy as given above by (21), (20), and (19), respectively.

Here $D_\mu \equiv \partial D/\partial\mu > 0$ reflects the increase in private donations induced by the increase in the matching rate μ. (In the case of (26), $D_\mu=(\delta'/\delta)D$.) The expression $D+\mu D_\mu$ gives the dollar increase in expenditure on the subsidy associated with a unit increase in μ. The first term on the right-hand side of (31)–(33) reflects the direct effect of the increase $D+\mu D_\mu$ in expenditure on the subsidy; this effect has the same sign and magnitude as would an equivalent expenditure on a lump-sum subsidy, as analyzed above. The second term on the right-hand side of (31)–(33) reflects the additional effect resulting from the increase in private donations induced by increasing μ.

Turning to the third term on the right-hand side of (32), we have, using the donation function (26),

$$D_n+(1+\mu)D_{n\mu}=-[\delta+(1+\mu)\delta']nP_n. \tag{34}$$

This expression is positive, and thus, since $NR_{nn}<0$ by virtue of the second-order condition, the final term in (32) is positive. This term reflects the incentive to increase n (and lower $\bar{P}$) given to the firm by virtue of the fact that, with a higher μ, the firm will effectively be able to capture a larger fraction of the increase in consumer surplus created by such a move. The final term in (33) derives from the increase in n reflected in the final term in (32), and will be positive whenever $P > C_n$.

It follows from (33) that, in terms of our welfare measure S, a donation subsidy will always be superior to an equivalent expenditure on a lump-sum subsidy in any case in which a lump-sum subsidy would itself be justifiable (i.e., where $dS/dL > 0$). The extent by which the donation subsidy dominates an equivalent lump-sum subsidy is given by the second and third terms on the right-hand side of (33), reflecting, respectively, the increase in private donations and the increase in the donation matching rate μ.

The Audience Maximizer

For the audience maximizer we have

$$\frac{dq}{d\mu} = \frac{dq}{dL} D + \mu D_\mu] + \frac{dq}{dL} D_\mu - \frac{NR_{q\mu}}{NR_{qq}} \tag{35}$$

$$\frac{dn}{d\mu} = \frac{dn}{dL} [D + \mu D_\mu] + \frac{dn}{dL} D_\mu \tag{36}$$

$$\frac{dS}{d\mu} = \frac{dS}{dL} [D + \mu D_\mu] + \frac{dS}{dL} D_\mu + \left[\int_0^n P_q(v, q) dv - nP_q \right] \frac{-NR_{q\mu}}{NR_{qq}}, \tag{37}$$

where dq/dL, dn/dL, and dS/dL are the effects of a unit increase in the lump-sum subsidy as given by (24), (23), and (19).

The interpretation of the first two terms on the right-hand side of (35)–(37) parallels that given for (31)–(33) above. Using the donation function (26), the final term in (35) becomes

$$\frac{-NR_{q\mu}}{NR_{qq}} = \frac{-[\delta + (1+\mu)\delta'] \left[\int_0^n P_q(v, q) dv - nP_q \right]}{NR_{qq}}, \tag{38}$$

which has the same sign as P_{qn} (since $NR_{qq} < 0$ by virtue of the second-order condition). This term reflects the increased incentive to adjust quality to conform to the tastes of inframarginal donors that the firm faces owing to the larger fraction of consumer surplus that it can (in effect) capture with a higher value of μ. The final term in (37) reflects the same phenomenon. Using (26), that term becomes

$$\left[\int_0^n P_q(v, q) dv - nP_q \right] \frac{-NR_{q\mu}}{NR_{qq}} = - \frac{[\delta + (1+\mu)\delta'] \left[\int_0^n P_q(v, q) dv - nP_q \right]^2}{NR_{qq}}. \tag{39}$$

This term will always be nonnegative, reflecting the fact that bringing quality more into line with average, as opposed to marginal, audience members will always enhance consumer welfare as measured by S.

It follows from (37), then, that whenever $dS/dL \geq 0$, a lump-sum subsidy is dominated by a donation subsidy of equivalent amount—or, in other words, for the audience maximizer as for the quality maximizer, a donation subsidy is to be preferred to a lump-sum subsidy whenever a subsidy of either type is justifiable at all.

Summary

The advantages of the donation subsidy here are two-fold. First, by inducing further donations it yields to the firm a larger increase in revenue per dollar of subsidy than does the lump-sum subsidy. Note, in this connection, that since part of the increased revenues due to a donation subsidy come from donors who benefit from—and value highly—the performances involved, donation subsidies also have stronger equitable appeal than do lump-sum subsidies, at least where public funds are the source of the subsidy.[43]

Second, a subsidy geared to donations gives the firm an additional incentive to attract donations. Since we have been assuming that donations are proportional to consumer surplus, this means that with a donation subsidy the firm has an incentive to adjust its quality and price (or, equivalently here, audience size) closer to the levels that maximize consumer welfare.

TICKET SUBSIDIES AND TAXES

Admissions subsidies for the performing arts might also seem attractive.[44] Such subsidies might take either of two forms. First, the subsidy can be offered on the basis of a fixed amount per admission, regardless of the price charged for admission. Second, the subsidy can be designed to match total admissions (ticket) receipts on a fixed percentage basis, similar to the donation subsidy discussed above. In both cases incentives will be created for the organization that are absent in the case of a lump-sum subsidy.

At present neither of these types of admission subsidies is common. However, a negative subsidy applied to total ticket receipts, in the form of a sales tax on theatre tickets, has commonly been applied to commercial performing arts groups and sometimes to nonprofit organizations as well. Since the effects of such a tax are precisely the reverse of those resulting from a subsidy of the same type, analysis of the subsidy also yields an analysis of the tax.

The Model

I shall confine myself here to analysis of a per-receipts subsidy. Rather similar results follow from an analysis of a subsidy of a fixed amount per admission.

Let σ represent the rate at which ticket receipts are matched by the ticket receipts subsidy, so that the total amount expended through this subsidy is σnP. The firm's nonprofit constraint becomes

$$(1+\sigma)nP+D-C=0. \tag{40}$$

The Quality Maximizer

Proceeding as in the analysis of the donation subsidy, the effects of increasing the ticket subsidy rate for the quality maximizer are:

$$\frac{dq}{d\sigma}=\frac{dq}{dL}\,nP \tag{41}$$

$$\frac{dn}{d\sigma}=\frac{dn}{dL}\,nP-\frac{P+nP_n}{NR_{nn}} \tag{42}$$

$$\frac{dS}{d\sigma}=\frac{dS}{dL}\,nP-(P-C_n)\,\frac{P+nP_n}{NR_{nn}}\,. \tag{43}$$

The expression nP here represents the dollar increase in expenditure on the ticket subsidy associated with a unit increase in σ. The first term on the right-hand side in (41)–(43) gives the direct effect of the increase nP in the amount of the subsidy; it is the same as the effect of an equivalent expenditure on a lump-sum subsidy. The final term in (42) will be positive if the firm is operating where demand is elastic ($nP_n/P>-1$), and negative otherwise, reflecting the fact that the net-revenue-maximizing value of n (which is the value of n chosen by the quality maximizer) changes with σ. It follows from (42) that a ticket subsidy will actually lead to a *smaller* increase in audience size (and thus, from (43), a smaller increase in welfare) than would an equivalent lump-sum subsidy if (as is possible) the quality maximizer is operating in the inelastic portion of the demand curve.[45]

The Audience Maximizer

For the audience maximizer we have

$$\frac{dq}{d\sigma}=\frac{dq}{dL}\,nP-\frac{nP_q}{NR_{qq}} \tag{44}$$

$$\frac{dn}{d\sigma}=\frac{dn}{dL}\,nP \tag{45}$$

$$\frac{dS}{d\sigma}=\frac{dS}{dL}\,nP-\left[\int_0^n P_q(v,\,q)dv-nP_q\right]\frac{nP_q}{NR_{qq}}\,. \tag{46}$$

Since $nP_q/NR_{qq}<0$, it follows from (44) that a ticket subsidy will lead to a larger increase in quality than will an equivalent expenditure on a lump-sum subsidy. The reason for this is that increasing σ increases P_q, and hence raises the level of q that maximizes net revenue. As the final term in (46) indicates, this (additional) increase in q will raise, rather than lower, welfare only if $P_{qn}<0$.

Summary

Interestingly, for the audience-maximizing firm a ticket subsidy has no greater effect on audience size than does a lump-sum subsidy, while for the quality maximizer a ticket subsidy may actually lead to a smaller audience than would a lump-sum subsidy. For both the audience maximizer and the quality maximizer, there is a range of cases in which a ticket subsidy is dominated by a lump-sum subsidy in terms of our welfare measure *S*. From the results of the analyses of donation subsidies we can in turn conclude that there is a much larger class of cases in which a ticket subsidy is dominated by a donation subsidy—though there may be instances in which a ticket subsidy is superior to both donation and lump-sum subsidies.

CONCLUSION

The live performing arts are commonly characterized by fixed costs that are high relative to marginal costs, and by overall demand that is relatively small. As a consequence, performing arts groups often must engage in price discrimination if they are to survive without subsidy. The opportunities for effective discrimination through ticket pricing are limited, however. Therefore, nonprofit firms, which can, in effect, employ a system of voluntary price discrimination, can often survive in areas of the performing arts where for-profit firms cannot.

In many cases, free-rider incentives presumably keep donations below the level necessary for efficient production. In such cases, public subsidies can be justified on efficiency grounds, although such subsidies clearly present problems of equity.

As it is, the arts in the United States, including the performing arts, receive public subsidies that compare favorably in amount with those provided in other industrialized democracies.[46] The United States is unique, however, in providing most of its public subsidies in the form of matching grants for private donations. This policy has a great deal to recommend it. Donation subsidies not only serve to increase the level of private contributions, but may also cause performing arts groups to pay greater attention to the desires of inframarginal consumers.

NOTES

1. See Thomas G. Moore, *The Economics of the American Theater* (Durham: University of North Carolina Press, 1968), 12.

2. Among theatres, nonprofits are most commonly to be found off Broadway and in local and regional stock and repertory companies; they are primarily a development of the period since World War II. Moore, op. cit., 16–20, 100; William J. Baumol and William G. Bowen, *Performing Arts: The Economic Dilemma* (Cambridge: M.I.T. Press, 1968), 57–60. On the institutional history of symphony orchestras, see M. Mayernik, "Rhapsody in Red: The Eco-

nomic Future of the Philadelphia Orchestra" (unpublished manuscript, Department of Economics, University of Pennsylvania, Spring 1976), 19.

3. Baumol and Bowen, op. cit., 147–157.

4. Henry Hansmann, "The Role of Nonprofit Enterprise," *Yale Law Journal* 89 (1980): 848–854; Burton A. Weisbrod, "Toward a Theory of the Voluntary Nonprofit Sector in a Three-Sector Economy," in E. Phelps, ed., *Altruism, Morality, and Economic Theory* (New York: Russell Sage Foundation, 1975).

5. Baumol and Bowen, op. cit., chapter 16; Dick Netzer, *The Subsidized Muse* (Cambridge: Cambridge University Press, 1978), Chapter 2.

6. Moore, op. cit., Chapter 8, and A. T. Peacock, "Welfare Economics and Public Subsidies to the Arts," in M. Blaug, ed., *The Economics of the Arts* (London: Westview, 1976), are also skeptical about the magnitude of the public benefits involved.

As noted later, however, a performing arts production is to an important extent a public good *for those individuals who are among the audience.* Thus, if someone who has already purchased a subscription to the Metropolitan Opera makes a donation to that organization, the improvement in the quality of the performances that the donation permits will be enjoyed as a public good by all others who also hold subscriptions.

7. Direct data on the proportion of donations coming from audience members are apparently unavailable. Some indication is provided, however, by the evidence, discussed later in the chapter, indicating that a substantial percentage of those who attend also contribute.

8. Baumol and Bowen, op. cit., Chapter 4.

9. Baumol and Bowen, op. cit., 272–278.

10. Moore, op. cit., 120–121, also alludes briefly to contributions as a means of price discrimination, though he does not pursue the issue.

11. It is difficult to obtain useful data comparing fixed costs with variable costs for productions by performing arts groups. Existing studies of economies of scale in the nonprofit performing arts simply correlate cost per performance with the total number of performances per year for different organizations (e.g., symphony orchestras or theatre groups) without taking into account the number of different productions represented by those performances. See Baumol and Bowen, op. cit., Chapter 8, and S. Globerman and S. H. Books, "Statistical Cost Functions for Performing Arts Organizations," *Southern Economic Journal* 5 (1976): 1–26. Data on Broadway theatre assembled by Moore, op. cit., Chapter 3, are, however, suggestive; they show that, for the 1960–1961 season, weekly operating cost—i.e., the (variable) cost of a week's performances—for a show was, on average, less than one-fifth as large as the (fixed) cost of producing the show.

12. Here and in what follows I assume that nonprofit performing arts firms have some degree of monopoly power, and thus face downward-sloping demand curves. This is in keeping with the observation that demand is limited and fixed costs are high, thus presumably making competition unworkable. It is also in keeping with the very limited competition that in fact prevails among the nonprofit performing arts; even New York City supports only one major symphony orchestra, two substantial opera companies, and a handful of (highly differentiated) dance groups.

13. See the analysis of essentially the same issue in a different context offered in Sidney Winter, "A Problem" (unpublished manuscript, May 1968). It also follows from Winter's analysis that, when constructing a new theatre, there may well be gains to be had from creating a high ratio of bad seats to good seats, even if it would be as cheap or cheaper to construct a larger proportion of good seats for the same total capacity.

14. Similarly, the performing arts are not well situated to take advantage of the type of two-part tariffs described by Walter Oi, "A Disneyland Dilemma: Two-Part Tariffs for a Mickey Mouse Monopoly," *Quarterly Journal of Economics* 85 (1971): 77–96, because many people wish to attend only one performance by a given organization and because it is difficult to make tickets nontransferable.

15. See note 6.

16. Baumol and Bowen, op. cit., 307–308.

17. To some extent, contributions undoubtedly represent an effort to buy recognition and

status. Many organizations in the performing arts exploit this motivation quite consciously by publicizing the names of donors and by arranging special social events for them. But the development of the performing arts as a locus for such conspicuous giving seems most probably a consequence rather than a cause of their nonprofit, donatively financed status.

18. Moore, op. cit., Chapter 1 and Table A-6.

19. D. Gordon, "Why the Movie Majors Are Major," in T. Balio, ed., *The American Film Industry* (Madison: University of Wisconsin Press, 1976).

20. Hansmann, op. cit., 877–879.

21. Baumol and Bowen, op. cit., 277, report that their interviews with managerial personnel in fact revealed a fear that increased ticket prices would lead to reduced contributions. Although Baumol and Bowen devote little attention to this relationship between contributions and ticket prices, they offer no alternative explanation for the tendency to set prices at a level where demand is inelastic, other than the possibility that management feels that by keeping prices low they are fulfilling a social obligation to make the performing arts available to as much of the populace as possible. The behavior of a firm that has the latter objective, yet is dependent upon donative financing, is explored later in this chapter.

22. Baumol and Bowen, op. cit., Chapters 8, 9.

23. Baumol and Bowen, op. cit., Chapter 3.

24. In terms of constant dollars, average productions costs for Broadway theatre increased by 236 percent between 1927 and 1961, whereas weekly operating costs increased by only 80 percent. This relative increase in production costs was evidently responsible for the fact that the length of run required for a Broadway show to make a profit roughly tripled over this period. Moore, op. cit., 11–12, 34.

25. A more detailed discussion appears in Hansmann, op. cit.

26. There are areas other than the performing arts in which similar factors seem to be at work. For example, one of the most interesting and most obvious examples of the type of voluntary price discrimination described here is provided by New York's Metropolitan Museum of Art, which requires that every visitor pay some amount to gain admission but leaves each visitor entirely free to determine how much to pay. In this connection it should be noted that museums are seemingly characterized by an even higher ratio of fixed costs to marginal costs than are the performing arts, yet, like performing arts groups, are in a relatively poor position to implement nonvoluntary price discrimination.

27. Robert Brustein, "The Metropolitan Opera—The High Price of Being Best," The *New York Times* February 12, 1978, sec. 2, p. 1, cols. 1 and 6.

28. In Broadway theatre each production is usually organized as a separate "firm." Baumol and Bowen, op. cit., 20. Most nonprofit performing arts organizations, in contrast, are relatively permanent and produce a large number of productions. (This difference in structure is presumably explainable at least in part by the need for nonprofit groups to develop strong and stable reputations that will provide assurance to potential donors.) Because I shall not be concerned with the effect that one production has upon demand for another, the number of productions that a given organization undertakes will not be important here.

29. An important issue that will be avoided here is the degree to which an organization can and will use some of its income to solicit further donations.

30. For other models of nonprofit firms (in particular, hospitals) with similar objective functions, see Joseph Newhouse, "Toward a Theory of Nonprofit Institutions: An Economic Model of a Hospital," *American Economic Review* 60 (1970): 64–74; M. Feldstein, "Hospital Price Inflation: A Study of Nonprofit Price Dynamics," *American Economic Review* 61 (1971): 853–872.

31. The second-order condition, both here and for the altered models of the firm below, is

$$\lambda[2NR_nNR_qNR_{nq} - NR_n^2NR_{qq} - NR_q^2NR_{nn}] + 2NR_nNR_qU_{nq} - NR_n^2U_{qq} - NR_q^2U_{nn} > 0.$$

32. This is a necessary but not a sufficient condition for the quality maximizer to operate at the constrained social optimum. If, for example, the locus $S_q = 0$ lies below the locus $NR_q = 0$—the conditions for which are explored below—it is possible that the constrained

social optimum will be at the quality-*minimizing* point f rather than the quality-*maximizing* point a in Figure 1.1 when donative behavior is such that $D_n = -nP_n$.

A similar qualification applies to the discussion of the audience maximizer below.

33. A. Michael Spence, "Monopoly, Quality and Regulation," *Bell Journal of Economics* 6 (1975): 417–429; E. Sheshinksi, "Price, Quality and Quantity Regulation in Monopoly Situations," *Economica* 43 (1976): 127–137.

34. See Baumol and Bowen, op. cit., 253–257, for a discussion of the desire of performing arts groups to perform contemporary works, and of the adverse consequences this has for demand.

35. The level of q at which $P_q(n, q)$ reaches zero should presumably depend on n. For very low values of n, at which point one is dealing only with true enthusiasts, P_q might even remain positive for all values of q.

36. Baumol and Bowen, op. cit., Chapter 16; Netzer, op. cit., Chapter 2.

37. Moore, op. cit., 120–121, 122, also makes a brief, though puzzlingly dismissive, reference to "price discrimination" as a possible rationale for performing arts subsidies, by which he evidently means something like the declining-average-cost rationale suggested here.

I should emphasize that I am speaking here only of subsidies for the performance of existing works. Subsidies to authors and composers for the creation of new works are an entirely different matter. It is often extremely difficult for artists to capture for themselves even a small fraction of the benefits society derives from their work, and thus there is much to be said for subsidizing them. The fact that public acceptance of new works often lags considerably behind their creation, and that it is probably helpful to artists to see their work performed when they produce it, may also lead to some justification for subsidies to performing arts groups that are specifically earmarked for performance of new works. (The Ford Foundation, for example, has sometimes pursued this course. Ford Foundation, *The Finances of the Performing Arts* [New York: The Ford Foundation, 1974].)

38. As in the discussion of the economic behavior of the basic model, the results here and below can be reinterpreted for the case in which q represents quality of the second type by assuming, instead, that $C_q = 0$ and that, beyond some level of q, $P_q < 0$.

39. As an example, consider a quality-maximizing firm that faces a demand function $n = \sqrt{q}[A - P]$ or equivalently the inverse demand function $P = A - n/\sqrt{q}$, so that $P_{qn} > 0$. Assume also that the firm's cost function takes the simple form $C = q + n$ and that the subsidy level L is initially zero. Solving the first-order conditions for q and n and substituting these values into (19) gives $dS/dL = -1/(2-\delta)$. Thus here $dS/dL < 0$ for all values of δ between 0 and 1. (In this example $dq/dL = 2 > 0$, $dn/dL = 2/(A-1) > 0$.)

Note that here $P - C_n = (A-1)[(1-\delta)/(2-\delta)]$, and therefore $P > C_n$ so long as $A > 1$, $0 \leq \delta < 1$.

40. For example, assume that an audience maximizer faces the demand and cost functions in the preceding note, and assume that initially $L = 0$. Then $dS/dL = (2-5\delta)/3(2-\delta)$, so that $dS/dL < 0$ for $\delta > 2/5$. Here $P - C_n = (A-1)(2-3\delta)/3(2-\delta)$, so $P > C_n$ whenever $\delta < 2/3$ and $A > 1$. In this case (assuming $A > 1$), $dn/dL = 3/(A-1) > 0$, $dq/dL = 4/3 > 0$, $S_n = (A-1)(2-3\delta)/3(2-\delta) > 0$ for $\delta < 2/3$ and $S_n < 0$ for $1 \geq 2/3$, $S_q = -(1-\delta)/(2-\delta) < 0$ for $0 \leq \delta < 1$.

41. Netzer, op. cit., 44, 95, estimates the cost to the federal government of the deduction for gifts to arts organizations as $400 million or more for 1975, whereas he estimates total direct public support of the arts at all governmental levels as just under $300 million.

42. Martin Feldstein, "The Income Tax and Charitable Contributions: Part I—Aggregate and Distributional Effects," *National Tax Journal* 28 (1975): 81–99; Feldstein, "The Income Tax and Charitable Contributions: Part II—The Impact on Religious, Educational, and Other Organizations," *National Tax Journal* 28 (1975): 209–226; Martin Feldstein and C. Clotfelter, "Tax Incentives and Charitable Contributions in the United States," *Journal of Public Economics* 5 (1976): 1–26.

43. The donation subsidy model here has a matching rate that does not vary from one donor to another—as would be the case with a uniform tax credit, and as is typically the case with NEA grants. The subsidies channeled through the charitable deduction under the personal income tax, in contrast, involve a matching rate that ranges from 0 to 70 percent,

depending upon the donor's tax bracket. Such a deduction may well be dominated, in terms of both equity and efficiency, by a tax credit of equivalent amount. See H. Hochman and J. Rodgers, "The Optimal Tax Treatment of Charitable Contributions," *National Tax Journal* 30 (1977): 1–18.

44. Netzer, op. cit., 32–33.

45. In the model developed here, the quality maximizer will operate where $nP_n/P < -1$ when marginal cost (C_n) is low and the increase in donations (D_n) in response to lower ticket prices is relatively large [see (5)].

46. Netzer, op. cit., 50–52.

2

Cultural Entrepreneurship in Nineteenth-Century Boston

PAUL J. DiMAGGIO

Sociological and political discussions of culture have been predicated on a strong dichotomy between high culture—what goes on in museums, opera houses, symphony halls and theatres—and popular culture, of both the folk and commercial varieties. Such culture critics as Dwight MacDonald and Theodor Adorno have based on this dichotomy thorough-going critiques of popular culture and the mass media.[1] Defenders of popular culture have questioned the normative aspect of the critique of popular culture, but have, for the most part, accepted the basic categories.[2] The distinction between high and popular culture has been implicit, as well, in the discussion of public policy towards culture in both the United States and Great Britain.[3]

Yet high and popular culture can be defined neither by qualities inherent to the work of art, nor, as some have argued, by simple reference to the class character of their publics. The distinction between high and popular culture, in its American version, emerged in the period between 1850 and 1900 out of the efforts of urban elites to build organizational forms that, first, isolated high culture and, second, differentiated it from popular culture. Americans did not merely adopt available European models. Instead they groped their way to a workable distinction. Not until two distinct organizational forms—the private or semiprivate, nonprofit cultural institution and the commercial popular-culture industry—took shape did the

This paper originally appeared in *Media, Culture and Society* 4 (1982): 33–50, Copyright © by Academic Press Inc. (London) Limited. For advice and encouragement, I am indebted to Randall Collins, David Karen, Michael Schudson, Ann Swidler, and to the members of Professor Mary Douglas's "Mass Media and Mythology" seminar at the New York University Institute for the Humanities, of Theda Skocpol's graduate research seminar at Harvard University, and of Paul Hirsch's production-of-culture session at the 1980 "Social Theory and the Arts" conference in Chicago. Research and institutional support from the Andrew W. Mellon Foundation and from Yale University's Program on Non-Profit Organizations is gratefully acknowledged.

high/popular-culture dichotomy emerge in its modern form. Once these organizational models developed, the first in the bosom of elite urban status communities, the second in the relative impersonality of emerging regional and national markets, they shaped the role that cultural institutions would play, the careers of artists, the nature of the works created and performed, and the purposes and publics that cultural organizations would serve.

In this paper I will address only one side of this process of classification, the institutionalization of high culture and the creation of distinctly high-cultural organizations. While high culture could be defined only in opposition to popular culture, it is the process by which urban elites forged an institutional system embodying their ideas about the high arts that will engage us here. In order to grasp the extent to which the creation of modern high-cultural institutions was a task that involved elites as an organic group, we will focus on that process in one American city. Boston in the nineteenth century was the most active center of American culture; and its elite—the Boston Brahmins—constituted the most well defined status group of any of the urban upper classes of this period. For this reason the processes with which I am concerned appear here in particularly clear relief.[4]

When we look at Boston before 1850 we see a culture defined by the pulpit, the lectern and a collection of artistic efforts, amateurish by modern standards, in which effort rarely was made to distinguish between art and entertainment, or between culture and commerce. The arts in Boston were not self-conscious; they drew few boundaries. While intellectuals and ministers distinguished culture that elevated the spirit from that which debased it, there was relatively little agreement on what works or genres constituted which.[5] Harvard's Pierian Sodality mixed popular songs with student compositions and works by European fine-arts composers. The Philharmonic Society played classical concerts, but also backed visiting popular vocalists. Throughout this period, most of Boston music was in the hands of commercial entrepreneurs. Gottlieb Graupner, the city's leading impresario in the 1830s, sold sheet music and instruments, published songs and promoted concerts at which religious, classical and popular tunes mingled freely. (One typical performance included a bit of Italian opera, a devotional song by Mrs. Graupner, a piece of European fine-art music, "Bluebell of Scotland" and "The Origin of Common Nails," recited by Mr. Bernard, a comedian.) The two exceptions, the Handel and Haydn Society and the Harvard Musical Association, founded in the 1840s and 1850s respectively, were associations of amateurs and professionals that appealed only to a relatively narrow segment of the elite.

The visual arts were also organized on a largely commercial basis in this era. In the 1840s, the American Art Union sold paintings by national lottery.[6] These lotteries were succeeded, in Boston, New York and Philadelphia, by private galleries. Museums were modelled on Barnum's: fine art was interspersed among such curiosities as bearded women and mutant animals, and popular entertainments were offered for the price of admission to a clientele that included working people as well as the upper middle class.[7] Founded as a commercial venture in 1841, Moses Kemball's Boston Museum exhibited works by such painters as Sully and Peale alongside Chinese curiosities, stuffed animals, mermaids and dwarves. For the entrance fee visitors could also attend the Boston Museum Theatre, which presented works by Dickens and Shakespeare as well as performances by gymnasts and contortionists, and brought to Boston the leading players of the American and British stage.[8] The promiscuous combination of genres that later would be considered incompatible was not uncommon. As late as the 1880s, American circuses employed Shakespearian clowns who recited the bard's lines in full clown make-up.[9]

By 1910, high and popular culture were encountered far less frequently in the same settings. The distinction toward which Boston's clerics and critics had groped 50 years before had emerged in institutional form. The Boston Symphony Orchestra was a permanent aggregation, wresting the favor of Boston's upper class decisively from the commercial and cooperative ensembles with which it first competed. The Museum of Fine Arts, founded in 1873, was at the center of the city's artistic life, its exhibitions complemented by those of Harvard and the eccentric Mrs. Gardner. Music and art critics might disagree on the merits of individual conductors or painters; but they were united in an aesthetic ideology that distinguished sharply between the nobility of art and the vulgarity of mere entertainment. The distinction between true art, distributed by not-for-profit corporations managed by artistic professionals and governed closely by prosperous and influential trustees, and popular entertainment, sponsored by entrepreneurs and distributed via the market to whomever would buy it, had taken a form that has persisted to the present. So, too, had the social distinctions that would differentiate the publics for high and popular culture.

The sacralization of art, the definition of high culture and its opposite, popular culture and the institutionalization of this classification, was the work of men and women whom I refer to as *cultural capitalists*. I use the term in two senses to describe the capitalists (and the professionals whose wealth came from the participation of their families in the industrial ventures—textiles, railroads and mining—of the day) who founded the museums and the symphony orchestras that embodied and elaborated the high-cultural ideal. They were capitalists in the sense that their wealth came from the management of industrial enterprises from which they extracted a profit, and cultural capitalists in that they invested some of these profits in the foundation and maintenance of distinctly cultural enterprises. They also—and this is the second sense in which I use the term—were collectors of what Bourdieu has called "cultural capital," knowledge and familiarity with styles and genres that are socially valued and that confer prestige upon those who have mastered them.[10] It was the vision of the founders of the institutions that have become, in effect, the treasuries of cultural capital upon which their descendants have drawn that defined the nature of cultural capital in American society.[11]

To create an institutional high culture, Boston's upper class had to accomplish three concurrent, but analytically distinct, projects: entrepreneurship, classification and framing. By entrepreneurship, I mean the creation of an organizational form that members of the elite could control and govern. By classification, I refer to the erection of strong and clearly defined boundaries between art and entertainment, the definition of a high art that elites and segments of the middle class could appropriate as their own cultural property; and the acknowledgment of that classification's legitimacy by other classes and the state. Finally, I use the term framing to refer to the development of a new etiquette of appropriation, a new relationship between the audience and the work of art.[12] The focus of this paper will be on the first of these three processes.

THE PREDECESSORS: ORGANIZATIONAL MODELS BEFORE THE GILDED AGE

By the close of the Civil War, Boston was in many ways the hub of America's cultural life. But, as Martin Green has illustrated, the unity of the city's economic and cultural elite, the relative vibrancy of Harvard and the vitality of the communal cultural associations of the elite—the Handel and Haydn Society, the Athenaeum, the Dante Circle, the singing clubs—made Boston unique among America's cities.[13] Godkin called Boston "the one place in America where wealth and the knowledge of how to use it are apt to coincide."[14]

Yet at the close of the Civil War, Boston lacked the organizational arrangements that could sustain a public "high culture" distinct and insulated from more popular forms. As we have seen, the boundaries between high art and mass art were poorly drawn; artists and performers had not yet segmented elite and popular markets. It is not that the wealthy were uninterested in art. Henry Lee Higginson, later head of the Lee, Higginson brokerage house and founder of the Boston Symphony Orchestra, could reminisce of his not atypical student days in Cambridge in the mid-1850s: "We had been to the Italian opera, getting there seats for twenty-five cents in the upper gallery enjoying it highly. I had an inborn taste for music, which was nourished by a few concerts in Boston and by the opera."[15] His wife recollected:

> There were private theatricals, sometimes in German, there was a German class, and there were readings which finished with a delightful social gathering in the evening. He [Higginson] belonged to a private singing club in Boston, and often went to James Savage's room in Holworthy, where there was much informal singing and music.[16]

Many young Brahmins, like Higginson, spent time in Europe, studying art or music.[17] And many more learned and played music in or around Boston, or attended public lectures on the arts.[18]

Nor was there a lack of theories about the nature of good art. Although aesthetic philosophies blossomed after the high-culture institutions were established, even the mid-1850s nurtured aesthetic philosophers like Brook Farmer John S. Dwight, editor of *Dwight's Journal of Music*. Some Bostonians were aware of the latest developments in European music and acquainted with classical standards in the visual arts.

High culture (and by this I mean a strongly classified, consensually defined body of art distinct from "popular" fare) failed to develop in Boston prior to the 1870s because the organizational models through which art was distributed were not equipped to define and sustain such a body and a view of art. Each of the three major models for organizing the distribution of aesthetic experience before 1870—the for-profit firm, the cooperative enterprise and the communal association—was flawed in some important way.

The problems of the privately owned, for-profit firm are most obvious. As Weber has argued, the market declassifies culture: presenters of cultural events mix genres and cross boundaries to reach out to larger audiences.[19] The Boston Museum, founded in the 1840s, mixed fine art and sideshow oddities, Shakespeare and theatrical ephemera. For-profit galleries exhibited art as spectacle: when James Jackson Jarves showed his fine collection of Italian primitives at Derby's Institute of Fine Arts in New York, "the decor of this . . . dazzlingly ornate commercial emporium . . . caused much more favorable comment than Jarves' queer old pictures."[20]

If anything, commerce was even less favorable to the insulation of high art in the performance media. Fine-art theatre in Boston never seems to have got off the ground. And the numerous commercial orchestras that either resided in or toured Boston during this period mixed fine-arts and light music indiscriminately. A memoir of the period recalls a concert of the Germania Society (one of the better orchestras of this type): "One of the numbers was the 'Railway Gallop,'—composer forgotten—during the playing of which a little mock steam-engine kept scooting about the floor of the hall, with black cotton wool smoke coming out of the funnel." The same writer describes the memorable "evening when a fantasia on themes from Wallace's 'Maritana' was played as a duet for mouth harmonica and the Great Organ; a combination as the program informed us, 'never before attempted in the history of music!' "[21]

As with the visual arts, the commercial treatment of serious music tended to the extravagant rather than to the sacred. In 1869, an entrepreneur organized a Peace Jubilee to celebrate the end of the Civil War. A structure large enough to accommodate 30,000 people was built (at what would later be the first site of the Museum of Fine Arts) and "star" instrumentalists and vocalists were contracted to perform along with an orchestra of 1000 and a chorus of 10,000. As a finale, the orchestra (which included

330 strings, 75 drums and 83 tubas) played the anvil chorus with accompaniment from a squadron of firemen beating anvils, and the firing of live cannon.[22]

An alternative form of organization, embraced by some musical societies, was the worker's cooperative, in which each member had a vote, shared in the profits of the enterprise and elected a conductor from among their number.[23] The cooperative was vulnerable to market incentives. Perhaps more important, however, it was (also like its privately owned counterpart) unable to secure the complete allegiance of its members, who supported themselves by playing many different kinds of music in a wide range of settings. The early New York Philharmonic, for example, performed as a group only monthly. Members anticipated the concert "as a pleasant relief from more remunerative occupational duties, and the rehearsal periods were cluttered up with routine business matters, from which members could absent themselves with relative impunity."[24]

The lines dividing nonprofit, cooperative, for-profit and public enterprise were not as strong in the nineteenth century as they would become in the twentieth. Civic-minded guarantors might hold stock in commercial ventures with no hope of gaining a profit (e.g., Symphony Hall at the end of the century). The goals of the charitable corporation were usually defined into its charter, but otherwise it legally resembled its for-profit counterpart. Even less clearly defined was what I call the voluntary association: closed associations of individuals (sometimes incorporated, sometimes not) to further the aims of the participating members, rather than of the community as a whole. For associations like the Handel and Haydn Society, which might give public concerts, or the Athenaeum, which took an active role in public affairs, privateness was relative. But, ultimately, each was a voluntary and exclusive instrument of its members.

Why were these communal associations ill-suited to serve as the organizational bases for high culture in Boston? Why could the Athenaeum, a private library, or the Boston Art Club, which sponsored contemporary art shows, not have developed continuous programs of public exhibitions?[25] Could not the Handel and Haydn Society, the Harvard Musical Association (formed by Harvard graduates who wished to pursue after graduation musical interests developed in the College's Pierian Sodality) or one of the numerous singing circles have developed into a permanent orchestra? They faced no commercial temptations to study, exhibit or perform any but the highest art. (Indeed, the Harvard Musical Association's performances were so austere as to give rise to the proverb "dull as a symphony concert."[26])

None of them, however, could, by the late nineteenth century, claim to speak for the community as a whole, even if they chose to. Each represented only a fraction (although, in the case of Athenaeum, a very large and potent fraction) of the elite; and, in the case of the musical associations and the Art Club, members of the middle class and artistic professionals were active as well. The culture of an elite status group must be monopolized, it must be legitimate and it must be sacralized. Boston's cultural capitalists would have to find a form able to achieve all these aims: a single organizational base for each art form; institutions that could claim to serve the community, even as they defined the community to include only the elite and the upper-middle classes; and enough social distance between artist and audience, between performer and public, to permit the mystification necessary to define a body of artistic work as sacred.

This they did in the period between 1870 and 1900. By the end of the century, in art and music (but not in theatre[27]), the differences between high- and popular-culture artists and performers were becoming distinct, as were the physical settings in which high and popular art were presented.

The form that the distribution of high culture would take was the nonprofit corporation, governed by a self-perpetuating board of trustees who, eventually, would delegate most artistic decisions to professional artists or art historians.[28] The charitable corporation was not designed to define a high culture that elites could monopolize; nor are nonprofit organizations by their nature exclusive. But the nonprofit corporation had five virtues that enabled it to play a key role in this instance. First, the corporation was a familiar and successful tool by which nineteenth-century elites organized their affairs.[29] In the economic realm it enabled them to raise capital for such profitable ventures as the Calumet and Hecla Mines, the Western railroads and the telephone company. In the nonprofit arena, it had been a useful instrument for elite communal governance at Harvard, the Massachusetts General Hospital and a host of charitable institutions.[30] Second, by entrusting governance decisions to trustees who were committed either to providing financial support or to soliciting it from their peers, the nonprofit form effectively (if not completely) insulated museums and orchestras from the pressures of the market. Third, by vesting control in a well-integrated social and financial elite, the charitable corporation enabled its governors to rule without interference from the state or from other social classes. Fourth, those organizations whose trustees were able to enlist the support of the greater part of the elite could provide the stability needed for a necessarily lengthy process of defining art and developing ancillary institutions to insulate high-cultural from popular-cultural work, performance and careers. Finally, and less obviously, the goals of the charitable corporation, unlike those of the profit seeking firm, are diffuse and ambiguous enough to accommodate a range of conflicting purposes and changing ends. The broad charters of Boston's major cultural organizations permitted their missions to be redefined with time, and enabled their governors to claim (and to believe) that they pursued communitarian goals even as they institutionalized a view and vision of art that made elite culture less and less accessible to the vast majority of Boston's citizens.

THE CONTEXT OF CULTURAL CAPITALISM

In almost every literate society, dominant status groups or classes eventually have developed their own styles of art and the institutional means of supporting them. It was predictable that this would happen in the United States, despite the absence of an hereditary aristocracy. It is more difficult, however, to explain the timing of this process. Dwight and others wished (but failed) to start a permanent professional symphony orchestra from at least the late 1840s. The Athenaeum's proprietors tried to raise a public subscription to purchase the Jarves collection in the late 1850s, but they failed. What had changed to enable later efforts to succeed?

Consider, first, the simple increase in scale and wealth between 1800 and 1870. At the time of the revolution, Boston's population was under 10,000. By 1800 it had risen to 25,000; by 1846 it was 120,000. By 1870, over a quarter of a million people lived in Boston.[31] The increase in the size of the local cultural market facilitated a boom in theatre building in the 1830s,[32] a rise in the number and stability of book and music stores,[33] and the growth of markets for theatre, music, opera, dancing and equestrian shows.[34] The growth of population was accompanied by an increase in wealth. Boston's first fortunes were mercantile, the fruits of the China trade, large by local, but small by national standards. In 1840, Boston had but a handful of millionaires. By 1890, after post–Civil War booms in railroads, mining, banking and communications, there were 400.[35] Even the physical scale of the city changed during this period: beginning in 1856, developers began filling in the waters of the Back Bay, creating a huge tract of publicly owned land, partially devoted to civic and cultural buildings. As wealthy outlanders from Lawrence, Lynn and Lexington migrated to Beacon Hill and Cambridge, streetcars reduced the cost and the difficulty of travel to Boston from its suburbs.[36] In short, Boston was larger, wealthier and more compact in 1870 than it had been 50 years before.

With growth came challenges to the stability of the community and to the cultural authority of elites.[37] Irish immigrants flowed into Boston from the 1840s to work in the city's industrial enterprises;[38]industrial employment rolls doubled between 1845 and 1855.[39] With industry and immigration came disease, pauperism, alcoholism, rising infant mortality and vice. The Catholic Irish were, by provenance and religion, outside the consensus that the Brahmins had established. By 1900, 30 percent of Boston's residents were foreign-born and 70 percent were of foreign parentage.[40] By the close of the Civil War, Boston's immigrants were organizing to challenge the native elite in the political arena.[41]

If immigration and industrialization wrought traumatic changes in the city's social fabric, the political assault on Brahmin institutions by native populists proved even more frightening. The Know-Nothings who captured state government in the 1850s attacked the social exclusivity of Harvard College frontally, amending its charter and threatening state control over its governance, hiring and admissions policies.[42] Scalded by these attacks, Boston's leadership retreated from the public sector to found a system of nonprofit organizations that permitted them to maintain some control over the community even as they lost their command of its political institutions.[43]

Story argues persuasively that this political challenge, and the wave of institution-building that followed it, transformed the Brahmins from an elite into a social class.[44] As a social class, the Brahmins built institutions (schools, almshouses and charitable societies) aimed at securing control over the city's social life.[45] As a status group, they constructed organizations (clubs, prep schools and cultural institutions) to seal themselves off from their increasingly unruly environment. Thus Vernon Parrington's only partially accurate observation that "The Brahmins conceived the great business of life to be the erection of barriers against the intrusion of the unpleasant."[46] The creation of a network of private institutions that could define and monopolize high art was an essential part of this process of building cultural boundaries.

The Brahmin class, however, was neither large enough to constitute a public for large-scale arts organizations, nor was it content to keep its cultural achievements solely to itself. Alongside of, and complicating, the Brahmins' drive towards exclusivity was a conflicting desire, as they saw it, to educate the community. The growth of the middle class during this period—a class that was economically and socially closer to the working class and thus in greater need of differentiating itself from it culturally—provided a natural clientele for Boston's inchoate high culture. While we have all too little information about the nature of the visitors to Boston's Museum or of the audiences for the Symphony, it seems certain from contemporary accounts (and sheer arithmetic) that many of them were middle class. The same impulse that created the markets for etiquette and instruction books in the mid-nineteenth century helped populate the galleries and concert halls of the century's last quarter.[47]

CULTURAL ENTREPRENEURSHIP: THE MUSEUM OF FINE ARTS AND THE BOSTON SYMPHONY ORCHESTRA

The first step in the creation of a high culture was the centralization of artistic activities within institutions controlled by Boston's cultural capitalists. This was accomplished with the foundings of the Museum of Fine Arts and the Boston Symphony Orchestra. These institutions were to provide a framework, in the visual arts and music, respectively, for the definition of high art, for its segregation from popular forms and for the elaboration of an etiquette of appropriation.

Bostonians had sought to found a museum for some time before 1870. In 1858, the state legislature, dominated by factions unfriendly to Boston's elite, refused to provide Back Bay land for a similar venture.[48] The immediate impetus for the Museum, however, was a bequest by Colonel Timothy Bigelow Lawrence of an armor collection too large for the Athenaeum's small gallery to accommodate. Three years earlier the Athenaeum's Fine Arts Committee had suggested that the galleries be expanded, but nothing had been done. With the Lawrence bequest, and his widow's offer to contribute a wing to a new gallery, the trustees voted that the present is a proper time for making an appeal to the public and especially to the friends of the fine Arts, to raise the sum required to make available Mrs. Lawrence's proposed donation, and, if possible, to provide even larger means to carry out so noble a design in the confident hope that it may be attended with success. . . .[49]

A new museum promised to solve problems for several of Boston's elite institutions: Harvard had a collection of prints for which it sought a fire-safe depository, and the Massachusetts Institute of Technology and the American Social Science Association possessed collections of architectural casts too large for them to store conveniently. After a series of meetings between the Athenaeum trustees and other public and private decision makers, it was decided to raise money for a museum on a tract of land in the Back Bay. (The land, owned by the Boston Water Power Company, was made available through the intervention of Mathias Denman Ross, a local developer who was keenly aware of the effects of public and cultural buildings on the value of nearby real estate.) In 1870 the state legislature chartered the enterprise and, with the help of the Athenaeum, which sponsored exhibitions throughout this period, fund-raising began.[50]

The initial aspirations of the Museum founders were somewhat modest. The key figure in the founding was Charles Callahan Perkins, a great-nephew of a China-trade magnate, kinsman of the chairman of the Athenaeum's Fine Arts Committee and himself President of the Boston Art Club. Perkins wrote two books on Italian sculpture in the 1860s, championed arts education in Boston's public schools and served as head of the American Social Science Association's arts-education panel in 1869. (He had studied painting and sculpture in Europe for almost 10 years, before concluding that he lacked the creativity to be a good artist.) Perkins, in a report to the ASSA had asserted "the feasibility of establishing a regular Museum of Art at moderate expense," with primarily educational aims. Since Boston's collections had few originals, he recommended that the new collection consist of reproductions, primarily plaster casts of sculpture and architecture.

The breadth of response to the first appeal for funds for the museum is striking. Although the economy was not robust, $261,425 was collected for the building. Of this amount, the largest gift was $25,000, only two were larger than $5000 and all but $100,000 came from over 1000 gifts of less than $2000 from such sources as local newspapers, public-school teachers and workers at a piano factory. (By contrast, when the Museum sought to raise $400,000 for new galleries and an endowment 15 years later, $218,000 of the initial $240,000 in contributions came from a mere 58 donors.[51])

One reason for the breadth of early support was that the Museum, although in private hands, was to be a professedly communitarian and educational venture. The Board of Trustees contained a large segment of the Brahmin class: All but one of the first 23 trustees were proprietors of the Athenaeum; 11 were members of the Saturday Club, while many others were members of the Somerset and St. Botolph's clubs; most were graduates of Harvard and many were active in its affairs. The public nature of the Board was further emphasized by the inclusion on it of permanent and *ex officio* appointments: from Harvard, MIT and the Athenaeum; the Mayor, the Chairman of the Boston Public Library's board, the trustee of the Lowell Institute, the Secretary of the State Board of Education and the Superintendent of Boston's schools. The trustees dedicated the institution to education; one hoped that the breadth of the board's membership would ensure that the Museum's managers would be "prevented from squandering their funds upon the private fancies of would-be connoisseurs." Indeed, the articles of incorporation required that the Museum be open free of charge at least four times a month. The public responded by flooding the Museum on free weekend days in the early years.[52]

The centralization of the visual arts around a museum required only the provision of a building and an institution controlled by a board of civic-minded members of the elite. The Museum functioned on a relatively small budget in its early years, under the direction of Charles Greely Loring, a Harvard graduate and Civil War general, who had studied Egyptology when his physician sent him to the banks of the Nile. The Museum's founders, facing the need to raise substantial funds, organized both private and public support carefully, mobilizing a consensus in favor of their project from the onset.

By contrast, the Boston Symphony Orchestra was, for its first years at least, a one-man operation, forced to wrest hegemony over Boston's musical life from several contenders, each with its own coterie of elite support. That Henry Lee Higginson, a partner in the brokerage firm of Lee, Higginson, was able to do so was a consequence of the soundness of his organizational vision, the firmness of his commitment, and, equally important, his centrality to Boston's economic and social elite.

In a sense, Higginson began as a relative outsider. Although his father, founder of the family firm, made a fortune in shipping, Henry was the first of his line to matriculate at Harvard; but soon he dropped out (claiming poor vision), visiting Europe and returning to private tutelage in Cambridge. Upon completing his education, he studied music in Europe for several years, ultimately against the wishes of his father, as their tense and sometimes acrimonious correspondence suggests.[53] After an accident lamed his arm, he returned to the United States for good, fought in the Civil War, married a daughter of the Harvard scientist Louis Agassiz and, following a disastrous venture in southern farming and a lucrative investment in the Calumet and Hecla copper mines, finally joined his father's State Street firm.[54]

Higginson was a knowledgeable student of music, and a follower of the aesthetic doctrines of John S. Dwight. As early as 1840, Dwight had called for the founding of a permanent orchestra in Boston. "This promises something," he wrote of an amateur performance.

> We could not but feel that the materials that evening collected might, if they could be kept together through the year, and induced to practice, form an orchestra worthy to execute the grand works of Haydn and Mozart. . . . To secure these

ends might not a plan of this kind be realized? Let a few of our most accomplished and refined musicians institute a series of cheap instrumental concerts. . . . Let them engage to perform quartettes, etc., occasionally a symphony, buy the best masters and no others. Let them repeat the best and most characteristic pieces enough to make them a study to the audiences.[55]

A number of ensembles attempted to realize Dwight's ambitions. But it was Higginson's organizational skills (and his money) that gave Boston the nation's first permanent, philanthropically supported and governed, full-season symphony orchestra. In achieving the dream of a large permanent orchestra devoted to fine-arts music, Higginson faced and overcame two challenges: first, establishing control over fine-arts music in Boston as a whole; and, second, enforcing internal discipline over the orchestra's members. Against him were arrayed the supporters of Boston's existing ensembles, principally the Philharmonia and the Harvard Musical Association, and the city's musicians, jealous of their personal and professional autonomy.

Higginson published his plans for the orchestra in a column, headed "In the Interest of Good Music," that appeared in several of Boston's newspapers:

Notwithstanding the development of musical taste in Boston, we have never yet possessed a full and permanent orchestra, offering the best music at low prices, such as may be found in all the large European cities. . . . The essential condition of such orchestras is their stability, whereas ours are necessarily shifting and uncertain, because we are dependent upon musicians whose work and time are largely pledged elsewhere. To obviate this difficulty the following plan is offered. It is an effort made simply in the interest of good music, and though individual in as much as it is independent of societies or clubs, it is in no way antagonistic to any previously existing musical organization.[56]

In this last sentence, Higginson treads on delicate ground. He goes on to praise, specifically, the Handel and Haydn Society and the Harvard Musical Association, the two musical societies with the closest Brahmin connections, while indicating implicitly that there will be no further need for the services of the latter. To launch this new enterprise, Higginson proposes to spend, annually, $20,000 of his own money until the orchestra becomes self-supporting.

Despite a measure of public incredulity, and some resentment at Higginson's choice of European conductor, George Henschel, over local candidates, the BSO opened in December 1881 to the enthusiastic response of the musical public. (The demand for tickets was great; lines formed outside the box office the evening before they went on sale.) The social complexion of the first night's audience is indicated by a report in a Boston newspaper that "the spirit of the music so affected the audience that when the English national air was recognized in Weber's Festival Overture, the people arose en masse and remained standing until the close." By employing local musicians and permitting them to play with the Philharmonic

Society and the Harvard Musical Association (both of which, like the BSO, offered about 20 concerts that season), Higginson earned the gratitude of the city's music lovers.

The trouble began in February 1882, when the players received Higginson's terms for the following season. To continue to work for the Symphony, they would be required to make themselves available for rehearsals and performances from October through April, four days a week, and to play for no other conductor or musical association. (The Handel and Haydn Society, which had strong ties to the Athenaeum, was exempted from this prohibition.) The implications of the contract, which the players resisted unsuccessfully, were clear: Boston's other orchestras, lacking the salaries that Higginson's subsidies permitted, would be unable to compete for the services of Boston's musicians. (To make matters worse, a number of the city's journeymen musicians received no offers form Higginson at all.)

The response of the press, particularly of the Brahmin *Transcript,* suggests that loyalists of the other ensembles responded to Higginson's actions with outrage. The *Transcript* editorialized of Higginson

> He thus "makes a corner" in orchestral players, and monopolizes these for his own concerts and those of the Handel and Haydn Society. . . . Mr. Higginson's gift becomes an imposition, it is something that we must receive, or else we look musical starvation in the face. It is as if a man should make a poor friend a present of several baskets of champagne and, at the same time, cut off his whole water supply.[57]

A more populist newspaper complained that the "monopoly of music" was "an idea that could scarcely have emanated from any association except that of deluded wealth with arrant charlatanism." Even *Music,* a New York publication originally friendly to Higginson's efforts, called his contract

> a direct stab at the older organizations and rival conductors of Boston. It means that one or two organizations may make efforts to place their concerts on the off days which Mr. Henschel has been pleased to allow them, but some must be left in the cold, orchestraless and forlorn. . . . The manner in which the proposal was made was also one that forbodes tyranny. Some of the oldest members of the Orchestra, men whose service to music in Boston have entitled them to deference and respect, were omitted altogether, and will be left out of the new organization. It was intimated strongly that in case the offer was rejected by the men, their places would be filled from the ranks of European orchestras.[58]

Higginson and his orchestra weathered the storm. Attendance stayed up and, within a year, his was the only orchestral association in Boston, coexisting peacefully with the smaller Handel and Haydn Society. In order to achieve the kind of ensemble he desired, however, Higginson had to ensure that his musicians would commit their time and their attention to the BSO alone, and accept his (and his agent's, the conductor's) authority as inviolate. Since, in the past, all musicians, whatever their affiliations, were freelances upon whom no single obligation weighed supreme, accomplishing these aspirations required a fundamental change in the relationship between musicians and their employers.

In part, effecting this internal monopolization of attention was simply a matter of gaining an external monopoly of classical-music performance. With the surrender of the Philharmonic Society and the Harvard Musical Association, two major competitors for the working time of Boston's musicians disappeared. Nonetheless, while his musicians were now more dependent upon the BSO for their livelihoods, and thus more amenable to his demands, his control over the work force was still challenged by the availability of light-music or dance engagements, teaching commitments and the tradition of lax discipline to which the players were accustomed.

Throughout his life, Higginson fought to maintain control over the Orchestra's employees, and the issue of discipline was foremost in his mind from the beginning. In an early plan for the Orchestra, he suggested engaging a conductor and eight to ten exceptionally good younger musicians from outside Boston at a fixed salary, "who would be ready at my call to play anywhere, and then to draw around them the best of our Boston musicians, thus refreshing and renewing the present orchestra, and getting more nearly possession of it . . ." At that time, exclusive employment contracts were so rare that the more timid Henschel, after agreeing to serve as conductor, tried to convince Higginson to abandon his insistence on total commitment. "I assure you," he wrote as the first orchestra was being assembled,

> that is the best thing we can do, and if you have any confidence in my judgment, pray drop all conditions in the contract except those relating to our own welfare. I mean now the conditions of discipline, etc.[59]

Despite his frequent assertions that he yielded in all cases to his conductors' advice on orchestral matters, Higginson, as we have seen, insisted on exclusive contracts in the orchestra's second year, threatening to break any strike with the importation of European players. Although he won that battle, he nonetheless replaced the locals gradually, over the course of the next decade, with new men with few Boston ties, mostly European, of greater technical accomplishment, upon whose loyalty he could count.[60]

In this, Higginson was not merely following a European model. "My contracts," he wrote an associate in 1888, "are very strong, indeed much stronger than European contracts usually are . . ."[61] Characteristic of the orchestra contract was section 12:

> If said musician fails to play to the satisfaction of said Higginson, said Higginson may dismiss said musician from the Orchestra, paying his salary to the time of dismissal, and shall not be liable to pay him any compensation or damages for such dismissal.[62]

Higginson was undeniably an autocrat. In later years he rejected the suggestions of friends to place the Orchestra under a board of trustees; and he used the threat of discontinuing his annual subventions as a bludgeon to forestall the unionization of the players. Yet Higginson accomplished what all orchestras would have to achieve if orchestral work was to be separated permanently from the playing of popular music and Dwight's dream of a permanent orchestra devoted to high-art music achieved: the creation of a permanent musical work force, under exclusive contract, willing to accept without question the authority of the conductor.

THE BRAHMINS AS AN ORGANIZATION-FORMING CLASS

The Museum of Fine Arts and the Boston Symphony Orchestra were both organizations embedded in a social class, formal organizations whose official structure was draped around the ongoing life of the group that governed, patronized and staffed them.[63] They were not separate products of different segments of an elite; or of artists and critics who mobilized wealthy men to bankroll their causes. Rather they were the creations of a densely connected self-conscious social group intensely unified by multiple ties among its members based in kinship, commerce, club life and participation in a wide range of philanthropic associations. Indeed, if, as Stinchcombe has argued, there are "organization-forming organizations"—organizations that spawn off other organizations in profusion—there are also organization-forming status groups, and the Brahmins were one of these.[64] This they could be not just because of their cultural or religious convictions (to which Green, Baltzell and Hall have called attention[65]), but because they were integrated by their families' marriages, their Harvard educations, their joint business ventures, their memberships in a web of social clubs and their trusteeships of charitable and cultural organizations. This integration is exemplified in the associations of Higginson, and in the ties between the Museum and the Orchestra during the last 20 years of the nineteenth century.

It is likely that Higginson's keen instinct for brokerage—and the obligations he accrued as principal in one of Boston's two major houses—served him well in his efforts to establish the Orchestra. At first glance, Higginson's achievement in creating America's first elite-governed permanent symphony orchestra in Boston appears to be the work of a rugged individualist. On closer inspection, we see that it was precisely Higginson's centrality to the Brahmin social structure that enabled him to succeed. Only a lone, centrally located entrepreneur could have done what Higginson did, because to do so ruffled so many feathers: a committee would have compromised with the supporters of other musical associations and with the patrons of the more established local musicians. Nonetheless, if Higginson's youthful marginality permitted the attempt, it was his eventual centrality that enabled him to succeed. His career illustrates the importance of kinship, commerce, clubs and philanthropy in Boston elite life. Ties in each of these areas reinforced those in the others; each facilitated the success of the Orchestra, and each brought him into close connection with the cultural capitalists active in the MFA and led, eventually, to his selection as a Museum trustee.

Higginson was born a cousin to some of the leading families in Boston: the Cabots, the Lowells, the Perkins, the Morses, the Jacksons, the Channings and the Paines, among others.[66] (The first four of these families produced trustees of the Museum of Fine Arts during Higginson's lifetime. His kinsman Frances W. Higginson was also a Museum trustee.) In Cambridge, he was close to Charles Lowell and, after his first European adventure, he studied with Samuel Eliot, a cousin of Harvard President Charles W. Eliot, and later a trustee of the Museum. During this period, he spent a great deal of time in the salon-like household of Louis Agassiz, befriending the scientist's son and marrying his daughter. So close did Henry remain to his Harvard classmates that, despite his withdrawal after freshmen year, they permitted him to take part in their class's Commencement exercises.

When Henry went into business, he brought his family and college ties with him. A contemporary said of the Lee, Higginson firm, it "owed in some measure to family alliances its well-advised connections with the best financial enterprises of the day."[67] Indeed, Higginson's first successful speculation was his investment in the Calumet and Hecla mines, at the behest of his in-laws Agassiz and Shaw (the latter an early donor of paintings to the Museum). The family firm was instrumental in the development of the western railroads, through the efforts of cousin Charles Jackson Paine. In this enterprise, Higginson associated with John M. Forbes and with Charles H. Perkins (kinsman of the MFA founder). Higginson was so intimate with the latter that he invested Perkins' money without consultation. Lee, Higginson made a fortune in the telephone company, and Higginson, in later years, was a director of General Electric. In some of these ventures, the firm cooperated with other Boston financiers. Higginson was on close terms with his competitors, Kidder of Kidder, Peabody (the Museum's first treasurer) and Endicott, President of the New England Trust and Suffolk Savings (and the Museum's second Treasurer). Gardiner Martin Lane was a partner in Lee, Higginson when he resigned his position to assume the Museum's presidency in 1907.

Higginson was also an active clubman, a member of the Tavern Club (and its President for 20 years), the Wednesday Evening Club, the Wintersnight, Friday Night and Officers Clubs, New York's Knickerbocker Club and, from 1893, the Saturday Club. Among his Tavern Club colleagues were Harvard's Charles Eliot Norton (spiritual godfather of the Museum's aesthetes), William Dean Howells and Henry Lee. At the Friday Club he consorted with Howells, William James and Henry Adams. At the Saturday Club, his clubmates included the MFA's Thomas Gold Appleton and Martin Brimmer.

In the 1890s, Higginson's career in Boston philanthropy blossomed. (By now he was on the MFA's Board. Earlier, when the Museum's first President, Martin Brimmer, asked Charles Eliot Norton if Higginson should be invited, Norton wrote back that "Higginson would be excellent, but he never attends meetings."[68]) He lavished most of his attention (beyond that devoted to the Orchestra) on Harvard, which elected him a Fellow in 1893. He gave Harvard Soldiers Field and a new student union, was Treasurer of Radcliffe College, played a key role in the founding of the Graduate School of Business, patronized the medical school and gave anonymous gifts to deserving faculties.[69] Higginson's position as Fellow of Harvard placed him at the summit of Boston's institutional life and undoubtedly reinforced his contacts with the Museum's trustees and friends. His personal art collection, which included Turners, Corots and Rodins, encouraged such interactions as well. (In 1893, he donated a valuable Dutch master to the MFA.)

Thus was the Orchestra's founder embedded in the Brahmin community. When Lee, Higginson furnished an emergency loan of $17,000 to the Museum of Fine Arts in 1889, with little prospect of repayment, was this because he was on the Board; was it a consequence of Higginson's kinship ties with the Cabots, Perkinses or Lowells; his business alliances with Kidder or Endicott; his club friendship with Norton; Harvard ties to the Eliots? The range of possibilities renders the question trivial and illustrates how closely knit was Higginson's world.

In 1893, when Higginson demanded that Boston build him a new and suitable Symphony Hall, lest he abandon the Orchestra to bankruptcy and dissolution, the initial appeal for funds was signed by a broad cross section of the city's elite: his friends and kinsmen Agassiz, Lodge, Lowell, Lee and John Lowell Gardner; Harvard's Eliot, Norton, Longfellow, Shattuck and Parkman; Peabody of Kidder Peabody, to name a few. Present on the list were at least four of Higginson's fellow MFA trustees: the President (Martin Brimmer), the Treasurer (by now, John L. Gardner), Eliot and Norton.[70] The group raised over $400,000, a substantial stake in that financially troubled year.

CONCLUSIONS

The Museum of Fine Arts and the Boston Symphony Orchestra were creations of the Brahmins, and the Brahmins alone. As such, their origins are easier to understand than were British or Continental efforts in which aristocrats and bourgeoisie played complex and interrelated roles.[71] The Brahmins were a status group, and as such they strove towards exclusivity, towards the definition of a prestigious culture that they could monopolize as their own. Yet they were also a social class, and they were concerned, as is any dominant social class, with establishing hegemony over those they dominated. Some Marxist students of culture have misinterpreted the cultural institutions as efforts to dictate taste or to inculcate the masses with the ideas of elites. Certainly, the cultural capitalists, consummate organizers and intelligent men and women, were wise enough to understand the impossibility of socializing the masses in institutions from which they effectively were barred. Their concern with education, however, was not simply window-dressing or an effort at public relations. Higginson, for example, devoted much of his fortune to American universities and secondary schools. He once wrote a kinsman, from whom he sought a donation of $100,000 for Harvard, "Educate, and save ourselves and our families and our money from the mobs!"[72] Moreover, a secret or thoroughly esoteric culture could not have served to legitimate the status of American elites; it would be necessary to share it, at least partially. The tension between monopolization and hegemony, between exclusivity and legitimation, was a constant counterpoint to the efforts at classification of American urban elites.

This explains, in part, the initial emphasis on education at the Museum of Fine Arts. Yet, from the first, the Museum managers sought to educate through distinguishing true from vulgar art—at first, cautiously, later with more confidence. In the years that followed they would place increased emphasis on the original art that became available to them, until they abandoned reproductions altogether and with them their emphasis on education. In a less dramatic way, the Orchestra, which began with an artistic mandate, would further classify the contents of its programs and frame the aesthetic experience in the years to come.

In structure, however, the Museum and the Orchestra were similar innovations. Each was private, controlled by members of the Brahmin class, and established on the corporate model, dependent on private philanthropy and relatively long-range financial planning; each was sparely staffed and relied for much of its management on elite volunteers; and each counted among its founders wealthy men with considerable scholarly or artistic credentials who were centrally located in Boston's elite social structure. The Museum was established under broad auspices for the education of the community as a whole; the Orchestra was created by one man in the service of art and of those in the community with the sophistication or motivation to appreciate it. Within 40 years, the logic of cultural capitalism would moderate sharply, if not eliminate, these historically grounded differences. The Symphony would come to resemble the Museum in charter and governance, and the Museum would abandon its broad social mission in favor of aestheticism and an elite clientele.

The creation of the MFA, the BSO and similar organizations throughout the United States formed a base through which the ideal of high culture could be given institutional flesh. The alliance between class and culture that emerged was defined by, and thus inseparable from, its organizational mediation. As a consequence, the classification "high culture/popular culture" is comprehensible only in its dual sense as characterizing both a ritual classification and the organizational systems that give that classification meaning.

NOTES

1. Dwight MacDonald, "A Theory of Mass Culture," in Bernard Rosenberg and David M. White, eds., *Mass Culture: The Popular Arts in America* (Glencoe, Ill.: The Free Press, 1957); and T. W. Adorno, "On Popular Music," *Studies in Philosophy and Social Science* 9 (1941).

2. Herbert J. Gans, *Popular Culture and High Culture* (New York: Basic Books, 1974); Leo Lowenthal, *Literature, Popular Culture and Society* (Englewood Cliffs, N.J.: Prentice-Hall, 1961).

3. Paul DiMaggio and Michael Useem, "Cultural Property and Public Policy: Emerging Tensions in Government Support for the Arts," *Social Research* 45 (1978): 356–389.

4. The process, in other U.S. cities, was to a large extent influenced by the Boston model. A final, more mundane, consideration recommends Boston as the focus of this study: The prolixity of nineteenth-century Boston's men and women of letters and the dedication and quality of its local historians make Boston an ideal site for such an enterprise.

5. Christopher Hatch, "Music for America: A Cultural Controversy of the 1850s," *American Quarterly* 14 (1962): 578–586; and Neil Harris, *The Artist in American Society: The Formative Years, 1790–1860* (New York: Braziller, 1966).

6. Russell Lynnes, *The Tastemakers* (New York: Grosset and Dunlap, 1953).

7. P. T. Barnum, *Struggles and Triumphs; Or Forty Years Recollections* (Buffalo, N.Y.: The Courier Company, 1879); Neil Harris, *Humbug: The Art of P. T. Barnum* (Boston: Little, Brown, 1973).

8. C. McGlinchee, *The First Decade of the Boston Museum* (Boston: Bruce Humphries, 1940).

9. Dexter W. Fellows and A. A. Freeman, *This Way to the Big Show: The Life of Dexter Fellows* (New York: Viking Press, 1936).

10. Pierre Bourdieu and Jean-Claude Passeron; *Reproduction in Education, Society and Culture* (Beverly Hills, Calif.: Sage Publications, 1977); Pierre Bourdieu and Jean-Claude Passeron, *The Inheritors: French Students and Their Relation to Culture* (Chicago: University of Chicago Press, 1979).

11. In a third sense, "cultural capitalist" might refer to the entrepreneurs of popular culture—the Barnums, the Keiths, the Shuberts and others—who turned culture into profits. Although we will not consider this group at any length, we must remember that it was in opposition to their activities that the former defined their own.

12. My debt to Basil Bernstein and to Mary Douglas is evident here. My use of the terms "classification" and "framing" is similar to Bernstein's. See Basil Bernstein, "On the Classification and Framing of Educational Knowledge" and "Ritual in Education," both in *Class, Codes and Control*, Vol. 3 (London: Routledge and Kegan Paul, 1975); and Mary Douglas, *Purity and Danger: An Analysis of Pollution and Taboo* (London: Routledge and Kegan Paul, 1966).

13. Martin Green, *The Problem of Boston* (New York: Norton, 1966).

14. Ibid., 41.

15. Bliss Perry, *The Life and Letters of Henry Lee Higginson* (Boston: Atlantic Monthly Press, 1921), 29.

16. Ibid., 81.

17. See, e.g., Henry Adams, *The Education of Henry Adams: An Autobiography* (New York: Book League of America, 1928).

18. G. M. Whipple, *A Sketch of Musical Societies of Salem* (Salem, Mass.: Essex Institute, n. d.).

19. Max Weber, *Economy and Society*, Vol. 2 (New York: Bedminster Press: 1968), sec. 9.

20. Nathaniel Burt, *Palaces for the People* (Boston: Little, Brown, 1977), 57.

21. William F. Apthorp, quoted in Mark A. D. Howe, *The Boston Symphony Orchestra: An Historical Sketch* (Boston: Houghton Mifflin, 1914).

22. W. A. Fisher, *Notes on Music in Old Boston* (Boston: Oliver Ditson, 1918), 45–46.

23. For more detailed descriptions of this form, see Stephen R. Couch, "Class, Politics, and Symphony Orchestras," *Society* 14 (1976): 24–29; and John H. Mueller, *The American Symphony Orchestra: A Social History of Musical Taste* (Bloomington, Ind.: Indiana University Press, 1951).

24. Mueller, ibid., 41.

25. Boston Art Club, *Constitution and By-Laws of the Boston Art Club, with a Sketch of Its History (Boston: E. H. Trulan, 1878).*

26. *Howe,* op. cit., 8.

27. Twentieth Century Club, *The Amusement Situation in Boston* (Boston: Twentieth Century Club, 1910); Jack Poggi, *Theater in America: The Impact of Economic Forces, 1870–1967* (Ithaca, N.Y.: Cornell University Press, 1968).

28. Vera L. Zolberg, "The Art Institute of Chicago: The Sociology of a Cultural Institution," (Ph.D. diss., Department of Sociology, University of Chicago, 1974); and "Conflicting Visions of American Art Museums," *Theory and Society* 10 (1981): 103–125.

29. George M. Fredrickson, *The Inner Civil War: Northern Intellectuals and the Crisis of the Union (New York: Harper & Row, 1965); Ronald Story, The Forging of an Aristocracy: Harvard and the Boston Upper Class, 1800–1870* (Middletown, Conn.: Wesleyan University Press, 1980); Peter Dobkin Hall, *The Organization of American Culture* (New York: New York University Press, 1982).

30. Story, ibid..

31. R. Lane, *Policing the City: Boston, 1822–1885* (New York: Atheneum, 1975).

32. Russell B. Nye, *The Cultural Life of the New Nation, 1776–1830* (New York: Harper & Row, 1960), 264.

33. Fisher, op. cit., 30.

34. Nye, op. cit., 143.

35. Frederic C. Jaher, "The Boston Brahmins in the Age of Industrial Capitalism," in Frederic C. Jaher, ed., *The Age of Industrialism in America* (New York: Oxford University Press, 1968); Frederic C. Jaher, "Nineteenth-Century Elites in Boston and New York," *Journal of Social History* 6 (1972):32–77; Story, op. cit.

36. Sam Bass Warner, *Streetcar Suburbs: The Process of Growth in Boston, 1870–1900* (New York: Atheneum, 1970).

37. Paul Starr, *The Social Transformation of American Medicine* (New York: Basic Books, 1982).

38. Oscar Handlin, *Boston's Immigrants, 1790–1880* (New York: Atheneum, 1972); Stephen Thernstrom, *Poverty and Progress: Social Mobility in a Nineteenth-Century City* (New York: Atheneum, 1972).

39. Handlin, ibid.

40. Green, op. cit., 102.

41. Barbara M. Solomon, *Ancestors and Immigrants* (New York: John Wiley, 1956).

42. Story, op. cit.

43. Shiverick notes the contrast between the founding of the public library in the 1850s and that of the private art museum 20 years later, both enterprises in which Athenaeum members were central. See Nathan C. Shiverick, "The Social Reorganization of Boston," in A. W. Williams, *A Social History of the Greater Boston Clubs* (New York: Barre Press, 1970).

44. I use the term "class" to refer to a self-conscious elite united by bonds of economic interest, kinship and culture. For similar views of class, see E. P. Thompson, *The Making of the English Working Class* (New York: Random House, 1966); and Story, op. cit., xi.

45. N. J. Huggins, *Protestants Against Poverty: Boston's Charities, 1870–1900* (Westport, Conn.: Greenwood, 1971); and Morris Vogel, *The Invention of the Modern Hospital* (Chicago: University of Chicago Press, 1981).

46. Quoted in Shiverick, op. cit., 129.

47. Nye, op. cit.; Ann Douglas, *The Feminization of American Culture* (New York: Avon, 1978).

48. Neil Harris, "The Gilded Age Revisited: Boston and the Museum Movement," *American Quarterly* 14 (1962): 548.

49. Walter Muir Whitehill, *Museum of Fine Arts, Boston: A Centennial History* (Cambridge, Harvard University Press, 1970), 6–8.

50. This section relies heavily upon Walter Muir Whitehill's classic two-volume history of the Museum (ibid.) and, to a lesser extent, on Neil Harris' fine paper (1962, op. cit.) for its facts, albeit not for their interpretation.

51. Whitehill, ibid., 42.

52. Harris, 1962, op. cit., 48–52.

53. Perry, op. cit., 121–135.

54. In Henry Adams's words, "Higginson, after a desperate struggle, was forced into State Street." In later years, Higginson told a relative that "he never walked into 44 State Street without wanting to sit down on the doorstep and cry." See Adams, op. cit., 210; and ibid., 135.

55. Howe, op. cit., 4–5.

56. Ibid., 41.

57. Ibid., 67–69.

58. Ibid., 28.

59. Perry, op. cit., 299.

60. Howe, op. cit., 121–123.

61. Perry, op. cit., 398.

62. Ibid.

63. In James Thompson's terms, they were organizations whose resource dependencies all coincided. For their financial support, for their governance and for their clients, they looked to a class whose members were "functionally interdependent and interact[ed] regularly with respect to religious, economic, recreational, and governmental matters." See James D. Thompson, *Organizations in Action* (New York: McGraw-Hill, 1967), 27.

64. Arthur L. Stinchcombe, "Social Structure and Organizations," in James G. March, ed., *Handbook of Organizations* (Chicago: Rand McNally, 1965).

65. Green, op. cit.; E. Digby Baltzell, *Puritan Boston and Quaker Philadelphia* (New York: Free Press, 1979); Hall, op. cit.

66. Perry, op. cit., 14.

67. Ibid., 272.

68. Harris, 1962, op. cit., 551.

69. Higginson, whose vision extended beyond Boston, also gave generously to Princeton, Williams, the University of Virginia and Middlesex and sent the Orchestra to play, at his expense, at Williams, Princeton and Yale.

70. Higginson's relationship with Gardner and his mildly scandalous wife Isabella Stewart Gardner is revealing. When Isabella, a New Yorker, entered Boston society in the 1880s, she was accorded a frosty reception. According to Morris Carter, her biographer and the first director of her collection, she won social acceptance by employing the BSO to entertain at one of her parties, an action that would have required Higginson's approval. After her palace opened (more or less) to the public in 1909, Higginson presented her with a book compiled by her admirers. See Morris Carter, *Isabella Stewart Gardner and Fenway Court* (Boston: Houghton Mifflin, 1925); and Green, op. cit., 112.

71. Janet Wolff, "The Problem of Ideology in the Sociology of Art: A Case Study of Manchester in the Nineteenth Century," *Media, Culture and Society* 4 (1982): 63–76.

72. Quoted in Perry, op. cit., 329.

II

BETWEEN THE MARKET AND THE PUBLIC PURSE

3

Can Culture Survive the Marketplace?

PAUL J. DiMAGGIO

THE CHALLENGE OF THE 1980s

The inauguration of the Reagan administration in January 1981 brought a chill to the art world. For the President and his Office of Management and the Budget recommended severe reductions in the federal government's support for the arts and humanities. Even worse, many feared that the administration would eventually seek to eliminate altogether the National Endowments for the Arts and the Humanities.

To beneficiaries of the Endowments' support, it seemed as if the administration might roll back 15 years of progress in federal assistance to the arts. During the 25 years between the demise of the New Deal WPA Arts Projects in the early 1940s and the establishment of the National Endowments for the Arts and the Humanities in 1965, federal support for the arts in the United States had been virtually limited to the indirect yield of tax deductions for contributions to (and exemption from taxation of most revenues of) nonprofit arts organizations. Between the agency's creation in 1965 and 1980, the budget of the National Endowment for the Arts (NEA) grew from $2.5 million to over $150 million, as a wide range of other programs—the Humanities Endowment, the Kennedy Center, the Corporation for Public Broadcasting, the Museum Services Institute, the Comprehensive Education and Training Act (CETA), Housing and Urban Development block grants, and others—sprang up to bring total direct federal

This paper is reprinted, with permission, in revised and updated form, from the *Journal of Arts Management and Law* 13 (Spring 1983): 61–87. It was originally prepared as a background document for the forum "Can Culture Survive the Marketplace?" which took place at the Institute of Politics of the John F. Kennedy School of Government of Harvard University on April 21, 1983, under the sponsorship of the Kennedy School and the Massachusetts Council on the Arts and Humanities. Jonathan Moore, Nancy Perkins, and Robert Solow provided helpful reactions to a memorandum on which the paper was based. I am grateful to Anthony Keller and John Simon for careful and astute editorial readings of an earlier draft; and to the Andrew W. Mellon Foundation, the Ford Foundation, and the Yale Program on Non-Profit Organizations for support of research on which the paper draws. Nonetheless, the analysis and opinions expressed here are my responsibility alone and are not necessarily shared by any of the persons or organizations to whom thanks are due.

support for the arts to a level well above that. With the growth of federal investment in the arts there emerged a concomitant and directly related increase in state aid, from less than $3 million in 1968 to over $120 million in 1981. Municipal support for the arts, more difficult to measure, also rose sharply during this period. Much of this public support—between $300 and $350 million by 1980—was directed to private nonprofit organizations: art museums, orchestras, theatre, dance, and opera companies, nonprofit local arts agencies, and neighborhood arts organizations.[1]

Partly in response to this infusion of public support, but also in response to rises in disposable income, the coming of age of the baby-boom generation, and the huge increase in enrollments in colleges and universities in the 1960s, arts organizations increased both in scale and in number between 1960 and 1980. According to the National Endowment for the Arts, between 1965 and 1980, the number of professional orchestras increased from 58 to 144; opera companies from 27 to 65; dance companies from 37 to 200; large theatre companies from 12 to 70; and community arts agencies from 125 to nearly 2000.[2] On top of the growth in numbers was a growth in the budget and scale of existing organizations, with substantial investment in new plant and in greater administrative intensity. By 1980, according to Lester Salamon of the Urban Institute, nonprofit arts organizations had total revenues of some $2.6 billion.[3] Although it is not clear that these developments constituted a "boom"—annual consumer spending levels for the arts had not, for example, increased dramatically as a percentage of real income or kept pace with such truly booming items as health care—the growth was real nonetheless.

The psychological impact of the Reagan budget proposals, then, must be understood in terms of the orientation toward expansion during the two previous, heady decades. The original administration budget plans would have cut federal support to nonprofit cultural organizations (in 1980 dollars) by at least 60 percent from the level of the final year of the Carter administration. Had they been enacted, the proposals would have hurt arts organizations by reducing the federal funds they received. The Economic Recovery Plan, as a whole, also threatened arts organizations in three other ways. First, reductions in taxes of individuals in high brackets would increase the cost of giving, and many people believed that this would make individual donations decline.[4] Second, even deeper cuts in federal support for other program areas—in particular the social services, community development, and environmental programs—would place strong pressure on foundations and corporate patrons to transfer support to these fields. By increasing the level of competition for private support, the administration's program could reduce the share of private funds allocated to the arts and increase the fund-seeking costs of nonprofit organizations operating in an increasingly competitive funding environment. Third, cuts in federal support for the arts (and social services more generally) were believed likely to trickle down to the states: Smaller federal budgets, it was thought, would be reflected in reduced (or at least stagnant) levels of state and local cultural spending.

To arts supporters in an expansionist mood, such developments were discouraging indeed. And to organizations suffering from liabilities of newness or from expenses incurred by recent expansion, such cuts seemed to pose critical threats. As we shall see below, however, a softening in the administration's position on the arts and the President's inability to get all of the budget cuts he wanted from Congress both rendered some (but not all) of those fears exaggerated. Even in 1980, many such fears reflected a lack of understanding of the place of the federal contribution in the total mosaic of arts organizations' revenues.

The federal contribution to the arts, even in 1980, was small relative to the federal share of support for nonprofit activity in other realms. The Urban Institute estimated that federal programs provided 12 percent of the revenues of nonprofit cultural organizations in fiscal year 1980 and that reductions in federal support would lead to annual decreases in sector revenues of 8 percent.[5] (By contrast, nonprofit organizations in the social services and community development fields stood to lose a quarter of their total revenues as a result of the proposed federal cutbacks.) Other studies indicated that nonprofit arts organizations received, on average, between 5 and 10 percent of their budgets from the federal government.[6]

These figures, however, failed to tell the whole story. Any reduction in public support for the arts would not affect all organizations equally. While public funds constitute between 10 and 20 percent of the budgets of traditional arts organizations, public monies account for almost 50 percent of the revenues of local arts agencies. Experimental and neighborhood programs also were (and remain) particularly dependent upon public funds. Among the traditional institutions, with the exception of orchestras, smaller organizations are hardest hit by cuts in public monies. But declines in public support are most crippling for arts programs aimed at nontraditional publics such as rural or minority people; federal assistance for these agencies came largely from those public social programs that suffered the deepest cuts. Thus, it is precisely that sector of the arts world that has done the most to increase access to the arts—smaller and nontraditional organizations—that stand most at risk when public budgets fall.[7]

CULTURE, SURVIVAL, AND VALUES

The administration's efforts provided an occasion to address, more systematically than usual, the question of the responsibilities of the public and private sectors to the arts. As administration spokespersons hailed "private initiatives," sometimes as if they had invented them, called for increased levels of individual and corporate giving, and pressed "earned-income enhancement" upon arts organizations as an antidote to smaller government grants, critics wondered whether private and public dollars were as fungible as such exhortations implied. In other words, can private dollars—donated or earned through sale of services—be substituted for public without fundamentally changing the composition of organizations, programs, and activities that constitute the nonprofit arts sector in the United States? Can culture survive the marketplace? In the pages that follow, I shall address the opportunities and challenges that arts organizations and their supporters face in several funding arenas. I shall try, as well, to place these questions in a broader policy perspective, since the issue of how decision makers in a pluralistic society can best allocate responsibility for the support of its cultures is likely to remain with us long after the Economic Recovery Plan has disappeared into the history texts.

In one respect, the answer to the question posed above is an easy one. Culture not only can survive the marketplace; much of it—our literary and nonfiction book production, cinema, popular music, interior design, photography, and cuisine, to name but a few cases—has flourished in it, at least quantitatively. Many other segments of U.S. culture—folk music and dance, humor, language, styles of speech and popular expression—have done perfectly well by ignoring the economic marketplace. Religions have prospered relying on the tithes of their members. An impressive edifice of law has been built up by government, with the assistance of schools of law and law firms. United States science has reached heights of discovery through a partnership of government and universities, and is practiced successfully (although the norms and goals are different) in profit-seeking corporations as well.

Now many of the people reading this are likely to be interested in one particular kind of culture, high culture, and by this they mean the familiar areas of music, literature, drama, the dance, and the visual arts. I raise the preceding examples not as an exercise in semantic troublemaking, but to address three points. First of all, in our search for models for the organization and sustenance of culture we need not look very far. The production of popular culture, folk culture, religion, science, and law provide an array of alternative approaches and offer some hints as to their advantages and drawbacks. Second, high culture, by which I mean those art forms primarily produced in or distributed by nonprofit organizations, accounts for only a small part of our national culture (or cultures) and should be viewed from the perspective of the whole.[8] Third, we need not worry about the survival of culture, because culture always survives. What we are really concerned about is *the sort of* culture that will survive.

In order to talk about what kind of public policy can best contribute to the growth and flourishing of the arts, we must first agree that the arts are sufficiently important to warrant the attention of policy makers and the expenditure of public dollars. I will not discuss fully here the reasons I believe that there is a public interest in the well-being of the arts. But I will make explicit a few values that I think are important, because any discussion of arts policy must proceed with reference to the values that policy should maximize. I make no effort here to place priorities on these values. There are probably others; different individuals will place different weights on different ones; and, in practice, they quickly become tangled up with one another. But the multiplicity of values that cultural policy addresses is complicating, because one must consider trade-offs among them. If there were only one goal of public support for the arts, policy making would be much easier.

Excellence

Everyone talks about excellence, but few can define it. Suffice it to say that, among those who create and criticize any art form, some work is perceived as better—more skilled, more sophisticated, more adventurous, evocative of more profound responses—than other work. Some quality differentials in both execution and presentation are apparent to almost everyone; discerning others is better left to experts. Nonetheless, nearly everyone agrees that support for the arts from any source should encourage excellence, however defined, and discourage mediocrity. A common fallacy is that some art forms or genres are intrinsically more excellent than others. This position tends to underlie discourse on the arts even though it is, on the face of it, indefensible. There is, or could be, excellence in any artistic genre, form, or medium.

Conservation

Another aim of cultural policy might be the conservation of great works (and even merely good works, if they embody styles or ideas not elsewhere available) of the past. First of all, great art still delights and inspires or shocks and surprises. More important, we can think of art works as the genes of culture: Progress in art depends, in part, on the availability to contemporary artists of models from the whole of art history.

Access

In a democracy, most people agree that great works of culture should be accessible to everyone. It has been argued that efforts to acquaint the poor or ethnic minorities with high culture represent a patronizing form of cultural colonization; if such efforts are mishandled this may be the case. But if we see culture as, in Kenneth Burke's words, "equipment for living," as a kind of currency or capital, then acquaintance with a variety of cultural forms makes people better equipped and richer than they otherwise would be.

Innovation

We need not accept the analogy between progress in art and progress in science to agree that most art forms require constant innovation and that innovative art should be given the room it needs to survive and a chance to make its mark.

Pluralism and Diversity
A commitment to pluralism has been a traditional part of the American heritage. Justice Holmes called attention to the public interest in protecting the free marketplace of ideas, and others have noted the importance of protecting the multiple cultures that constitute our national culture. In government-policy terms, a commitment to pluralism is a matter of equity: Why should artists working in traditional European forms be given the resources to create excellent work while artists who work in other forms must respond to the dictates of the market? But there is a larger public interest in supporting pluralism. For just as mainstream high-culture art can be a resource for poor or minority people, so can ethnic or non-mainstream art be a resource for ethnic majorities and the well-to-do.

Participation
There may also be a public interest in developing the skills and inclinations that people need to make art as well as to consume it. Participation in cultural activities can give individuals opportunities to act on their environments, to stretch their imaginations, and to enhance their expressive abilities. (Ironically, many of those who criticize public agencies most severely for supporting amateur or participatory programs are the same people who take seriously the work of mass-culture critics like Dwight MacDonald and Ortega y Gasset, who warned that the mass media were narcotizing the public into a passive lump, ill-suited to citizenship in a democracy.)

I shall refer to this incomplete list from time to time to suggest that different forms of support for the arts and different ways of organizing artistic production and distribution are more or less supportive of different values. In the section that follows, I shall discuss several models of the ways in which supporters of the arts—private patrons, foundations, corporations, and government—might divide up the philanthropic turf.

THE DIVISION OF LABOR AMONG FUNDING SOURCES

Let us start with two principles of cultural policy:

1. *The uncertainty principle. (We can never be sure what is going to work.)* At the core of the evaluation of any work of art is an area of uncertainty. What one generation or group of critics thinks has promise may turn out to be sterile; what they think is barren may be hailed by another generation as great art, or may lead to the creation of great art. To see that this is the case, we need only to read art or music history. The French Impressionists were roundly condemned until they developed their own distribution system and inspired their own critics. When the music of Brahms was first played in this country, concert halls emptied out and critics called it atonal rubbish. This is not to say that one should be completely relativistic. What it does mean is that any system of cultural pa-

tronage should have some looseness in it, some play, some opportunity for odd works to fall between the cracks. If the Brahmses and Impressionists of our era are to survive, we need to foster a variety of patronage principles and a variety of relatively autonomous patronage sources.

While this may seem obvious, it is at odds with customary ways of thinking about policy, and is one of the things that makes cultural policy differ from social, military, or fiscal policy. Ordinarily we know what we want to achieve (e.g., well-fed children, missiles that go where they are aimed, taxes that are reliably collected) and we try to design an airtight system to achieve it. By contrast, in supporting culture, maintaining a sizeable element of randomness is essential.

2. *The constraint principle. (All organizations face constraints.)* No one can decide how or what culture should be funded and then instruct someone to follow his or her blueprint. Aside from private patrons, all funders of the arts are organizations, and all organizations have their own agendas, their own traditions, and their own supporters to whom they are beholden. Governments must please voters, corporations must appease shareholders, foundation staff must justify their actions to their trustees, and the trustees must justify them to themselves and to their associates. We can condemn such constraints and create master plans that ignore them; or we can recognize the varying limits that different sectors face and try to build them into our plans. The former is the rational engineering approach; the latter is more akin to Buddhism and Oriental methods of self-defense.

There are currently at least four popular prescriptive models of how the sectors that support the arts should interact with one another. The first model is that government lead and others follow. The second is that corporations and private foundations lead, calling upon government when they need its financial clout. The third model proposes a partnership among government, business, and foundations to set policy collectively. A fourth approach is to discern a natural division of labor among funding sectors and to build policy upon that.

Government as Leader

Because the National Endowment for the Arts is this country's single largest arts funder, it is alleged that the NEA has, in effect, been setting the priorities that foundation and corporate donors follow. The mechanisms for this are said to be two: First, large challenge grants, requiring three-to-one matches from private sources, permit recipient organizations to pressure other donors for support. Second, Endowment grants act as seals of approval, signifying to nonexpert funders that an arts organization is worthy of patronage.

The principal defense of having government (in the form of the Arts Endowment) set policy, while foundations and corporations follow, is that the NEA has the resources to assemble the professional panels necessary to give objective and knowledgeable reviews of competing proposals. The costs of information are so high, so this argument goes, that the Endowment becomes a clearinghouse and a vehicle for the professional arts community, in effect, to make the decisions—much as scientists decide on the relative merits of applicants to the National Science Foundation. Their decisions, it is argued, are fairer than less informed decisions by lay people could be, and thus their examples warrant following.

There is some merit to this argument and much merit to the panel system itself. Yet, even if one dismisses accusations that certain panels are "stacked" with advocates of one or another artistic position, there are three things wrong with it. First, the most important allocational decisions—allocation of agency resources among artistic disciplines and Endowment programs—are made by the agency director and staff (with the advice and consent of the National Council), not by panelists. These allocations are in large part political—as, in a broad sense, they should be, given the impossibility of comparing the merits of different artistic disciplines. But if it is impossible for a government agency to avoid making allocational decisions that are responsive to politics, this does not mean that other funders should abide by them. Second, this model violates *the uncertainty principle,* according to which even peer judgment cannot be relied upon to select, in every case, the art that should be funded. While we may agree that peer review is the best single decision-making strategy, we would still want to preserve some areas in which decisions were eccentric, quirky, or perverse enough occasionally to aid the potentially important artist or organization whose merit no sane or fair-minded contemporary would recognize. Third, this model violates *the constraint principle.* In practice, other agencies could not, for long, follow the lead of government, even if they wanted to. They are subject to different constraints and could not get away with it. (Imagine, for example, Exxon supporting [as the NEA did] the production of Erica Jong's *Fear of Flying.*)

Private Sector as Leader

Angered by pressure from challenge-grant recipients, some foundation and corporate arts supporters have countered that the private sector should call the tune, enlisting government financial aid when this is necessary. According to this model, best articulated in a Heritage Foundation paper on arts policy, private decision makers should generate projects, and government agencies should help fund them. This approach appeals to those who distrust government; what is more, it acknowledges the uncertainty principle. If funding decisions emerge from a variety of centers, each with its own decision rules, they will, presumably, be more diverse than those that come out of one or two public agencies.

Yet, ultimately, this model is as impractical as the government-leadership approach. First, one questions the wisdom of placing public money in the hands of many of those who might generate plans and proposals. While McNeil Lowry and the Ford Foundation of the 1960s originated programs that government could have matched with equanimity, we can all think of examples of private decision making less worthy of government endorsement. Second, this method also violates the constraint principle. A government agency that simply ratified private-sector funding decisions would lack a broad constituency among either artists or legislators and would probably perish. Third, the generation of initiatives from the private sector would quickly outrun the ability of government to fund them: Decisions would have to be made, peer review would be established, and the current system would be restored.

Partnership

The Arts Endowment often describes its policies as based upon a partnership among government, business, foundations, and the arts. The partnership approach is rhetorically appealing; but the goal of genuinely shared decision making at the national level is unattainable, and probably undesirable. First, any funding system that seeks consensus among all support sectors violates the uncertainty principle. Second, the partnership idea violates the constraint principle—different funding sources diverge not out of perversity but because they face different incentives, different pressures, and attract different kinds of people. One is tempted to suggest that any cultural project that requires the enthusiastic support of people in each funding sector is probably not worth funding (a suggestion to which the recent history of public television lends some support).

Natural Division of Labor

A final model is to let each support sector do what it is inclined to do and what it does best. This approach acknowledges the uncertainty principle in that it recognizes the value of multiple funding sources using a variety of decision rules. It also acknowledges the constraint principle in that it entails a patronage system designed around the constraints that differing funders face. Its major flaw is that there may be some values that none of the funding sectors are likely to address. One role of government in such a system should be to identify the values (and organizations that embody them) that are being served poorly; to encourage funders who can to support those values; and, when possible, to itself act as patron of the last resort, in addition to its normal patronage functions.

Up to now, I have discussed the arts funding system as a mosaic whole. If we accept the premises of the natural-division-of-labor model—and the attentive reader will notice that I have stacked the rhetorical deck in this direction—then our attention is focused on the pieces that compose this mosaic. Designing strategies of arts support that can meet the challenges described in this paper's first section requires an appreciation on the part of foundations, corporations, or government agencies of the constraints on other funding sectors, the resources that they command, and the preferences that are likely to guide their decisions. The next section provides such an overview.

PATTERNS OF PRIVATE AND PUBLIC PATRONAGE

The post-World War II era has been one of ever-greater institutional complexity in the arts, as in most other regions of the voluntary sector. Organizations in every artistic discipline have grown, both in budget and staff size and in the number of programs that they offer. Growth, and crises brought on by overly rapid expansion, have increased the budgetary needs of established institutions and have made the work of administering them much more complex.

Even more important, the number of arts organizations—and the number of kinds of arts organizations—grew exponentially during the 1960s and 1970s. Cultural industries that barely existed during the 1950s—the nonprofit resident theatre movement, dance, and chamber music, and neighborhood and community arts—spawned literally thousands of new organizations. And even the older, more staid arts fields expanded as well. (Fully one-third of the art museums active in 1980 had been founded in the previous 20 years.)[9] This supply-side cultural explosion has brought about new economies of scale and new levels of competition for audiences, grants, and trustees.

A third kind of complexity has been the differentiation of the arts organization's funding environment. Where the private patron once reigned supreme, the contemporary executive director or fund-raiser must know how to raise money from three levels of government, private foundations, and corporations as well as from the individual donor. Indeed, arts support has undergone an institutional revolution during the past 25 years, a revolution with which we are still coming to terms.

The complex budgetary ecology of the arts thus consists of several interdependent dimensions. Let us consider, one at a time, the major factors in the arts' funding environment: private patrons, corporate patrons, private foundations, and government agencies. In each case, I shall attempt to assess what the scale of giving has been to date and what it is likely to be in the future. Second, based on information that is of necessity fragmentary and often anecdotal, I shall sketch the constraints that each of these funding sources faces and the kinds of values that their giving programs are likely to address.

Private Patrons

Private giving by living individuals has increased markedly, from approximately $7 billion in 1956 to more than $66 billion in 1985. Although there are no reliable figures on the proportion of individual giving directed to the arts, we know that it is relatively small. (The largest recipient, by far, is organized religion.) Nonetheless, this amount still represents the greatest share of private (unearned) support for arts organizations. (Even if just 3 percent of individual contributions support the arts, the total, over $1.8 billion, would greatly exceed the combined grants of private foundations, corporations, and all levels of government.) Donations as a percentage of real income declined between 1970 and 1980 but increased sharply with the economic recovery of 1983, returning to early 1970s levels.[10]

What are the prospects for individual donations to arts organizations? In part, this depends on the state of the economy, which influences donated funds from all sources. In part, it also depends on the effects of changes in the federal tax laws, about which there are several opinions. The conventional view, associated with economists Martin Feldstein and Charles Clotfelder, is that individual givers respond to the *price of giving;* that is, to the income forgone by making a deductible contribution. Donors in high tax brackets give up less money when they make a deductible contribution than do individuals in lower tax brackets (because, had they not donated the income, it would have been subject to a higher rate of taxation). According to Clotfelder, tax cuts discourage donations (as would, of course, elimination of the charitable contribution deduction) by making it more expensive to give.[11]

By contrast, Yale economist Gabriel Rudney has argued that contributions are affected not only by the price of giving but also by the amount of discretionary income that donors have available. In this view, tax reductions may have relatively small effect on individual donations because they simultaneously raise the cost of charitable donations (which makes giving decline) and increase taxpayers' discretionary income (which makes giving increase).[12] Note, however, that almost all economists would expect changes in the cost of giving that do *not* increase discretionary income (e.g., elimination of the charitable deduction) to make charitable donations decline.

What does this mean for the arts? Too few years have passed since the Reagan tax cuts, our theories are too speculative, and data on individual donations are too poor in quality, to reach any confident conclusions. But there are some reasons for concern.

For one thing, evidence is emerging that younger people of means (the famous "Yuppies") have different and less favorable attitudes towards giving than do older individuals of comparable wealth.[13] (Whether these attitudes will change as the Yuppies age is an open question.)

For another, changes in the tax laws may have the strongest negative effect on the giving of precisely those donors who are most likely to contribute to arts organizations: people of wealth and upper-middle-class professionals. Using a sample of IRS returns from the 1970s, Rudney and two colleagues found that the dampening effect of the cost of giving on donations was greatest for high-income donors, whereas the positive impact of discretionary income was most substantial for the less wealthy.[14] The early returns from the first Reagan tax cut were consistent with their findings. According to the American Association of Fund-Raising Counsel, between 1981 and 1984 the average taxpayer with a family income of less that $50,000 gave more to charity; whereas the average taxpayer with a family income of grater than $50,000 gave less.[15]

Such dampening effects of taxes on giving may be counteracted by more aggressive fund-raising by arts organizations large enough to afford it. Preliminary analyses by economist Richard Steinberg of data from the late 1970s suggest that the arts sector, especially in comparison to other nonprofit industries, was spending less than an optimal amount on fund-raising (i.e., the marginal return to organizations in the sector of an extra dollar spent on fund-raising was substantially greater than $1.00).[16] There is some evidence that some arts organizations are investing more in fund-raising than they used to, and that this investment may be paying off. The Theatre Communications Group, for example, reports that individual contributions to its constituency of resident theatres more than doubled between the 1980–81 and 1983–84 seasons.[17]

What purposes and values do private donations sustain? Private patrons are usually immersed in a dense and influential set of relationships with other patrons. Most private giving, fund-raisers say, occurs when a person is solicited for a cause by someone that he or she respects. Families develop relationships with local institutions—the leading museum or orchestra in their community, in particular—that span generations. Families of newer wealth may seek, consciously or unconsciously, to establish their social positions through affiliation with institutions supported by established social elites. (Modern volunteers are able to rank a community's boards of trustees and "women's committees" by prestige and to pursue "volunteer careers" that take them from the less to the more prestigious of these groups.)[18]

The bulk of individual giving goes to large and prestigious organizations (in big cities) and to more modest, but locally prestigious, ones in smaller places. Art museums and symphony orchestras have the advantage here, although groups excluded from traditional boards on social grounds have often been among the leading constituents of resident theatres, museums of modern art, dance companies, and chamber orchestras. Larger, older, and more established arts organizations have the advantage as well, because they can afford to employ professional fund-raisers to pursue individual contributions.

Where the major institutions are of high quality, individual support furthers the values of excellence and of conservation. In smaller cities with less professionally developed institutions, such support may further the aim of geographic access by providing art for local citizens. Because private patrons are often willing to support capital expansion—which requires expanded programming to at least a broader middle-class audience—limited increase in access may occur in this way as well. Except for those cases in which socially excluded donors have established experimental alternative organizations, private patronage, as a rule, is less supportive of the value of innovation and not supportive at all of pluralism, diversity, participation, or excellence outside of the established artistic disciplines. The recent increase in private giving is unlikely to have helped the nontraditional, experimental, or neighborhood-based organizations that were placed most at risk by reductions in federal support for the arts.

Corporate Philanthropists

Between 1975 and 1985, business philanthropy has been a rapidly growing area of private giving, more than tripling in just ten years.[19] The levels of corporations' charitable contributions are tied closely to their profits. When profits rise, so do donations (but not as markedly as profits). When profits fall, contributions follow them (but, again, less sharply).[20]

During the recession of the early 1980s, it was apparent that companies had buffered their contributions programs from the short-term effects of hard times. Although absolute growth slowed, donations as a percentage of the declining pretax net income of firms increased more than 50 percent, to the unprecedented level of 1.76 percent in 1982. As good times returned, the dollar amount of corporate donations resumed its rise, but the percentage that this figure represented of company earnings declined. (Preliminary estimates for 1985 show lower profits and a higher percentage of contributions.)[21]

When President Reagan announced his plans to reduce sharply the federal role in the arts, many arts organizations turned to business for help; and many observers, believing that companies would have to give their highest priority to the victims of the administration's elimination of federal social programs, expected them to be rebuffed. In fact, neither the ambitions of arts advocates nor the fears of the doomsayers have proven correct. During the past four years, support for the arts has held more or less steady at about 10.5 to 12 percent of company contributions, rising slightly between 1980 and 1981, declining modestly in 1982, holding constant in 1983, and declining again in 1984. This means that the arts received about $400 million in grants from business in 1984, approximately as much from independent foundations as from all levels of government.[22]

This stability represents a setback for the arts in comparison to the heady rise in both the arts' share of the corporate dollar and in absolute support during the 1970s. The American Association of Fund-Raising Counsel reports that respondents to its 1982 survey of company foundations planned to reduce arts spending in favor of more support for education, health, and social services.[23] The fact that the 1982 and 1984 declines in the percentage of corporate contributions going to the arts were mild ones may simply represent a lag between intentions and action.

Indeed, a study of Massachusetts company contributions officers by Michael Useem and Stephen Kutner indicates that the honeymoon between corporations and the arts may be nearing an end, albeit one more likely to culminate in stable marriage than divorce. Useem and Kutner report that of the companies they surveyed, the ones that gave the largest proportion of their contributions to the arts were the ones with relatively "old-fashioned" approaches to philanthropy: those with smaller, less professionalized giving programs and those in which the chief executive officer played a particularly active role in both setting policy and choosing recipients.[24]

Corporate support tends to be allocated according to three somewhat different models. In the more traditional firms, it works much like private patronage; aid is given to causes when friends of the CEO ask him or her to assist. In other corporations, aid to the arts is, in effect, a public relations expense. (Indeed, in a few firms it has been part of the public relations budget.) In the more progressive companies, philanthropy is becoming professionalized: Philanthropic staff resist, as best they can, efforts by executives to deploy corporate dollars to their favorite causes; and, to the extent their usually stretched resources permit, attempt to plan coherent giving strategies that address community or national needs by drawing on the special strengths of their firms. Professional staff of corporate giving departments and company foundations seem particularly oriented, first, towards addressing community social and educational needs; and, second, to devising giving programs that are related to the core activities of their firms.[25] This latter emphasis often discourages gifts to the arts.

Observers of corporate philanthropy are unanimous in believing that the pace of professionalization has already begun to rise and will continue to accelerate. If this is the case, and if Useem's and Kutner's findings prove applicable beyond Massachusetts, company support for the arts may, at best, hold steady at its current levels as a percentage of total giving. Whether the absolute magnitude of corporate support rises will continue to depend upon the state of the economy.

Probably no donors face more pressing constraints than do corporate philanthropists. Company giving staff work in profit-making, usually publicly held, organizations that must justify their actions to directors and shareholders. Grant decision makers themselves must justify their choices to corporate superiors. Although corporate foundations often provide limited autonomy to staff and do serve to buffer donation levels from short-term fluctuations in company net income, they are usually dependent on year-to-year budgetary decisions by the parent company.

Despite some notable exceptions, corporate programs in the arts tend to be either conservative or commercial. Both Useem, and Kutner in their Massachusetts study, and sociologist Joseph Galaskiewicz, in a study of corporate philanthropy in the Twin Cities, discovered that corporate giving staff exert a strong influence on one another's points of view, and that a gift to an arts organization by a leading firm may serve as a more powerful imprimatur than an NEA or private foundation grant.[26]

What is more, even where company philanthropy is administratively separated from public relations, business philanthropists must exercise caution lest their gifts embarrass their firms. Company dollars tend to go towards traditional arts organizations in cities where companies are headquartered or maintain plants; and to large, visible organizations that promise to deliver large, visible things, like popular public television series and blockbuster art exhibits. Corporate support for art that is controversial is difficult for firms to justify.

Data collected by the Conference Board, a business group, on the 1982 arts and culture contributions of 534 major American companies illustrate this point. Of those gifts the recipients of which were identified, over 45 percent were devoted to music (including opera) or museums, and 16 percent to public television and radio. Cultural centers and theatres each received about 9 percent of the total, arts councils or united arts funds approximately 8 percent, and dance companies a scant 3 percent of company gifts.[27] Moreover, according to a survey undertaken by Kenneth Goody for the Rockefeller Foundation, when they do support arts organizations, corporations are more likely to provide general support or administrative aid than assistance to artistic projects.[28]

On balance, corporate funding may enhance the value of excellence as traditionally defined. (On the other hand, some corporate-supported blockbusters have been allegedly of substandard artistic quality, museum directors complain that certain corporate funders meddle intolerably in exhibit design, and curators bemoan the influence of traveling exhibitions on the quality of their working lives.) Company donations undoubtedly support the value of access, to the middle class at least. And, in some instances (e.g., the Kool jazz festivals), they tend to aid certain kinds of pluralism. Occasional corporate support for local arts councils and festivals may enhance participation as well. Corporations are generally ill equipped and little inclined to support serious innovation or experimental work, access beyond the middle class, or pluralism that extends beyond already popular or commercial forms. Nontraditional or highly innovative arts organizations, neighborhood arts groups, or arts organizations that serve minorities and the poor can expect little assistance from the business sector.

Private Foundations

The private foundation share of private philanthropy, which doubled between 1955 and 1970, fell to 5.7 percent in 1980, just ahead of the share of corporations.[29] Of all sources of philanthropy, private foundation grants grew most slowly during the 1970s. Increased assets (associated with a buoyant stock market) led to a substantial rise in foundation grant-making between 1980 and 1985.[30] In the long run, however, barring dramatic change in the tax laws, the long-term rate of growth is likely to be modest. Foundations have devoted approximately 14 to 15 percent of their outlays to cultural activities (a broad classification of which roughly half to two-thirds comprises the arts) in recent years.[31] Foundations, like other donors, have been pressed to address social welfare needs arising from federal budget cuts; but, through 1984 at least, they apparently have not reallocated support from the arts to do so.

The passivity of many arts fund-raisers with regard to foundations has been odd in comparison to the hope invested in corporate philanthropy, since the two sectors disburse roughly similar quantities of funds to the arts. Indeed, the constraints on foundations are probably less uniform than are the constraints on private patrons, corporations, or government agencies. Every foundation must support activities that are consistent with the laws that regulate foundations and with its own charter. Every foundation's staff must support programs that are acceptable to its trustees. And every foundation must solve certain problems of administration, including the trade-off between gathering costly information in order to make informed decisions, on the one hand, and keeping administrative costs in check, on the other.

Within the foundation community one can find programs of grant-making to the arts that support almost every conceivable value. Some private foundations support fellowships for individual artists; others aid community arts activities; still others provide assistance for conservation in the visual arts. Most private foundation arts support, however, is given with little fanfare to major traditional organizations, especially art museums and orchestras, in the foundation's home community.[32] Thus, although the potential for diversity in foundation grant programs is great, and often evident in the programs of some of the larger or better known private foundations, relatively few private foundations have exploited that potential to serve as sources of philanthropic "risk capital" for worthy but unpredictable experimental programs.

Government

The Reagan administration initially aimed to reduce the federal presence in the arts dramatically, proposing to cut the budget of the NEA by almost 50 percent. Stymied by Congress in this effort, the administration has settled for a slow war of attrition, eliminating those social programs like CETA that provided incidental support for the arts, attempting to terminate the National Institute for Museum Services, and seeking ever-smaller reductions in the Arts Endowment budget.

The effects of these policies have been threefold. First, and most widely appreciated, the budget of the National Endowment for the Arts, the after-inflation growth of which stalled during the Carter administration, has continued to stagnate. (By fiscal year 1985, annual appropriations for the NEA stood at approximately $163 million, in deflated dollars about where they were in the middle 1970s.)[33] The Hodsoll administration has, for the most part, eschewed ideological appointments and bold innovations, carrying out the same kinds of policies as did its predecessors, albeit with a slightly more conservative flavor. The decline in real dollars appears to have been distributed relatively evenly among the Endowment's major programs.[34]

Second, the first half of the 1980s has witnessed a quiet change in the center of gravity of public arts support from the federal government to the states. Federal appropriations for the Arts Endowment, which in 1980 exceeded state appropriations for state arts agencies by approximately 50 percent, now roughly equal those of the states, which have been on the rise.[35] (For 1984, the states appropriated $137 million. According to the National Assembly of State Arts Agencies, the figure for 1985 is over $160 million.[36]) Because more than 20 percent of the Endowment budget is passed to the states, state resources are now greater than those of the NEA. State agencies are more likely than the Endowment to fund smaller, established organizations; and several states are moving towards more routine general operating support for major (by state standards) established institutions. State agencies also provide more support than the federal government to local arts agencies and, although the amount is small, to neighborhood or participatory programs.[37]

Third, the widely publicized struggles over the budgets of the NEA and the Museum Services Institute obscured a more dramatic elimination of social programs that had provided special support for neighborhood and community arts organizations, which receive little direct assistance form the NEA. In particular, the elimination of CETA, which had paid salaries of staff ranging from secretaries at neighborhood arts agencies to at least one director of a small art museum, seems likely to have hurt disproportionately the smallest and most vulnerable organizations. Similarly, limits on federal support for municipal social programs eliminated another source of contracts for neighborhood, minority, and educational arts organizations.[38]

Hard data on the effects of the changing public role on the budgets of arts organizations are few. According to the American Symphony Orchestra League and the Theatre Communications Group, public support, as a proportion of total budgets, has declined somewhat for orchestras and theatres while, within the public sector, state support has come to play a slightly greater role than federal.[39] But the size of these changes is modest. Studies of local nonprofit sectors by Lester Salamon and his associates at the Urban Institute indicate that government support for the extremely broad category of art, culture, and recreation declined slightly in some cities, more in others (like Atlanta, which suffered an 18 percent decrease) between 1980 and 1982, but that this decline may have slowed or halted with the 1983 recovery.[40] Although the situation varied from place to place, in general changes were not marked.

Of course, such studies do not permit us to look at the effects of changes in public funding on specific kinds of arts organizations. In general, cuts in public support are more likely to hurt relatively small organizations in a discipline than very large ones, and experimental rather than traditional institutions (e.g., the 30 developmental theatres that the Theatre Communications Group reports have closed since 1980).[41] In particular, it is likely that cuts in social programs have taken their toll on neighborhood and minority arts groups. But data of high quality are simply unavailable.

Public arts programs, by their nature, entail an emphasis on accountability and geographic access. It is also politically essential for them to court the organized arts lobbies, which are dominated by the largest established organizations: art museums, symphony orchestras, and, in some states, resident theatres. These dual imperatives—to support the wealthiest and to provide access—create tension for public agencies when resources are not expanding. Some state agencies have resolved this tension by focusing on support for the largest and most powerful institutions while maintaining some assistance for organizations in "underserved" parts of their states and for organizations serving organized minority constituencies. In its five-year plan, the Endowment emphasized its support for the more established experimental organizations, which have less access to corporate and individual contributions than their more conventional peers.[42]

The constraints under which public arts agencies operate generate certain dynamics that have been resistant to changes in administration. First, public grants tend to be relatively widely dispersed, in a manner that enables agencies to hold together their constituencies. Second, relatedly, public agencies are more likely than other institutional donors to support organizations in arts-poor areas, thus increasing access to the arts among the middle class. Third, partly because of pressures for their own accountability and partly because of limits on their own resources, public agencies, like many corporations and private foundations, have been active in encouraging arts organizations to become more administratively efficient, to stretch grant dollars further. Fourth, public arts agencies are more likely than private foundations or corporations to support the development of art forms in fields that, like jazz or folk arts, extend their appeal beyond the upper-middle-class constituency of most traditional arts organizations. In practice, the Endowment and many state arts agencies have acknowledged a special responsibility to the experimental and innovative. But this is only one part of their collective mission. Because it is one that seems to survive as a matter of conscience rather than as a political imperative, it must be constantly defended.[43]

In short, then, the highly decentralized U.S. system of direct public assistance for the arts supports a wider range of values than most other funding sectors: excellence in both traditional and, to some extent, nontraditional art forms; innovation; access for the broad middle class and, to a lesser extent, others; diversity; at the federal level, conservation; and, at the local level, participation. Because the Arts Endowment, with its system of peer review, has been until now somewhat insulated from political pressures from outside the world of the arts; and because direct public support in the United States is so decentralized (and thus public agencies are subject to different constraints from place to place), the public contribution is potentially important beyond its size. On the other hand, because they support so many purposes, public agencies can address no single one of them as concertedly as can private foundations, at least at current levels of funding.

Summary

This review of the sectors that share the role of funding the arts has made two facts apparent. First, the financial outlook for the arts is neither particularly buoyant nor, for the arts in the aggregate, particularly grim. During the 1970s, support from private foundations declined relative to that from other sources, but support from the federal government and corporations increased markedly. During the early 1980s, federal support has shrunk, but continued increases in corporate and state support and in earned income have made up the difference. In the aggregate, the pluralistic U.S. system of support for the arts is relatively stable and capable of maintaining the current level of artistic activity.

What we have seen is that there are natural markets in the funding community for some kinds of values—those of excellence (for which I presume all funders strive), conservation (in the sense of the preservation, display and performance of traditional great works), and access (for residents of small cities and the broad middle class but not for minorities or the poor). Other values—diversity, participation, and limited pluralism—have received public support but are now threatened by reductions in government budgets. Still other values—in particular, innovation, scholarship, and diversity in the strongest sense—have few natural allies. Scholarly endeavors, like those of curators and recreators of medieval or nonwestern music, tend to be insufficiently glamorous for corporate and many government donors and have yet to engage the interest of many foundations. Few funders in any sector have considered seriously providing the infrastructure necessary to support the artistic development of minority, uninstitutionalized, or folk cultural forms. Innovative art work is risky and usually unpopular; and innovative arts organizations tend to have troublesome management structures that fit poorly with (public and private) bureaucratic requirements. What is more, artists, who are central to innovation, have been seriously neglected. Notwithstanding the existence of a few excellent foundations, Arts Endowment, and state arts agency programs that support creative artists, the bulk of arts-support activity in the United States proceeds as if the arts can do perfectly well without them.

One challenge, then, both for the next several years and beyond, will be for private and public cultural policy makers to devise systems for addressing some of the less marketable values of arts policy and to encourage those donors who can afford to be different to resist the temptation to follow the philanthropic crowd. In particular, I suspect that foundations and government agencies are in a potentially strong position to influence the arts-support system by example and by supporting programs that no one else will fund.

ART IN THE MARKETPLACE

Up to now, I have taken the basic structure of the U.S. arts support system as given. What are the alternatives to the system of artistic patronage that has developed in the United States? The obvious ones, if we look at how other advanced industrial societies of both the market and socialist varieties support the arts, involve a much larger government role. Yet the Reagan administration has argued that government's participation in supporting the arts, already less central than in any of this country's friends or foes around the world, should become smaller still. Government support for the arts, according to a comparative study by Yale economist John Michael Montias, accounts for 77 percent of revenues of nonprofit performing arts organizations in Austria, 73 percent in the Netherlands, 68 percent in France, 86 percent in Germany, and 90 percent in Sweden. By comparison, the figure in the United States is closer to 15 percent. Even the indirect support given through government tax deductions for gifts to 501(c)(3) (charitable) nonprofit organizations does not begin to compensate for this difference.[44]

At this point, the possibility of a public role of European scale in the U.S. arts-support system seems too remote to warrant a full-fledged discussion of its pros and cons. Instead, I shall consider the alternative to which the arts and other nonprofit organizations have been urged: increased reliance on earned income and the economic marketplace.

Increased Earned Income

Arts organizations can pursue at least two kinds of earned income. The first is nontaxable income from activities related to their core missions: for example, museum admissions or membership fees, performing-arts subscription or single-ticket sales, orchestra recording contracts, and theatre television productions. The second is taxable "unrelated business income" of the sort accrued by museum stores that sell a broad range of gifts and consumer goods, or by museums that buy and sell real estate. Arts administrators have become increasingly attuned to the first kind of earned income and are beginning to be more alert to opportunities for the second.

Related earned income plays a crucial role in the finances of most contemporary arts organizations. On average, large resident theatres earn 65 to 70 percent of their operating income (smaller, experimental theatres earn between 35 and 45 percent); orchestras, 45 to 60 percent; opera companies, 45 to 55 percent; dance companies, 55 to 65 percent; presenting organizations, about 65 percent; art museums, approximately 33 percent; local arts agencies and service organizations, 30 to 40 percent; and neighborhood and minority arts organizations, approximately 20 percent.[45]

In recent years, the established arts organizations have become more sophisticated in promotion, ticket pricing, and building a subscription base, and the results have paid off handsomely with increased attendance and income. Indeed, economist William Baumol notes that performing-arts organizations have suffered far less from the "inflation disease" over the past decade than many had predicted. Part of the reason has to do with greater sophistication with respect to marketing. (The rest has to do with declining cast sizes, production standards, and performer salaries.)[46]

Nonetheless, into the swelling chorus of advocates of earned income as a solution to the arts' ills, it is important to contribute a few discordant notes of skepticism. First of all, increasing earned income is not a viable strategy for organizations whose purpose it is to serve low-income persons who cannot afford to pay for their services. Increased earned income may also be a poor solution for organizations seeking to lure potential audience members into the arts; or for local arts agencies providing technical assistance for small, struggling producing groups. Earned income enhancement, as it is sometimes called, also holds out little promise for organizations—choral societies, avant-garde musical ensembles or theatre companies, or highly specialized art museums—that deal in genuinely unpopular art forms. Organizations whose potential audience is small and can be reached by word of mouth have little to gain by investing in elaborate marketing schemes. Thus, many organizations most severely affected by federal budget cuts do not have available to them a direct market option.

Second, earned income growth may be a mixed blessing for arts organizations concerned with achieving their core artistic missions. The nonprofit form exists precisely because the government and many of its citizens believed that some important social goals could not be achieved by the market. Organizations that let conductors rehearse new works for hours, curators who write books about obscure artists, fiction writers attempting first novels, and actors who engage in time-consuming theatre games all behave irrationally in economic terms: Their behavior costs more than its results can contribute to revenues, even with the cleverest marketing director.[47]

Third, and perhaps most important, is the problem of what students of management call *goal displacement.* When goals like artistic excellence or the service of new publics are difficult to accomplish, they may be displaced by goals that *can* be achieved. New staff are needed to perform new administrative functions; and such staff (except for the occasional saint) very naturally become advocates for the importance of their functions, and for policies that make it easier for them to do their work.

Take, for example, the case of subscription campaigns in the performing arts. Subscription audiences can enhance the stability of theatres by making it easier for them to plan full seasons and to maintain a constant cash flow. When the match between the interests of subscribers and the artistic goals of the theatre is a good one, they can be quite helpful.

But consider this only slightly overdrawn example of a theatre whose artistic director and staff have avant-garde aspirations. An ingenious marketing plan recruits a sizeable subscription audience for two years. The theatre uses the income to extend its season, to hire new administrative staff, and to spearhead a capital campaign that enables it to move into a larger house. At this point the trouble begins: The subscribers tire of the theatre and its challenging repertoire, and few new subscribers can be reached. By now, however, the company has accrued too many obligations to do without them.The managing director (with the director of marketing at his or her elbow) asks the artistic director to substitute a currently popular Broadway hit for an expensive production of a difficult new play about growing up Portuguese in Northern Ireland. The artistic director accedes.

The Broadway hit keeps the company afloat but does not revive its finances sufficiently. The next year a trustee asks the artistic director to do *A Christmas Carol* (to charm subscribers and coax single-ticket buyers away from the local ballet's production of *The Nutcracker*). The artistic director and some of the actors resign. The next year the new artistic director introduces a Noel Coward play, a musical version of *The Werewolf of London,* and, as a sop to the original subscribers, a new production of *That Championship Season.* (In order to justify a hoped-for foundation grant, the company may also do *Othello* and something by Ted Talley.) The organization has survived, but its original purposes (and most of its original personnel and audience) have been forsaken.

If this hypothetical case study seems too coarsely drawn, consider the real implications of dependence upon recording contracts for one major orchestra. (This example comes from a book by political scientist Edward Arian, who played in the Philadelphia Orchestra before he wrote about it.) In the period Arian describes, the orchestra, which surpassed all others in income from recording contracts, programmed concerts with pieces scheduled for recording in order to economize on rehearsal time. According to Arian, the need to cater to popular taste in selecting pieces to record created a "circle of conservatism" that "continues to feed upon itself."[48]

The point of these stories is not that arts organizations that devise exhibits and hold performances that appeal to large audiences cannot or should not market their programs more effectively. They should. But only certain kinds of organizations can benefit significantly from increases in earned income. What is critical is that trustees and managers assess carefully the implications for their organization's core goals before implementing techniques to enhance earned income, and that funders be sensitive to these same considerations.

Enhancement of unrelated business income is more difficult, but for some organizations it may be more promising since it is easier to insulate core activities from unrelated business efforts. Art museums have earned money from stores and restaurants; museums, performing-arts organizations, and even neighborhood arts groups have received income from real estate investments. The potential for such entrepreneurship, even given the constraints of tax and nonprofit corporations law, is probably significant for many organizations. Nonetheless, success in a business unrelated to one's core activity is often elusive (as executives of expansive conglomerates will attest), and the administrative costs are substantial. What is more, such ventures are subject to the tax on unrelated business income and may also attract IRS scrutiny of an organization's other activities.

More radical market solutions

The association of art, or at least "high culture," and the market may seem strange or even horrifying to those of us who were raised on Matthew Arnold and T. S. Eliot. Yet, if one looks at the origins of American high culture, one finds that the nonprofit/for-profit division of labor that now exists is neither as natural nor as hallowed by tradition as it seems. Our first major museums—those of the Peales and, a little later, of P. T. Barnum and his many imitators—were decisively for-profit. Yet they exhibited fine art, produced theatre of high quality (including Shakespeare and Gilbert and Sullivan, whose operettas were first seen in America at the for-profit Boston Museum), and hosted touring European "classical" vocalists and fine-arts dancers. The first American orchestras were for-profit, sometimes musicians' cooperatives, sometimes established by entrepreneurs: Gottlieb Graupner, whose Boston Philharmonic is said to be the first American symphony orchestra, was also a popular-song publisher and singer. The nonprofit form came to the arts relatively late—after the Civil War—and was not entirely dominant until much later. (A profit-making entrepreneur toured 12 English-language opera companies in the first decade of this century; and some commentators saw the Shubert organization as the hope of classical music into the teens.)

And if we look at our high-culture industries today, we soon see that nonprofit organization is not the only form. Indeed, in art, classical music, and even theatre, our museums, symphonies, and resident stages are only the nonprofit jewels in a for-profit crown. Museums are enmeshed in a web of for-profit galleries and dealers, supported by the sales of art books published by for-profit publishers and postcards manufactured by for-profit cardmakers. Some symphony orchestras draw income from recording contracts (with for-profit record companies), play on instruments manufactured and sold in for-profit enterprises, and use sheet music produced by for-profit publishers; and much classical music is played by small ensembles that are legally profit-seeking partnerships. Broadway theatres, many summer theatres, and the rapidly proliferating dinner theatres are for-profit; as are talent agencies, the theatrical press, and theatre-supply stores. what is more, many theatre plants are still owned and operated, for a profit, by real-estate entrepreneurs. How determinant are the obstacles (for they are certainly formidable) either to backward integration of nonprofit arts organizations into profit-making related fields that could subsidize their activities or to forward integration by for-profit producers of materials into presentation or exhibition?

The familiar explanations for the rise of nonprofit organizations do not fit well in the case of nonprofit enterprise in the arts in the United States. "Market failure," for example, is not a satisfactory account. The commercial orchestras of the nineteenth century can be said to have failed only in retrospect. In their time, they made a profit. Not until nonprofit entrepreneurs like Henry Higginson (founder of the Boston Symphony Orchestra) developed the permanent, first-rate, solely classical symphony orchestra, which before had existed only in the imaginations of a few music-lovers, could orchestras be said to be economically non-self-supporting (and then only because Higginson's subsidized model drove its for-profit competitors out of business).

The rise of nonprofits in the arts was, I suspect, the result of two coinciding impulses: those of artists and critics for organizations that would provide the maximum of freedom from market constraints and those of emergent urban elites for a prestigious culture that they could dominate and call their own. Although the demands of the former are stronger and better articulated than ever, the existence of institutions devoted to purifying an exclusive high culture is probably of less importance to our current national upper class than to the local elites of the beginning of this century, particularly now that the massive rise in higher education has made the arts accessible to more and more Americans. So although the professional apparatus of high culture has never been better institutionalized, the social constituency for the distinction between high and popular culture, and between nonprofit and for-profit enterprise in the arts, may be eroding.

Indeed, the for-profit sector already supports some values that we might want arts policy to achieve. Augustin Girard, for many years a member of the French Ministry of Culture and now "Minister de la Qualite de la Vie" for France, has argued that, while French public agencies sought in vain to increase the audience for that country's arts organizations, commercial culture industries achieved that goal behind the back of public policy. According to Girard, we should reject "cultural policies (that) have borne on classical dissemination methods and have aimed at democratizing the institutions reserved until now to an elite" and emphasize, instead, efforts supporting and influencing the development of what he calls the cultural industries, by subsidizing less profitable but meritorious products, providing tax relief and tax shelters in combination with regulations requiring certain public-service investments, and increasing the availability of investment capital to cultural entrepreneurs.[49]

Lest one be carried away by Girard's euphoria, note that he addresses only one goal of policy, that of increasing access; he writes of France, which differs from the United States in numerous respects; and he ignores the possibility that mass-communications approaches could drive out of business small performing-arts organizations that provide much of the diversity and innovation in our culture. Moreover, his arguments are irrelevant to the concerns of neighborhood and community arts organizations and many others, as well. Nonetheless, his point is worth taking seriously, if skeptically.

I offer these remarks in order to provoke thought and discussion and because the state of our knowledge about the intersectoral division of labor does not warrant very firm or scientific conclusions. We know rather little about why some art forms do well on the market and some do poorly. It is not enough to say that popular forms survive and unpopular ones fail: What this assertion ignores is the power of market segmentation. Markets are created by entrepreneurs; they do not exist in nature. Thus American popular music became dramatically more innovative and diverse when the radio industry began segmenting markets by age, ethnicity, region, and race.[50] Where markets for an art form are highly segmented, pluralism and often innovation thrive. Where mass markets are sought, pluralism, innovation, and, from the standpoint of many artists and consumers, excellence suffer. Yet little is known about the ways in which markets become segmented, or about the subtle but important relationship between the evolution of markets and the evolution of artistic genres.

Neither do we understand the manner in which expectations about the scale and quality of artistic performance develop. It is probably too late to go back to the standards of nineteenth-century orchestras which, with their slimmer staffing, uneven rehearsal schedules, and members who played in several ensembles at once, could make a profit (so long as they did not face subsidized competition); nor would we necessarily want to. But an understanding of the factors that lead to norms of performance might suggest fruitful opportunities for experimentation.

By way of summary, consider the following six points:

1. The current allocation of cultural activities between the for-profit and nonprofit sectors is neither natural nor incontrovertible.
2. Some arts organizations that are now nonprofit may be able to support themselves on the market (perhaps with a consequent loss of innovativeness).
3. In some cases, creative efforts to forge or segment profitable markets for currently unprofitable cultural products might work.
4. In other cases, creative recombinations of core and ancillary cultural activities through backward vertical integration by nonprofits or forward integration by for-profits might permit profitmaking activities to subsidize meritorious money-losing ones.
5. Some plausible aims of cultural policy are assisted, to varying degrees, by the market sector already.
6. Market solutions will do nothing to address problems of access for persons with little discretionary income; problems of diversity and survival of art forms without large markets; or, indeed, most of the other values with which cultural policy is concerned.

CONCLUSION

I began with a discussion of the Reagan administration's plans for the federal arts budget in the 1980s, and with these I will conclude. We have seen that the costs of the budget cuts originally proposed for arts organizations would have been substantial but not, in the aggregate, catastrophic. We have seen, as well, that, barring an unlikely conjuncture of fortuitous developments, the revenue gap that would have resulted would not have been filled by private philanthropy.

We have also seen that the natural division of labor among funding sources—the varying constraints that hem in any person or organization in the philanthropic field—combine to make new income least available to precisely those organization most likely to be harmed deeply by sharp reductions in public assistance to the arts: those organizations that address, primarily, the values of innovation, pluralism, diversity, and excellence in unconventional kinds of art. Such organizations are likely to remain less attractive than traditional institutions to private patrons and corporate donors. And they are particularly unlikely to find much salvation in pursuit of earned income.

In nurturing innovation, pluralism, and diversity, private foundations and government are best equipped to play a central role. As Kingman Brewster has written, "Let the government take its place as a full partner along with other angels; but let it be willing to march in when other angels fear to tread alone."[51]

In the long run, the welfare of the arts may depend on the emergence of a new intersectoral division of labor among nonprofit, for-profit, and public enterprise in the production and distribution of culture, broadly defined, and on the craftsmanship with which this new order is wrought. In this longer process, corporate and private foundations may play an important and constructive role if they display the daring necessary to provide risk capital to both nonprofit and for-profit enterpreneurs. And government must have the courage and wisdom to take fuller responsibility for the pursuit of those purposes that neither the market nor private philanthropy can be expected to support.

NOTES

1. Paul J. DiMaggio, "The Impact of Public Funding on Organizations in the Arts," (Yale Program on Non-Profit Organizations Working Paper 31, New Haven, Conn. July 1981), 3–7.

2. Livingston Biddle, "America for the arts," *Cultural Post* 6, 3 (Sept./Oct. 1980): 1ff. These figures ride on a fairly restrictive definition of "professional" and probably underestimate considerably the number of organizations with paid artistic staff in both periods.

3. Lester M. Salamon and Alan J. Abramson, *The Federal Budget and the Nonprofit Sector* (Washington, D.C.: The Urban Institute, 1982), 32. These figures do not include the impact of the demise of CETA and other programs that, though not cultural in orientation, to some degree supported arts organizations.

4. Charles Clotfelder and Lester Salamon, *The Federal Government and the Nonprofit Sector: Impact of the 1981 Tax Act on Individual Charitable Giving* (Washington, D.C.: The Urban Institute, 1981).

5. Salamon and Abramson, op. cit., 44.

6. DiMaggio, op. cit., 8–11.

7. Ibid.

8. Throughout this paper I used the term "high culture" loosely to refer to those artistic efforts supported by private philanthropy and government. As I explain below, history shows us that the designation "high" refers not to intrinsic features of an art form or genre but to its social status and to the manner in which artistic work is organized and distributed. One of the distinctive aspects of our current cultural landscape is the increased ambiguity, to which both public arts support and broader social trends have contributed, surrounding the classifications "high versus low" or "high versus popular" culture. For a broader discussion of this topic, see my chapter, "Cultural Entrepreneurship in Nineteenth-Century Boston" (chapter 2, this volume).

9. Paul J. DiMaggio, "The Nonprofit Instrument and the Influence of the Marrketplace on Policies in the Arts," in W. McNeil Lowry, ed., *The Arts and Public Policy in the United States* (Englewood Cliffs, N.J.: Prentice-Hall, 1984), 71. (The data come from the author's

analysis of the data from the National Center for Educational Statistics' Museum Program Survey 1979).

10. American Association of Fund-Raising Counsel, *Giving USA: Annual Report 1986* (New York: American Association of Fund-Raising Counsel, 1986), 10–17.

11. See, e.g., Clotfelder and Salamon, op. cit.

12. Barry Dennis, Gabriel Rudney, and Roy Wyscarver, "Charitable Contributions: The Discretionary Income Hypothesis" (Yale Program on Non-Profit Organizations Working Paper 63, New Haven, Conn., January 1983).

13. Arthur H. White, *The Charitable Behavior of Americans* (Washington, D.C.: Independent Sector, 1986). 14. Dennis, Rudney, and Wyscarver, op. cit.

15. American Association of Fund-Raising Counsel, op. cit., 13.

16. Richard Steinberg, "Economic and Empiric Analysis of Fundraising Behavior by Nonprofit Firms" (Yale Program on Non-Profit Organizations Working Paper 76, New Haven, Conn., September 1983).

17. Theatre Communications Group, *Theatre Facts 1984,* insert to *American Theatre* 1 (March 1985): 7.

18. Based on conversations with managers of and volunteers for arts organizations in several northeastern and California cities.

19. American Association of Fund-Raising Counsel, op. cit., 33.

20. Ibid., 33.

21. Ibid.

22. Ibid., 38.

23. American Association of Fund-Raising Counsel, *Giving USA: Annual Report 1984* (New York: American Association of Fund-Raising Counsel, 1984), 34.

24. Michael Useem and Stephen I. Kutner, "Corporate Contributions to Culture and the Arts" (Chapter 4, this volume).

25. Joseph Galaskiewicz, *Social Organization of an Urban Grants Economy: A Study of Business Philanthropy and Nonprofit Organizations* (Orlando, Florida: Academic Press, 1985).

26. Ibid.

27. American Association of Fund-Raising Counsel, *Giving USA: Annual Report 1985* (New York: American Association of Fund-Raising Counsel, 1985), 37. Similarly, a detailed study of corporate arts support in Chicago found that more than 50 percent of all company arts dollars went directly to museums, symphony orchestras, or opera. By comparison, theatre, the dance, individual artists, arts education, and arts fairs received a combined total of only 10 percent. See Chicago Council on Fine Arts, *Corporate Support of the Arts 1977* (Chicago: Chicago Council on Fine Arts, 1977).

28. Kenneth Goody, "The Funding of the Arts and Artists, Humanities and Humanists in the United States" (Report to the Rockefeller Foundation, November 1983, mimeographed).

29. American Association of Fund-Raising Counsel, *Giving USA: Annual Report 1982* (New York: American Association of Fund-Raising Counsel, 1982), 8. For a more comprehensive treatment of the role of private foundations in support of the arts, see Paul J. DiMaggio, "Support for the Arts from Independent Foundations" (Chapter 5, this volume).

30. American Association of Fund-Raising Counsel, 1986, op. cit., 42.

31. Ibid., 30–31.

32. See DiMaggio, "Support for the Arts," op. cit.

33. Robert Holley, "1985 NEA Pie Divided," *American Theatre* 1 (March 1985): 18.

34. Ibid.

35. Robert Holley, "An '85 Leap for State Arts Funding," *American Theatre* 1 (March 1985): 17.

36. "Update," Insert in *National Assembly of State Arts Agencies News* 5 (May 1985).

37. See, e.g., James Backas, "The State Arts Council Movement" (Background paper prepared for the National Partnership Meeting sponsored by the National Endowment for the Arts and the National Assembly of State Arts Agencies, June 23–25, 1980, Washington, D.C.), 23–34.

38. Regrettably, precise data on these effects are unavailable. CETA's administrative pro-

cedures were so decentralized and poorly monitored that estimates of its contribution to the arts vary by an order of magnitude. And no one has studied rigorously the plight of neighborhood and minority arts organizations—which, unlike more established groups, have no collective data-gathering capacity.

39. Theatre Communications Group, op. cit., 10.

40. See the following reports, all published by the Urban Institute Press, Washington, D.C., in 1984: Paul G. Lippert, Michael Gutowski, and Lester M. Salamon, *The Atlanta Nonprofit Sector in a Time of Government Retrenchment;* Michael Gutowski, Lester M. Salamon, and Karen Pitman, *The Pittsburgh Nonprofit Sector in a Time of Government Retrenchment;* Paul Harder, James C. Musselwhite, Jr., and Lester M. Salamon, *Government Spending and the Nonprofit Sector in San Francisco;* Kristen A. Gronbjerg, James C. Musselwhite, Jr., and Lester M. Salamon, *Government Spending and the Nonprofit Sector in Cook County/Chicago;* and Diane M. Disney, Madeleine H. Kimmich, and James C. Musselwhite, Jr., *Partners in Public Service: Government and the Nonprofit Sector in Rhode Island.*

41. Theatre Communications Group, op. cit., 1.

42. National Endowment for the Arts, *Five-Year Planning Document, 1986–1990* (Washington, D.C.: National Endowment for the Arts, 1984).

43. In 1985, the House of Representatives, stimulated by objections to grants made to several poets whose work was identified as "obscene," considered but rejected an amendment to the reauthorization bill for the National Endowment for the Arts that would have prohibited that agency's funding of work that (in the American Association of Museums' paraphrase) "might be judged offensive to a large segment of the population"—a standard that, if rigidly applied, would limit drastically the federal government's ability to support experimental artwork. See Ruth Hargraves, *AAM Legislative Service Bulletin,* August 27, 1985.

44. J. Michael Montias, "Public Support for the Performing Arts in Europe and the United States" (Chapter 14, this volume).

45. DiMaggio, 1984, op. cit., 63.

46. Hilda Baumol and William J. Baumol, "The Family of the Arts," in Baumol and Baumol, eds., *Inflation and the Performing Arts* (New York: New York University Press, 1984), 4–13. One suspects that there is room for continued growth in these areas, and that many arts organizations that have not yet employed modern marketing methods can benefit from doing so. See Paul M. Hirsch and Harry L. Davis, "Art Arts Administrators Really Serious About Marketing?" in Michael Mokwa and William Dawson, eds., *Marketing and the Arts* (New York: Praeger, 1979).

47. See DiMaggio, 1984, op. cit. for a more thorough discussion of these issues.

48. Edward A. Arian, *Brahms, Beethoven and Bureaucracy* (University, Ala.: University of Alabama Press, 1971), 23.

49. Augustin Girard, "Policy and the Arts: The Forgotten Cultural Industries," *Journal of Cultural Economics* 5 (1981): 61–68.

50. Richard A. Peterson and David Berger, "Cycles in Symbol Production: The Case of Popular Music," *American Sociological Review* 40 (1975): 158–173.

51. Kingman Brewster, "Paternalism, Populism, and Patronage" (Sotheby Lecture, Victoria and Albert Museum, London, 1978).

4

Corporate Contributions to Culture and the Arts: *The Organization of Giving and the Influence of the Chief Executive Officer and of Other Firms on Company Contributions in Massachusetts*

MICHAEL USEEM and STEPHEN I. KUTNER

Corporate contributions to the nonprofit sector have been on a nearly continuous rise since World War II. Business philanthropic gifts totalled $38 million in 1940 but multiplied more than tenfold within the next two decades, reaching $482 million by 1960. By 1980 annual corporate contributions topped $2.6 billion, and by 1982 corporate giving exceeded $3 billion. In recent years, the growth rate in corporate philanthropy has outstripped that of all other forms of private giving.[1]

Despite the increase, corporate largesse remains a comparatively small source of income for most nonprofit organizations. Of the $116 billion in revenues received in fiscal 1980 by nonprofit organizations other than religious organizations, only 22 percent came from all types of private giving, with corporate support providing a mere 2 percent. A survey conducted in 1982–83 of 3400 nonprofit organizations found that whereas government funds constituted 39 percent of revenues, direct company gifts supplied only 3 percent. In the case of colleges and universities, major beneficiaries of corporate philanthropy, company support accounted for only 1.3 percent of higher education's total expenditures in 1982–83. Sim-

The study on which this chapter is based has been supported by a grant from the Graduate School of Boston University, and research assistance has been rendered by Mary E. Beasley, Sandra J. Soslowsky, and Molly Zane. Helpful suggestions in preparing this chapter were provided by Paul DiMaggio, Meryl Louis, and Christine Rossell.

ilar patterns prevail among the nation's cultural organizations: In 1978–79, only 2.8 percent of the income of 18 major theatres derived from corporate gifts, and among 31 major orchestras the proportion was a scant 0.7 percent.[2]

Spread evenly, corporate contributions would be of relatively small moment for many nonprofit organizations. Yet most cultural, educational, and other nonprofit organizations receive no business underwriting at all, while a relatively small number receive much. For the favored few, the value of expanded corporate sponsorship can occupy a large place in development planning. But for nearly all, the potential value of company backing has acquired a new importance in an era of government austerity for the nonprofit sector.

The value of corporate money has become all the more significant because there is simply more of it. The rate of corporate giving is driven by the level of company income, and corporate earnings are on the rise. When a company's profits increase by $1 million over the previous year's income, for instance, the firm's giving can be expected to rise by nearly $10,000. Though the recession of the late 1970s and early 1980s retarded the rate of growth in the income of many companies, by 1984 most major firms were basking in multimillion dollar earnings increases. During a period in which government funding was down and corporate income up, the importance of business gifts to the nonprofit sector loomed greater than ever.[3]

For cultural and educational organizations, corporate giving was of particular salience, since they received more than half (52.1 percent in 1982) of the donated money. Moreover, culture and the arts were the area of greatest relative expansion during the 1970s, growing from 5.3 percent of total company contributions in 1970 to 11.4 percent in 1982. Education's share, which stood at 40.2 percent in 1970, had dropped to a low of 34.9 percent in 1973; but since the mid-1970s education has also been on an upward slope, reaching 40.7 percent of total corporate giving in 1982. By 1982, a commitment to contributing at least some funds to education and culture had spread to more large companies than had commitments to any other type of giving. Among 255 major firms participating in a 1981–82 national survey, 70 percent gave to culture and the arts, and 84 percent to education.[4]

The nonprofit sector thus intensified its courting of the profit sector during the early 1980s and, by fortuitous coincidence, corporations were themselves discovering new value in a strengthened relationship. For their own reasons, many companies came to view universities, ballet companies, art museums, and other nonprofit organizations as agencies with which association could further company goals. A philosophy of corporate social responsibility, accepted by growing numbers of senior managers, imbued giving with noble purpose. For the more narrowly oriented company pragmatists, the invention of the business-nonprofit partnership provided a self-interested rationale for increased giving as well. The giving spirit of both groups of managers was fueled in any case by the economic recovery, which had placed far more disposable cash in the hands of most corporations.

The intensifying importance of corporate philanthropy for both the suppliers and the demanders has been accompanied by a quiet but profound transformation in the organization of corporate giving. As company giving has grown, it has been accompanied by a gradual process of routinization and professionalization. Although this could lead to a reduction in the direct role of senior management in giving programs, we shall argue that it does not. The contributions process becomes more systematized as it becomes larger, but it does not become more insulated from top direction. Moreover, we also shall argue that as programs grow and become professionalized, they become more, not less, responsive to influences from outside the corporation, primarily from other corporations. The general expansion of corporate contributions has been accompanied by the emergence of a shared management culture that stresses giving, and companies whose programs do not measure up to the norm are encouraged to give more.

This chapter focuses on three central features of the evolving internal organization of corporate giving: the bureaucratization of the contributions process, the critical role of the chief executive in guiding the giving program, and the mutually reinforcing influence of firms on one another's contributions levels. These are the major organizational elements shaping both the level of a company's giving and the kinds of applicants on which its generosity is bestowed. They are the organizational filters through which successful applications from nonprofit organizations must ultimately pass. This chapter evaluates their influence on overall giving practices, practices that generally characterize corporate giving whether it be to education, culture, or other nonprofit areas. The chapter also directs attention to several distinctive features of corporate giving to culture and the arts.

To offer a more detailed appraisal of these organizational elements, we have chosen to focus on company giving in the Commonwealth of Massachusetts. We concentrate on a single state for both pragmatic and conceptual reasons. The organizational elements could not be adequately examined without the acquisition of information directly from the companies themselves, and focusing on firms in a single state considerably reduced our research costs. The limited geographic focus also permitted more direct analysis of the relative influence of outside organizations on company giving programs. The kinds of companies active in Massachusetts and their record of philanthropy are not precise replicas of the national patterns. Generalizations to other states and to the nation are necessarily tentative. Still, most of the organizational issues that are the subject of this analysis are applicable to major companies throughout the country.[5]

Our analysis is based on a direct survey that we conducted of 62 of the major Massachusetts companies in 1984. An initial list of the major firms was compiled from a roster of corporations in the state that had at least 1000 employees, and from the membership rosters of two of the state's major business associations, the Massachusetts High Technology Council (MHTC) and the Massachusetts Business Roundtable. The former includes most of the Commonwealth's manufacturers of high technology products, a key sector in the state, and the latter includes most of the state's largest firms.

With a consolidated list of corporations from these three sources, we contacted each by telephone in an attempt to identify an individual responsible for or knowledgeable about its giving program. The 126 companies for which we succeeded constitute the study population. Of these, 62 firms returned usable survey forms, for a response rate of just under 50 percent. Larger companies were moderately more likely to respond than smaller firms. Of the 39 companies that were members of the MHTC but were neither members of the Roundtable nor large employers, for instance, 36 percent responded, below the overall rate. There is thus a small upward bias in size, but the participating companies constitute a reasonably representative cross-section of the state's leading firms.

THE GROWTH AND PROFESSIONALIZATION OF COMPANY GIVING PROGRAMS

Companies making small contributions to the nonprofit sector generally allocate money on a relatively ad hoc basis, with few fixed rules and procedures for setting priorities and selecting recipients. A common pattern is for a lump sum to be set aside for parceling out by the company's chief executive or senior managers. Gifts are usually made in response to requests received directly by top managers, and largely in accord with their personal preferences.

As a company's giving program reaches a level in which ad hoc decisions by top management are no longer feasible, it typically introduces new procedures and organizational units designed to systematize the contributions process. Four elements are commonly found in highly developed giving programs. First, staff specialists are appointed to manage the contributions program. Second, the criteria for selecting recipients and the procedures for deciding among competing requests are encoded in written statements. Third, matching-gift programs are established to incorporate employee preferences into company allocations. Finally, a company foundation is established to partially insulate the giving program against the annual vagaries of company income.

The proportion of major Massachusetts companies studied that had adopted each of these elements is shown in Table 4.1. Half of the state's companies had one or more full-time professional contributions staff members; half had programs guided by written policy and procedure statements; half maintained matching-gift programs; and about a third operated a company foundation. Of the matching-gift programs, employee gifts to college and university were the favored form, matched by company gifts

Table 4.1 The Number and Percentage of Massachusetts Companies Maintaining a Professional Staff, Written Statement, Company Foundation, and Matching-Gift Program to Guide Their Allocation of Gifts to Nonprofit Organizations

Organizational Element	Number of Firms	Percentage of Firms
Professional Contributions Staff		
None	19	30.7%
One part-time	10	16.2
One full-time	12	19.4
More than one full-time	21	33.9
Written Contributions Statement		
Yes	30	48.4
No	32	51.6
Company Foundation		
Yes	21	33.9
No	41	66.1
Matching-Gift Program		
Yes	31	50.0
No	31	50.0

in the case of 27 of the 31 companies with such programs. Gifts to cultural organizations were matched by 10 of the 31 companies, and gifts to other nonprofit institutions were matched by 8 firms.

The larger the contributions program, the more likely are companies to have incorporated each of these elements. This can be seen if we divide the companies into three groups—the third whose 1983 contributions were less than $75,000, the third whose contributions ranged from $75,000 to less than $500,000, and the third with contributions exceeding $500,000 (nine companies gave more than $1 million). The proportion of the firms in these ranked groups possessing each of the organizational elements is displayed in Table 4.2.[6]

Virtually none of the firms with small annual contributions budgets had incorporated any of the major organizational elements into their programs. By contrast, most of the companies with large programs had incorporated all four. As the magnitude of company giving programs increases, so too does the degree of organizational professionalization.

The magnitude of company giving is a direct function of the company's pretax net income. The "1-percent rule" has prevailed for the past three decades, and it provides a convenient way to estimate a firm's contribution budget: Major companies have on average allocated one percent of their pretax income to philanthropic purposes. Thus, as a company's income pushes above the $50 million level, for instance, a contributions budget rising above the $500,000 level can also be expected.

The findings here imply that as a company's annual earnings begin to

Table 4.2 Percentage of Companies with Small, Medium, and Large Contributions Programs That Have Incorporated Major Organizational Elements into the Giving Process

Size of Contribution Program	Organizational Elements			
	Staff Size over 1.5	Written Statement	Matching-Gift Program	Company Foundation
Under $75,000 (10 to 12 companies)	10.0%	8.3%	8.3%	8.3%
$75,000–$500,000 (12 to 13 companies)	41.7	38.5	38.5	41.7
Over $500,000 (12 to 13 companies)	69.2	84.6	66.7	84.6
Statistical Significance of Relationship	$p=.03$	$p=.0005$	$p=.03$	$p=.002$

exceed $50 million, it is highly likely that it will have moved to appoint a full-time staff professional, set forth its giving procedures in writing, and establish matching-gift and foundation programs to facilitate the giving. In contrast, for a company whose pretax annual income falls below $7.5 million, and whose contributions budget is thus likely to fall below $75,000, the probability is high that it will have adopted none of these organizational elements to guide its giving. For a company whose pretax income lies between $7.5 million and $50 million, it is likely that the giving program will be in transition, moving from the largely ad hoc procedures characteristic of small firms toward the organized procedures instituted by most large firms.[7]

The expansion and professionalization of company programs contains implications as well for the composition of giving. In professionalized companies, policies are more subject to the norms prevailing within the corporate community. Thus, as giving programs develop, a convergence toward the corporate mean can be expected. National surveys of major corporations by the Conference Board reveal that there is less variability in the overall percentage giving levels among the largest U.S. corporations. Our survey of Massachusetts firms reveals that there is also less dispersion in the amounts allocated to the major fields of activity among corporations with the largest programs.

Again dividing the Massachusetts firms into three groups according to the size of their contributions program, we find, as anticipated, that large programs distribute their monies more conventionally than do small programs. Among firms with small programs (under $75,000 annually), the typical firm allocated approximately 10 percent to education, far below the prevailing national norm for major companies of 31 percent. The typical (median) figure for middle-sized programs ($75,000 to $500,000) was 22 percent. For large programs (over $500,000) it was 29 percent, just short of the 31-percent national norm. Conversely, the typical firm with a small contributions program gave 20 percent of its gift money to culture and the arts, far above the norm. The characteristic firm with a middle-sized program gave 12 percent of its budget to culture and the arts. For firms with large programs, the median figure was 10 percent, nearly the same as the national norm for major companies of 9 percent.

The growth and professionalization of company giving, then, is accompanied by greater conformity to the conventions of the profession. Among our Massachusetts firms, growth and professionalization translate into a smaller share of company gifts to culture and the arts, and a larger share to education. Once a company program reaches about $500,000 annually, however, further growth is no longer associated with diminishing proportions for culture and the arts. A survey of 534 firms in 1982 by the Conference Board reveals that the median percentage of the gifts budget allocated to culture and the arts is about the same—around 9 percent—for firms whose contributions budgets are $0.5 million to $1 million, $1 million to $5 million, or over $5 million.[8]

Growth and professionalization of corporate giving is also accompanied by declining variability in the recipients selected for largesse. As we shall see, companies whose annual program budgets exceed $500,000 are nearly twice as likely as companies with budgets under $75,000 to report that other companies influence their own decisions in setting giving levels and in selecting grant recipients in culture and the arts. Companies with small programs are thus more likely to follow their own guidance, whereas firms with large programs are more prone to listen to the counsel of their corporate brethren. An unanticipated consequence of the growth and professionalization of company giving may be more channeling of corporate gifts to recognized cultural organizations, and less to experimental groups.

THE INFLUENCE OF THE CHIEF EXECUTIVE ON COMPANY GIVING PROGRAMS

The systematization of corporate giving practices as firms grow large may well reduce opportunity for executive discretion. When philanthropic programs are small and ad hoc, the funds and thus most decisions remain in the hands of top management. When programs become large and routinized, senior management's discretion may be limited by the very rules it has prescribed. It may be limited as a matter of managerial priorities, as well. A contribution budget constitutes a tiny fraction of any company's spending plans. As a percentage of the firm's total annual budget, the gifts budget typically averages less than one-tenth of 1 percent. If sheer relative scale is a portent of senior management attention, a giving program should receive scant top attention at best. As a company's contributions budget grows, then, the converse side of increasing organizational routinization may be decreasing senior management guidance.

Among Massachusetts companies studied, however, this is not the case.

Table 4.3 Relative Influence of Company Personnel and Units in Setting Company Giving Policies and in Selecting Gift Recipients

Individual or Unit	Percentage of Companies Reporting Modest or Strong Influence on*	
	Gift Program Policies	Selection of Recipients
Chief Executive Officer	69.3%	61.2%
Contributions Office	48.4	48.3
Committee of Executives	30.6	30.6
Board of Directors	29.1	19.4
Public Affairs Office	17.7	24.2
Nonexempt Employees	9.7	14.5
Advertising Office	1.6	1.6

NOTE: Companies were asked, "How important or influential are the following units and individuals in the contribution decision-making process? Distinguish between decisions that (1) set general program policies, and (2) select specific recipients for program support." Three levels of potential influence were designated as strong, modest, and little or none.
*Number of companies on which percentages are based = 62.

Despite the relatively small place of contributions budgets in all of the companies' spending plans, top management continues nonetheless to exercise a strong hand. The chief executive officers (CEOs) of three-fifths of the firms, for instance, still review recommendations for specific contributions if they exceed a minimum amount. In the case of half of these firms, the minimum amount is a mere $500.

Similarly, most firms report that the single most important influence in the setting of company giving policies—and even in selecting recipients—is the chief executive. Companies were asked to identify the influence of the contributions staff, the chief executive, the board of directors, and other units on their giving programs. The chief executive emerges as the central figure, as can be seen in Table 4.3.

In two-thirds of the companies, the chief executives exercised significant influence on both the policies of the giving program and the distribution of its monies. The contributions offices had a strong voice in only half of the firms, and all other organizational units and groups, including other executives, the board of directors, and non-exempt employees, exercised still less voice.

Still, it is arguable that the chief executive's influence will be comparatively less on the largest gift programs, as contributions offices create formal procedures to guide the giving process. Here, too, the evidence is contrary. Again dividing the companies into three groups according to the size of their contributions budget, we see that the chief executive is as involved in gift decisions among the largest as among the smallest contributors (Table 4.4).

Most of the companies with programs of all three sizes report that their chief executive is centrally involved in setting policies and selecting recipients. The involvement of the chief executive is not a diminishing function

Table 4.4 The Influence of the Chief Executive and Contributions Office on Contributions Decisions in Firms with Small, Medium, and Large Contributions Programs

Size of Contribution Program	Percentage of Companies Reporting Strong or Modest Influence of			
	Chief Executive on		Contributions Office on	
	Program Policies	Selection of Recipients	Program Policies	Selection of Recipients
Under $75,000 (12 companies)	75.0%	58.3%	16.7%	16.7%
$75,000–$500,000 (13 companies)	100.0	84.6	76.9	76.9
Over $500,000 (13 companies)	84.6	76.9	61.5	61.5
Statistical Significance of Relationship	n.s.	n.s.	$p = .008$	$p = .008$

NOTE: n.s. signifies that the differences are not statistically significant.

of program size. The influence of the contributions office, on the other hand, is an increasing function of the annual giving, at least as it enters the range of $75,000 to $500,000. The chief executive comes to share power over the company's giving with the contributions office, but it is not a power that is significantly diminished by the rise of a professional contributions staff and office. Routinization of giving as a company grows large is not accompanied by any withdrawal of top managerial guidance.

Not only is the chief executive active in the life of most giving programs, but the top manager's level of interest can have a decisive bearing on the scale of the giving programs. This should be anticipated from the findings of research on corporate innovation in a range of social programs. In one investigation, for instance, researcher Michael Merenda studied exemplary efforts in corporate social responsibility among five companies or divisions of companies based in Massachusetts. The programs included an effort by General Electric to increase minority representation among its managerial ranks, Raytheon's establishment of an inner-city job training center, Cabot Corporation's expansion of its corporate contributions, Eastern Gas and Fuel's evolution of a system of social audit and reporting, and Hancock's program to assist the Boston School System through a troubled period of court-ordered desegregation. To explain why the companies chose to start the new social programs at the time each did, the researcher located the final cause in each instance not in predisposing company characteristics but in the personal interest taken by top management. In all five cases, concludes Merenda, "the chief executive is the pivotal figure when it comes to the initiation of voluntary social programs."[9]

If top leadership is critical to starting contribution programs, continuing commitment from the chief executive may be equally important for sus-

Table 4.5 Percentage of Companies with More Active Chief Executive That Have Increased Their Contributions Budget During the Past Two Years

Level of Involvement of Chief Executive in Contribution Program	Rate of Annual Increase of Contribution Budget, Past Two Years: Zero or Decrease	1 to 12 Percent	More than 12 Percent	Statistical Significance
Role of CEO in Setting Contributions Policies				
More active (17 companies)	29.4%	23.5%	47.1%	$p = .09$
No change or less active (45 companies)	51.1	28.9	20.0	
Attitude of CEO toward Contributions Budget				
Encourages larger budget (28 companies)	25.0	32.1	42.9	$p = .009$
No change (34 companies)	61.8	23.5	14.7	

taining their growth. This is evident in our study of Massachusetts company giving. To identify whether its chief executive had become more active, we asked each company the question, "During the past two years, has the chief executive officer taken a more or less active role in setting contribution policies?" We also asked each company whether, during that time period, its contribution budget had increased or decreased. For the sake of comparison, we divide firms into three groups according to trends in their contribution budgets: 28 companies whose budgets had decreased or remained constant, 21 companies whose budgets had increased by a modest 1 to 12 percent per year, and 17 companies whose budgets had grown by more than 12 percent annually.

Table 4.5 reveals that companies led by chief executive officers with deepening engagement in the giving programs during the past two years also tend to be companies with sharply rising contributions budgets. Of those companies with accelerating involvement of the chief executive, nearly half had annual budget growth rates exceeding 12 percent; of those firms whose chief executive had not become more active, only one in five had such high rates of expansion. If we compare two companies, one with an increasingly interested chief executive and the other without, the evidence implies that the first company is more than twice as likely as the second firm to make pronounced increases in its gifts program.

The differences are even greater when we compare firms whose CEO has been explicitly encouraging enhanced contributions with those whose CEO has favored no growth. Companies were asked, "During the past two fiscal years, has the chief executive encouraged or discouraged larger contributions budgets?" The lower half of Table 4.5 reveals that, if a company was led by an executive pushing for increases, it was three times

Table 4.6 Percentage of Companies Placing Importance on Culture and the Arts for Business, by Support of Chief Executive for Increased Contributions to Culture and the Arts

Level of CEO Encouragement for Company Expansion of Culture and Arts Contributions	Percentage of Companies Reporting Strong or Modest Importance of Culture and the Arts in the Region to			
	Help Recruit Managers	Improve Quality of Life	Improve Business Climate	Make Managers More Effective
CEO Encourages More Gifts (17 companies)	76.4%	94.1%	88.3%	76.5%
CEO Does Not Encourage More (45 companies)	35.6	60.0	51.1	24.3
Statistical Significance of Relationship	$p = .01$	$p = .02$	$p = .02$	$p = .003$

more likely than a company with a more passive executive to be operating a rapidly expanding gifts program.

The role of the chief executive is also critical in determining the allocations of gift monies among the major fields of activity. Paralleling the above question, companies were also asked if the chief executive had encouraged greater spending for culture and the arts during the two preceding years. Of the 45 companies reporting no special encouragement by the firm's top officer, 22 percent allocated a larger share of their contributions to culture and the arts in 1983 than in 1981. By contrast, of the 17 companies whose chief executive had pushed for increases, 47 percent gave a larger percentage of their 1983 gifts to culture and the arts. Enterprises with a chief executive who backed more spending on culture and the arts were more than twice as likely to have enlarged the proportion of the gifts budget bestowed on the same.

The rationale for enhanced cultural giving is not an arbitrary expression of executive preference but is rooted in an encompassing belief system concerning the value of the arts to the contributing firm. A flourishing cultural climate is viewed as valuable for both employee morale and the climate of business. This is evident if we again compare companies headed by chief executives who had been pushing for enhanced spending on culture with companies whose top officers had not. To understand their motivation for contributing to culture and the arts, companies were asked the importance of having a "strong set of cultural, arts and humanities institutions and organizations in Massachusetts or a city close to your location" for four company interests: (1) recruiting new managers, (2) enhancing the quality of life of employees and managers, (3) improving the business climate in the region, and (4) making managers who become familiar with the arts more effective in their work. The proportions of the companies reporting a strong or modest importance for each factor are shown in Table 4.6.

Of the companies whose chief executive had not been pressing for increased company contributions to culture, 36 percent indicated that a favorable cultural climate in the state was important for recruiting new managers. By contrast, of the companies led by top officers who had been encouraging more cultural gifts, 76 percent reported that the cultural climate was important for managerial recruitment. Similar differences in company outlook on the value of culture and arts in Massachusetts prevail for the three other areas of potential value to business.

The intensity of involvement of a chief executive is also a strong predictor of expected future growth in a company's giving. Firms were asked to forecast the size of their following year's contribution budgets compared to their spending levels at the time of the survey. Again, firms whose chief executive had become more active in the contributions programs were nearly twice as likely as other companies to anticipate growth of more than 12 percent. Similarly, companies whose chief executive had been pushing for increases were three times more likely than other companies to expect substantial contributions increases.

Despite the professionalization of giving among larger companies, the attitude of top management toward contributions to the nonprofit sector thus remains a decisive determinant of the level and distribution of giving among Massachusetts firms. The critical role of top management in determining a company's scale of giving is characteristic of large firms throughout the nation as well. A national survey of 229 major companies in 1980–81, for example, asked the firms to identify the factors that most influenced their level of corporate contributions. The single most important of 12 major factors identified (including the company's current and past earnings, the volume of requests, and the size of the firm relative to the community), was the "discretion of the chief executive officer." More than two-thirds of the corporations rated this as a key determinant of the level of giving. Similarly, interviews with 219 chief executives of another set of companies in 1981–82 reveal the same trend: four-fifths of the CEOs report that their own influence on giving levels was decisive. Still another study shows the importance of chief executives in steering company monies to specific recipients. The arts contributions of 69 major companies in Minneapolis and St. Paul were strongly skewed toward cultural organizations whose governing board included the contributing company's chief executive.[10]

The importance of the chief executive's attitude for the health of a company's giving program is implicit in the strategies of a range of campaigns to enhance company philanthropy. In recent years, the federal government, state agencies, and associations of both corporations and nonprofit organizations have launched various efforts to increase corporate giving. During the 1980s, the Reagan administration has fostered the concept of "new federalism," through which its reductions of support for many nonprofit institutions were to be replaced in part by expanded private subvention that federal exhortations were to stimulate. At the national level, for example, the National Endowment for the Arts in 1982 established an Office of Private Partnership to increase private support for the arts, and the White House founded the President's Committee on the Arts and Humanities to achieve the same. Illustrative of programs at the state level, the Massachusetts Council on the Arts and Humanities launched a "Corporate Support Project" in 1982 to encourage more company giving in the Commonwealth. Within the business world itself, the Business Committee for the Arts and the Council for Financial Aid to Education have long promoted more company largesse. The Independent Sector and other associations of nonprofit organizations have led similar efforts to foster more private giving.[11]

These campaigns typically work with top management as both agents and targets of change. Chief executives and other senior managers are invited to join advisory boards, and they are convened for evenings with fellow business leaders already committed to more corporate giving. To reward the meritorious and inspire the laggards, awards and honors are bestowed upon those managers and companies whose contributions have been exemplary. The Business Committee for the Arts, for example, conducts regional seminars for business executives to convert the unconvinced, and it recognizes a number of companies at an annual awards banquet for their outstanding contributions to the arts.

The present study confirms the validity of such strategies. The evidence implies that an especially effective means of leveraging more company giving is through changing the outlook of the chief executive. Although larger giving programs are well bureaucratized, and although even the largest programs still occupy only a tiny place in the spending plans of most firms, the attitude of the chief executive remains critical. Strengthening the chief executive's appreciation for the value of giving, heightening his or her understanding of the benefits in giving to such specific areas as culture and the arts, and ensuring that both translate into the budget and policies of the contributions office are among the most certain avenues for change. Yet though the channel for change is clear, far less certain is any nonbusiness organization's ability to gain access to the channel. Chief executives often listen to one another on corporate giving, but voices from outside their inner circles sound far fainter.

THE INFLUENCE OF COMPANIES ON ONE ANOTHER

Outside access to both the chief executive and the contributions office is first accorded chief executives and contributions officers of other companies. In serving on several corporate boards and in taking active part in trade association activities, senior managers from a range of companies routinely encounter one another far more often than they do directors of nonprofit organizations. Similarly, because of their shared concerns, contribution officers usually turn first to one another for advice on the level and target of their firms' giving.

Table 4.7 The Influence of Outside Organizations on the Level and Target of Contributions by Massachusetts Companies

Outside Organization	Percentage of Companies Reporting Modest or Strong Influence of Outside Organization on Own Decisions
Government Agencies	
National Endowment for the Arts	14.5%
National Endowment for the Humanities	11.3
Massachusetts Council for the Arts and Humanities	21.1
Nonprofit Association	
Massachusetts Cultural Alliance	21.0
Business Associations	
Business Committee for the Arts	6.4
Conference Board	21.0
Other Corporations in the Region	51.6

NOTE: Number of companies on which percentages are based = 62.

The special influence that companies have on one another's giving policies is evident in our survey of Massachusetts firms. For this analysis, we focus on corporate giving to culture and the arts. The leading organizations active in encouraging corporate giving in the cultural field include three government agencies: the National Endowment for the Arts, the National Endowment for the Humanities, and the state art agencies (in Massachusetts, the Massachusetts Council on the Arts and Humanities). Other organizations include the major state association of nonprofit organizations concerned with corporate giving, the Massachusetts Cultural Alliance, and two business associations: the Business Committee for the Arts, a national organization devoted to increasing private support for cultural activities, and the Conference Board, an organization that does not advocate increased corporate giving but does publish the definitive set of statistics on annual company giving, to which many firms look for guidance. Finally, we include among our list of potentially influential outside organizations other corporations in the region. Our survey question asked each company "how important or helpful are [these] outside organizations in setting contribution budget levels or in identifying suitable gift recipients in the area of culture, the arts and humanities?" Findings on the relative influence of the outside organizations are displayed in Table 4.7.

Fewer than one company in five singles out the two national endowments or the Business Committee for the Arts as having significant influence on their giving policies. About one in five attributes substantial influence to the Massachusetts Council on the Arts and Humanities, the Massachusetts Cultural Alliance, and the Conference Board. But one company in two identifies other corporations as influencing its decisions. The most important single external source of influence on a firm's giving is thus the giving of other firms.

Table 4.8 The Influence of an Outside Organization's Earlier Grant to an Applicant on the Evaluation of the Applicant's Merits by Massachusetts Companies

Outside Organization	Percentage of Companies Reporting Modest or Strong Influence of Outside Organization on Own Decisions
National Endowment for the Arts	29.0%
National Endowment for the Humanities	27.4
Massachusetts Council for the Arts and Humanities	33.9
Another Major Corporation	50.0

NOTE: Number of Companies on which percentages are based = 62.

An identical conclusion emerges in examining the influence of outside organizations when a company is selecting gift recipients from among its many applicants. The volume of requests to companies is so great that companies must frequently take decisions in the absence of fully adequate information. Firms have neither the time nor the means for a thorough review of all prospective recipients' past performance, constituency, or internal management. Given this lack of comprehensive information, a frequently employed short-hand indicator of merit is whether the applicant has previously received grants or gifts from other organizations of stature.

In reviewing gift requests, Massachusetts companies report being influenced by an applicant organization's success in obtaining support from the two national endowments, the state arts council, and other corporations. To assay the relative significance of each, companies were asked, "How important is the fact that an applicant has already received a grant from one of [these] organizations in helping you to assess the merit of [the applicant's] program?" Table 4.8 reports the proportion of the firms attributing significant influence to each.

Again, we see that the most influential outside organization is another corporation rather than a public agency. If another firm has already made a grant to an applicant, it is a legitimating factor for half of the companies surveyed, a substantially higher proportion than if the outside organization is one of the three government granters. Still, it is notable that the imprimaturs of the two national endowments and the state arts council are not without weight. A third of the firms attribute significant influence to grant actions by the Massachusetts Council on the Arts and Humanities, and nearly similar amounts ascribe importance to support from the National Endowments for the Arts and for the Humanities.

In relying on the confirming decisions of other firms, Massachusetts corporations are using a strategy common to companies across the country. Nearly a third of the corporate executives responsible for giving programs of 440 major firms reported in response to a 1975 survey by the Conference Board that "peer company comparisons" were a major factor in setting the contribution dollar level. Similarly, a survey of 229 large firms in

1980–81 revealed that most corporations are well informed about the giving policies and practices of other companies: One-third of the companies solicited giving information from other firms, and four in five were aware of the other firms' contributions policies. Two-thirds of the companies report that pressure from other firms was a very important influence on their own giving decisions.[12]

The relationship between internal decision making and reliance on external information creates an upward spiral of mutual influence. If a company's chief executive is pressing for expanded funding for culture and the arts, the company frequently turns to other companies for guidance. This is evident among the Massachusetts companies. Of the firms whose chief executives have been urging greater spending on culture and the arts during the previous two years, four out of five report that other companies in the region had influenced their own contribution budgets in culture and the arts. By contrast, of the firms whose chief executives had not been urging greater spending in this area, only two out of five report that they had been open to the influence of other firms.[13]

As companies newly active in culture and the arts turn to other firms for guidance in giving, the guidance is not only technical but also normative. They obtain assistance in establishing program procedures, but they also open themselves to pressure to shoulder greater responsibility for the health of the nonprofit sector. And they take it to heart. This can be seen if we divide the Massachusetts companies into two groups: those that attribute significant influence to area corporations in establishing their own budget levels in culture and the arts and those that do not. We then compare the relative increase of arts and culture funding in these firms' overall contributions budgets during the two preceding years. Of the companies responsive to outside influence on their arts giving by other companies, 41 percent devoted a greater share of their contribution budget to culture than two years before. Of the companies unresponsive to outside company influence, however, only 17 percent had increased the proportion of their gifts budget going to culture. Similar findings are obtained if we use the actual dollar increases in gifts for culture and the arts in place of the percentage increases.

When top managers push their corporations to take a more active role in funding culture and the arts, then, the firms look to already active companies for guidance. In doing so, they open themselves to more pressure for more giving, since major donors have evolved a shared corporate culture stressing the value of giving to culture and the arts. Once a company chooses to open its decision making to suggestions from the business community, the mutually reinforcing effects propel continued growth in its own giving. And its upward growth in turn encourages other companies to give still more of their monies. Study of corporate giving in a number of American cities confirms the upward mutual reinforcement among business firms elsewhere. All other things being equal, a company will increase its contributions if other firms in the region have already done so.[14]

The process is akin to that of economic "takeoff"; once a threshold of development is reached, economic growth acquires an accelerating momentum of its own. Once a company initiates significant giving to culture and the arts, its support is launched on an accelerating curve. The company enters a world in which additional cultural giving is valued, and the chief executive joins a circuit in which art is a medium of conversation. For public agencies and nonprofit organizations concerned with strategies for enhancing corporate contributions to the arts, then, the single most important achievement is to move a company above the starting threshold. Once so moved, the internal dynamics of the corporate community can be expected to carry the company forward thereafter.

THE FORMALIZATION OF CORPORATE GIVING WITHOUT AUTONOMY

Corporate contributions have been on a growth curve for several decades. As giving programs have grown in scale, they have grown in organization as well. When a firm's annual giving budget reaches $500,000 or more, it generally moves to formalize its program: Contribution specialists are hired, written procedures are set forth, matching-gift programs are established, and company foundations are created. The company also moves to bring its division of gift monies among education, culture, and the other major areas into greater conformity with the prevailing corporate norms. As more firms rise into this giving bracket, as is certain over time, the formalization and normalization of corporate giving will increasingly prevail.

The professionalization we have witnessed in the contributions program is characteristic, as well, of other programs by which corporations seek to influence social and political affairs. Similar trends are evident in the organization of corporate public affairs offices and in the operation of political action committees. As companies have intensified their social and political outreach in recent years, they have also formalized the bureaucracy through which activities are administered.[15]

There is seeming irony, however, in other changes in the contributions process. According to classical theory, bureaucratization of a company program should create a more impersonal and autonomous administrative system. Individual preferences, whether expressed by those of low or high station, are in principle subordinated to dispassionate and rule-guided decision making. Theorists would also expect increasingly bureaucratic programs to be more insulated from outside pressures, especially if they are to take calculating actions in the furtherance of company interests.

Yet we have seen that the rise of more formal organization in the contributions process is not accompanied by a decline in the direct personal influence of the firm's chief executive. The CEO's influence on the giving process, ranging from the setting of budget outlines down to approving grants as small as $500, is nearly undiminished as contribution budgets grow large. And the chief executive's personal involvement, we have found, makes a major difference. When the personal interest is strong, giving programs prosper; when the personal interest in the arts is strong, cultural giving prospers.

Moreover, the rise of more formal organization is accompanied by greater openness to outside influence. This becomes evident if we divide our companies into three groups according to the size of their contribution budgets, as done earlier, and then compare the openness of the three groups to the influence of other firms in setting contribution levels and in identifying grant recipients in culture and the arts. Of the companies with small contributions programs (under $75,000 annually), 42 percent report that other firms had modest or strong influence on their own decisions. Of companies with middle-range budgets ($75,000 to $500,000), 69 percent report such influence. Among corporations with large contribution budgets (over $500,000), 77 percent indicate their openness to guidance from other corporations. A similar difference is found in a study of corporate giving to culture and the arts in Minneapolis and St. Paul. Only 5 percent of the Twin Cities' smaller firms frequently share information on nonprofit organizations they are considering funding, but 40 percent of the larger firms do so. As a by-product, the managers of large contributions programs come to share similar knowledge and attitudes about the arts community, a mind set that is not shared, however, among the managers of smaller giving programs. Contrary to what organizational theory might suggest, larger programs with more formal organization are also those most subject to outside influence by the business community. Program autonomy is inversely related to program size and formalization.[16]

As companies enter the ranks of major contributors, they increasingly look to one another for cues on how to structure their giving. Corporate contribution programs are thus likely to become more uniform in administration as they grow large. They also become more subject to pressures to increase giving as they acquire greater sensitivity to the norms of the corporate community. The norms of the era suggest that responsible firms will give at least 1 percent of their pretax earnings, and some business leaders are urging levels of 2 and even 5 percent. Because of corporate openness to one another's influence in this area of decision making, as companies become significant contributors, and most major companies do, we can expect substantial convergence in the structure, level, and distribution of their philanthropic programs.

Although the convergence in corporate practices may lead companies to give more and to give in similar ways, it may at the same time make it more difficult for organizations unfamiliar to business to become the recipients. To overcome this problem, securing the endorsement of the chief executives of several companies can be a critical first step for an organization embarking on a corporate development campaign. As we have seen, the top officers' active interest can decisively move their companies to make grants. This in turn can encourage other firms to be more forthcoming, especially if the endorsing chief executives are willing to approach senior management of other firms on behalf of the fund-raising campaign. Whether a cultural organization is large or small, established or new, drawing on the networks of mutual influence within the highest circles of corporate management may have become the single most effective means of attracting and sustaining corporate support.

NOTES

1. Time-series figures on aggregate corporate giving are reported in Kathryn Troy, *Annual Survey of Corporate Contributions, 1984 Edition* (New York: Conference Board, 1984). See also American Association of Fund-Raising Counsel, *Giving USA: 1984 Annual Report* (New York: American Association of Fund-Raising Counsel, 1984).

2. Lester M. Salamon and Alan J. Abramson, *The Federal Budget and the Nonprofit Sector* (Washington, D.C.: Urban Institute Press, 1982); American Association of Fund-Raising Counsel, *Giving USA: 1983 Annual Report* (New York: American Association of Fund-Raising Counsel, 1983); Nonprofit Sector Project, *Progress Report No. 3* (Washington, D.C.: The Urban Institute, 1983); Council for Financial Aid to Education, *Corporate Support of Education, 1982* (New York: Council for Financial Aid to Education, 1984); Samuel Schwarz and Mary G. Peters, *Growth of Arts and Cultural Organizations in the Decade of the 1970's* (Washington, D.C.: Research Division, National Endowment for the Arts, 1983).

3. Katherine Maddox McElroy and John J. Siegfried, "The Effect of Firm Size on Corporate Philanthropy," *Quarterly Journal of Economics and Business* 25 (Summer 1985): 18–26; Michael Useem, "Corporate Philanthropy," in Walter W. Powell, ed., *The Handbook of Non-Profit Organizations* (New Haven, Conn.: Yale University Press, 1987).

4. Troy, 1984, op. cit.; Council for Financial Aid to Education, 1984, op. cit.; Paul DiMaggio, "Can Culture Survive the Marketplace?" (Chapter 3, this volume); Arthur H. White and John S. Bartolomeo, "The Attitudes of Corporate Philanthropy in America," in *Corporate Philanthropy*, edited by Council on Foundations (Washington, D.C.: Council on Foundations, 1982).

5. Contributions by Massachusetts companies generally mirror national patterns. Limited available evidence suggests, however, that Boston-area companies give above-average amounts to educational institutions but below-average levels to cultural organizations (Michelle Garvin, "Analysis of Corporate Support for the Arts in Massachusetts" [Boston: Massachusetts Council on the Arts and Humanities, 1982]; Council for Financial Aid to Education, 1984, op. cit.).

6. One-third of the companies did not report their 1983 contribution budget total, and they have been excluded from this analysis. Budget totals do not include employee contributions in matching-gift programs.

7. On the relationship between corporations' pretax income and philanthropic giving, see Hayden W. Smith, *A Profile of Corporate Contributions* (New York: Council for Financial Aid to Education, 1983), and Troy, 1984, op. cit.. General information on the organization and management of contributions programs by large corporations can be found in Kathryn Troy, *Managing Corporate Contributions* (New York: Conference Board, 1980), and Anne Klepper, "Profiles of the Corporate Contributions Professional," *Corporate Philanthropy*, edited by Council on Foundations (Washington, D.C.: Council on Foundations, 1982).

8. Troy, 1984, op. cit.; Smith, 1983, op. cit.

9. Michael J. Merenda, "The Process of Corporate Social Involvement: Five Case Studies," in Lee E. Preston, ed., *Research in Corporate Social Performance and Policy*, Vol. 3 (Greenwich, Conn.: JAI Press, 1981), 17–41.

10. John J. Siegfried, Katherine Maddox McElroy, and Diane Biernot-Fawkes, "The Management of Corporate Contributions," in Lee Preston, ed., *Research in Corporate Social Per-*

formance and Policy, Vol. 5 (Greenwich, Conn.: JAI Press, 1983); White and Bartolomeo, 1982, op. cit.; Joseph Galaskiewicz, *Social Organization of an Urban Grants Economy: A Study of Business Philanthropy and Nonprofit Organizations* (New York: Academic Press, 1985).

11. *Cultural Post,* "President's Committee Holds Meeting" 8, 5 (December 1982): 1ff.; Frank Hodsoll, "Prospects for Private Arts Support," *Cultural Post* 8, 7 (March/April 1983): 2. The programs of the National Endowment for the Arts, Massachusetts Council on the Arts and Humanities, Council for Financial Aid to Education, Business Committee for the Arts, and The Independent Sector to increase corporate giving are described in the organizations' annual reports, newsletters, and various publications. They can be obtained by writing the National Endowment for the Arts, 2401 E St., N.W., Washington, D.C. 20506; Massachusetts Council on the Arts and Humanities, One Ashburton Place, Boston, Mass. 02108; Council for Financial Aid to Education, 680 Fifth Avenue, New York, N.Y. 10019; Business Committee for the Arts, 1501 Broadway, New York, N.Y. 10036; and The Independent Sector, 1828 L Street, N.W., Washington, D.C. 20036.

12. James F. Harris and Anne Klepper, *Corporate Philanthropic Public Service Activities* (New York: Conference Board, 1976); John J. Siegfried and Katherine Maddox McElroy, "Corporate Philanthropy in America: 1980," (unpublished manuscript, Department of Economics and Business Administration, Vanderbilt University, 1981); McElroy and Siegfried, 1985, op. cit..

13. The survey asked, "During the past two fiscal years, has the chief executive encouraged or discouraged larger contribution budgets and greater spending for . . . culture, arts and humanities?"

14. Siegfried et al., 1983, op. cit.

15. James S. Post, Edwin A. Murray, Jr., Robert B. Dickie, and John F. Mahon, "Managing Public Affairs: The Public Affairs Function," *California Management Review* 26 (Fall 1983): 135–150; Edward Handler and John R. Mulkern, *Business in Politics* (Lexington, Mass.: Heath, 1982); Michael Useem, *The Inner Circle: Large Corporations and the Rise of Business Political Activity in the U.S. and U.K..* (New York: Oxford University Press, 1984).

16. Joseph Galaskiewicz, 1985, op. cit.

5

Support for the Arts from Independent Foundations

PAUL J. DiMAGGIO

Foundations represent the oldest institutional source of contributed revenues to nonprofit arts organizations. The Carnegie Corporation of New York, the Rockefeller philanthropies, and other private foundations assisted the arts as early as the 1920s; by contrast, corporations first discovered culture in the 1950s, and government assistance to nonprofit cultural enterprises did not come into its own until the early 1960s.[1] Private foundations today continue to support performing and visual arts organizations, at levels comparable to corporate and public contributions.[2] Moreover, because some foundation programs focus their grants on specific and well-formulated objectives that most other patrons neglect, they exert an influence above and beyond the size of their contributions.

Given the centrality of philanthropic foundations to the support of the arts, it is surprising how little attention their role has received in recent years, from the academy or from the art world itself, especially compared with the verbiage and concern lavished upon government and, especially, the corporate sector. This chapter is a modest effort to address this imbalance by discussing the evolution of foundations' support for the arts; by reporting data, tabulated from a study that until now has been unexploited

The research reported in this chapter was supported by the Ford Foundation and the Yale Program on Non-Profit Organizations. I am indebted to Ruth Mayleas of the Ford Foundation for carefully reading draft materials and alerting me to several errors of interpretation of aggregate statistics; to Patricia Read of the Foundation Center for providing proofs of the Center's 1985 report on giving to the arts and for guiding me through the Center's excellent collections; to Karla Shepard of the Commonwealth Fund for a helpful response to a question about the data that she collected and organized; to Fritz Mosher of the Carnegie Corporation for providing materials on that foundation's early programs in the arts; and to John G. Simon for an exceptionally careful and helpful editorial review. A major debt that I cannot fully acknowledge (in the interest of protecting anonymity) is to the 10 foundation program officers and 1 trustee who consented to be interviewed for the project of which this chapter is one product. Needless to say, none of the people or organizations to whom thanks are due is responsible for, or should be presumed to agree with, any of the opinions or interpretations expressed in this chapter.

by students of the arts, on all appropriations made by 47 of the 54 largest independent foundations at six points between 1955 and 1979;[3] and by analyzing, in as much detail as available data permit, the allocation of arts and culture grants to different kinds of purposes and organizations during the early 1980s. I focus in this paper on lessons from the aggregate statistics, rather than, as is more conventional, notable national foundation programs of assistance to the arts. Although the portrait thus presented is less colorful than that which an emphasis on exemplary programs would yield, it is also more globally accurate, depicting the broad valleys as well as the peaks of the foundation world.

In particular, a more global perspective calls attention to a paradox. Independent foundations are, in many respects, uniquely organized to act independently. Yet, as we shall see, the most visible foundation patrons of the arts—the Ford Foundation, the Rockefeller Foundation, the Andrew W. Mellon Foundation, and a few others at both the national and local levels—are quite atypical in their attention to planning, goals, and program development and in their willingness to support activities that are either experimental or in other respects comparatively unattractive to most agencies that assist nonprofit arts organizations. In other words, despite the apparent autonomy of the private foundation and diversity of the foundation universe, most foundation arts dollars go quietly to major established institutions, in most cases symphony orchestras and art museums, for capital projects, endowment building, or operating support. To explain this paradoxical finding we shall adopt an organizational perspective that emphasizes, on the one hand, the embeddedness of private foundations in local leadership networks and, on the other, the costs of acquiring reliable information about alternative courses of action.

THE DEVELOPMENT OF FOUNDATION SUPPORT FOR THE ARTS

Foundations, almost from their inception, have made grants to the arts, although the popularity of arts organizations as recipients of foundation support has increased since World War II. The earliest systematic data on the scope of this support come from Eduard Lindemann's pathfinding study of the grant-making of 80 independent and 20 community foundations between 1921 and 1930.[4] According to Lindemann, the foundations he studied, which collectively controlled the bulk of foundation assets of the time, gave a total of between $117,000 and $971,000 a year, or approximately 1 percent of all foundation disbursements for the decade, to "aesthetic" organizations and programs. In 1931, the Twentieth Century Fund's *American Foundations and Their Fields* reported that 13 of 122 private foundations were active in the field of "aesthetics," more than made grants for the physical sciences, the humanities, government, race relations, agriculture, city planning, or housing. These 13 foundations, 5 of which were among the 20 largest, provided $1.39 million of support in 1930, or 2.7

percent of total foundation disbursements for that year.[5] As the Depression deepened, giving to "aesthetics" declined until it reached $740,000 in 1933, remaining at roughly that level through 1940 (after which no data are available until 1955).[6]

The style and substance of early foundation cultural giving varied from foundation to foundation. The Juilliard Foundation harbored most of its assets to support its own musical academy; and when, in keeping with the terms of Juilliard's bequest, it began to assist the debt-ridden Metropolitan Opera in 1933, its officers intervened forcefully, demanding administrative reforms and seats on the Opera's board of trustees.[7] By contrast, the programs of the Carnegie Corporation, the General Education Board, which assisted industrial arts and design projects, and the Rockefeller Foundation, which supported playwrights and film projects (and even made a grant to the national office of the Federal Theatre Project to purchase an offset printer), were less interventionist in nature.[8]

Private foundation arts support was dominated throughout the 1920s and 1930s by the wide-ranging activities of the Carnegie Corporation of New York under Frederick Keppel, who assumed Carnegie's presidency in 1923. Not until the height of the Ford Foundation's programs of support for theatre, orchestras, and dance during the 1960s would one foundation again have such a decisive influence on the institutional development of U.S. culture.

Consider 1930, which, despite the Depression, was a typical year in the Carnegie program, with expenditures of $417,000 on the arts. If one subtracts from the national total the Juilliard Foundation's operating support for the Juilliard School of Music and the General Education Board's assistance for "the industrial arts," Carnegie's contribution represents 82 percent of all independent foundation spending on "aesthetics."[9] By the time Keppel retired in 1941, Carnegie had made grants and provided fellowships of approximately $13.5 million in support of arts activities.

A report to the Carnegie Corporation notes that the arts program had "been more concerned with educating people to appreciate the arts than with training professional artists or financing the creation of art works."[10] Nonetheless, the Corporation's grants were widely distributed. Carnegie provided graduate fellowships to many of the leading art historians and museum directors of this century; distributed "teaching sets" of art books, photographs, and slides to 302 U.S. colleges and high schools; gave similar sets of music books, records, scores, phonographs and record cabinets to 356 U.S. universities and secondary schools; and helped endow music departments in almost 20 U.S. colleges and universities. The Carnegie Corporation gave substantial operating assistance to the American Association of Museums; and it also supported the American Association for Adult Education, the American Federation of Arts, and the College Art Association, respectively, to investigate the role of music and museums in adult education, assist the Little Theatre movement, and circulate exhibitions. The program even made grants to three of the first community arts councils, those of Santa Barbara, Cedar Rapids, Iowa, and Owatonna, Minnesota.[11]

Despite their somewhat scattered character, Carnegie's grants appear to have played an important role in disseminating and institutionalizing the high culture that museums, orchestras, and other arts institutions had begun to define toward the end of the nineteenth century. To a lesser extent, through subsidization of studies and books on the role of the arts in U.S. society, Carnegie supported the emerging union of the arts and universities, encouraged the professionalization of museum and orchestra management, and pressed upon trustees the view, more novel at that time than it is today, that they owed a responsibility to the public.

After Carnegie's almost complete withdrawal in 1943, foundations provided only modest support for the arts for several years. When R. Emerson Andrews wrote his classic volume, *Philanthropic Giving,* in the late 1940s, he reported little foundation giving to the arts aside from grants and fellowships to visual artists, musicians, and composers from a few small foundations.[12]

Foundations did make occasional grants to nonprofit arts organizations throughout this period. But only in 1957, with the inauguration of the Ford Foundation's arts programs under the direction of W. McNeil Lowry, did the private foundation once again become a major force in the arts. The aim of the Ford program was nothing short of revitalizing the performing arts throughout the United States: in the case of orchestral music, stabilizing symphony orchestras around the country; in the cases of dance and theatre, creating new industries where none existed. The scale of Ford support and the instruments the Foundation used to achieve its ends varied. But a distinctive and consistent set of purposes were evident throughout the Lowry years. First, the Ford program sponsored the diffusion of classical music, opera, theatre, and the dance throughout the United States by supporting—and in some cases helping to create—strong regional institutions. Second, unlike Keppel at Carnegie, who sought to coax the universities into adopting the arts, Lowry sought direction primarily from artists and artistic directors, and focused Ford's attention on nurturing environments that could attend both to artists' material and to their creative needs. Third, the Ford Foundation sought to help performing artists by assisting the nonprofit cultural institutions that employed them; and by encouraging these institutions to build stable paying audiences and, especially in later years, to institute financial-management reforms.

The dominance of the Ford Foundation arts programs throughout the late 1950s and 1960s was quantitative as well as philosophical. The scale of that Foundation's appropriations was unprecedented and, until the maturation of the National Endowment for the Arts, unmatched by any other public or private patron. Beginning in 1962, the Foundation made over $14 million in grants to enable 13 resident theatres to "reach and maintain new levels of artistic achievement and financial stability"; provided, in the late 1960s and early 1970s, approximately $6 million in support for minority theatre institutions; in the 1970s, made over $10 million in cash reserve grants to 29 resident theatres (these were multiyear matching grants aimed at eliminating deficits and establishing accounts to buffer the recipients from cash-flow problems); and in 1961 created the Theatre Communications Group, a service organization for the resident stage, which received more than $3 million in Ford support during its first two decades. In the dance, the Foundation appropriated over $12 million in support of seven ballet companies in 1963, and in the 1970s granted more than $7 million for a cash reserve program for 15 ballet and dance organizations. In the early 1960s the Foundation gave over $4 million to 16 civic opera companies, adding $8.5 million to this amount in cash-reserve grants during the 1970s. In its most spectacular display of financial largesse, in 1966 the Ford Foundation appropriated $80.2 million in support for 61 symphony orchestras across the United States. The purpose of these grants was to eliminate deficits and to enable the orchestras to expand their activities and to achieve a modicum of financial stability.[13]

Substantial as these figures are, they represent just a portion of Ford's giving to the arts and omit what were, in some disciplines, substantial programs of support for creative artists, for the production of new works by Americans, for documentation, and for professional training. Few parts of the performing-arts world were untouched by the Foundation's gifts. Although the Ford Foundation was criticized in some quarters for pushing the theatres' institutional development at the cost of artistic growth and audience diversity,[14] or for encouraging wage inflation in the symphony orchestra,[15] the Ford programs represented an application of private funds to artistic development that was unique in magnitude and scope and unusually broad in vision.

The Rockefeller Foundation also began to fund the arts in the late 1950s, at first focusing its attention on Lincoln Center and then broadening the program (which in 1963 came under the direction of former Oberlin College Music Dean Norman Lloyd) to professional training in universities, fellowship programs for creative artists, and support for innovative and experimental organizations and programs. Although its total expenditure between 1964 and 1972 amounted to only $24 million—less than one third the size of Ford's 1966 orchestra appropriation alone—the Rockefeller Foundation funded many innovative ventures. Moreover, it supported the values of artistic professionalism that the Ford Foundation also embraced, albeit, in contrast to Ford, with a special emphasis on the universities.

Since the late 1960s, other foundations have come to view the arts as an important category of foundation philanthropy. A review of the key players in the 1970s and 1980s would find Ford and Rockefeller remaining at the forefront; it might also mention the Andrew W. Mellon Foundation, with its commitment to visual-arts conservation and its multiyear projects in support of artistic and administrative development in museums and the performing arts; the Kresge Foundation's support for capital expansion in university and independent arts organizations; the John Simon Guggenheim Foundation's longstanding fellowship assistance for artists; the JDR 3rd Fund's and Rockefeller Brothers Fund's work in arts education and international cultural exchange; the Getty Foundation's massive operating programs in support of scholarship, conservation, and arts education; and wide-ranging and often thoughtfully designed programs of local giving by the Hewlett Foundation, the MacArthur Foundation, the Mabel Pew Myrin Trust, the Ahmanson Foundation, and others. But, as we shall see, a series of descriptive vignettes would be misleading in so far as it suggested that such foundation programs are typical. A more balanced view requires inspection of aggregate statistics on foundation giving.

SUPPORT FOR THE ARTS FROM MAJOR FOUNDATIONS, 1955–79

Fortunately, aggregate statistics on foundation giving are available from a study by Karla Shepard of grant-making by major private foundations. Shepard's figures cover all grants made by 47 of the 54 largest foundations in 1955, 1960, 1965, 1970, 1975, and 1979.[16]

The figures must be interpreted with some caution. First, because there is double-counting of grants that fit into more than one category, the only non-overlapping totals are for "arts, culture, and the humanities," a very broad classification of which the arts represent only a portion. Thus the reader should note that these aggregate totals include many grants to such organizations as libraries, university English departments, and public television stations that supported activities one would not conventionally associate with the arts. (Data are also reported for more finely drawn categories; but these more narrowly defined figures cannot be summed to yield total support for the arts because of the problem of double-counting.)

Second, both the broad totals and the subcategory figures are based on appropriations for each year rather than on the number of grant dollars actually paid out in that year. Because many foundations appropriate funds in a single year that will be paid out over a period of two, three, or even more years, data on appropriations are likely to exhibit more marked fluctuation than would data on actual grant expenditures. Consequently, we cannot be certain to what extent changes in appropriations as measured every five years reflect trends or simply document exceptional patterns of appropriations in selected years. Because the Ford Foundation's grants represent a large portion of all arts giving over much of the period studied, and because the Ford Foundation tended to commit most of its arts spending in the form of multiyear appropriations, the problem is especially grave. Fortunately, Shepard also calculates totals *excluding* the Ford Foundation. Because these latter figures aggregate the appropriations of many smaller foundations, none of which accounted for a large share of arts funding, they are likely to "smooth out" fluctuations and thus be relatively reliable.

Despite these limitations, the data provide a useful overview of the grants of foundations that collectively accounted for 35 percent of all grant dollars in 1979.[17] Table 5.1 displays the *number* of grants to arts, culture, and the humanities (and, below this figure, the percentage of grants), in the aggregate and by arts subcategory between 1955 and 1979. Table 5.2 depicts the *size of appropriations* (and the percentage for each subcategory of all appropriated dollars) over that period. Because Ford Foundation appropriations accounted for such a high proportion of all grant-making activity by foundations during much of the period reviewed, data for all foundations and data for all foundations *excluding Ford* are presented separately in rows 2 and 4. Because inflation makes comparison of dollar amounts misleading, most of the discussion below will focus on the percentage share of total foundation appropriations allocated to different subcategories of the arts.

Note, first, that the number of foundation grants for arts, culture, and the humanities grew from 485 in 1955 to 2032 in 1979; while grant dollars expanded from almost $13 million in 1955 to $147 million in 1979. Although the percentage of all grants going to arts, culture, and the humanities rose only modestly during this period, from 21 percent in 1955 to 28 percent in 1979, the rise in the percentage of foundation dollars contributed to this category climbed more sharply, from almost 10 percent to almost 21 percent.

The increase in the percentage of resources appropriated for the arts, culture, and the humanities was sharpest between 1955 and 1960, then rose smoothly and steadily for the next twenty years. This trend is somewhat illusory, however, a product of changes both in the Ford Foundation's giving patterns and in Ford's share of all foundation disbursements. If we exclude the Ford Foundation's grants, we discover a sharp rise in giving to the arts, culture, and humanities (as a share of all foundation appropriations) between 1955 and 1960, another rise in 1965, a sizable decline in 1970, and then stabilization at just above 1965 levels in 1975 and 1979.[18]

The aggregate figures, of course, tell only part of the story. Giving to subcategories of "the arts, culture, and humanities" classification developed at different rates. In the discussion that follows, these subcategories are taken to constitute "the arts": general arts (a heading that includes arts councils, arts centers, and other multidisciplinary programs); visual arts; architecture; dance; music; theatre; media and communications; and museums. (Data are also presented by recipient, as opposed to field of interest, for museums, performing arts groups, and art councils/consortia.)

Although double-counting precludes precise estimates, the arts component appears to have increased over the period Shepard studied from about one-third to one-half of all arts, culture, and humanities dollars. The most established fields in 1955 were those of music and museums, which received 0.5 and 1 percent, respectively, of all foundation expenditures. By contrast, less than two-tenths of a percent of foundation appropriations were directed to general arts, architecture, or dance; and just three tenths to theatre.

Between 1955 and 1975, all of the arts areas grew as a percentage of

Table 5.1 Number of Grants Made by 47 Major Foundations, 1955–1979

Category	1955	1960	1965	1970	1975	1979
All Grants	2289	3237	3805	4357	6161	7320
	2014	2554	3262	3367	5264	6326
Grants for Arts/	485	801	919	994	1697	2032
Culture/Humanities	460	637	837	826	1540	1813
	21.2%	24.8	24.2	22.8	27.5	27.8
	22.8%	24.9	25.7	24.5	29.3	28.7
Subclassification by Field of Interest						
General Arts	4	16	28	47	85	123
	4	12	25	39	74	105
	0.2%	0.5	0.7	1.1	1.4	1.7
	0.2%	0.5	0.8	1.2	1.4	1.7
Visual Arts	23	52	83	88	118	181
	23	44	73	82	106	173
	1.0%	1.6	2.2	2.0	1.9	2.5
	1.1%	1.7	2.2	2.4	2.0	2.7
Architecture	3	15	25	18	36	78
	1	12	20	14	34	63
	0.1%	0.5	0.7	0.4	0.6	1.1
	0.0%	0.5	0.6	0.4	0.6	1.0
Dance	1	9	10	22	42	59
	1	9	7	17	40	43
	0.0%	0.3	0.3	0.5	0.7	0.8
	0.0%	0.4	0.2	0.5	0.8	0.7
Music	44	83	87	118	148	213
	44	73	80	106	139	194
	1.9%	2.6	2.3	2.7	2.4	2.9
	2.2%	2.9	2.5	3.1	2.6	3.1
Theatre	7	25	45	69	121	175
	7	18	40	51	113	139
	0.3%	0.8	1.2	1.6	2.0	2.4
	0.3%	0.7	1.2	1.5	2.1	2.2
Media/Communications	28	97	88	162	223	283
	17	29	70	95	173	221
	1.2%	3.0	2.3	3.7	3.6	3.9
	0.8%	1.1	2.1	2.8	3.4	3.5
Museums	28	32	48	71	103	148
	28	30	48	69	97	145
	1.2%	1.0	1.3	1.6	1.7	2.0
	1.4%	1.2	1.5	2.0	1.8	2.3
Subclassification by Type of Recipient Institution						
Museum	30	36	60	83	123	157
	30	33	57	76	117	152
	1.3%	1.1	1.6	1.9	2.0	2.1
	1.5%	1.3	1.7	2.3	2.2	2.4
Performing	24	61	77	103	188	291
Arts Group	24	54	70	85	182	254
	1.0%	1.9	2.0	2.4	3.1	4.0
	1.2%	2.1	2.1	2.5	3.5	4.0

Category	1955	1960	1965	1970	1975	1979
Arts Council/	2	6	17	21	62	96
Consortium	2	5	17	15	53	79
	0.1%	0.2	0.4	0.5	1.0	1.3
	0.1%	0.2	0.5	0.4	1.0	1.2

Row 1: Number of grants from 47 major foundations. *Row 2:* Number of grants, *excluding* grants by the Ford Foundation. *Row 3:* Percentage of all grants to category in left-hand column. *Row 4:* Percentage of grants to category in left-hand column, *excluding* those of Ford Foundations.
Note: Because of multiple classification of certain grants, subcategories cannot be summed to total.
SOURCE: Printouts on file at the Foundation Center Library in New York from Study of Foundation Grant-Making by Karla Shepard, sponsored by the Twentieth Century Fund.

foundation appropriations. Dance funding, virtually nonexistent in 1955, reached 0.7 percent by 1965; theatre funding increased from 1 in every 333 foundation grant dollars in 1955 to 1 of every 67 by 1965. Support for music increased more slowly, from 0.5 to 1.5 percent of foundation expenditures over the total period. Museum assistance increased from 1.0 to 2.8 percent of total grants, and grants for the visual arts, which represented 1 in every 500 grant dollars in 1955 accounted for 1 in 50 by 1979.

As we have seen, the Ford Foundation's role in performing-arts assistance during this period was substantial. The Ford Foundation appropriated more than all other 46 major foundations combined for dance in 1965 and 1970, for music in 1965, and for theatre in 1965 and 1970. Consequently, the share of all grant dollars going for dance, music, and theatre all peak in 1965 as a product of Ford's spending and decline thereafter (although music and theatre nearly recover by 1979).

To what extent was Ford leading the field in its allocation of grant dollars? In dance, Ford's entry in the early 1960s appears to coincide with a marked decline in support, as a percentage of all grant dollars, from other foundations: indeed, dance played as large a role in the budgets of other major foundations in 1960 as it would through 1979. In music, the trajectories of Ford and of other support were similar (although the fluctuation in Ford's pattern was more marked): up in 1965, down during the early and mid-1970s, and up again in 1979. Support for the theatre doubled as a proportion of other foundations' grants between 1960 and 1965, as the Ford program grew; but then fell off sharply between 1965 and 1970.

These figures warrant two observations. First, the Ford Foundation's performing-arts expenditures of the 1960s and 1970s, though remarkable for their size, national scope, and degree of focus, were largely consistent with more general trends in foundation giving during this period. Second, the extent of Ford's grant-making was so great relative to that of other foundations between 1955 and 1975 that any figures on foundation giving to the arts during this period that include the Ford Foundation's grants are likely to be misleading. Including Ford depresses the share of foundation grants going towards the performing arts in 1955 and inflates them by the mid-1960s. Excluding the Ford Foundation's contributions, the rise

Table 5.2 Dollars Appropriated, in Millions, by 47 Major Foundations, 1955–1979

Category	1955	1960	1965	1970	1975	1979
All Grants	$132.43M	301.33	505.03	575.55	680.26	718.54
	72.37M	132.99	202.36	321.75	494.59	634.43
Grants for Arts/ Culture/Humanities	$12.65M	42.00	76.66	99.98	125.81	147.10
	9.26M	23.62	40.00	48.18	99.78	128.76
	9.5%	13.9	15.2	17.4	18.5	20.5
	12.8%	17.8	19.8	15.2	20.2	20.3
Subclassification by Field of Interest						
General Arts	$0.09M	1.92	3.68	4.84	12.05	15.18
	0.09M	0.76	3.51	4.07	4.03	8.94
	0.1%	0.6	0.7	0.8	1.8	2.1
	0.1%	0.6	1.7	1.3	0.8	1.4
Visual Arts	$0.22M	2.54	6.32	5.48	14.53	14.87
	0.22M	2.13	4.67	4.16	14.17	14.79
	0.2%	0.8	1.3	1.0	2.1	2.1
	0.3%	1.6	2.3	1.3	2.9	2.3
Architecture	$0.11M	1.10	1.06	4.14	2.71	4.78
	$0.01M	0.92	0.51	2.98	2.66	3.41
	0.1%	0.4	0.2	0.7	0.4	0.7
	0.0%	0.7	0.3	0.9	0.5	0.5
Dance	$0.03M	0.72	3.60	1.74	2.62	2.27
	$0.03M	0.72	1.68	0.68	2.45	1.35
	0.0%	0.2	0.7	0.3	0.4	0.3
	0.0%	0.5	0.1	0.2	0.5	0.2
Music	$0.71M	1.81	8.44	5.04	5.36	10.88
	$0.71M	1.35	2.59	3.66	5.02	9.65
	0.5%	0.6	1.7	0.9	0.8	1.5
	1.0%	1.0	1.3	1.1	1.0	1.5
Theatre	$0.42M	1.72	7.34	6.66	7.80	10.08
	$0.42M	0.95	2.91	2.62	4.23	6.62
	0.3%	0.6	1.5	1.2	1.1	1.4
	0.6%	0.7	1.4	0.8	0.9	1.0
Media/Communications	$3.31M	9.69	16.57	33.83	26.31	21.37
	$0.64M	1.72	4.40	3.75	8.46	12.39
	2.5%	3.2	3.3	5.9	3.9	3.0
	0.9%	1.3	2.2	1.2	1.7	2.0
Museums	$1.36M	3.47	2.11	7.70	20.12	20.15
	$1.36M	3.43	2.11	7.13	19.96	20.11
	1.0%	1.2	0.4	1.3	3.0	2.8
	1.9%	2.6	1.0	2.2	4.0	3.2
Subclassification by Type of Recipient Institution						
Museum	$0.49M	2.41	3.04	7.59	22.89	20.78
	$0.49M	2.36	3.00	6.97	22.74	20.72
	0.4%	0.8	0.6	1.3	3.4	2.9
	0.7%	1.8	1.5	2.2	4.6	3.3

Table 5.2 Dollars Appropriated, in Millions, by 47 Major Foundations, 1955–1979 (*continued*)

Category	1955	1960	1965	1970	1975	1979
	$0.70M	2.22	7.14	6.20	11.65	14.35
	$0.70M	1.46	2.46	3.34	8.78	12.01
	0.5%	0.7	1.4	1.1	1.7	2.0
Performing Arts Group	1.0%	1.1	1.2	1.0	1.8	1.9
	$0.03M	0.46	0.24	1.74	2.79	3.25
	$0.03M	0.41	0.24	1.14	2.26	2.75
Arts Council/	0.0%	0.2	0.0	0.3	0.4	0.5
Consortium	0.0%	0.3	0.1	0.4	0.5	0.4

Row 1: Grant appropriations, in millions, of 47 major foundations. *Row 2:* Grant appropriations, *excluding* those of the Ford Foundation. *Row 3:* Percentage of all grant dollars to category in left-hand column. *Row 4:* Percentage of all appropriations to category in left-hand column, *excluding* grants by Ford Foundation.

Note: Because of multiple classification of certain grants, subcategories cannot be summed to total.

SOURCE: Printouts on file at the Foundation Center Library in New York from Study of Foundation Grant-Making by Karla Shepard, sponsored by the Twentieth Century Fund.

in foundation support for the performing arts was relatively modest. By contrast, increases in assistance to the visual arts and museums fields of interest as a share of the foundation grant dollar were more marked.

The 1960s and 1970s were a time of ferment and expansion in the arts. As foundation grant-making to arts organizations increased, so did the number of applicants. How did this affect the size of the grants that foundations made in support of the arts?

We can gain some clues to this by calculating the dollar size of the average grant by subcategory from the information in Shepard's tables. (The results of these calculations are exhibited in Table 5.3.) Because the pattern for Ford Foundation grants is idiosyncratic, we shall consider only the figures for all foundations, excluding Ford. The average foundation grant for all purposes grew steadily between 1955 and 1979 (although the increases stopped keeping up with inflation after 1970). The same was true of grants to the aggregate category of arts, culture, and the humanities. Note that the rate of growth in the latter category was faster and steadier, however. Whereas in 1955, the average arts, culture, and humanities grant amounted to approximately 45 percent of the average dollar amount of all foundation grants, by 1979 the ratio was over seven tenths. Like other grants, however, grants for the arts, culture, and humanities became smaller, in real-dollar terms, during the 1970s.

Because averages are easily distorted by exceptionally large grants where the number of grants is small, data on changes by subcategory may be deceptive. Nonetheless, we can learn something by observing persistent change in those subcategories with the greatest number of grants. Music grants increased markedly in size between 1960 and 1965. Although they declined relative to inflation thereafter, the real value of the average grant was still larger in 1979 than it was in 1960. By contrast, grants in support of theatre fluctuated throughout this period but declined markedly in real

Table 5.3 Average Size, in Thousands of Dollars, of Appropriations Made by 47 Major Independent Foundations, 1955–79

Category	1955	1960	1965	1970	1975	1979
All Grants	$57.9G	93.1	132.7	132.1	110.4	98.2
	$35.9G	52.1	62.0	95.6	94.0	100.3
Grants for Arts/	$26.1G	52.4	83.4	100.6	74.1	72.4
Culture/Humanities	$20.1G	37.1	47.8	58.3	64.8	71.0
Subclassification by Field of Interest						
General Arts	$22.5G	120.0	131.4	103.0	141.8	123.4
	$22.5G	63.3	140.4	104.4	54.5	85.1
Visual Arts	$ 9.6G	48.9	76.1	62.3	123.1	82.2
	$ 9.6G	48.4	64.0	50.7	133.7	85.5
Architecture	$36.7G	73.3	42.4	230.0	75.3	61.3
	$10.0G	76.7	75.5	212.9	78.2	54.1
Dance	$30.0G	80.0	360.0	79.1	62.4	38.5
	$30.0G	80.0	240.0	40.0	61.3	31.4
Music	$16.1G	20.7	97.0	42.7	36.2	51.1
	$16.1G	13.0	32.4	34.5	36.1	49.7
Theatre	$60.0G	68.8	163.1	96.5	64.5	57.6
	$60.0G	52.8	36.4	51.4	37.4	47.6
Media/Communications	$118.2G	99.9	188.3	208.8	118.0	75.5
	$ 37.7G	59.3	62.9	39.5	48.9	56.1
Museums	$48.6G	108.4	44.0	108.5	195.3	136.2
	$48.6G	114.3	44.0	103.3	205.8	138.7
Subclassification by Type of Recipient Institution						
Museum	$16.0G	66.9	60.7	91.5	186.1	132.4
	$16.0G	71.5	52.6	91.7	194.3	136.3
Performing Arts Group	$29.2G	36.4	92.7	60.2	62.0	49.3
	$29.2G	27.0	35.1	39.3	48.2	47.3
Arts Council/	$15.0G	76.7	14.1	82.9	45.0	33.9
Consortium	$15.0G	82.0	14.1	76.0	42.6	34.8

Row 1: Average size of appropriations from 47 major foundations. *Row 2:* Average size of grants, *excluding* appropriations by the Ford Foundation.
SOURCE: Calculated by author from printouts on file at the Foundation Center Library in New York from Study of Foundation Grant-Making by Karla Shepard, sponsored by the Twentieth Century Fund.

dollars. In short, many foundations responded to the increase in demand for grants by making more but smaller grants to performing-arts institutions.

FOUNDATION SUPPORT FOR THE ARTS SINCE 1980

Data on foundation support for the arts between 1980 and 1984 are exhibited in Table 5.4. Because the Foundation Center, which collects these

Table 5.4 Foundation Grants to Cultural Activities, 1980–84

Category	1980	1981	1982	1983	1984
General Arts	$23.8	52.3	37.2	69.1	44.9
	534	776	778	1075	1181
	2.0%	4.2	2.5	3.9	2.7
Art/Architecture	$36.3	43.1	57.4	48.8	50.5
	498	554	683	745	761
	3.0%	3.4	3.9	2.7	3.1
History	$16.9	12.8	17.5	22.5	21.3
	328	360	401	461	496
	1.4%	1.0	1.2	1.3	1.3
Language/Literature	$9.8	20.1	12.4	20.5	14.6
	227	302	347	405	487
	0.8%	1.6	0.8	1.1	0.9
Media/Communications	$27.0	20.9	28.3	40.2	24.6
	492	399	563	591	577
	2.3%	1.7	1.9	2.2	1.5
Music	$23.4	24.5	35.7	47.5	44.1
	640	799	892	1012	1082
	2.0%	1.9	2.4	2.6	2.7
Theatre/Dance	$23.7	18.8	20.3	28.8	28.1
	602	688	771	862	958
	2.0%	1.5	1.4	1.6	1.8
All Arts and Culture					
Dollars:	$160.8	192.6	208.7	277.3	229.0
Percent:	13.5	15.3	14.1	15.4	14.0

Row 1: Appropriations, in millions of dollars. *Row 2:* Number of grants. *Row 3:* Percentage of all appropriations of $5000 or more by reporting independent, community, and company foundations.
SOURCE: Foundation Center Statistical Summary, New Series.

data, changed its system of classification and reporting to one similar but not identical to the Shepard system; because the Foundation Center data are from a larger number of foundations, including community and some corporate foundations; and because the Center tabulates only grants of $5000 or more, these figures are not precisely comparable to those for prior years. Moreover, because the Foundation Center reports are based on a slightly different number and set of foundations from year to year, comparability within this table of dollar amounts and numbers of grants is not perfect. Nonetheless, because the foundations represented account for the majority of grant dollars, comparability of the percentage of appropriations allocated to different categories of spending is reasonably reliable. Thus, we shall focus on this figure.

With the onset of the Reagan administration's budget reductions in federal social programs, many observers predicted that the arts' share of the foundation dollar would decline as foundations responded to the needs of financially strapped social-service agencies.[19] In fact, during the first year of the Reagan administration, private foundation support for "cultural activities" (a rubric that includes general arts, art and architecture, history, language and literature, media and communications, music, and theatre and dance) increased markedly, from 13.5 to 15.3 percent of grant dollars. Between 1981 and 1982, culture's share of the foundation dollar receded; in 1983 it surpassed the 1981 level; and in 1984 it declined to 14 percent.[20]

Because these aggregate figures include many grants for such purposes as education in the humanities or public-service programming for public television, it is important to go beyond these totals to inspect finer recipient categories. Since 1980, grants in support of the theatre and the dance have declined slightly as a percentage of foundation outlays, with the largest drop between 1980 and 1981; while the share of grants in support of music has increased by more than 33 percent. Proportional support for art and architecture appears to have held more or less steady. The share of grants to media and communications projects has declined, while the heterogeneous "general" category has fluctuated widely from year to year. Despite the decline in funding for the broad category of "cultural activities" between 1983 and 1984, the shares of music, theatre and dance, and art and architecture all increased.

Thus there is no evidence of a wholesale reallocation of foundation appropriations from the arts to human services or other beneficiaries. Indeed, the early 1980s were good to foundation support of the arts because foundation assets, which stagnated throughout the 1970s, expanded dramatically after 1979. Grant-making followed suit, with appropriations (to all areas) increasing from $2.42 billion in 1979 to $4.36 billion in 1984.[21] Consequently, the arts benefited from maintaining a stable slice of a rapidly growing pie.

WHICH FOUNDATIONS SUPPORT THE ARTS—AND WHICH ARTS DO THEY SUPPORT?

Aggregate data are useful because they highlight the contours of the foundation sector's allocations and permit us to identify trends. But aggregate data also obscure a great deal of information about the kinds of arts activities that foundations support. In order to understand who benefits from foundation assistance to the arts, it is necessary to look at the grants and grant-makers themselves.

Sixty-nine foundations are recorded as reporting grants of $1 million or more to arts organizations in the 1984 and 1985 editions of the Foundation Center directory, *Grants for Arts and Cultural Programs*.[22] The 1984 list is based on grants of more than $5000 made, for the most part, in 1982 or early 1983, whereas the 1985 list is based on such grants made, in most cases, in 1983 or early 1984. These reports are only rough guides to foundation activity, compiled for the purpose of assisting grant-seekers.

Nonetheless they provide a useful, if rough, overview to the meaning of the aggregate figures.

The amount of turnover on the list between 1984 and 1985 is notable and suggests the episodic quality of much giving to the arts. The Ford Foundation, which headed the list of the 10 largest arts funders in 1984, in part as a result of a large grant to the National Arts Stabilization Fund, is absent in 1985.[23] (Ford's total also included grants of $4.5 million to the Social Science Research Council and $2.5 million to the American Council of Learned Societies.) Indeed, only 4 foundations were in the top 10 in both years. Of these, 2 (Andrew W. Mellon and Kresge) are independent foundations; 1, Atlantic Richfield, is a corporate foundation; and 1, the San Francisco Foundation, a community foundation.

Most of the 10 foundations reporting the most arts and culture grants in the 1984 listing gave locally and concentrated their funding on a few major institutions, usually universities, public television stations, orchestras, or art museums. The Pew Memorial Trust, for example, did most of its grant-making in Philadelphia. Almost two thirds of its 1984 total represented grants to public television; of the remaining $7.2 million, more than half consisted of two grants to the Philadelphia Museum of Art. Of the $2.65 million distributed outside Philadelphia, more than half supported an arts and technology center at the Massachusetts Institute of Technology.

Some foundations focus intently on a small domain. For example, all $8.16 million in grants from Palo Alto's Systems Development Foundation were to universities for computer music projects "leading to artistically expressive inexpensive instruments," according to the Foundation Center directory. All but $5,000 of the Don and Sybil Harrington Foundation's $4.7 million constituted a single grant to the Metropolitan Opera.

Other leading arts supporters concentrate on a single community or region. For example, the Cullen Foundation made all of its grants ($7.7 million) in Houston. The Lilly Endowment spent all but $114,000 of its arts assistance ($5.1 million, including $3 million in grants to the Indiana State Symphony) in Indianapolis. The Brown Foundation (Houston, $9 million), the Krannert Charitable Trust (Indianapolis, $5 million), the Ahmanson Foundation (Los Angeles, $4 million), and the William Penn Foundation (Philadelphia, $3.4 million) were similarly local in orientation. In sum, of those foundations reported among the top 10 supporters of cultural activities in either the 1984 or 1985 directories, only the Ford Foundation, the Andrew W. Mellon Foundation, the Kresge Foundation, and the Atlantic Richfield Foundation had ongoing national programs of support for the arts.

The tendency for foundation grants to be concentrated, both geographically and by recipient, is also observed if we look at foundation assistance to theatre, dance, orchestras and musical performances, and museums. Only seven foundations reported grants of $1 million or more to theatres.[24] Of these, the three leaders, Mellon, Ford, and Kresge, had national programs.

(Kresge's focused on construction grants, many for university theatres or theatre departments.) The remaining four were all local, two of them community foundations. The Brown and William Penn Foundations were each among the top ten because of a single grant. Of 17 other foundations reporting grants of $200,000 or more in support of the theatre, 3 were community and 2 were corporate foundations. Aside from the corporate foundations, only one—the Rockefeller Foundation—was national in orientation.

Only 16 foundations reported more than $100,000 in grants supporting the dance.[25] Of these 16, 3 were community foundations and 2 were corporate foundations. Of the others, 3 foundations—Hewlett, Starr, and Stiemke—made only one grant each. Of the remaining 8, only the Ford, Kresge, and Rockefeller Foundations were national in orientation. The largest dance funder, the Mabel Pew Myrin Trust ($1.1 million), gave grants to a variety of dance organizations in the Philadelphia metropolitan area, as well as one small grant to the Joffrey Ballet.

The 1984 Foundation Center directory of grants for orchestras and musical performances includes 27 foundations that reported grants totalling $400,000 or more in this category.[26] Of these, 5 were company foundations and 3 were community foundations. Of the 10 leading music donors, only the Ford Foundation was truly national. (The Atlantic Richfield Foundation made grants to orchestras throughout the United States, but primarily in the West.) Giving in this area was highly concentrated: Of the almost $18 million provided by the ten leading donors, more than $13 million was represented by a mere seven grants; and of the latter amount, three grants to a single institution, the Metropolitan Opera, accounted for nearly half. The pattern of few, large grants to one or two major institutions was replicated among the smaller donors.

Grants totalling $1 million or more were reported from 21 foundations in the Foundation Center's 1984 museums listing.[27] Of these, 20 were independent foundations, one (The Houston Foundation) a community foundation. None of the 10 major givers was national in focus. Most of them made just a few very large grants to favored local museums.

Several notable conclusions emerge from this review:

1. Although the total of foundation support for "cultural activities" is high, many of these activities (public television, university research, libraries) are only marginally relevant to either the performing or the visual arts. Support for the performing and visual arts probably represents about half to two-thirds of all foundation support for "cultural activities."

2. The vast majority of foundation arts dollars is given locally. The percentage originating in private foundations with organized national arts programs is probably about 5 percent. Although a few locally oriented foundations support a diversity of organizations, and a handful approach arts giving systematically, most local support is concentrated on the largest, most prestigious, and most artistically conventional institutions. These generalizations apply with special force to support for orchestras and art

museums (which receive the major share of foundation support), and less so to support for theatres and dance companies.

3. Much—perhaps most—foundation support for the arts is episodic and represents large grants to major capital campaigns. Such support is concentrated on the largest, most prestigious, and most artistically conventional institutions.

4. Because most foundation support for the arts is locally oriented, such support is geographically uneven. Arts organizations in cities with robust foundation communities like those of Philadelphia, Minneapolis, San Francisco, and Houston have greater access to philanthropic capital than do institutions in such cities as Atlanta, Kansas City, Cincinnati, or (at least until the recent intervention of the National Arts Stabilization Fund) Boston, where local philanthropies have maintained a less vigorous commitment to the arts.

5. Only a very small share of the foundation dollar goes to experimental arts organizations, minority arts organizations, artists, or community-oriented organizations. In a paper prepared for the Rockefeller Foundation, Kenneth Goody reported that only one sixth of the foundations with arts programs that he surveyed responded without qualification that they gave any support at all to the avant-garde or to new and emerging groups. Fewer than 10 percent reported providing direct grants in support of artist fellowships.[28] In a review undertaken for the Arts Endowment's Expansion Arts Division, the Foundation Center found just over $28 million in independent, community, or corporate foundation grants in its 1982 index targeted to all of the following categories, all very broadly defined: "smaller arts organizations that focus on a minority population, support aspiring professionals, are community-based in a rural or urban area, or are education-oriented"; education, outreach, or community-oriented activities of major arts institutions; arts centers and arts councils; and technical assistance for "smaller" arts organizations.[29]

The relatively few private foundations that do support artists, experimental or innovative organizations, minority institutions, and educational or community-based activities, and the very few that have long-term, national, focused, and systematically developed program commitments, have an influence and visibility that far exceed their proportional share of the foundation dollar. But why are these foundations such a small minority of all private foundations that give to the arts?

THE POTENTIAL OF THE INDEPENDENT FOUNDATION

Private foundations are widely believed to possess a flexibility in their grantmaking that public agencies and corporations lack. In his introduction to the Andrew W. Mellon Foundation's 1980 *Annual Report*, for example, Mellon President John E. Sawyer noted that, unlike public agencies, independent foundations can respond rapidly to new needs, change or terminate programs that are not working, fund "counter-cyclically" to counteract swings in government or corporate attention, and support projects and goals with long-term or uncertain payoffs.[30] Similarly, a history of the JDR 3rd Fund's Asian Cultural Program reports that "whereas official cultural exchange programs often operate with much caution, emphasizing established artists and scholars, the Fund has been able to support a large number of young people who showed talent, but were only beginning their professional development."[31] Writing as the federal government was organizing the National Endowment for the Arts, drama critic Brooks Atkinson proclaimed,

> If Congress appropriates money for the arts it will, quite rightly, influence or control them . . . Foundations are better equipped to help the theatre, for they are represented by officers whose training and experience make artistic judgments a normal procedure . . . Most of the foundations would not be startled by reckless ideas and bizarre styles of production . . . On the basis of what the foundations have already achieved in the theatre, I put my confidence in their taste and their hands.[32]

The remainder of this chapter is based in large part on interviews with program officers (and one trustee) of 10 independent foundations that give to the arts, either nationally or in the community in which the foundation is located.[33] These informants, several of whom had previously worked in other sectors, echoed these views. Comparing his current employer to the federal government, one informant reported, "We can afford to take different kinds of risks, to make long-term commitments. We can respond to things that we might not have thought of when we started." Another program officer with federal-government experience noted that he had been able to alter his program quickly when it stopped meeting the foundation's expectations; by contrast, in government he would have had to carry on despite disappointing results.

An independent foundation program officer who had worked as a junior staff member in a corporate foundation appreciated her ability to maintain well-defined guidelines and to make large grants systematically and without external interference. By contrast, her previous employer's grants were small and made "almost entirely at random." Unlike the independent foundation, she reported, even the most professionally administered company foundations must answer to employees, shareholders, and the chief executive officer.

Autonomy and insulation from external pressure are the factors that foundation staff spoke of most frequently in explaining the greater flexibility they perceived in independent foundations than in government or corporations. One program officer welcomed his ability to make large grants without the concern for regional distribution required of grant-makers in the federal government. Private foundations possess the ability to focus resources to a greater extent than do governments (which must maintain legislative coalitions), corporations (which must enhance, or at least not damage, the corporate image), and community foundations (which bear an encyclopedic responsibility within their charitable domains).

The relative autonomy of independent foundations also enables them to act without undue concern for public relations. With no corporate sponsor to please, independent foundations can contribute funds quietly to vital behind-the-scenes efforts, like scholarship, art conservation, or the training of younger artists, that lack the gloss of blockbuster exhibits or new wings for performing arts centers.

Finally, the independence of the private foundation gives it the potential to take risks, for if the enterprises in which it invests fail, trustees and staff have only to answer to themselves. As one informant said of a program supporting artists, "If two thirds of the people we support are forgotten in twenty years, that's the chance we must take to help the one third that will make an impact on their fields."

If the individual independent foundation has flexibility and the freedom to experiment, the foundation sector is believed to possess collectively a diversity that enables it to sustain an unusual range of purposes and activities. The heterogeneity of foundation charters, missions, and trustee orientations may permit more variation among foundation programs than among public agencies (which share certain common political imperatives) or corporations (which are subject to profit incentives and the constraints these pose).

CONSTRAINTS ON FOUNDATION PROGRAMS OF SUPPORT FOR THE ARTS

But if the universe of foundations contains programs that support almost every imaginable artistic pursuit, from the Metropolitan Opera to electronic music, from the National Gallery to alternative spaces, from the Guthrie Theatre to Alternate Roots, on balance, relatively few of the hundreds of independent foundations that give to the arts have lived up to the promise of the sector to make a difference for enterprises that other patrons will not support. As we have seen, the number of national programs in the arts can be counted on one hand and together account for approximately $1 in every $20 of foundation grants to the arts. Even if one adds to these few institutions those foundations that maintain ongoing and systematic programs of assistance to local artists and arts organizations, it is doubtful that the total rises far above 10 percent of all foundation arts disbursements.

All organizations, even private foundations, face constraints. Discussions of the flexibility and autonomy of private foundations often overlook this fact, consequently treating a relative advantage as an absolute dispensation from the cares of the world.

In fact, foundations, their trustees, and their program officers are constrained in the kinds of programs that they can develop in support of the arts. These constraints may be neither so dramatic nor so invariant as those facing their counterparts in the public or corporate sectors, but they are nonetheless real and may help to explain why imaginative and courageous programs of artistic philanthropy are so unusual, so rarely replicated, and thus so critical for the field as a whole. Let us consider a few of the possible factors that may constrain foundation programs of giving in the arts.

Federal and state laws regulating private grant-making foundations set broad parameters around foundation activities. But in practice they seem to present few obstacles for most program officers or trustees concerned with the arts.

Foundation missions and traditions pose more significant constraints, but these vary from foundation to foundation. Those foundations that pride themselves on maintaining trim staffs are unlikely to mount fellowship programs, which are staff-intensive (although they may support fellowship programs through operating nonprofit organizations). Program officers working for foundations that have traditionally supported certain disciplines or institutions may find it difficult to abandon old commitments. For the most part, however, foundation interests pose opportunities for arts programs as well as constraints. The arts program of one foundation that is international in orientation, for example, was able to build on the strengths of the foundation as a whole to mount programs of international cultural exchange.

Internal politics present a more formidable constraint to many larger foundations. The staff interviewed for this study varied in the emphasis they lay on building and maintaining an internal constituency. The director of one major program noted that he attempts to stay attuned to the preferences of the trustees, to respond to their cues in his program development efforts, and to convince his fellow program directors of the importance of the foundation's activities in the arts. By contrast, the director of another major program noted that she receives little input from the foundation's trustees and works largely by herself, submitting new program proposals to the trustees only after they have been fully developed.

In the long run, arts programs that have strong constituencies on boards of trustees, that are strongly anchored in the more general mission of a foundation, and the staff of which interact vigorously with their peers would seem to have stronger survival chances than those that operate more autonomously. In private foundations, as in many relatively small and informal organizations, the strong identification of a program with its director sometimes creates crises of commitment when the program officer steps down. (Grants to the arts by one locally oriented foundation, for example, declined by one half when a program officer who served as the arts' internal advocate resigned.) Where program officers are able to decentralize their organization's memory of and commitment to an arts program, such succession crises are more likely to be avoided.

Budgetary change represents another constraint and, in some cases, an opportunity. The systematic approach to program development characteristic of foundations like Ford, Rockefeller, and Mellon is, as I have noted, rare among most donors to the arts. Most foundations, especially local ones, with sustained commitments to the arts begin with grants to established institutions, often museums and orchestras, of the sort favored by the more conservative trustees; they expand their programs only when the assets and disbursements of the foundation are climbing. Because new programs and new kinds of grantees are most easily accommodated when their initiation does not require a reallocation of resources, foundation growth provides avenues for innovative grant-making and external leverage that are unavailable during times of stasis or retrenchment.

Trustee preferences, and the preferences of those with whom trustees regularly come into contact, represent a major constraint on arts-program staff. Many of the informants for this study reported that their trustees were more conservative in their tastes and grant-making inclinations than were they themselves. Two mentioned that trustees would not permit them to make direct grants to artists. "Grants to organizations are much safer than direct grants to genius," said one. Another indicated that she would like to support smaller and less tested organizations than her trustees would permit: "We place our emphasis at the higher end of the field. We cannot do much with the avant-garde, the more experimental, the dizzier end of the field. . . . I couldn't get away with that." A third noted that trustee opposition precluded foundation assistance to nontraditional and minority arts organizations. Another reported that trustees associate the avant-garde with "bare bosoms and four-letter words."

Trustee conservatism may be a matter of personal taste; or it may result from the pressures with which the trustee comes in contact in his or her daily routine. If foundation trustees are usually, in practice, free from legal or material retribution for their institution's policies, they are nonetheless subject to all of the forms of interpersonal control (esteem and disesteem, embarrassment and pride, condemnation and praise, raised eyebrows and pats on the back) by which people regulate one another's behavior. Because most foundations' trustees are persons of wealth and status and many are business executives, the worlds that they as a group inhabit are likely to be more conservative than those of scholars or practicing artists. The influence of trustee conservatism is probably strengthened by the widespread belief that cultivated people should have "tastes" in the arts (although they may remain respectably unopinionated about such program areas as medical research or environmental affairs).

Peer pressure on trustees is likely to be most intense in foundations that recruit their trustees from and make most of their grants in a single community. Under such circumstances, trustees are likely to be held more often to account for their foundations' actions and to be subject to more concerted pressure from supporters of grantees or would-be grantees. (A program officer at one locally oriented foundation reported his constant struggles against backers of major capital campaigns, who try to persuade trustees to commandeer the arts budget for their favored causes.) This is undoubtedly one reason why most (but not all) local grant-making focuses on the major established institutions.

Trustees are not, of course, invariably conservative, and staff are sometimes able to maneuver around trustee tastes. Much of the diversity in the foundation world reflects variation in the values and preferences of foundation trustees. Some innovative programs—for example, one foundation's program of assistance to film and video organizations—begin as trustee suggestions. Moreover, trustees of many mature foundations defer to the programmatic judgments of staff and of professionals in the field.

What is more, foundation staff are often able to combat trustee recalcitrance through a combination of advocacy and gentle guile. Foundations that make small grants at a staff member's or president's discretion may experiment with such grants to prove the worth of an initiative. One program officer reported drawing on a long-standing regional commitment of her foundation in order to support an innovative organization that would otherwise have been ineligible for support. Another program officer reported funding certain difficult-to-classify avant-garde performing companies under a program category devised to assist more conventional organizations.

THE PROBLEM OF INFORMATION

The cost of information—of getting it and of evaluating it—is as substantial a constraint on foundation innovativeness as any other. If trustee preferences are more binding upon local foundations, information limits may press harder on national programs, where the number of potential grantees—and the distance between foundation officer and grantee—is likely to be greater. As the Rockefeller Panel on the Performing Arts wrote in 1965, "Because decisions on arts applications involve judgments of quality in an area where there are few absolute standards, there is perhaps greater uncertainty about making grants than in the traditional areas of foundation support."[34]

Given the uncertainty surrounding the evaluation of artistic work, and the ambiguity of much of the information that foundation officers receive, defining the needs of a field and selecting grant recipients is both difficult and expensive. Indeed, the only respect in which the federal government was compared favorably to independent foundations in grant-making was in its unparalleled access to information. One informant noted that when he was a federal employee, "information rolled across my desk in barrels every day." As a foundation program director, maintaining contact with and access to information from the field has been more difficult. (Another informant, who had worked in the arts, complained of finding her old friends suddenly guarded in their comments when she assumed a grant-making role.)

Because it takes time to collect and to evaluate, information is expensive. Almost all of the program officers interviewed for this study described strategies they use to contain information costs (although few of them put it in these terms); and many of them noted the trade-off between minimizing expenditures on information and maximizing the openness of their programs to all talented grant-seekers.

One strategy for containing information costs is to develop such narrow guidelines that for any round of grants the universe of potential grantees is finite and knowable. Indeed, one informant prefers setting limits on her programs that may appear arbitrary precisely because such limits save time and money, permitting the foundation to spend more on grant-making, and potential applicants to invest their proposal-writing time effectively. Such a strategy, which works well to conserve information costs, would not be appropriate for a foundation that sought to identify new talent; to make fine distinctions among a great many potential applicants; or to encourage the best small, new, or innovative organizations. (The most widely cited argument against individual award and fellowship programs is that gathering sufficient information to make fair and intelligent decisions on individual applicants is extraordinarily expensive.)

A few of the major foundations that support the arts invest in program officers who come with years of experience and extensive personal networks, or they provide sufficient travel budgets and staff assistance to enable program directors to forge such connections. In other cases, however, program officers draw on the expertise of a few individuals who are believed to be "central" to a field, either hiring them as consultants or seeking their advice informally. This is a sensible economic strategy; indeed, it is difficult to imagine an affordable alternative for any but the wealthiest foundations. But such consultants, formal or informal, may, after a while, constitute an invisible college upon which many different foundations rely. If many foundations draw on the same invisible college, and if members of that group influence one another as well, program officers may believe that they are making independent and convergent discoveries about the field when, in fact, they are all hearing the same conventional wisdom from the same sources. At worst, such a system may come to resemble a game of "whisper down the lane," with chance remarks fed back into the pipeline and magnified, and rumor replacing research as a basis for decision.

The problem of information is exacerbated, of course, by the fact that evaluations of artistic work are likely to be ambiguous. Although almost all program officers wish to fund excellent programs and artists, few have the resources to visit each of the organizations they might assist or to convene rotating panels for peer review. Under such circumstances, some informants reported seeking less ambiguous data to help them distinguish among applicants: information on attendance figures, earned-income statistics, and meeting-attendance records of the applicants' trustees. (Without supplementary information on quality, such practices would lead to grants to organizations that mount popular productions and exhibitions and select board members who, for whatever reasons, are willing to attend meetings. Whether such organizations also produce high-quality art is a moot point.)

Princeton economist Joseph Stiglitz has distinguished between "polyarchies," in which each actor has the discretion to accept or reject a potential project (or proposal), and hierarchies, in which projects are taken from a pool only once, with those selected by the lower level passed on to the next, which re-examines and then approves or vetoes them.[35]

According to Stiglitz, one can demonstrate mathematically that a hierarchy rejects more good projects than a polyarchy and that a polyarchy accepts more bad ones. "Under the plausible assumption," writes Stiglitz, "that there are more bad projects than good projects—after all, it it easier to think up bad ideas than good ideas—polyarchy performs better than hierarchy."[36]

The universe of independent foundations is clearly a "polyarchy" by Stiglitz's definition. If a proposal is rejected by one foundation, it stays in the pool to be considered by others. Such a decentralized system seems especially tailored for a field like the arts, where merit is difficult to define and, until established, may be difficult to discover. The success of a decentralized system in nurturing the arts, however, requires that foundations value and sustain their diversity and flexibility. For the more similar are the standards, decision procedures, and information sources of members of a polyarchy, the more such a polyarchy will tend, in practice, towards hierarchy, and the less likely it will be to find the "scarce new ideas" of which Stiglitz writes.

CONCLUSION

Independent foundations, because of their autonomy, flexibility, and diversity, have played a critical role in the arts by supporting those purposes and programs of merit that other funders have been constrained to neglect. Yet private foundations are themselves constrained. Relatively few of them live up to their potential to be different and to take the risks that others refuse. Despite the comparatively high visibility of the few independent foundations that maintain creative, national programs of support for the arts, the persistence of the foundation role cannot be taken for granted. Most foundation dollars go to established traditional institutions, most often art museums and symphony orchestras, in the foundation's home community, frequently in support of building or endowment campaigns. Few foundation grants support access to and participation in the arts for the poor and working poor; conservation or preservation of performances in such performing arts as dance, theatre, or improvisational music; or assistance for innovative artists and arts organizations. Nor are there many that support programs and organizations that promote the values of pluralism and diversity through presentation of genres that, like jazz performance and composition or ethnic dance, are associated with specific racial or nationality groups or, like performance art and video art, have emerged out of the hybridization of classic and commercial culture. The resources of the relatively few foundations that do support such activities are stretched extremely thin.

If private foundations are as autonomous and as flexible as they appear to be, then why does the foundation sector, taken as a whole, display so little variation in its funding of the arts? For locally oriented foundations the answer may lie in the networks of reciprocity in which trustees are embedded, networks that reinforce aesthetic conservatism and that impel foundations to assist the most powerful and traditional institutions. For foundations that are large enough to operate at the national level, conformity is encouraged by the high cost of reliable information and by the strategies that many foundations employ to contain those costs.

The Rockefeller Panel, anticipating a steeper rise in the arts' share of the foundation dollar than has in fact occurred, called for a division of labor between the national and local foundation in which the former assisted experimental projects and demonstration programs and the latter devoted itself to "the steady general support of performing arts organizations at the community level."[37] There is a logic to this position, but one that relies on the willingness of the large foundations to act nationally in support of the arts and the readiness of the local foundations to support a broader range of cultural endeavors than most of them currently embrace. The nationalization of boards of trustees that are currently composed of members from the same city or region may, eventually, weaken bonds of local obligation in some local foundations. A few others may design means of gathering information that permit them to act more independently and daringly than they have thus far. Until that happens, however, private foundations with creative and systematic programs of giving to the arts are more likely to remain an important, influential, but small minority in the foundation universe.

NOTES

1. Some corporations did attend to the cultural life of their workers during the heyday of welfare capitalism, but such programs fell by the wayside during the Depression and, at any rate, are not comparable to the organized programs of assistance to nonprofit cultural enterprises mounted by corporate philanthropists over the past 25 years. Similarly, the federal government sponsored major arts projects during the WPA era, local governments have supported public entertainments for most of this century, and both have commissioned memorials and public architecture throughout our history. But only with the creation of the state arts councils and the National Endowment for the Arts has the major share of this activity been pursued through nonprofit, rather than public, enterprises.

2. The reader is warned that a substantial amount of guesswork lies behind this statement. Taking the American Association of Fund-Raising Counsel's projection of $4.36 billion in foundations disbursements for 1984; estimating a percentage of all grants going to the arts

from the Foundation Center's breakdown of grants of $5000 or more from reporting foundations; and assuming that the same percentage applies to foundations that do not report their grants to the Foundation Center—a contestable but plausible procedure, we arrive at an estimate of from $325 to $350 million for 1984, a figure similar to the value of all public support for the arts and somewhat higher than the total of corporate contributions. Data come from the American Association of Fund-Raising Counsel, *Giving USA: 1985 Annual Report* (New York: American Association of Fund-Raising Counsel, 1985), 30–31, 42.

3. These data, which are from printouts on file at the Foundation Center Library in New York, were collected by Karla Shepard as part of a study sponsored by the Twentieth Century Fund.

4. Eduard C. Lindeman, *Wealth and Culture: A Study of One Hundred Foundations and Community Trusts and Their Operation During the Decade 1921–1930* (New York: Harcourt, Brace and Company, 1936).

5. *American Foundations and Their Fields, 1931* (New York: Twentieth Century Fund, 1931), 12.

6. *American Foundations and Their Fields.* Editions for 1931, 1932, 1934 (New York: Twentieth Century Fund), 1937, and 1940 (New York: Raymond Rich Associates).

7. Irving Kolodin, *The Metropolitan Opera: 1883–1935* (New York: Oxford University Press, 1936), 449–450, 477–478.

8. On General Education Board, see *American Foundations and Their Fields, 1931,* op. cit.; on Rockefeller Foundation's film and playwright grants, see Malcolm L. Richardson, "Historical Review of Foundation Activities in the Arts and Humanities" (Report to the Rockefeller Foundation Arts and Humanities Division, July 1983, mimeographed), 3–4; on Rockefeller WPA grant, see William F. McDonald, *Federal Relief Administration and the Arts: The Origins and Administrative History of the Arts Projects of the Works Progress Administration* (Colombus, Ohio: Ohio State University Press, 1969), 580.

9. *American Foundations and Their Fields, 1931,* op. cit.

10. Brenda Jubin, *Program in the Arts, 1911–1967* (New York: The Carnegie Corporation, 1968), 2.

11. Ibid.

12. F. Emerson Andrews, *Philanthropic Giving* (New York: Russell Sage Foundation, 1950), 211–212.

13. The Ford Foundation, "Activities in the Creative and Performing Arts" (mimeographed, n.d.).

14. Richard Schechner, "Ford, Rockefeller, and Theatre," *Tulane Drama Review* 10, no. 1 (Fall 1965): 23–49.

15. Dick Netzer, *The Subsidized Muse: Public Support for the Arts in the United States* (New York: Cambridge University Press, 1978), 106–107; The Ford Foundation, *Sharps and Flats: A Report on Ford Foundation Assistance to American Music* (New York: The Ford Foundation, 1980).

16. Tables in this paper are based on printouts from Shepard's study that are on file at the Foundation Center Library in New York. The printouts contain information on all categories of foundation giving during the period Shepard studied.

17. Moreover, data compiled by the Foundation Center (*Grants Index*, New York, 1982) indicate that the distribution of grants across subcategories of arts spending by the largest and by other foundations is quite similar. To the extent that this was also the case during the period Shepard studied, her figures are likely to be representative of the allocations of smaller foundations, as well.

18. Because the Ford Foundation's programs were so massive and because much support was given in the form of multiyear appropriations, the data excluding the Ford Foundation are more reliable guides to trends in support of the arts among large foundations as a group than are the data including Ford's appropriations. For example, Shepard's data do not include the $80 million appropriated by the Ford Foundation in support of U.S. symphony orchestras because that appropriation was made in 1966, a year not covered by her study.

19. See Paul J. DiMaggio, "Can Culture Survive the Marketplace?" (Chapter 3, this volume).
20. Foundation Center, *Statistical Summary, New Series* (New York, Foundation Center, 1985).
21. Ibid.
22. Foundation Center, *Grants for Arts and Cultural Programs,* (New York: Foundation Center, 1984).
23. The Ford Foundation's grant was actually made in autumn, 1984; were reporting times more consistent than required by the purposes for which the Foundation Center collects these data, its grant would have been included in the 1985 listing.
24. Foundation Center, *Comsearch Printouts: Theatre, 1984* (New York: Foundation Center, 1984).
25. Foundation Center, *Comsearch Printouts: Dance, 1984* (New York: Foundation Center, 1984).
26. Foundation Center, *Comsearch Printouts: Orchestras and Musical Performances, 1984* (New York: Foundation Center, 1984).
27. Foundation Center, *Comsearch Printouts: Museums, 1984* (New York: Foundation Center, 1984).
28. Kenneth Goody, "The Funding of the Arts and Artists, Humanities and Humanists, in the United States" (Report to the Rockefeller Foundation, November 1983, mimeographed).
29. The Foundation Center, *Public/Private Cooperation: Funding for Small and Emerging Arts Programs* (New York: Foundation Center, 1983).
30. John E. Sawyer, "1980 President's Report," *Report of the Andrew W. Mellon Foundation, 1980* (New York: Andrew W. Mellon Foundation, 1980), 8–11.
31. The JDR 3rd Fund, *The JDR 3rd Fund and Asia: 1963–1975* (New York: JDR 3rd Fund, 1977).
32. Brooks Atkinson, "American Foundations and the Theatre," Chapter 22 in Warren Weaver, *U.S. Philanthropic Foundations: Their History, Structure, Management, and Record* (New York: Harper & Row, 1967), 314–315.
33. Interviews ranged from 35 minutes to 2 hours in length, with a median duration of 1 hour and 15 minutes.
34. Rockefeller Panel on the Performing Arts, *The Performing Arts: Problems and Prospects* (New York: McGraw-Hill, 1965), 107.
35. Joseph Stiglitz, "Information and Economic Analysis: A Perspective" (Hoover Institution Working Paper in Economics E-84-16, December 1984).
36. Ibid.
37. Rockefeller Panel, op. cit., 99–103.

6

Public Provision of the Performing Arts: *A Case Study of The Federal Theatre Project in Connecticut*

ELIZABETH A. CAVENDISH

The establishment in 1935 of the Federal Theatre Project as one of the Four Arts Projects under Federal One, a section of the Works Progress Administration, marked the United States government's first major venture in the arts.[1] The Project was a relief measure and providing work to unemployed theatre artists was its first priority. It was not meant to serve as a prototype for a federal theatre, although this idea soon surfaced. Nor was it dedicated, at its inception, to artistic excellence or innovation, although these values soon became prominent in the thinking of many participants. In short, the Federal Theatre transcended its original goals without abandoning them. Yet in trying to fulfill too many missions and to justify itself to too many publics, the Project foundered. As it did, it became a symbol that has shaped discourse about public involvement in the arts since the 1930s. For conservatives, the Federal Theatre Project, with its much publicized productions of radical plays, became a lightening rod embodying their deepest fears about federal intrusion into culture. For the left, it became a symbol of a benign state supporting the pursuit of radical change through the arts.

The Theatre Project has remained a symbol because our image of it is shaped by memories of participants who tend to eulogize the Project,[2] by histories that focus on the Project's controversial New York units,[3] by the self-congratulatory publications of the Project itself, or by hostile articles in the contemporary conservative press. In general, students of the Proj-

This chapter represents an extensive revision of the author's senior thesis in American Studies at Yale College.

ects, the press, and Project officials themselves have focused in their accounts on atypical incidents and, usually, on the New York Project.

The continuing focus on New York, which employed the largest number of workers, permeated even contemporary discussion in other states. When workers in the New York Arts Projects struck for job security and against pay cuts, the strikes were reported throughout Connecticut. Communist activity in New York was covered by the same Connecticut press that ignored the state's own, less political, Theatre Project. Strikes and Communists came to represent the whole Theatre Project during the 1930s, and in many secondary sources thereafter.

In practice, the Federal Theatre was beset with marked internal tensions that both supporters and critics have tended to ignore. Project personnel minimized the conflict between the relief mission and artistic excellence or social relevance, in a way that audiences and critics confronted by the performances of worn-out vaudeville actors could not.[4] Project Director Hallie Flanagan could inveigh from Washington against the "small but precious" character of American theatre without facing the need, as her lieutenants in most states and communities did, of garnering the support of middle-class professionals for their projects' survival.[5] The leadership in Washington could write about the Project's efforts to provide an alternative to mass culture for the common man, while local directors imitated commercial theatre and even began to quest for profitability.[6]

To be sure, the Federal Theatre Project did transcend its original relief goal to foster a spirit of cultural responsibility. Many units of the Project were committed to producing plays that were popular, innovative, or of special local interest. New York's productions of *Professor Mamlock, Dr. Faustus,* and *Murder in the Cathedral* are theatrical landmarks. The simultaneous opening of Sinclair Lewis' *It Can't Happen Here* in 18 cities marked a feat of national theatrical organization. *The Living Newspaper,* a fast-paced multimedia review of current events, represented the emergence of a new theatrical form. In some midwestern cities, the Federal Theatre's performances reached nearly every citizen. And the Theatre Project offered diverse programs, from drama in foreign language to children's theatre, undeniably broadening access to culture and helping to preserve and expand the nation's dramatic heritage.

Many of the criticisms leveled at the Project were also apt. As conservatives complained, some productions were tawdry, unsophisticated, or amateurish, and some units wasted public money. Moreover, Communists were active in parts of the Project and leftist propaganda plays were indeed produced.

Yet the Project was too complex to be understood in terms of the pat slogans of either the left (community involvement, pluralistic drama, social awareness, innovation) or the right (inefficiency, creeping socialism, amateurishness, Communism, propaganda). For the Federal Theatre Project meant very different things in most communities. If the project in New York City, with that city's huge community of theatre artists and vital, organized leftist movements could pursue its members' social agenda at least for a few years, in most of the United States project leaders devoted their efforts to building enough community support to enable their organizations to survive from one year to the next. Survival, in most locales, required balancing the many conflicting priorities of the Theatre Project against one another and against the diverse demands of several potential constituencies. The results, although less dramatic than those of the New York experience, were more typical and may have more to teach us about the limits and possibilities of public enterprise in the performing arts.

THE CONNECTICUT THEATRE PROJECT: AN OVERVIEW

Shifting focus from the Federal Theatre Project's national ideals to its local operation depletes the Project of much of its allure and reveals an organization concerned with the daily problems of raising resources and maintaining legitimacy. To be sure, the Connecticut Project could boast of many accomplishments. Its first unit, opening in New Haven in January 1936 and closing in June of that year, presented two works by Connecticut playwrights, a children's drama, three vaudeville performances, and eight other productions to a total of over 13,000 viewers.[7] In March, the Project opened units in Bridgeport and Hartford. The former produced 28 plays before closing in September 1937; a separate Bridgeport vaudeville unit put on 94. Hartford's unit recorded 35 productions before its demise in April 1939, operating consistently on schedule and with financial support from the municipal government.[8] Hartford also maintained a "Negro Experimental Group," one of three black ensembles then operating in Connecticut.[9] Exemplifying its commitment to decentralizing access to theatre, the Project established workshop units in such small cities as New London, Norwalk, and Southington, sending productions of classics and other plays on tour to even smaller places.[10] The Connecticut Project took pride, as well, in the airing of its "Theatre of the Air" programs on six local stations, in its presentation of six plays by young playwrights, and in its alumni who found employment in broadcasting or on the commercial stage.

Moreover, the Connecticut Project adhered successfully to the federal guideline that less than 10 percent of its budget go towards nonlabor expenses (although 14 percent, above the national limit, went to supervisory personnel). Gross receipts for the Connecticut Project totalled more than $20,000, and more than 80,000 people were admitted to performances free of charge.[11] The Connecticut Project employed 421 persons in its first year,[12] although, like the Projects in other states, federal cutbacks reduced this figure to 115 by 1938.[13]

Highlights of the Connecticut Theatre Project include the Bridgeport production of Sinclair Lewis' *It Can't Happen Here* and the electrifying *Living Newspaper* exposé of tenement housing, *One-Third of a Nation.*

William Dubois' *Haiti* attracted attention because whites and blacks shared the stage, as they rarely did in the commercial theatre, while the Harlem Unit's touring production of *Macbeth* in Hartford drew the largest audience.

Yet despite these achievements, the Federal Theatre in Connecticut was vexed by a constant struggle for support and survival. Tensions between the desire to provide access for the poorest and the attempt to earn enough money to supplement federal funds, between the drive to mount socially relevant drama and the effort to obtain political support from the powerful and well-to-do, and between the demands of work relief and the aspirations of the Project's artists were unremitting.

TENSIONS OF MISSION AND INTERNAL PROCESS

The creation of a new organization, with few if any models upon which to draw, is never an easy task. For the Connecticut Federal Theatre Project, the job was complicated by the multiplicity of goals that participants could pursue and by constant ambiguity about the role of central authority in the local units' activities.

Directors with Goals in a Goal-less Organization

In some locations, Federal Theatre Project units were committed to a consistent and overriding ideal of what theatre should be. By contrast, in Connecticut, artistic policy vacillated. Few of the plays that the Connecticut Project produced illuminated the social crisis of the Depression. Few represented the best of contemporary drama or the classics. Nor was the Project dedicated to experimental plays, techniques, or interpretation. It was not even democratic in its choice of mediocre plays, for the Connecticut units avoided producing labor or ethnic drama, favoring stock revivals or imitations of fluffy Broadway hits.

The Federal Theatre in Connecticut often strove to imitate the commercial theatre from which it might have felt liberated. The ideal of "profitability" persisted in the minds of Connecticut leaders, even though they were free of the financial and artistic demands of Broadway. Connecticut was the first state to charge admission to Theatre productions, and Project leaders boasted more of their increased receipts than of diversified or enlarged attendance.

The impact of this commercial-mindedness on the creative process was substantial. In November 1936, State Director Gertrude Don Dero, in a memorandum to all local production directors, decreed that "there will be no further experimentation without basically sound reasons," and exhorted the directors to adhere to "the best business principles."[14] Moreover, Don Dero wanted hits to spark community interest: She appreciated

It Can't happen Here not, like national Project Director Flanagan, for its powerful anti-Fascist message, but because of its salutary impact on attendance.[15]

Local directors followed Don Dero's lead. Eager to make the Hartford Civic Repertory a self-sufficient unit, its first director boasted of attendance by "the finest class of people in the city."[16] Described in press and internal memoranda as "dead wood," a man who "concentrated on mediocre stock revivals,"[17] he was soon replaced by the former director of the Bridgeport unit, noted for his affection for "snappy Broadway scripts."[18] A few months later, the Hartford unit announced that it would experiment with new plays, condescendingly contrasting itself to the local private "little theatres," with their emphasis on Broadway successes.[19] The unit abandoned this policy only one month later to present *The Curtain Rises,* a Viennese comedy.[20]

Yet the Hartford unit demonstrated more stability than its counterpart in Bridgeport, which swayed under seven directors in only 18 months. Cecil Spooner, the first, brought artless direction and charges of nepotism, although audiences seemed to like her *Shanghai Sal.* Homer Mason, temporary head of vaudeville productions, offered such eternal plays as *House of Fear,* and *The Trial of Mary Dugan.* Local critics smiled when Walter Klavun introduced Broadway's higher grade of frivolity, then gasped when Ann Ayers tackled social issues with *It Can't Happen Here.* Her successor, Charles Atkins, attempted to base the productions in American life and Bridgeport's community, including local ethnic choirs in one production and presenting two plays by Connecticut authors. Wilton Graff carried on his predecessor's style briefly before yielding to L. Anderson, who guided Bridgeport's last two productions, *Live Dolls on the Moon* (with puppets) and *Help Yourself.* The Bridgeport unit was closed on short notice when state Project headquarters moved to Hartford.

The brisk pace of directorial turnover had numerous origins: Don Dero's dissatisfaction with the artistic policy of one director, a commercial job offer for another, a lateral move within the Project for a third, and a flagrant judgmental error in yet another director's production of her husband's plays, on which he collected royalties. The rapid progression of directors indicates the operational irrelevance of Washington's pronouncements of mission to the local level. By and large, the goals of the Connecticut Federal Theatre's units were the goals of their directors; and, like the directors, they changed rapidly.

Grassroots Drama and Central Control

The Federal Theatre in Connecticut was vexed, as well, by constant tensions between localism and centralism. Supporters of a permanent public theatre sought central direction and concentration of the best talent at a single site. But the national Project sought to bring drama to the disenfranchised, wherever they might live. The Connecticut Project attempted to reconcile this tension by centralizing its administration, while sometimes trying to increase access to culture.

At times, however, the conflict between localism and centralism was less a matter of ideals than of practical politics. When headquarters moved from Bridgeport to Hartford, consolidating the project, the Bridgeport press complained bitterly.[21] (Local loyalties had flared earlier when more experienced New York workers displaced Bridgeport citizens on the Project staff.)[22]

Throughout the Project's brief life, conflicts between local Projects and the state-level directorate rent the day-to-day process of artistic work. The question of who controlled the choice of plays exemplified these struggles. Official procedures permitted scripts to be considered at the local level, but once chosen, they were to be sent immediately for state review, accompanied by a report of the director's artistic and promotional plans for the production. The state, in turn, forwarded the recommended plays and supporting materials to Washington, for yet another review.[23] (Local theatres could avoid red tape by choosing plays already approved by the National Project's Bureau of Contracts and Play Rentals in New York.)[24]

Such efforts at administrative centralization were not always successful. For example, Hallie Flanagan's lieutenant, David Lane, was surprised to find *The Streets of New York* opening in Bridgeport in November 1936.[25] Washington responded with a flurry of harsh letters, which in turn generated scolding memos from Don Dero, upbraiding local directors for "vital violations" of administrative procedure.[26]

In addition to their attempts to monitor the selection of plays, federal Project officials occasionally intervened in the staging of presentations. For instance, the Federal Theatre Project's Assistant Director for the East wrote Don Dero about the White House scene in *It Can't Happen Here:* "You may stage the White House scene in a hotel room, and if you do not refer to the White House by name, you may play the scene."[27] Hiram Motherwell, assistant director for the Federal Project, ordered Hartford's production of *For Crying Out Loud* terminated on the grounds that "it lacks sufficient merit to justify its performance on government funds. Please cancel production plans and hunt for a play of more definite dramatic interest."[28] Although such isolated incidents as the suppression of *Ethiopia* in New York attracted more national attention, in Connecticut, attempts to maintain artistic control represented an ongoing process.

Federal and state Project officials' efforts at creative control may not have made the local units any less "free" than their commercial counterparts, bridling under the "censorship" of the market. Certainly, the Project units affirmed the views of neither the government nor their patrons and at times offered alternatives to commercial fare. What is more, unlike the effects of the private market, the Federal Theatre Project's sporadic attempts at censorship were decried in the press and subject to ongoing public debate. Unfortunately, this public debate regarding censorship never expanded into a broader consideration by the press of the systematic biases and exclusions of private theatre.

Connecticut Theatre Project officials manifested a general unease about their federal superiors, editing reviews of favorable snippets and compiling folders of laudatory letters from professionals and leaders of private organizations. That their discomfort may have been warranted is indicated by the replacement of Director Don Dero with Charles La Rue in September 1937. (The local press hailed the departure of Don Dero, whom they termed a theatrical "egg layer," as a "revolution" in the project.[29]) La Rue, an experienced actor, director, promotional manager, and financial executive, had directed the Theatre Project in Nebraska and Iowa.

La Rue had little time to make an impact on Connecticut theatre. In April 1939, the Connecticut Project was abruptly concluded. (In a few months, red-baiting investigations by congressional opponents of the New Deal led to the demise of the Federal Theatre on the national level.) Thus the Theatre Project, originally committed to decentralizing drama and then to establishing a national theatre, became embroiled in the conflicting interests of local audiences and actors, and of local, state, and federal officials, including, eventually, Congress.

THE STRUGGLE FOR LEGITIMACY

The contradiction at the heart of the Theatre Project was the battle between its need to establish itself and its urge to democratize the stage. Was the Project to be a part of the cultural system of the past, a basis for a national theatre with a politically potent constituency? Or was it to be an attempt at cultural democracy, a national theatre for the shirt-sleeved people whose pictures covered the Project's in-house publication, *Federal Theatre?* The Connecticut Federal Theatre Project found itself trapped between accepted notions of who should attend theatre, and in what style, and the national Project's democratic ideals of opening culture to all Americans. In Connecticut the Project tried to build its legitimacy, against the slings of a largely unsympathetic conservative press, by reaching out to social influentials. In these unsuccessful efforts, it moved far from the social agenda that the national project had inaugurated.

The Local Press and the Connecticut Project

The Connecticut press tended to treat the Federal Project as just another commercial theatre. Rarely did a writer evaluate the Project as a whole or commend its contributions to democracy. When it did not benignly miss the point of the Project, the Connecticut press usually opposed it. Anti–New Deal editors used the Project as a symbol of boondoggling and selected wire service dispatches that portrayed it in a hostile light. By contrast, drama critics held their political diatribes for those few Project plays that addressed political themes. More destructively, however, these critics used the standards of the conventional upper-middle-class stage to evaluate the Project's work: Their reports focused on who attended the plays, what they wore, who starred in the performances, and whether the Connecticut Federal Theatre was as good as Broadway. Thus Connecticut residents had little access to the Theatre Project's own definition of its goals. Indeed, the Connecticut Project came to echo the reviewers' preoccupations in its own press releases.

The debate over the star system highlights the persistent tensions among the Project's ideals, the press's beliefs, and popular conceptions of theatre. The Federal Theatre was strategically and philosophically opposed to the star system: Its official purpose was to employ unemployed actors (among whom stars were conspicuously absent), and many participants were actively committed to theatre as collective effort.

Yet personalities, not edifying content, attract audiences, as Hartford drama critics never tired of reminding the Theatre's management. Critic Edward Brainard compared the theatre's star system to that of baseball and the movies and emphasized the crucial importance of celebrities in encouraging repeat attendance.[30] Despite some efforts at accommodation, the Project's own press releases usually stressed the name and theme of the play in a valiant effort to oppose the star system.

If the critics decried the Federal Theatre's promotional methods, they were discomfited by the broadly inclusive audiences that these methods attracted. Critic Brainard, after proclaiming that he was a Republican, went on to criticize the audience's "rudeness," explaining that "the motion pictures have made bad children out of the customers."[31] Similarly, columnist Jess Benton of the Bridgeport *Herald* devoted almost as much space to the Project's audiences as to its players' acting. In a harshly negative review of Bridgeport's *Blind Alley,* Benton expressed irritation at the "distractions supplied by the audience," whose wholehearted enjoyment of the play was expressed in spontaneous curtain calls.[32]

For some, the audiences were a novelty. Ethel Beckwith of the Bridgeport *Post* congratulated the Bridgeport unit on filling the theatre where "only ghosts had been for the past ten years," and noted that the new theatregoers "preferred to leave their ermine wraps at home . . . Cocktail breath and chatting debutantes were absent at the large and lusty reception." (Nonetheless, the review was accompanied by pictures of men and women in evening dress, and Beckwith included the names of luminaries in attendance.)[33] Only eight months later, *Countess Fairfield,* a local society writer, relegated the Bridgeport Theatre to those who did not "bother" with ties and tails. She noted how different the audiences were in Bridgeport than in New Haven and remarked wistfully, "but then every town can't have a college." The "Countess" did not wish to seem undemocratic;

but she wrote for people who dreaded the influx of working class audiences for social drama: "Despite the fears of some and the DISMAY of others, the play went over with a bang."[34]

One of the few early supporters of the Connecticut Federal Theatre was Julian B. Tuthill, drama critic for the Hartford *Times*. Tuthill organized a theatre party "to acquaint Hartford with the work of the Government Civic Repertory Company which is operating . . . as part of the Federal Theatre Project." Tuthill reported that his companions "never dreamed anything so inexpensive could be so good."[35] Six months later Tuthill challenged the community to "set aside their snobbishness . . . and go and applaud and appreciate the work that is being done by the excellent acting company."[36] Few traditional theatre attenders heeded his plea. For the most part, the public stayed away from the shows that the critics admired, and the critics panned the programs that the public liked.

The conservatism of the press was perhaps most evident in critics' treatment of Hartford's Negro unit. Though critics often looked favorably on the productions, they did so with condescension, using them as occasions to discourse on race, the audience, or the significance of government support for black drama. For example, when black Connecticut playwright Ward Courtney produced his second play with the Negro unit, an application to the contemporary United States of themes from classical Greek drama, Hartford *Times* critic Charles Niles evinced surprise: "No one can ever accuse the Negro artist of not working hard or of a lack of earnestness in every one of his or her productions."[37] White critics evaluated black productions as spectacle rather than art. The Negro unit's plays might be interesting if they revealed "Negro moods and manners," but the critics rarely confessed to enjoying them.[38] They were most favorable when discussing the members of the Negro unit as entertainers at children's camps and block parties: ". . . children were delighted by the Negro Unit's songs and dances, their strange positions and weird faces."[39]

The Federal Theatre in Connecticut presented many kinds of plays: murder mysteries, comedies, religious pageants, historical epics, musicals, classics, puppet shows, children's plays, and works by Shakespeare, O'Neill and Dos Passos. But the press focused its attention on the social dramas, especially Sinclair Lewis's *It Can't Happen Here* and the *Living Newspaper*'s critique of slum housing, *One-Third of a Nation*. In Connecticut, these two plays came to epitomize the Federal Theatre, their popularity intensifying the perceived threat of the works themselves.

The critics used a variety of stratagems to condemn these productions. Bridgeport critic Benton accused the audiences of staying at Lewis's play only to "ogle lovely Ellen Love."[40] Hartford's Tuthill dismissed *It Can't Happen Here* as "trivial," contending angrily that "No, it *can't* happen here."[41] Six of eight local reviews labeled the production "propaganda," a "vote-getting ballyhoo" by "Democratic propagandists."[42]

In none of its comments on the play did the Connecticut press note what the Theatre Project's federal leadership regarded as most important about the production: the fact that it opened simultaneously around the country, enabling thousands of people to hear its message at once. Flanagan regarded Lewis's work as patriotic, and the Theatre Project's production as evidence of the potential of a permanent national theatre.[43] This theme was lost on the local reviewers.

By 1939, Connecticut's critics were even more explicit about their distaste for *One-Third of a Nation*, despite their admiration for its production values. The New Haven *Journal-Courier*, for example, condemned the playwrights for ignoring the "genetical" aspects of tenement crime, disease, fire, and filth.[44] The Yale *Daily News* complained that *One-Third* failed to present the point of view of the landlord and favored "the abolition of the profit motive." "This," it intoned, "is the message of the Theatre representing our National Government."[45] To this political refrain, the Hartford *Courant* added the charge that the play was not really "art."[46]

The press cared little for the characters represented in the *Living Newspaper*'s production, so different were they from the upper- and middle-class denizens of polite drama. In breaking down the barriers between art and politics, the Federal Theatre's social dramas had been "frankly subversive." Noting cuts in the Federal Theatre's budget in 1937, the Greenwich *Times* editorialized that the "middle-classers aren't going to finance attacks on their philosophy."[47]

The Federal Theatre's efforts to justify itself to the press were futile because the social classes the press represented were suspicious of artists and ideologically committed to the separation of art and politics and to minimal government. Theatre was one of their prerogatives and they did not want government interfering or widening its thematic or social scope. Indeed, if Connecticut's drama critics were hard on the Theatre Project, at least they acknowledged its occasional successes. By contrast, Connecticut's small-town press rarely covered the Connecticut Project at all, preferring to run wire-service reports on the latest scandals in the New York Project.

Charges of "Un-American activities" appeared in Connecticut's news pages long before the opening of the 1938 Dies Committee hearings on the Federal Theatre. The New London *Day* reported anonymous "persistent complaints" against the Federal Theatre's "Communist" propaganda, its ribaldry and jocular treatment of U.S. history, and demanded that the money appropriated for the Project be spent on "enterprises fundamentally American in character."[48] Publication of such pieces in early 1936, when the Connecticut Project was only a few months old, demonstrate the press's visceral ideological opposition. Before long, the Project was criticized, as well, for competing with private enterprise, even though commercial theatre had been moribund in the state for at least a decade.[49]

During the Dies Committee hearings, more than 15 Connecticut papers published Associated Press coverage on a regular basis, running lengthy articles almost daily for more than two weeks. The charges reprinted were various, often fanciful, and, where based on fact, usually applicable only to New York: for example, that the Project advocated "some form of collectivism" and was a "hot-bed of Communism,"[50] that Project leftists forced employees to join Communist organizations, and that they even told "small blonde Sally Saunders to go out with a Negro."[51] In addition to providing such generous coverage to the Dies Committee, Connecticut's press was less inclined than New York's newspapers to question ill-founded charges or to report the rebuttals from the Project's defenders.

In short, Connecticut's newspapers, with few exceptions, either palpably opposed the Project from its inception, or, evaluating the Project in the customary terms of commercial drama, soon came to oppose it. With the exception of a single interview by Julian Tuthill of the director of the Hartford unit, the Connecticut press thoroughly concealed the ideals of the Theatre Project.[52] Again with the exception of Tuthill, it failed to report the formation of Citizens' Committees to integrate the Project into their communities. Nor did Connecticut's journalists cover the bulk of the Federal Theatre's diverse programs at CCC camps, children's camps, schools, and hospitals. Although the Federal Theatre in Connecticut produced four children's plays and one touring puppet company, only two articles featured this creative program, and even these did not accord the Federal Theatre itself much notice.[53] The press' trivial or sensationalistic concerns also hampered what could have been a great benefit of the project—increasing awareness of the public importance of culture, who controls it, and whose culture is being reflected in public performances. Instead, journalists' preoccupation with the social dramas and the New York scandals undermined the public standing of the Connecticut Project.

Efforts at Self-Promotion

Rejected by much of the press in advance, the Federal Theatre Project in Connecticut had to attempt to tell its own story through advertising and press releases. In so doing, the Project faced the dilemma of attempting to satisfy its critics while maintaining strong ideals and community roots. Promotional materials consistently demonstrated a sincere effort to reach out to those who had not attended theatre in the past. At the same time, the Theatre Project actively sought the favor of long-time theatre patrons and the socially prominent.

It is significant that although promotion plans for each play were to be registered with state-level Project authorities, devising and implementing these plans were left to the local units, who, it was believed, were in close touch with their communities. Yet the local units, whether stung by hostility of local influentials or stuck in the assumptions of the commercial stage, rarely promoted the Project as a vital force in community culture. Rather than cultivate a new constituency for the theatre through Project-oriented ads or series subscription sales, they tended to seek audiences for particular shows. Moreover, members of the audience would presumably see shows most likely to appeal to them, shows rooted in their own cultural experience. If series seats had been sold, however, they would have been exposed to different forms of culture.

The Project's early advertisements were exceptionally restrained by the promotional standards of the period's cinemas and commercial theatres; however, as the Project evolved, it used more of the marketing techniques current in the 1930s. The Connecticut Theatre advertised in a wide range of publications: the major newspapers, small-town papers such as the Jewett City *Press* and the Torrington *Register,* and special-interest publications including the Hartford *Insurance Girl* and the Bridgeport *Sporting News.*

Radio was the Project's most effective promotional tool. The Theatre Project performed scenes from its plays in production over the air, and often used its fifteen- to thirty-minute radio blocks to proclaim the goals and announce the accomplishments of the Project nationally. In addition, the Project ran daily spots over a variety of stations.[54]

Throughout Connecticut, however, local units tended to overlook their natural constituency of labor and ethnic groups in favor of the white-collar public. In Bridgeport, for example, promotional efforts were focused on the press and on contacts with such civic clubs as the YMCA and the Jewish Women's Council.[55] The New Haven unit cultivated the most elite audience, focusing its direct-mail promotional efforts on Yale Department Chairs, a list of 1,000 prominent New Haven citizens, and a separate list of previous theatre patrons. It also sent notices to language and history teachers at local high schools. For its production of *A Would Be Gentleman,* New Haven supplemented this routine by blanketing Yale students and several clubs and organizations with promotional material.[56]

Southington's short-lived unit devised a comprehensive plan that was approved by Federal Director Hallie Flanagan herself. The prospectus for the Southington Federal Theatre declared the unit's intent to stage its plays for "the rank and file of our people in the community." Yet the unit's promotional plan excluded labor and ethnic groups. Instead, promotion focused on an effort to persuade local civic organizations to sponsor blocks of one hundred tickets each, presumably to distribute among their members. All leaders of civic groups, including the DAR, were to be approached, and ministers would be asked to announce upcoming productions from their pulpits.[57]

The use of national press releases for local promotion was often hampered by an unsympathetic press. For example, the announced opening of the national Project's Bureau of Research and Publication, which was to provide opportunities for young American playwrights to produce their work, was treated in Connecticut's local papers as a story about additional red tape or support for amateurism.[58]

Thus the Connecticut Federal Theatre's efforts at self-promotion faltered on the hostility of the press and the Project's own reticence about its programs and goals. If local critics erred in treating the Project as just another theatre, so the production-oriented publicity of the Connecticut units reinforced the critics' disposition.

The Development of Community Sponsorship

Despite problems with the press and publicity, the Connecticut Project had another avenue open to it in its struggle to establish itself in the community. The Federal Theatre sought to establish itself as a vital cultural force in American communities. Toward this end, the Project cultivated individual and organizational sponsors to enhance its integration at the local level. In Connecticut, where the Federal Theatre had received such a tepid initial welcome, the sponsorship program was especially important.

Federal Assistant Director Hiram Motherwell urged state officials to develop the sponsors program to resolve the local conflicts that he predicted were inevitable. Motherwell suggested that sponsors be employed to explain the purpose of the Federal Theatre to the press and to secure the support of local political officials. The Project also looked to sponsors for advice in planning, loans of skilled workers, office space, scripts, and even donations: As early as 1936, Washington hoped that sponsors could help to transform the Project into a self-sufficient, independent institution.[59]

Motherwell's aspirations rested on an unrealistic confidence in the possibilities of class harmony, and some ambiguity regarding the social background of the projected sponsors. On the one hand, they were to represent the culturally active, those convinced "of the necessity of supporting arts as a cultural necessity in American civilization." On the other hand, they "should include persons truly representative of the communities."[60] But in Connecticut a "truly representative" committee would include many who thought that government had no business in the arts, especially if it intended to democratize participation.

At first, Connecticut's Theatre Project was able to lure a broad cross-section of supporters into lending their names to a cause about which they knew little. Yet some conflict was evident from the start. Julian Tuthill, the Hartford critic, headed the effort to secure sponsors. Early in 1936 he complained that "many prominent people do not want on yet."[61] He also wished to avoid the practice of using Little Theatre volunteers to develop sponsors lists, lest the Project be considered amateurish.[62] This preoccupation with professionalism led the Connecticut Theatre to ignore a natural constituency: If the Project would not work with those who already labored on behalf of theatre, how could it establish itself among those who cared little for art?

By April 1, 1936, Hartford's Sponsoring Committee included few social luminaries and none of the initial supporters. Among the sponsors were salesmen, clerks, dressmakers, a housekeeper, a domestic, a stenographer, a bookkeeper, three secretaries, and several former theatre workers and professional writers. Less than three weeks later, however, a new list emerged, shorter and consisting almost exclusively of the socially prominent. The Governor, the Mayor, and such influentials as "Mrs. Mary M. Hooker, Direct Descendant of the first settler of Hartford, Prominent society leader." Thus the Project's divergent concepts of its constituency were reflected in the lists of sponsors.

The composition of the sponsoring committees, sometimes called Citizen Committees, in other Connecticut cities likewise demonstrates early acceptance—and often rapid abandonment—of the Project by at least some members of the local elite. Committees in Bridgeport, New Haven, and New London contained few working people. In Bridgeport, for example, the citizen committee boasted many whose principal credential seemed to be high social standing, as well as several presidents of civic clubs. On none of the lists did member affiliations indicate the presence of a single labor leader, despite the national Project's desire to cultivate a labor audience and the need for labor cooperation in facilitating productions. Similarly, sponsors lists overlooked Connecticut's ethnic or religious minorities, with the exception of the Knights of Columbus. Recognizably Jewish names were absent from the Hartford, New Haven, New London, and Norwalk lists. In New Haven, Yale men and women dominated the list of sponsors (notwithstanding which fact Yale was reluctant to provide office space to the local unit).[63] In Norwalk, religious leaders of mainstream Protestant denominations were quick to lend their names.[64] Similarly, in New London, religious leaders, business executives and professionals constituted the list.[65] Thus, from the beginning, the Connecticut Project's preoccupation with establishing its legitimacy among community leadership outweighed the national focus on reaching out to disenfranchised constituencies.

In addition to enlisting these individual sponsors, the federal leadership directed state projects to secure organizational sponsors for every play. Because the Project could devote only 10 percent of its budget to nonlabor costs, these sponsors were expected to pay for certain material expenses.[66] Federal officials hoped that potential sponsors might be motivated by positive publicity and, in the unlikely event that the play turned a profit, by the fact that the sponsoring organizations would share half of the net receipts.

Connecticut units entered into a few creative partnerships with organizational sponsors, but ignored important constituencies. The Norwalk Workshop Unit, for example, sponsored a cosmetics workshop in cooperation with a local business.[67] In Hartford, the St. Justin's Ladies Guild sponsored a play on Catholic themes, and in Bridgeport similar groups supported religious drama.[68] In Altrusia, a "leading women's organization" sponsored a performance of a "Nativity Play" and other local organizations gave practical support: The Polish Choir, French Soloists, Schwachischer Maennerchor, St. Mary's Boys' Choir, and the Russian Symphonic Choir all lent their talents to the production.[69] Cooperation with Connecticut's ethnic communities would seem to have offered an important means, employed by the Federal Theatre in other states, through which the Connecticut Project might have established itself. Yet instances of this kind of collaboration were rare in Connecticut.

Similarly, labor groups were rarely solicited for sponsorship of the Connecticut Theatre's productions. The notable exception was the 1938 production of *It Can't Happen Here,* which the International Workers' Order and the New Haven Citywide Council for Slum Clearance cosponsored and the Hartford and New Haven Housing Authorities, the Social and Labor Legislation Conference, the Workers' Alliance, the American League for Peace and Democracy, the NAACP, and a variety of other unions and advocacy organizations endorsed.[70]

In its sponsorship program, as in the rest of its activities, the Connecticut Theatre was rent by a shifting conception of its constituency. By 1937, the Project had lost the support of Connecticut's conservative community leaders. At this point, should the Project have abandoned its efforts at wooing influentials and focused exclusively upon ethnic and labor support? Political realities demanded that it maintain the appearance of working for the whole community, even when the community was too fragmented for the Project to satisfy all tastes.

CONCLUSION: THE FEDERAL THEATRE AS SUBSTANCE AND SYMBOL

The Connecticut Project bears little resemblance to the symbolic theatre of the Project's radical enthusiasts or rightist detractors. Amorphous and variable, the Connecticut Theatre reflected the struggles of individual leaders to create and establish a legitimate institution under a range of administrative restraints. Those in Connecticut who, like Julian Tuthill, seized on the Project because they supported some of its ideals usually became disappointed. Those who opposed its ideals were never convinced and maintained their ideological hostility throughout the Project's existence.

Although Connecticut lacked the New York units' problems, scandals, and artistic achievements, certain events became emblematic in establishing the Connecticut Theatre's image. *One-Third of a Nation* brought pertinent drama before new and enthusiastic audiences. Yet it also embodied the Project's opponents' worst fears and objections. The shrill reaction to the play reflected its effect on its audiences. The juxtaposition of Senate leaders and street-dwelling indigents jarred critics' perceptions. The play flouted long-standing traditions that government should be treated with reverence, that art should likewise be revered, and that politics and art should never meet.

The Connecticut Project never solved the problem of patronage, nor did it ever free itself from administrative infighting. It was a public institution in an era in which "public" and "private" were poor guides to behavior. (Ironically, a commercial movie studio purchased the rights to the Federal

Theatre's *It Can't Happen Here* but refrained from producing it for fear of government retribution.) The *Living Newspaper's One-Third of a Nation* represented government creation of a new art form and earned sponsorship from a wide range of community, labor, and political groups. Yet this very sponsorship, so valuable in cultivating the Project's image as a daring experiment, undoubtedly eroded the support of the professional and business middle classes, of captains of industry, of civic and arts organizations, and of the traditional consumers of high culture alike.

The loss of these groups' support points to the fatal flaw of the Project in Connecticut: its failure to win the unquestioned support of any significant group or class in the communities in which it operated. Only sporadically cultivating its natural allies in labor and ethnic organizations, the Project vainly courted social influentials. Moreover, it failed to garner the support of liberals in universities and churches who might have encouraged ticket sales, benefit performances, and political lobbies.

Thus Connecticut's leadership strove for commercial respectability and encouraged local directors to adhere to "business principles" and to forswear experimentation; in so doing, it set aside a public theatre's greatest asset, its exemption from the demands of profitability. Local directors, too, often brought a professional, conventional view of theatre to the units. To a great extent, the Connecticut Theatre's leadership and many of its local directors had as slim a grasp of the Project's distinctive mission and possibilities as did the newspaper critics who evaluated it in commercial terms.

As the Project suffered from its failure to establish a political base or a devoted audience; it labored at the same time under intractable problems of administration. Project administrators and directors constantly fought, nagged and gossiped over personal peccadillos and artistic mission. The project vacillated artistically, producing a repertoire utterly lacking in consistency.

In its failure to make good on the Project's initial ideals, the Connecticut Theatre missed the opportunity to encourage regular theatre going among new publics. And in the era of talking cinema's greatest popularity, the existing theatregoing audience was too small to support a national theatre. What is more, the traditional theatregoers embraced the stage as an expression of an exclusive culture, as an escape from the irritations of their own working lives. Most emphatically, they did not want the relief work of others impinging upon their leisure. Confronted by the hostility of community leaders, the Connecticut Project reacted by abandoning its initial ideals, by neglecting its most natural constituencies, and by questing endlessly for the political legitimacy it would never find. In the course of its misadventures, however, it employed thousands of theatre workers during the depth of the Depression, provided presentations to thousands who might otherwise have never seen them, and helped to sponsor the production of a significant new dramatic literature. The Federal Theatre in Connecticut is neither the angel of leftist mythology nor the devil of conservative demonology. In its more human face, it reflects the ability of a public enterprise to do much good—albeit, in this case, usually inconsistently and often ineptly—under adverse circumstances.

NOTES

1. President Taft's Fine Arts Commission and the 1934 Section on Fine Arts of the New Deal preceded it on a much smaller scale.

2. See, e.g., Hallie Flanagan, *Arena* (New York: Duell, Stone and Pearce, 1940); Milton Meltzner, *Violins and Shovels: The WPA Arts Projects* (New York: Delacorte Press, 1976); Francis V. O'Connor, *Art for the Millions: Essays from the 1930's by Artists and Administrators of the WPA Federal Art Project* (Greenwich, Conn. New York Graphics Society, 1973).

3. See, e.g., John O'Connor and Lorraine Brown, *Free, Adult, Uncensored: The Living History of the Federal Theatre Project* (Washington, D.C.: New Republic Books, 1978); Jay Williams, *Stage Left* (New York: Charles Scribner's Sons, 1974).

4. Hallie Flanagan, "A Report on the First Six Months," *Federal Theatre* 1, 4: 6.

5. Hallie Flanagan, "Federal Theatre Tomorrow," *Federal Theatre,* 2, 1: 6–26.

6. Hallie Flanagan, "What Are We Doing With Our Chance?," *Federal Theatre,* 2, 3: 5–6.

7. First Year Evaluations, Narrative Reports File; Box 98; Record Group 33, National Archives, Washington, D.C.

8. Charles La Rue, "Highlight History of the Connecticut Federal Theatre Project," May 1937–September 1, 1937," Box 596; Record Group 33, National Archives, Washington, D.C.

9. "WPA Adopts Gilpin Players at Workshop: Negro Unit to Be Used in Federal Theatre Plan," Hartford *Times,* September 11, 1936.

10. Stephen Hegarty, Narrative Reports, April 1, 1936 and May 31, 1936, Box 86; Record Group 33, National Archives, Washington, D.C.

11. George Gerwing, "Report on the History of the Connecticut Federal Theatre Project From Its Inception to Closing," May 23, 1939; Box 596; Record Group 33, National Archives, Washington, D.C.

12. First Year Evaluations, Narrative Reports File; Box 98; Record Group 33, National Archives, Washington, D.C.

13. Gerwing, op. cit.

14. Gertrude Don Dero to All Production Directors; National Office Correspondence Box 50; Record Group 33, National Archives, Washington, D.C.

15. Gertrude Don Dero to C. J. Mauntz, Director of Information, New York City; Connecticut Correspondence File; Box 50; Record Group 33, National Archives, Washington, D.C.

16. G. Lester Paul, Narrative Report, June 29, 1936; Box 50; Record Group 33, National Archives, Washington, D.C.

17. Don Dero to Hallie Flanagan, November 11, 1936, Connecticut Correspondence File: Box 50; Record Group 33, National Archives, Washington, D.C.

18. "Washington's Axe Nears Gertie's Neck," Bridgeport *Herald,* January 31, 1937.

19. Julian B. Tuthill, "Federal Theatre Will Experiment with New Plays," Hartford *Times,* February 18, 1936.

20. George Spelvin, "Federal Theatre Gets Off to a Fine Start at Avery," Hartford *Times,* September 29, 1937.

21. Humphrey Doulens, "Federal Theatre: Professionals in Bridgeport Are Obliged to Commute to Hartford at Own Expense in Change of Federal Theatre Setup—Homer Mason Is Out," Bridgeport *Post,* September 12, 1937.

22. Roger Doulens, "Norwalk's Passing Show," *The Sentinel,* South Norwalk, Conn., June

1936. Also Narrative Reports, September 23, 1938, Regions I and II; Box 90; Record Group 33, National Archives, Washington, D.C.

23. Memo No. 1, Gertrude Don Dero to all Production Directors, November 29, 1936; Connecticut Correspondence File; Box 50; Record Group 33, National Archives, Washington, D.C.

24. Jane de Hart Mathews, *The Federal Theatre 1935–1939: Plays, Relief and Politics* (Princeton; Princeton University Press, 1967).

25. David Lane to Walter Klavun, November 23, 1936. Box 50; Record Group 33, National Archives, Washington, D.C.

26. Gertrude Don Dero to Ann Ayers, John Drabkin, and Arthur Hoyt, Box 50; Record Group 33, National Archives, Washington, D.C.

27. William Stahl to Gertrude Don Dero, October 23, 1936; Box 50; Record Group 33, National Archives, Washington, D.C.

28. Hiram Motherwell, November 14, 1936; Box 50; Record Group 33, National Archives, Washington, D.C.

29. Helen Henderson, "So Gertie's Gone and WPA Thittur Hails 'Revolution'," Bridgeport *Herald,* September 5, 1937; "Axe Smacks Femme Fuehrer," Bridgeport *Herald,* September 5, 1937.

30. Edward Brainard, "In the Green Room," Hartford *Times,* September 3, 1936.

31. Edward Brainard, "In the Green Room," Hartford *Times,* November 10, 1936.

32. Jess Benton, "Public Enemy Wilts before Psychologist," Bridgeport *Herald,* May 28, 1936.

33. Ethel Beckwith, "Uncle Sam Goes into Legitimate Theatre Business in Bridgeport and Cecil Spooner's Company Packs 'Em in with Comedy." Bridgeport *Post,* March 10, 1936.

34. Countess Fairfield, "Society News," Bridgeport *Herald,* November 11, 1936.

35. Julian B. Tuthill, "Through the Movie Scope," Hartford *Times,* May 9, 1937.

36. Julian B. Tuthill, "Federal Theatre Hits High Mark in Finest Drama," Hartford *Times,* December 29, 1937.

37. Charles E. Niles, review of "Trilogy in Black," Hartford *Times,* June 19, 1937.

38. Julian B. Tuthill, "Play at Avery Tonight Soon to Become Movie," Hartford *Times,* November 8, 1937.

39. "Two Tennis Courts Put into Service at Camp Courant," Hartford *Courant,* August 17, 1937.

40. Jess Benton, "More and More Ado: 'It Can't Happen Here,'—Well, Maybe It Didn't," Bridgeport *Sunday Herald,* November 11, 1936.

41. Julian B. Tuthill, "The Play in Review: 'It Can't Happen Here,' " Hartford *Times,* October 28, 1936.

42. Jess Benton, op. cit., November 11, 1936. See also S. M. Trebor, " 'It Can't Happen Here' Did Happen at the Park Theatre," *Bridgeport Life,* October 31, 1936; and Al Jackson, "Thaytah, Tsk, Tsk!," Bridgeport *Herald,* October 11, 1936.

43. Hallie Flanagan, "Why Not Here?," *Federal Theatre* 2, 2: 5–6.

44. "Third of Nation Well Presented," New Haven *Journal-Courier,* January 30, 1939.

45. Lawrence R. Harper, "Playbill: Beating the Drum," Yale *Daily News,* January 30, 1939.

46. "WPA Offers Housing Play at Bushnell: 'One-Third of a Nation' Pictures Historical and Human Rights of Public Problem," Hartford *Courant,* January 20, 1939.

47. "Declining Federal Theatre," Greenwich *Times,* November 18, 1937.

48. "The New Freedom," New London *Day,* March 18, 1936.

49. "WPA Theatre Row," New London *Day,* May 31, 1938. Wire service story also printed in Greenwich *Times,* Bridgeport *Star,* Hartford *Times,* and Middletown *Press.*

50. "Federal Theatre Folk Called in Communist Quiz," Ansonia *Sentinel,* August 19, 1938; "Hazel Huffman Determined to Keep Subversive Elements out of FTP," Bridgeport Evening *Post,* August 20, 1938; "Calls Federal Theatre Project a Cesspool of UnAmericanism," AP dispatch in Willamantic *Chronicle,* Waterbury *Republican,* Torrington *Register,* Norwich

Bulletin, Bridgeport *Evening Post,* Bridgeport *Telegram,* Manchester *Herald,* Meriden *Record,* New Haven *Register,* and Hartford *Courant,* August 20, 1938.

51. "Reds Control Theatre Aid, Actor Tells House Group," New London *Day,* August 20, 1938.

52. Julian Tuthill, "Stage Fights Way to Front Despite Films" Hartford *Times,* June 7, 1936.

53. "Favorite 'Alice in Wonderland' to Tour Several Public Schools," New Haven *Register,* March 15, 1936; "Puppets to Go for Ride Wherever Children Are: 'Through the Looking Glass!' " Bridgeport *Post,* July 20, 1937.

54. Connecticut Narrative Reports, Boxes 86 and 596; Record Group 33, National Archives, Washington, D.C.

55. Semi-Monthly Report, Bridgeport, March 15, 1937; Box 596, Record Group 33, National Archives, Washington, D.C.

56. Weekly Reports, April and May 1936, New Haven; Box 86, Record Group 33, National Archives, Washington, D.C.

57. Southington Narrative Report, April 1, 1936; Box 86, Record Group 33, National Archives, Washington, D.C.

58. "State PWA [*sic*] Adds Bureau to Read Play Manuscripts," Stamford *Advocate,* September 24, 1936; "Encouragement for Unknown Play Writers," Waterbury *Democrat,* September 24, 1936.

59. Memo from Hiram Motherwell to Gertrude Don Dero, October 20, 1936, Connecticut Correspondence File; Box 50; Record Group 33, National Archives, Washington, D.C.

60. Hiram Motherwell, Memo to All State Directors and Supervisors Concerning Co-Sponsoring Committees, February 5, 1936; Record Group 33, National Archives, Washington, D.C.

61. Julian Tuthill, letter to Hiram Motherwell, February 24, 1936, Sponsor's File; Box 604; Record Group 33, National Archives, Washington, D.C.

62. Julian Tuthill, letter to Gertrude Don Dero, February 24, 1936, ibid.

63. Gertrude Don Dero to Hiram Motherwell, November 9, 1936; Box 50; Record Group 33, National Archives, Washington, D.C.; Sponsor's File; Box 604; Record Group 33, National Archives, Washington, D.C.

64. Cleveland Bronner, Narrative Report from Norwalk, April 15, 1936; box 86; Record Group 33, National Archives, Washington, D.C.

65. Citizen Committee, Connecticut File; Box 50; Record Group 33, National Archives, Washington, D.C.

66. Charles La Rue to William Stanger: "Division of Receipts at Bushnell," February 16, 1939; Box 596; Record Group 33, National Archives, Washington, D.C.

67. Narrative Report, May 13, 1936; box 86; Record Group 33, National Archives, Washington, D.C.

68. "St. Justin's Ladies Guild Will sponsor a Presentation of 'The First Legion' by Emmet Lavery," Hartford *Courant,* March 9, 1936.

69. Altrusia Narrative Report, December, 1936; Box 86; Record Group 33, National Archives, Washington, D.C.

70. "Federal Theatre Bringing Famous Play to Memorial," *The Prompter,* January 1939. Julian B. Tuthill, "Federal Theatre Has a Treat for Hartford," Hartford *Times,* January 10, 1939.

III

MANAGEMENT AND MISSION

7

From Impresario to Arts Administrator: *Formal Accountability in Nonprofit Cultural Organizations*

RICHARD A. PETERSON

In the decades following the American Civil War, the leading nonprofit organizations devoted to displaying art works or presenting artistic productions were being formed in the major urban centers of America.[1] Very early, the roles of aesthetic leadership—those of museum curator, symphony orchestra conductor, and theatrical director—were separated from the tasks of arts management, that is, the coordination of the wide range of "behind-the-scenes" activities from fund-raising to janitorial services. At its core, the function of this system was—and still is—to buffer the art world, where questions of aesthetic evaluation are primary, from the world of business, where questions of money-making, economic power, and social status predominate. For nearly a century, the characteristic style of the buffer role was that of the impresario, but over the past quarter of a century, the impresario has been replaced by the administrator in the management of all but the smallest and fledgling arts organizations.

This chapter will offer an explanation for the rapid displacement of the impresarial by the administrative style of arts management. If correct, the

My interest in the emergence of arts administration was focused in conversations with Rosanne Martorella in 1975. Her view of the process was first presented in 1977 at the 72nd annual meeting of the American Sociological Association as "Arts Management as a Function of Increasing Organizational Complexity." I was privileged to work in the Research Division of the National Endowment of the Arts during 1979–1980 and had the opportunity to observe and talk with numerous arts administrators working in the United States and Canada in a wide range of disciplines. In the years following, I kept a file on the topic and it was, therefore, with great pleasure that I accepted Paul DiMaggio's invitation to prepare this chapter. I gratefully acknowledge DiMaggio's numerous provocative comments, as well as those of Daniel Cornfield, Claire Peterson, and John Ryan, on this as well as on an earlier draft of the chapter which was presented as "Le Rôle du Controle Formel dans le Passage Rapide d'un Mode Entrepreneurial à un Mode Administratif de Management des Arts" at the 1985 annual meetings of the French Sociological Association.

explanation may have application well beyond the realm of the nonprofit arts. First, the impresarial and the administrative styles are characterized. Next, four factors within the dynamics of the organization and six factors in the organization's task environment are explored. Then the professionalization and institutionalization of the administrative style are detailed. Finally, several possible consequences of the new style of management for the arts are suggested.

THE IMPRESARIAL FORM OF MANAGEMENT

The first generation of nineteenth-century arts managers came from remarkably diverse backgrounds and practiced a range of leadership styles. The ones that succeeded most often, however, exhibited a managerial style that combined traditionalistic authority, charisma, and entrepreneurship. This leadership style will here be identified as *impresarial.*

Whether running a performance company or a museum, the nineteenth century fine arts impresario tended to have the following characteristics. He (rarely she) was reared in an upper-class or upwardly aspiring family. He led an adventurous early life, not connected with the arts. He deported himself in a commanding and flamboyant style that was tooled to flatter the wealthy and tyrannize subordinates, but he related to people on a personal, individualistic basis. Finally, the impresario combined the appearance of a selfless devotion to art with attention to the most minute managerial detail, thus personifying the company in his every activity over what was often, by modern standards, an extremely long job tenure.

Take, for example, General Luigi Palma di Cesnola, the first full-time director of the New York Metropolitan Museum of Art, who served from 1879 to 1904, a span of 25 years.[2] Cesnola's unlikely but useful preparation for the top museum job included military academy training in his home town of Turin, Italy, then military action in a local Italian campaign. After his faction lost the war, he left Italy to spend several years as a teacher of French and Italian in New York City, where he befriended many of the city's young people of wealth. With the outbreak of the U.S. Civil War, he raised and trained a cavalry unit, which then joined the Union Army. Extensive and often-decorated service followed, as Cesnola rose to the rank of Brigadier General, surviving a court-martial for misappropriation of funds and his capture by Confederate forces. After the war, he married a New York debutante, and the couple served for twelve years in both the United States and the Russian Consular services at various Mediterranean posts. While in diplomatic service on Cyprus he engaged in extensive digs as a self-taught archaeologist. Cesnola came to the attention of the Board of Directors of the Metropolitan Museum of Art when he returned to New York to sell his archaeological finds (a number of which later proved to have been fabricated from fragments of broken statues) to the museum and to oversee the mounting of the exhibit.

Cesnola governed the museum autocratically. He had a glass-faced office built for himself on the balcony of the original museum building, from which he could see most of the galleries. He regularly wore metal-studded shoes that telegraphed his coming, and museum guards were expected to snap to attention at his passing. Like other impresarios, Cesnola devoted most of his attention to cultivating trustees and other wealthy patrons of the arts, an activity vital to maintaining the regular flow of money and artwork donations. Perhaps more important to Cesnola personally, the good will of these people made it possible for him to acquire inferior works of art for the museum from his Italian dealer friends from whom, it was alleged, he derived regular hidden cash commissions. Thanks to the continuing support of influential board members, including the richest banker of the time, J. Pierpont Morgan, he was twice able to escape public disgrace on the charge of having sold the museum doctored art work from Crete. Cesnola was able to stay in office until his death in 1904, but within a decade of his passing, all of the suspect works had been removed from public display. Not all early impresarios were as scheming as Cesnola, but his mix of self-effacing service and self-serving entrepreneurship was not unusual.[3]

The museum and orchestra managers who assumed their first major directorships in the early decades of the twentieth century tended to have less flamboyant early careers than Cesnola, and most had had some direct experience in an artistic discipline. Nonetheless, their impresarial management style did not differ appreciably from that of their predecessors.

The career of Arthur Judson, who managed the Philadelphia and New York Philharmonic Orchestras from 1915 through 1956, provides a good example of the arts organization impresario of the twentieth century.[4] Judson took conservatory training on the violin, but judging himself not to be excellent enough to make a successful career as a violin virtuoso, he switched to music education and then became a writer for *Musical America*, soon moving to the business side of the magazine operation. He joined the Philadelphia Orchestra as business manager in 1915, just three years after it had hired the energetic and innovative conductor Leopold Stokowski.

The national attention that Stokowski brought to the orchestra made it possible to cultivate and keep the loyalties of the Philadelphia elite. Judson was able to convince one patron to defray the operating deficit of the orchestra for five years so that all the proceeds from the campaigns for donations would go directly to creating an endowment fund. A few years later, when he had been made manager of the New York Philharmonic Orchestra as well, Judson cultivated another patron who "was able to allocate to various board members the sums of money they were expected to contribute or raise and then write his own check for the remainder of the budget. Judson recalls that at the end of each season he would give the patron an accounting of the operations, whereupon he would cover the amount that was lacking."[5]

Using his position as manager of the Philadelphia and then the New

York orchestras, Judson was able to develop a thriving independent business as personal manager to solo and concert artists, classical music groups, and budding conductors. In using his organizational position for private gain, he followed in the footsteps of Charles Ellis and Henry Voegeli, who did much the same in Boston and Chicago, respectively.[6] Judson soon began to involve his artists and orchestras in the fledgling media of radio and phonograph recording. In the process he invested heavily in the Columbia Broadcasting System, and at the time of his death, his holdings of CBS stock were second only to those of CBS founder William Paley.[7]

Over the decades of the twentieth century the freedom and scope of the personalistic style of the impresario have gradually been curtailed. This change can be traced over one hundred years through the careers of Cesnola and Judson to Rudolph Bing who, after 23 years of service, retired as General Manager of the Metropolitan Opera Company in 1972.[8] In the years since 1960, however, a new sort of arts manager has rapidly come to the fore and has virtually displaced the impresario. The new type of manager is the arts *administrator*.

THE EMERGENCE OF ARTS ADMINISTRATION

The arts *administrator* differs markedly from the impresario in formal education, responsibilities, and managerial style. Whereas the impresario relied on personal ties and charm in an entrepreneurial environment, the arts administrator relies on the norms of formal accounting in an environment of numerous bureaucratically structured organizations and unstructured publics.

Education

Until the mid-twentieth century, training for prospective arts managers consisted largely of tutelage by active impresarios. Their professional obligations were closely linked to their social life: for museum managers, this meant wooing art collectors and maintaining rapport with wealthy museum trustees;[9] for performing arts managers, it meant compromising the interests of the chief donors with those of the artistic directors and personnel—conductors, choreographers, actors, singers, players, or dancers.[10]

Most of the twentieth-century arts managers working in the impresarial mode did, of course, have formal schooling. Paul Sachs, who joined the Fogg Museum soon after World War I, taught several generations of Harvard students who went on to direct virtually all of the major museums in America. The primary skill he taught his students, however, was how to talk to wealthy prospective patrons.[11]

For the new breed of arts administrators, such training was no longer adequate. Rather than develop management skills in the idiosyncratic crucible of a liberal arts education and personal experience, these new arts administrators have increasingly been taught through postgraduate professional training. The first two postgraduate programs developed to train arts administrators were founded in 1966 at Yale and Florida State University. Both of these programs specialized initially in the training of theatre managers, but most programs founded subsequently now train their students for management roles in any of the arts.

In 1976, a decade after the first programs were launched, Donner[12] reported 12 fully operational arts administration postgraduate training programs. By 1981, the number of programs had doubled;[13] twenty-three universities had postgraduate programs in performing arts administration, and there were another thirteen programs in what has come to be called "museology," that is, museum administration studies. In addition, a number of agencies provided short-term intensive courses for working administrators.[14]

The curriculum of the arts administration program at the University of Wisconsin at Madison offers a good insight into the range of skills the new type of arts manager is presumed to need. This program currently graduates more students each year than any other, and its curriculum has been used as the model for most of the programs that have been instituted since its founding in 1969. The Wisconsin program is an area of professional training in the business school. Wisconsin students are required to take what the program bulletin calls "foundation" courses: microeconomics, financial and administrative accounting, budgets and budgetary control, marketing, organizational behavior, legal aspects of business, and statistics. According to the Bulletin, courses in arts administration are also required.

> A two-semester seminar in arts administration is given the first year. The first semester is devoted to modules that are environmentally oriented, such as arts administrators and their organizational structures; government, business, education and labor and the arts; and boards of directors. The second semester focuses on 'How to' modules; planning and programming, contracting and negotiating, marketing the arts, and fund raising and development.[15]

The only vestige of the older apprenticeship model of training in this rationalistic new program is a half-year internship in an arts organization.

Responsibilities

Shestack[16] notes the different responsibilities of the impresario and the administrator. The museum director of the 1920s, he asserts, needed to be a connoisseur and a gentleman engaged in wooing art collectors and satisfying wealthy trustees. Shestack contrasts these duties and skills with those of the administrator of the post-1960 era. The latter must pay attention to managing the museum, garnering prestigious touring exhibits, and attracting more museum attenders. As Thomas W. Leavitt, who took the famous "museum class" at Harvard in the early 1950s, has noted, in 1954 we did not realize that we were near the end of an era in the evolution of art directors. Even today most of the directors of that time are remembered as being larger than life . . . with a few notable exceptions, the grand style was gradually replaced with businesslike attention to growth and service. Most of the great collections had been wooed and won, and the spirit of the late 50s and early 60s called for consolidation, building expansion, larger education departments, and efforts to excite a wider cross-section of the public into museums.[17]

In a "job description" for the contemporary symphony manager, Ralph Black, an official of the American Symphony Orchestra League, writing in *Symphony News,* states that "the responsibility of the manager is to be responsible."[18] In a 23-item checklist, he notes the wide range of things the administrator is responsible *for,* and an even wider range of constituencies, most of which did not exist as organized interest groups 40 years ago, the symphony administrator is responsible *to.*

Managerial Style

Although his career began before the new form of schooling, the managerial style of Ernest Fleischmann, Executive Director of the Los Angeles Philharmonic Orchestra, exemplifies the orientation of the arts administrator.[19] Trained both as a music conductor and as an accountant, Fleischmann has been applauded for successfully negotiating contractual arrangements with the musicians' union, the City of Los Angeles, record company executives, and the wealthy members of the orchestra's board of directors (Thompson, 1976).

Like other administrators, Fleischmann's managerial style has been that of the technical arbitrator bringing contending interests to agree through negotiation and compromise. Unlike his impresarial counterpart, whose style was based on flattering and cajoling the affluent elite while dominating performers and employees by an autocratic imposition of his will, the successful arts administrator relies on the ability to apply evenhandedly technical knowledge to obtain the best possible results for the arts organization and all interested parties.

EXPLANATIONS OF THE RISE OF ARTS ADMINISTRATION

Why did the impresarial form of arts management, which evolved slowly over the course of a century, so rapidly give way to the administrative form of arts management? There are a number of alternative theories that have been advanced by economists or sociologists to account for changes in organizations of all types. The set of four explanations considered first focuses on processes taking place in the structure of formal organizations themselves. After deficiences in each of these organization-focal explanations are demonstrated, evidence will be introduced that simultaneously brings into question all four explanations and points the way to a quite different sort of explanation, one that focuses on events taking place in the world beyond the boundaries of the nonprofit organization.

Internal Organizational Factors

Size

It is often assumed that as organizations grow larger, either in the number of employees or in the size of budgets, they tend, other things being equal, to become more bureaucratic.[20] Martorella[21] has used this idea to explain the emergence of arts administration.

Virtually all of the surviving nonprofit organizations have grown in size over the past 50 to 100 years. Size, by itself, cannot explain the growth of arts administration, however, because this growth has typically been gradual, and because for organizations founded before 1950, most growth preceded by decades the emergence of arts administration. The New York Philharmonic Orchestra, the New York Metropolitan Opera Company, and the New York Metropolitan Museum of Art all had employees numbering in the hundreds and annual budgets of over one million dollars well before the advent of arts administration.[22] In a comparative analysis of the evolution of New York and London orchestras over the past century, Couch[23] demonstrates that increases in size and budget have occurred in the orchestras of both cities but within the context of radically different managerial structures. Indeed, there has long been solid evidence that increasing size does not automatically lead to increasing bureaucracy, for as Dibble[24] has shown, large-scale units of government operated in sixteenth-century England without bureaucratization.

Task Complexity

It has been widely asserted that as organizations become more structurally complex, that is, as they take on a greater number of different tasks, they become more bureaucratic. Again the idea of increasing complexity has been identified by Martorella[25] as a cause of the emergence of arts administration.

Certainly the leading modern opera companies, orchestras, theaters, and museums are more complex than their earlier counterparts. Contemporary art museums, for example, in addition to displaying owned and loaned works of art, may include a library, dining hall, retail art store, theatre, chamber music hall, art restoration center, arts school, and may mount extensive educational programs for the general public.[26] The major orchestras, opera companies, theatres, and ballet companies have also become more structurally complex as they have taken on a plethora of auxiliary activities. But again, as in the case of size, change in complexity has come gradually in the past several decades, as Arian[27] has shown in the case of the Philadelphia Orchestra and Tomkins[28] has shown for the Metropolitan Museum of Art. Finally, as Gersuny and Rosengren[29] have shown for service organizations generally, complexity has grown gradually over the century, and thus it cannot be a primary cause of the rapid and widespread rise of arts administration since 1960.

Organizational Life Cycle

The two most influential early twentieth-century organization theorists, Max Weber and Robert Michels, asserted that the leadership of organizations goes through a more or less regular sequence of stages. Although they used different terms, both believed that organizations that begin with an egalitarian or entrepreneurial leadership style become more bureaucratic and oligarchic over time, because of the internal dynamics of organizational development and the succession of organizational leaders.[30]

The biographies of many arts organizations do reveal a loosely structured early stage when the organization is largely built by a charismatic individual or group, followed by several stages of increasing formalization as successors try to perpetuate the institution. From the life-cycle perspective arts administration may be interpreted as emerging during an advanced stage in the cycle of an arts organization's growth and institutionalization.

There are two major problems with this hypothesis, however. The first is that only in their earliest years do organizations show consistent patterns of change. Beyond the earliest stages, the biographies of arts organizations show a wide range of paths. Nowhere is this diversity of lines of development more evident than in the histories of twentieth-century American dance companies.[31]

The second major problem with the life-cycle hypothesis is that the arts administration style has been adopted by most art organizations during a specific historical period irrespective of the age or life-cycle stage of the arts organizations in question. This suggests, parallel to the findings of Meyer and Rowan,[32] that formalization was caused by external forces yet to be identified that affected all organizations in a field at the same time. We will return to this point below.

Cost Disease

In 1966, William J. Baumol and William G. Bowen published *Performing Arts: The Economic Dilemma.*[33] The crux of the dilemma as they see it is that, whereas productivity in the general economy has risen at a compound rate of 2.5 percent per year, thus doubling labor productivity every 29 years, the productivity of performing arts groups has risen very little. Today, just as in J. S. Bach's time, they note, it takes four instrumentalists to play quartet music. Nonetheless, because arts performers are consumers in the general economy, they expect their incomes to rise with the rising general standard of living. Since arts' productivity is rising very slowly, arts organizations must raise ticket prices and solicit increased donations to satisfy employee income expectations. This dynamic of slowly increasing productivity and rapidly increasing costs created what Baumol and Bowen called the "income gap," and the Baumols now call the "cost disease."[34] Although such a cost disease is endemic in any fixed-productivity sector of the economy like the performing arts, many people in the late 1960s argued that it had reached a critical point, and that to survive, arts organizations had to operate differently. The most common prescription for curing the cost disease included a call to make arts management more efficient through the use of business principles of administration.[35] The cost disease, though real enough, does not account for the rise of arts administration because it is not an epidemic that has broken out in recent decades. Rather, it was chronic throughout the ascendancy of the impresario as well.

Internal Factors in Concert

In this section, we have examined the proposition that the rise of arts administration can be explained by dynamics internal to individual arts organizations: growth in size, increasing complexity, organizational life cycle, and the cost disease. All four of these factors have been at work over the past century, and each tends to encourage greater bureaucratization in an individual organization. Thus, we would expect that for each arts organization, the lower the rate of increase in unit productivity and the older, larger, and more complex the organization is, the greater is the probability of the shift from the impresarial to the administrative style of arts management.

These intraorganizational factors are quite useful in explaining the differences in arts management style between individual organizations and among the several arts disciplines—symphony, opera, museums, theatre, and dance—through about 1960. Each of the disciplines tended to have a distinct pattern and rate of change in the four intraorganizational forces that constrain a change in leadership style.[36] After 1960, however, the trend toward formalization of organizations and the development of arts administration spread rapidly across all arts disciplines, irrespective of the size, age, and complexity of individual organizations. It is as if the form of arts management we call "arts administration" was caused by a contagious substance in the environment of all arts organizations. In the section of the chapter that follows, we will identify the etiology of the administrative style of arts management and the epidemiology of its spread.

Extraorganizational Factors

A number of agencies and interest groups in the task environment of contemporary arts organizations increasingly hold the organization and its managers formally accountable for action taken in the name of the arts organization. The demand for formal accountability in turn puts a premium on employing arts managers adept at working in the administrative rather than the impresarial mode. In this section, six extraorganizational factors that have fostered the growth of arts administration will be identified.

New Patrons and Unearned Income

From meager beginnings in the 1950s, and increasing rapidly especially since the founding of the National Endowments for the Arts and Humanities in the mid-1960s, local, state, and federal contributions have become of major importance to funding arts organizations. To a degree far greater than that of other patrons, government agencies require formal grant applications that follow explicit guidelines, evaluation according to universally applied standards, documented adherence to specified guidelines, and strict accountability for expenditures.[37] What is more, philanthropic foundations and corporate patrons, whose contributions to the arts have grown rapidly in the past two decades, rationalized their grant-making procedures during the same period. They have taken these steps in part to comply with tax law requirements and also to satisfy the emerging norm of formal accountability.

The difference between the earlier pattern of informal or personal accountability and the recent shift to formal accountability is clearly shown in a discussion of the development of local community funding for the arts by John Blaine, Chairman of the Board of the National Assembly of Community Art Agencies.

> In the prehistory of local public funding for the arts, say ten years ago or a bit longer, those local tax dollars that found their way into the operating budget of cultural institutions were usually accounted for in a line item buried deep within the budget of some large city or county agency. Accountability for how those dollars were spent was generally accomplished at a cocktail party, opening night or on some other occasion that brought public officials together with board members of cultural institutions.[38]

In a provocative article on the impact of public funding on organizations in the arts, Paul DiMaggio[39] has speculated on the consequences for arts organizations of receiving government funds. He hypothesizes that arts organizations that seek and receive government support will have to formulate formal statements of policies and plans, to institute formal audits of their accounts, and to increase the sizes of their administrative staffs accordingly.

The case of jazz, a field in which there have been few stable nonprofit organizations, demonstrates the difficulty of conforming to the requirements for receiving public funding. The government has faced great obstacles to granting money for the aesthetic development of jazz because jazz musicians typically work as shifting small assemblages of players rather than in a few large and stable institutions. In 1979 Ezra Laderman, then Director of the National Endowment for the Arts Music Program, pointed with pride to the fact that the Endowment was finally able to give $1 million for jazz. Laderman noted that "despite the popularity of, and demand for jazz, there are basic problems in assisting the field. Unlike other art forms that have a strong organizational base, jazz for the most part does not function within an organization form as do theaters or orchestras."[40]

DiMaggio and Powell[41] have developed a theory that places in context the problem the government has experienced in trying to give money for the development of jazz. They assert that all organizations that regularly interact with one another in what they call an organizational field, such as the art world, tend to become structurally isomorphic in order to facilitate interaction with each other. Since few nonprofit jazz organizations have had stable organizational structures with standard accounting procedures, it has been difficult for government agencies to recognize jazz aggregations with which it could interact on terms fitting its own procedures.

The DiMaggio-Powell hypothesis of increasing institutional isomorphism nicely fits the facts at hand. It serves to explain why the contemporary new patrons, including government, foundations, and corporations, which are all formally structured, require formal accountability of arts organizations and facilitate the emergence of arts administration. The hypothesis of organizational isomorphism also serves to explain why, before the new patronage existed, the boards of directors of arts organizations which were largely composed of wealthy, self-made individuals most successfully dealt with art impresarios who were themselves the entrepreneurs of arts management.

New Audiences

Following the old adage, "he who pays the piper calls the tune," new patrons should mean new audiences as well. The bulk of government, foundation, and corporate grants have not been given to cover regular operating expenses. Rather, most grants have been given to stimulate new programming aimed primarily at attracting audiences to the arts. Leavitt succinctly shows the importance of this shift in patrons.

> As the country-club atmosphere of museums disappeared, private funds became harder to solicit and we had to build cases for public tax support from cities, counties, states and, finally, the federal government. Virtually all of these funds from public sources were conditional upon our performing additional services for the public.[42]

A larger and more socially diverse range of arts consumers is sought by the new arts managers, less as an end in itself than to show the prospective new patrons that the arts organization is socially worthwhile. As a case in point, Cal Bean, Station Manager of WPLN, the National Public Radio affiliate in Nashville, told me in 1978 that the station had just hired a development director to increase substantially the number of listener-donors. This was being done not so much for the money that would be raised but so that the station would be eligible to apply for larger federal government grants.

On a grander scale, Salem[43] reports that the Seattle Opera Company launched a series of money-losing programs in the early 1970s in order to garner national attention and critical acclaim in the hope of receiving larger government grants. DiMaggio cites numerous additional examples to illustrate the organizational, aesthetic, and audience-building consequences of the emergence of what he calls a "grants economy" in the arts.[44]

Several popular commentators and art critics have elaborated on such assertions. For example, Lilla[45] contends that the new breed of business-school trained arts managers knows nothing of art. They make museums "user friendly" with illustrated brochures, shops, and flashy traveling exhibits that excite and pander to extra-aesthetic interests.

As noted earlier, however, the modern arts administrator is not committed to building a bigger and more diverse audience as an end in itself. Rather, the goal of arts administration is more often "budget maximization." Three examples suggest that administrators may abandon audience building if organizations can prosper by increasing revenues in other ways. For example, Robert Brustein[46] reports that the manager of the Lincoln Center's Beaumont Theatre in New York focused his attention on investing building-fund money rather than on raising the production money necessary to put on plays. Cox[47] found that most of the efforts of managers of New York's South Street Seaport Museum have gone into real estate development; only 5 percent of the museum's holdings are on display, and most of the museum's exhibit space is rented out for boutiques. Finally, Posner[48] reports that the Frank Lloyd Wright Foundation, created to support a Wisconsin retreat for aspiring architects, has neglected the retreat, instead building an ever-larger endowment fund by systematically selling original Frank Lloyd Wright drawings and prints. These three illustrations, though extreme, suggest that arts administrators give high priority to audience building only when it facilitates their primary goal of budget building.

New Sources of Earned Income

In the quest for new sources of funds, administrators have instituted, or tried to make demonstrably profitable, ancillary activities ranging from restaurants, publications, gift shops, and membership tours to music recording contracts, affiliated art schools, real estate ventures, and the aggressive investment of endowments. Even if these activities are not new, they are newly subject to rational accounting and managerial criteria that evaluate each activity not as a service that arguably ought to be supplied but as an independent "profit center" to be expanded, eliminated, or turned over to a concessionaire depending on its profitability.

Administrators are assisted in this process of calculation by a swelling legion of consultants. Vilker[49] outlines the range of services that can become distinct profit centers and the appropriate effectiveness/efficiency criteria to be applied to each activity. Troyer and Boisture[50] make more extensive inventory of "creative approaches to income production" and discuss ways of protecting nonprofit status and limiting tax exposure. Hendon's[51] study of the Akron Art Museum represents a comprehensive review of a museum as an economic enterprise.

The evolution of the dining facility at the Cheekwood Museum and Botanical Garden in Nashville provides a convenient case study of the evolving view of "services" in the transition from the impresarial to the administrative era.[52] Soon after the Cheek family donated their estate to a self-perpetuating board of directors in 1960, the kitchen was renovated to serve the needs of the for-members-only gala parties given in the mansion's main gallery. Later, the ladies auxiliary of the membership committee began to serve light lunches in what was called the "Pineapple Room." The ladies contributed their time and opened the dining room to the public as a fund-raising charity. The menu and style of service, however, discouraged anyone but members of their own social class from lunching there.

When it became difficult to find enough volunteers, a staff was hired to run the operation. In 1979 the newly hired, administratively trained museum manager found that the lunchroom was costing the museum more money than it took in. He wanted to shut down the operation, but the board of directors objected. Several years later, he was able to include a kitchen and dining room, both complying with the sanitary and safety codes that had been violated in the old facility, in a new building under construction. The administrator then contracted for the lunch service from a local affiliate of a nationally known food service catering firm, thereby ensuring income from a lease-fee while providing consistently good food without museum management needing to be involved on a day-to-day basis.

In reevaluating many of the services that museums and performing arts centers have long provided, arts administrators have come to view arts institutions as having revenue-generating resources well beyond the tea room and gift shop. For example, the New York Museum of Modern Art has sold the "air rights" above its new west wing to real estate developers for $17 million. The idea of art institutions as real estate has also been applied to orchestra halls. For example, the Buffalo Philharmonic Orchestra Company sold its performance hall to a group of investors organized as a limited partnership. The Orchestra was able to pay off its debts and increase its endowment with the proceeds of the sale, while the limited partners have received significant tax advantages from the arrangement.[53]

Laws, Regulations, and Codes

Legal regulation of organizations has grown steadily in this century, but the trend has accelerated rapidly since 1960 with the advent of a wide range of social legislation. The increasing salience of legal matters is suggested by the important place given to law in the education of arts administrators[54] and by the rapidly proliferating professional and practical literature devoted to legal matters relevant to the arts world.

The impresario could be expected to learn the provisions of copyright law, obscenity codes, fire insurance and labor regulations, inheritance tax, and the like while working on the job. The contemporary administrator, however, must be familiar with an ever-expanding and rapidly changing set of laws, regulations, and codes in order to compete successfully for a position in an arts organization. Consider, as an example, just those laws, regulations, and codes that relate to employees: labor laws, labor union contracts, worker compensation law, retirement plans, medical benefits insurance, employee tax law, equal employment opportunity regulations, workplace safety codes, record and television performance royalties, and others.

Personnel

The ability to deal with people was the long suit of the impresario. Styles varied from individual to individual, but the impresarial technique was a mixture of kid gloves and mailed fists. The former was usually extended to patrons and leading stars; the latter was more often shown to employees and social inferiors. All relationships, however, were on a personal and paternalistic basis. Contracts were typically sealed with a handshake and long-term informal understandings commonly developed.[55]

Contemporary arts administrators characteristically deal with personnel relations in a quite different way. Increasingly the services of featured performers are secured by formal written contracts negotiated with artists' business managers or professional management agencies. In similar fashion, the services of musicians and backstage technicians are increasingly obtained on terms set by formal union contracts. The numerous performer and stagehand strikes that have occurred in all of the performing arts over the past 20 years attest to the displacement of paternalistic personal relationships by formal contractual arrangements.[56] Baron, Dobbin, and Jennings[57] report findings parallel to our argument here. They found that professional personnel managers displaced their personalistic predecessors in the major manufacturing industries during the World War II era because of the plethora of new regulations promulgated by the federal government at that time.

Logistics

The rate of movement of artists and art works has increased dramatically over the past 20 years. The advent of jet air travel allows performers, conductors, and other key artistic personnel to pursue world-spanning careers on a week-by-week basis. Not only soloists, lead dancers, and actors move at this pace, but choreographers, directors, and conductors now often hold two or three major positions simultaneously.[58] With the mobilization of large, spectacular touring museum exhibits in the 1970s, the contemporary museum administrator now has logistical problems the complexity of which could not have been imagined by the early twentieth-century impresario.

Logistical problems are such that the financing and mounting of major productions must be planned years in advance. The 1980 New York Museum of Modern Art retrospective on Picasso, for example, required five years of negotiations with the governments of France and Spain as well as with dozens of museums and private collectors around the world. The old-style arts manager, such as Luigi Cesnola, gained experience on the parade ground and in battle as a cavalry officer and gentleman in full dash, able to make quick decisions intuitively. Now the new arts administrator, like the first director of the Tennessee Performing Arts Center in Nashville, an Air Force missile range officer, is more likely to have been trained to target audiences methodically and to calculate the probable artistic "bang per buck" for each of various alternative arts venues.

Extraorganizational Factors in Concert

We have identified government funding as the primary cause of the emergence of arts administration since 1960. If this interpretation is correct, why did the first massive infusion of federal government money into the arts during the New Deal government arts program of the late 1930s not foster the development of arts administration? To my knowledge, no study has focused on this question, but the nature of government support then was crucially different from the government's role in the contemporary era.

Support for the arts in the 1930s was just one small part of the general "jobs program" aimed at reducing the dramatically high level of unemployment.[59] Money was allocated by government functionaries to individual artists or for the production of large commissioned works. With few exceptions, grants were not made to existing arts organizations, and the organizations that were created depended almost entirely on government funding. Thus, when the program was terminated soon after the advent of World War II, the federal administrators were reassigned and the entire federal arts organizational apparatus disappeared.[60]

Since 1960, however, as we have described in this section of the chapter, six different factors in the environment or at the organization-environment boundary have increased the need for arts managers with administrative skills. Although each of the six factors has been discussed separately, they typically operate in concert, mutually reinforcing the drive toward formal accountability and increasing the need for arts managers with the orientation and skills of arts administration.

PROFESSIONALIZATION AND INSTITUTIONALIZATION OF ADMINISTRATIVE STYLE

To this point, we have described the emergence of arts administration as a consequence of abstract forces that increased the demand for administrative services, but several people and groups took an active interest in speeding the development of the administrative style as well. In this section of the chapter we focus on the things that have been done to create an arts organizational world more congenial to the administrative managerial style. The key processes involved are referred to by sociologists as institutionalization and professionalization.

With growing clarity over the first two decades following World War II, American arts world leaders perceived a situation full of new opportunities and new problems. First, there was a new feeling that the United States was, or could become, the center of creative effort in all the arts, ending the feeling of inferiority that American art world participants had chronically felt relative to European art. Second, attendance at arts events was steadily rising and numerous new arts organizations of all types were being founded or revitalized around the country. Third, the cohort of large donors who for the first third of the century had been able simply to underwrite the operating deficits of even the largest organizations could no longer play that role. Organization costs were rising, but more importantly, individual fortunes had been greatly diminished by the Great Depression, and the discretionary power of the wealthy was diminished by the workings of tax law that led to philanthropy being channeled to charities through family or corporate foundations. In consequence there was an increasing reliance on earned income and a concern for audience building.[61]

These changes sparked a widespread discussion of an economic crisis in the arts, which became focused in 1965 by Baumol and Bowen's concept of cost disease. There were calls for large new government subsidies to cure the cost disease. Influential voices, however, argued that it was not more money that was needed so much as better management practices within arts organizations.[62] The *administrative* model emerged by degrees as the appropriate one for the new-style arts manager.

Four phases can be identified in the effort to institutionalize arts administration and professionalize arts managers. First, in the early 1960s corporations began to loan management personnel to arts organizations to help with accounting, legal services, cost control, and fund-raising. To legitimate and coordinate this activity within the business world, the Business Committee for the Arts was formed in 1967. The "loaned expert" program continues today, despite the problems inherent in having someone used to the operating logic of a for-profit industry advising nonprofit arts organizations. Business Committee for the Arts president, Godwin McClellan, recounted an incident that illustrates the problem.[63] A major performing company received assistance from a loaned business expert to eliminate its operating deficits. The company then scheduled a tour of Brazil, thus creating a new deficit of $60,000. When the exasperated business consultant confronted the arts-organization director, the latter explained that he needed a sizable deficit in order to spark the annual fund-raising drive.

Second, to get beyond the "loaned expert," attention turned to retraining arts managers in the logic of administration. "Trade" or "service associations" modeled on the American Symphony Orchestra League were formed in part to pool managerial expertise and to support short courses in administrative techniques for practicing arts managers. From its inception, the National Endowment for the Arts subsidized existing trade associations and helped to found new ones. By 1979, the NEA could report, "At this time, we provide about five million dollars in operating support for more than seventy service organizations, and another two million dollars in project support to these organizations."[64]

Third, the decade of the 1970s saw the proliferation of graduate arts administration training programs based in schools of business. Collectively these are dedicated to developing a new generation of MBA-credentialed arts managers committed to the logic of administration.

Finally, the professionalization of arts administration has been buttressed by a proliferation of a quasi-scholarly and practical literature treating the full range of management concerns, from identifying potential audiences to cultural-area zoning. Two quarterly journals, *Art and the Law,* launched in 1975 by Volunteer Lawyers for the Arts, and the *Journal of Arts Management and Law* (formerly *Performing Arts Review*) exemplify the wealth of new knowledge being assembled for and by the emerging university-trained cadre of arts administrators.

The Institutionalization/Professionalization Cycle

As a number of scholars drawing on observations in the full range of for-profit and nonprofit organizations have noted, once underway the processes of institutionalization and professionalization tend to reinforce each other.[65] Among arts organizations the cycle has taken the following form. The new institutional patrons demand formal accountability of arts organizations. Once the principle of formal accountability is accepted among arts organizations, the amount of information required is rapidly increased. The National Endowment for the Arts, for example, now requires all organizations applying for grants to provide a substantial body of information about finances, personnel, budgets, and audiences that the organizations did not collect a decade ago.[66]

To keep up with the increasing demands, arts organizations borrow knowledgeable executives from business or retain their own managers. And business schools begin to educate arts managers, as already noted, to fill the rapidly growing demand for technically trained personnel. In the process, arts management jobs become more alike from one organization to the next in each arts discipline, and across all the arts as well. As job descriptions are standardized, it is easier for administrators to make careers for themselves by moving rapidly from organization to organization. The frequent need to fill vacated positions leads to a further standardization of job descriptions, which in turn facilitates job-hopping both from one arts organization to another and from outside the art world entirely. The advertisement for a Public Relations Director of the Pittsburgh Symphony Orchestra appearing in the July 15, 1985 *New York Times* suggests the range of interchangeability. "Seeking PR pro to take on new position. . . . Strong media background *required* with innovations and a keen interest in the Performing Arts. PR experience in that area *preferred*" [emphasis added].

The current trend toward standardized job descriptions and job-hopping is also illustrated by the feature "Musical Chairs" that appears regularly in *Symphony News*, the monthly publication of the American Symphony Orchestra League. During the three months of 1982 surveyed, less than one-tenth of the job changes noted were for conductors or other artistic personnel. Nine-tenths of the shifts involved administrators. Another pattern apparent in such lists of job moves is the large proportion that are transfers between different kinds of arts organizations, such as arts-displaying and arts-presenting organizations; service organizations; government, corporate, or foundation money-granting organizations; and private consulting firms. Such moves serve to broaden the perspective of the individual administrator and further facilitate the standardization of the arts management field. With each revolution of the standardization cycle, the universalized training of the administrator becomes progressively more salient, and the particularistic training of the impresario becomes less relevant and more anachronistic.[67]

CODA

Having distinguished two arts management styles, the impresarial and the administrative, and having explored numerous possible explanations for the rapid displacement of the former by the latter since 1960, this chapter concludes by raising questions about the possible consequences of this displacement for the arts.

Astute impresarios and administrators alike have disclaimed any influence on the aesthetic direction of the arts organization for which they work.[68] Yet, as Hart[69] has noted, it is as difficult to keep aesthetic and managerial decisions separate as it is to keep the legislative, executive, and judicial functions of government separate.

While it is easy to show instances of the aesthetic influence of particular managers of each era, it is more difficult to show a systematic difference between the effects of impresarios and administrators. The set of circumstances that induced the shift from impresario to administrator could have been responsible as well for all the changes in aesthetics during the same span of years. What follows, therefore, is necessarily a set of conjectures about the consequences of the activities of impresarios versus those of administrators.

We begin by recalling some of the key differences, previously discussed, between the prototypical impresario and the prototypical administrator. The former works in one arts discipline, learns by experience, expects long tenure in a position, and strives to please the wealthy members of the organization's board of directors. The latter is trained in a set of general skills, holds positions in several arts disciplines, expects to make a career moving from job to job, and strives to make a reputation in the field of arts management.[70]

Based on these differences one would suggest that, all other factors being equal, the collective impact of impresarios was to make the aesthetic thrust of individual arts organizations increasingly distinct from other organizations in the discipline and also relatively slow to change. In contrast, the collective influence of administrators should be to make the aesthetic thrust of arts organizations in a given discipline more nearly alike but, at the same time, to cause aesthetic fashions to follow each other more rapidly.[71]

How these antagonistic tendencies of aesthetic homogenization, on the one hand, and rapid aesthetic change, on the other, will work out in practice depends largely on forces acting on the environment of arts administrators, forces over which they have little control. Further careful study of the actions of arts administrators will greatly enrich our understanding of the dynamics of the arts world and expand our knowledge of the operation of nonprofit organizations in general.

NOTES

1. Prior to this development of nonprofit civic arts institutions, the few arts organizations that existed were typically established as profit-making concerns by enterprising entrepreneurs. Theodore Thomas was the most renowned entrepreneur of orchestral music and P. T. Barnum, before he founded "the world's greatest circus," established a for-profit museum in New York City. In addition to paintings and sculpture, his museum featured stuffed animals and primitive artifacts as well as oddities and freaks of all sorts. Thomas's activities are summarized by Philip Hart, *Orpheus in the New World* (New York: Norton, 1973), 10–47. Barnum's numerous exploits are chronicled by Neil Harris, *Humbug: The Art of P. T. Barnum* (Boston: Little, Brown, 1973). Paul J. DiMaggio has shown the shift to nonprofit civic cultural institutions in Boston, the city that led the way in this development, in his "Cultural Entrepreneurship in Nineteenth-Century Boston" (Chapter 2, this volume).

2. This description of Cesnola's life and activities is drawn from Calvin Tomkins, *Merchants and Masterpieces* (New York: E. P. Dutton, 1970), 49–59, and Elizabeth McFadden, *The Glitter and the Gold* (New York: Dial, 1971). As a semi-official historian of the Metropolitan Museum of Art, Tomkins only notes the charges of criminal activity made against Cesnola while director of the museum. In her biography, McFadden details all of the considerable evidence of Cesnola's misdeeds. What she does not make clear is why the powerful board members of the museum, including J. Pierpont Morgan, supported Cesnola to the end.

3. C. G. Loring, for example, the first manager of the Boston Museum of Fine Art, though a patrician Bostonian rather than a foreign aristocrat, had much the same early career as Cesnola, including distinguished service in the Civil War cavalry and years spent as an archaeological treasure hunter. See Paul J. DiMaggio, op. cit.; Nathaniel Burt, *Palaces for the People: A Social History of the American Art Museum* (Boston: Little, Brown, 1977); and Walter Muir Whitehill, *Museum of Fine Arts, Boston: A Centennial History* 2 vols. (Cambridge: Harvard University Press, 1970).

4. This description of Arthur Judson's life and work is drawn from Philip Hart, op. cit., 71–95.

5. Ibid., 84. Kurt Adler, who became the director of the San Francisco Opera Company in 1957, notes the vital importance of personal charm in the earlier days. He says of Gaetano Merola, a Neapolitan who was his predecessor, "Merola was a very attractive man. The ladies—the wealthy ladies and not only those who had no money—liked him. Without Merola and the gold rush heirs he attracted, there would be no opera in San Francisco today." Adler is quoted by Melvin B. Krauss, "Kurt Adler: Gambler at the Opera," *Wall Street Journal*, November 27, 1981, 24.

6. Ibid., 79.

7. Ibid., 80.
8. See Rudolph Bing, *5,000 Nights at the Opera* (New York: Doubleday, 1972).
9. See especially Nathaniel Burt, op. cit., 249–348, and Alan Shestack, "The Director: Scholar and Businessman, Educator and Lobbyist," *Museum News* (November/December, 1978).
10. Bing, op. cit.
11. Tomkins, op. cit., 255.
12. This information was compiled from *Arts Administration Training in the United States and Canada* (Madison, Wisc: Graduate School of Business, University of Wisconsin, June 1977, revised edition).
13. This information was compiled from *A Survey of Arts Administration Training* (New York: The American Council for the Arts, 1981).
14. Ibid., 72–76, lists 34 agencies that offered such courses and seminars in 1980.
15. *Bulletin* of the University of Wisconsin, Madison, Arts Administration Program.
16. Shestack, op. cit.
17. Thomas W. Leavitt, "The Beleaguered Director," 91–101 in Brian O'Doherty, ed., *Museums in Crisis* (New York: Braziller, 1972).
18. Ralph Black, "The Symphony Manager—A Job Description," *Symphony News* (September 1979): 12.
19. The great importance of having a manager with Fleischmann's mix of skills is suggested by the comment of Carlo Maria Giulini, then music director of the Los Angeles Philharmonic, when he was asked by an interviewer whether it was true that he had turned down numerous music directorships at other respected American orchestras. He replied, "Yes, because I couldn't find a rapport between my private life and what a music director in the United States is asked to do. First of all, the great number of concerts and programs, and then the involvement in financial problems and unions. But here in Los Angeles with Ernest Fleischmann I have an agreement that is good for my wishes, for my work and my life. . . . I am absolutely free from problems that are not my business and that I am not very good at solving."Giulini is quoted by Martin Bookspan in "Dialogue: Carlo Maria Giulini," *Symphony News* (February 1980): 19–20.
20. See especially Peter M. Blau, "A Formal Theory of Differentiation in Organizations," *American Sociological Review,* 35 (1970): 201–218.
21. Rosanne Martorella, "Rationality in the Management of Performing Arts Organizations," in Jack Kamerman and Rosanne Martorella, eds., *Performers and Performances* (South Hadley, Mass.: Bergin and Garvey, 1983), 95–108.
22. See respectively Hart, Bing, and Tomkins, op. cit.
23. Stephen R. Couch, "Patronage and Organizational Structure in Symphony Orchestras in London and New York," in Jack Kamerman and Rosanne Martorella, op. cit., 109–121.
24. Vernon K. Dibble, "The Organization of Traditional Authority: English County Government, 1558 to 1640," in James G. March, ed., *Handbook of Organizations* (Chicago: Rand-McNally, 1965), 879–909. But see Blau, op. cit., who argues that as organizations increase in size, the proportion of personnel in the administrative sector increases as well. Blau and his followers have not, however, suggested why a shift in managerial style such as that from impresarial to administrative should take place.
25. Martorella, op. cit., 97.
26. See especially Vera Zolberg, "Conflicting Visions in American Art Museums," *Theory and Society* 10 (1981): 103–125, and Mark Lilla, "The Great Museum Muddle," *New Republic* 8 (April 1985): 25–30.
27. Edward Arian, *Bach, Beethoven and Bureaucracy: The Case of the Philadelphia Orchestra* (University, Ala.: University of Alabama Press, 1971).
28. Tomkins, op. cit.
29. Carl Gersuny and William R. Rosengren, *The Service Society* (Cambridge, Mass.: Schenkman, 1973).
30. The most complete review of ideas relating to the idea that organizations, like individ-

uals, experience life-cycle stages is provided by John R. Kimberly and Robert H. Miles, *The Organizational Life Cycle* (San Francisco: Jossey-Bass, 1980).

31. This observation is based primarily on a reading of articles on dance criticism because dance companies have received markedly less scholarly attention than orchestras, museums, and theaters. A suggestion of the dynamics of dance company development can be gleaned from Leila Sussman, "Anatomy of the Dance Company Boom, 1958–1980," *Dance Research Journal* 16 2 (1984): 23–28; Joseph Mazo, *Dance is a Contact Sport* (New York: Saturday Review Press, 1975); Margaret J. Wyszomirski and Judith H. Balfe, "Coalition Theory and American Ballet," in Judith H. Balfe and Margaret J. Wyszomirski, eds., *Art, Ideology and Politics* (New York: Praeger, 1985), 210–236; and Dale Harris, "New Direction for the San Francisco Ballet," *Wall Street Journal* May 22, 1985, 26.

32. John W. Meyer and Brian Rowan, "Institutionalized Organizations: Formal Structure as Myth and Ceremony," *American Journal of Sociology* 83 (1977): 340–363.

33. William J. Baumol and William G. Bowen, *Performing Arts: The Economic Dilemma* (Cambridge, Mass.: MIT Press, 1966).

34. Ibid., 161–180, and Hilda Baumol and William J. Baumol, "The Mass Media and the Cost Disease," in William S. Hendon, Nancy K. Grant, and Douglas V. Shaw, eds., *The Economics of Cultural Industries* (Akron, Ohio: Association for Cultural Economics, 1984), 109–123. Hart, op. cit., 295–330, provides an excellent early application of the "cost disease" argument to a class of arts organizations, symphony orchestras.

35. This recommendation was made early by the Rockefeller Panel Report, *The Performing Arts: Problems and Prospects* (New York: McGraw-Hill, 1965), and was echoed in numerous subsequent policy statements. See, for example, Thomas J. Raymond and Stephen A. Greyser, "The Business of Managing the Arts," *Harvard Business Review* July (1978): 123–132.

36. See especially Jack Poggi, *Theater in America: The Impact of Economic Forces 1870–1967* (Ithaca: Cornell University Press, 1968); Kenneth Hudson, *A Social History of Museums* (New York: Macmillan, 1975); Karl E. Meyer, *The Art Museum: Power, Money, Ethics* (New York: Morrow, 1979); Bing, op. cit.; Hart, op. cit.; Mazo, op. cit.; and Burt, op. cit.

37. Lawrence D. Mankin, "The National Government and the Arts: From the Great Depression Until 1973" (Ph.D. diss., University of Illinois, Urbana, 1976); Charles R. Swaim, "The Fine Politics of Art: Organizational Behavior, Budgetary Strategy and Some Implications for Arts Policy" (Ph.D. diss., University of Colorado, Boulder, 1977); Dick Netzer, *The Subsidized Muse* (New York: Cambridge University Press, 1978); and Vera Zolberg, "Changing Patterns of Patronage in the Arts," in Jack Kamerman and Rosanne Martorella op. cit., 251–268.

38. John Blaine, "Accountability to the Hand That Feeds You," *Museum News*, (May 1979): 34.

39. Paul J. DiMaggio, "The Impact of Public Funding on Organizations in the Arts" (Yale Program on Non-Profit Organizations Working Paper 31, Yale University 1981).

40. *NEA News*, "Jazz Grants at $1 Million Mark," news release (Washington, D.C.: National Endowment for the Arts, September 1979), 2. The still largely unorganized state of the jazz field has been noted by D. Antoinette Handy, "Jazz Gets Organized," *NEA Arts Review* 2, 4 (1985): 18–20.

41. Paul J. DiMaggio and Walter W. Powell, "The Iron Cage Revisited: Institutional Isomorphism and Collective Rationality in Organizational Fields," *American Sociological Review* 48 (1983): 147–160.

42. Leavitt, op. cit., 95.

43. Mahmoud Salem, *Organizational Survival in the Performing Arts: The Making of the Seattle Opera* (New York: Praeger, 1976).

44. Paul J. DiMaggio, "Can Culture Survive the Marketplace?" (Chapter 3, this volume).

45. Lilla, op. cit., 26.

46. Robert Brustein, "Boards Versus Artists," *New Republic* (October 1983): 22–23.

47. Meg Cox, "All at Sea: New York Museum's Problems Show Snares in Mixing Culture, Commerce," *Wall Street Journal,* April 12, 1985, 12.

48. Ellen Posner, "Selling Frank Lloyd Wright, the Wrong Way," *Wall Street Journal,* February 5, 1985, 30.

49. Barbara Vilker, "The Development of Museum Management Tools," in David Cwi, ed., *Research in the Arts* (Baltimore: Johns Hopkins University, 1977), 67–68.

50. Thomas A. Troyer and Robert A. Boisture, "Charities in Fiscal Crisis: Creative Approaches to Income Production," *Journal of Arts Management and Law,* 20, 4 (1984): 32–54.

51. William S. Hendon, *Analyzing an Art Museum* (New York: Praeger, 1979).

52. The description of the development of the Nashville museum is taken from Roberta Keller, "Cheekwood Enters Era Four of Arts Administration" (Unpublished manuscript, Vanderbilt University, 1985).

53. Cynthia Saltzman, "Recession Impact Hits Art Organizations Hard," *Wall Street Journal,* December 7, 1982, 52.

54. See notes 12 and 13.

55. Bing, op. cit.

56. Archie Kleingartner and Kenneth Lloyd, "Labor-Management Relations in the Performing Arts: The Case of Los Angeles," *California Management Review,* 15 (1972): 128–132.

57. James N. Baron, Frank Dobbin, and P. Devereaux Jennings, "War and Peace: The Evolution of Modern Personnel Administration in U.S. Industry" Forthcoming, *American Journal of Sociology.*

58. Alan Rich, "Bigamy on the Orchestral Front," *New York* (February 28, 1972): 56; Jack Kamerman, "The Rationalization of Symphony Orchestra Conductors' Interpretive Style," in Jack Kamerman and Rosanne Martorella, op. cit., 161–181.

59. The following discuss the efforts of the federal government to foster the arts during the New Deal era: June Mathews, *The Federal Theater, 1935–39* (Princeton, N.J.: Princeton University Press, 1967); William F. McDonald, *Federal Relief Administration and the Arts* (Columbus, Ohio: Ohio State University, 1969); Jerre Mangione, *The Dream and the Deal; The Federal Writers' Project 1935–1943* (Boston: Little, Brown, 1972); Francis V. O'Connor, *Federal Support for the Visual Arts: The New Deal and Now* (Greenwich, Conn.: New York Graphic Society, 1971); Richard D. McKinzie, *The New Deal for Artists* (Princeton, N.J.: Princeton University Press, 1973); and Helen Townsend, "The Social Origins of the Federal Art Project," in Judith H. Balfe and Margaret J. Wyszomirski, op. cit., 264–292. Hypotheses concerning the quite different reasons for government support to the arts, the natural sciences, and social sciences are provided by Michael J. Useem, "Government Patronage of Science and the Arts," in Richard A. Peterson, ed., *The Production of Culture* (Beverly Hills, Calif.: Sage, 1976), 123–142.

60. The fact that the organizational apparatus developed to administer the federal arts projects was dismantled does not mean that government projects had no lasting effects. Some of the arts organizations that led the "arts boom" following World War II were begun with federal government support in the 1930s or at least survived the Great Depression only because of this aid. Hart, op. cit., provides numerous examples among symphony orchestras. What is more, most of the artistic and managerial leaders of the postwar arts world were able to pursue their chosen craft in the Depression years because of the federal arts administration money.

61. Leavitt, op. cit., 95–96; Hart, op. cit., 330–347; Burt, op. cit., 249–257; Meyer, op. cit., 31–36, 64–69.

62. The professionalization of arts managers was one of the recommendations of the Rockefeller Panel Report, op. cit., that according to Swaim, op. cit., was influential in shaping the structure of the National Endowment for the Arts. The need to upgrade the managerial skills of arts managers was a continuing theme through the 1970s. See, for example, Ichak Adizes & William McWhinney, "Arts, Society and Administration: The Role and Training

of Arts Administrators," *Arts in Society* 10, 3 (1973): 40–48; and Raymond and Greyser, op. cit.

63. Personal communication with Godwin McClellan at a Nashville Area Chamber of Commerce meeting, April 1978.

64. NEA Memorandum, "Service Organization Study" (Washington, D.C.: National Endowment for the Arts, 1979).

65. This process is discussed by Magali S. Larson, *The Rise of Professionalism: A Sociological Analysis* (Berkeley, Calif.: University of California Press, 1977), and Randall Collins, *The Credential Society* (New York: Academic Press, 1979). An even less sanguine interpretation of the institutionalization–professionalization process is provided by Daniel Moynihan in his study of the development of the welfare establishment, *Maximum Feasible Misunderstanding* (New York: Free Press, 1969).

66. The range and detail of information now gathered has been reviewed in the Spring 1984 issue of the *Journal of Arts Management and Law.*

67. See Zolberg, op. cit. A study of the careers and aspirations of arts managers of U.S. museums, resident theaters, symphony orchestras, and local arts agencies supported by the Research Division of the National Endowment for the Arts has been completed by Paul J. DiMaggio. In comparing the attitudes and experiences of older with younger arts managers, it presents a vivid picture of the development of administrative-style careerism among arts managers.

68. See for example Hart, op. cit., 77–79; and Black, op. cit., 12.

69. Hart, op. cit., 77.

70. The contrasting career orientations of the impresario and the administrator are much like the differences between the orientations of two types of community influentials identified by Robert Merton as "locals" and "cosmopolitans." See his *Social Theory and Social Science* (New York: Free Press, 1968 enlarged edition), 441–474.

71. No one yet has done the research necessary to detail the consequences for the arts of the shift in the styles of arts management, but there have been suggestive studies of the analogous processes that are occurring in the creative leadership of symphony orchestras. As late as 1950, virtually all of the major orchestras of the world had a distinct "sound" that distinguished each of them from all other orchestras. Now the major orchestras are indistinguishable from each other to all but the most practiced ear. According to knowledgeable commentators, the primary reason for this change is that orchestras that were once molded by a single strong conductor over a number of years now have to be able to shift their sound on demand to fit the expectations of a series of itinerant guest conductors so that a more nearly uniform international orchestral sound has emerged. These processes are described by Robert Faulkner, "Orchestra Interaction: Communication and Authority in an Artistic Organization," in Jack Kamerman and Rosanne Martorella, op. cit., 71–83; Jack Kamerman, "The Rationalization of Symphony Orchestra Conductors' Interpretive Style," in Jack Kamerman and Rosanne Martorella, op. cit., 161–181.

8

Tensions of Mission in American Art Museums

VERA L. ZOLBERG

The conflict between elitism and populism is a perennial feature of American art museums. Proponents of populism, or the democratization of access to the fine arts for the many, identify the public education function of art museums as their most important role. Elitists, on the other hand, consider collecting, preserving, and studying art works to be the museum's central purpose. Yet public education has been claimed as a basic function by American art museums since their founding. Almost all explicitly assume this obligation in their charters, reiterate the goal in public statements, and most have actually undertaken activities that they defined as educational. Nevertheless, until recently very few have systematically pursued this aim if it meant sacrificing the others. This essay looks at why museum people talk so much about their responsibility to a public about whom they remain deeply ambivalent. To understand the nature of this ambivalence it is not enough to recognize that art museums have other interests, though this is central to understanding the gap between the stated purpose and its realization. Neither is it sufficient to explain the outcomes in terms of intentions, real or imputed to important actors. Rather, it is important to examine the American art museum both as a unique institution and in the broader, changing societal context in which it has arisen and with which it interacts.

In countries such as the United States reformers consider it vital to enlarge access to cultural "goods" such as literacy, knowledge of all sorts, and appreciation of previously inaccessible forms of art. Rather than confine culture to an ascriptively based membership, they would make it an achievable right, potentially for everyone. In this light, as with schools, art museums are expected to expand the cultural horizons of previously excluded groups, "improving" taste even for those not to the manor born,

Reprinted from *Social Forces* 63 (December 1984). "American Art Museum: Sanctuary or Free-for-All" by Vera L. Zolberg.

and promoting moral uplift for those whose previous cultural experience was perceived as either grossly commercial or merely quaintly folkloric. They are expected to permit individuals to gain in enlightenment and become "civilized" while society, for its part, gains a reinforced cultural consensus particularly important in modern heterogeneous systems.[1] These aims, altruistic at one level, have been interpreted in a more critical manner, one arguing that certain groups monopolize the definitions, valuations, and access to certain symbolic products in their own interest, defining the culture of outgroups as parochial, insignificant, or ignoble.[2] Such an interpretation lends itself to an analysis suggesting that access to and understanding of what is socially defined as high culture are doled out in doses sufficient only to create respect for the symbolic goods which dominant status groups control. The result is to inculcate widespread respect for fine art, but little comprehension of it, thereby reinforcing the reliance of the uninitiated on those apparently more adept. To the extent that people acknowledge their own lack of accomplishment, they are made accomplices in their self-definition as inferior, and the cultural distinctions enhancing social inequality are legitimated.[3] In these terms, rather than social integration, the result of anything short of complete democratization is the maintenance of hegemony.[4]

Rather than attempt to adjudicate between these interpretations, either of which could plausibly be imposed on available data, I have chosen to focus on a middle-range level of analysis, with particular emphasis on the components of art museums that are most germane to the elitist-populist debate. To this end, I start by looking at the social uses of the art museum's focal concern, art works themselves; second, I examine the structural models—and antimodels—on which art museums are based, and which continue to orient their current structure; third, in order to judge the relative importance of their changing priorities I examine the internal stratification of their personnel, with attention to their educational staff; and fourth, the extent to which their public education policies are internally generated or chiefly reactions to external forces. In concluding, I will relate the character of art museums as formed by these components to the changing meanings of elitism and populism in the context of changing aesthetic categories.

ARTWORKS: STATUS SYMBOLS IN ORGANIZATIONAL CONFLICT

Works of art have long been luxury commodities, valued for their rarity, association with nobility, foreign cachet, and romantic genius. These attributes, extrinsic to the works' aesthetic substance, have been said to create an aura, contact with which, through ownership or appreciation, provides symbolic legitimation for high social status.[5] The extra-aesthetic character of art is no new discovery, having been variously analyzed since at least Veblen by Marxian and non-Marxian thinkers alike.[6]

As long as art works were visible mainly through religious or civic display, or owned *qua* art only by the few, they could serve to separate elites from others. But with increasing availability through mechanical reproduction, public display in museums, and education, they risk losing their distinctiveness as status indicators. It would not be surprising, therefore, to find that those who have had access to them through inheritance or early enculturation, or who have attained such access only with difficulty, might greet their mass diffusion with some reluctance.

In countries such as the United States, however, the idea that wide diffusion is necessary for full democratization, national integration, or as a right of full membership in society has come to be applied to fine art as well as to other "goods." In the case of the fine arts, the institution most clearly assigned a role to achieve this aim is the public art museum. More than other cultural institutions, such as symphony orchestras or opera companies, but much like public libraries and schools, it came to be the most prominent target of those promoting the democratization of culture.

American art museums are complex, multipurpose organizations and, typical of such organizations, in response to pressures from within and without, they have emphasized one goal over another at various times in their history.[7] They have been creatures of their trustees, elite institutions with conservatorial goals, selecting, preserving and displaying art works as monuments to their tastes. These are the reasons they were founded, though not the only reasons, nor are these ideas uncritically accepted today. Curators seek autonomy from their boards to pursue research and acquire works that they themselves consider important; dealers and collectors try to influence aesthetic choices; artists seek entry for their works; public groups demand a say in policy decisions; national museum organizations criticize the stodginess of trustees. The dissatisfaction that these demands reveal represents both internal dilemmas and the changing environmental pressures that impinge on art museums.

Dilemmas, as Blau and Scott suggest, are alternatives endemic in organizations which provide "a continual source of change in the system."[8]

For art museums, the chief dilemma is between adhering to what are claimed to be disinterested consummatory aesthetic values on the one hand and on the other effectively providing service to society at large. In response to the intensity of demands for public service, therefore, museums launch programs of education and outreach. But whether they succeed or fail, they create new problems and provoke new demands.

To meet them, however, museums run the risk of being accused of allowing fine art to degenerate into a "mere" commodity, or something akin to commercial entertainment. On the one hand, art museums have an interest in providing sanctuary for study or quiet appreciation; on the other, they are impelled to provide service to a broad public whose very presence jeopardizes this goal. The background for understanding this dilemma will be reviewed in the following examination of the structural models that contributed to the making of public art museums.[9]

STRUCTURAL PROTOTYPES OF ART MUSEUMS AND THEIR IMPLEMENTATION

Art museums as we know them did not spring fully formed into existence but are institutions based on a number of earlier kinds of display structures. Some of these were sacred, such as churches which exhibited miraculous relics, paintings, and statues of saints and biblical figures in order to inculcate parishioners with religious beliefs. Others included royal palaces filled with paintings, statuary, and tapestries, testifying to their owners' legitimacy and taste, and intended to impress courtiers and foreign dignitaries. Similar to and emulating palaces were the collections of the wealthy, nobles or commoners, of treasures, curiosities, art works, antiques, or scientifically interesting objects for their own and their invited guests' delectation. At less exalted levels, popular shows and fairs provided entertainment, either live or in the form of objects having to do with historical events, natural wonders, or freaks, for a paying public as essentially commercial ventures. To a lesser or greater degree and in varying proportions, most of these displays were supposed to provide moral uplift, education, and scholarship, as well as entertainment.[10] To the extent that these forms were models for museums, however, they endowed them with inherent contradictions: whether to be palaces for the few or churches for the many; to be institutes for scholarly curiosity or fairs for passive spectators; to cater for the leisure of the elite or entertain the general public.

In modern times museums were created as a form drawing on aspects of all these models but in sharp contrast to some of their features. Differentiating themselves from commercial entertainment, they claimed a disinterested, high cultural project as their *raison d'être*. While other types of museums followed the related scholarly disciplines of history, natural science, and technology, gaining legitimacy from developments in the interlinked growth of university scholarship and professional specialization,[11] art museums based their rationale on connoisseurship and art history. This differentiation did not happen purely automatically, nor only because of the inner dynamic of the disciplines that came to encompass them. In great part it occurred because of the desire of wealthy elites, with the concurrence and sometimes pressure of artists, scholars, and cultural entrepreneurs (some of whom were also wealthy), to create a culture for themselves untroubled by lower income groups and distinct from parochial religious aims or purely commercial enterprise.[12]

Although all museums followed this pattern, however, there were important differences in their orientations toward the general public. European museums, as under *anciens régimes,* took the course of serving as national monuments, providing scholarly and artistic patronage and edification for high status group members, and used both direct and indirect means, such as restricted hours, to discourage working people from attending. They were the reverse of purely commercial enterprises, where anyone was welcome for a fee. Though museums aspired to or claimed a high degree of seriousness, however, until the late nineteenth century their exhibits were not necessarily different in kind from displays at some of the more popular events, which were just as likely to attract "people of quality" as the general public.[13]

Because art collecting and patronage were viewed as private pleasures and hobbies to which the public should not be constrained to contribute,[14] not until the second half of the nineteenth century did the idea that government support of cultural institutions was a legitimate way to promote moral uplift for the citizenry take hold. In the United States it had to overcome the connection of the fine arts with luxury, impracticality, and aristocratic degeneracy. The arts had to be made acceptable to American democracy, where criteria of "condition," hierarchically differentiating citizens—except for blacks, both as slaves and, later, in Jim Crow legislation—had no legitimacy in law.[15] Instead of being defined as the natural appurtenance of an aristocracy, the arts had to become an acquired taste whose achievement by everyone ought to be fostered.

The American situation was complicated by increasing immigration which, from the mid-nineteenth century on, was creating a level of heterogeneity viewed with alarm not only by groups in direct competition for jobs but by business interests who, while profiting from the enlarged labor pool, feared deep societal cleavages based on culture, including language and religion. On the other hand, beyond these concerns, high income groups were also creating status distinctions to establish and reinforce their own social standing. To this end, among the means they adopted was the promotion of the very kind of art that had been considered inappropriate to egalitarianism. Given the complexity of interests and motives associated with these various groups, it is understandable that conflicting goals have been assigned to cultural institutions.

The first priority for most cultural institutions in any case was simply to get started and become established in a relatively inhospitable environment. Their founders, gifted amateurs, social climbers, hobbyists, or all of these combined, acting as entrepreneurs in that they made use of existing prototypical elements which they recombined in new ways, succeeded in creating the distinctively American art museums. Until the middle of the nineteenth century, even the fine arts had been profit-making operations. Nevertheless, the idea that there was a type of art that could not appeal to everyone, but that was worth supporting even if it did not return a profit, slowly took root. Combining patriotism and moral uplift with didactic purposes, the founders applied them to "difficult" art and "serious" music which, by their inaccessibility except to those willing to work and train their faculties, surpassed mere entertainment and provided leisure activity that insulated them from undesirable contacts.[16]

Because of external pressure from popularizers and social reformers, as well as from some inside the institutions, however, museum founders also undertook to proselytize the unconvinced. But this project was not unambiguously undertaken as a primary goal in all art museums, the rhetoric of democracy notwithstanding. As with symphony societies, opera companies, libraries, and schools, it did not necessarily mean bringing culture to *all* the people. In art museums public initiation or education was likely to be confined to creating art schools for professionals, classes for amateurs, paid lectures for interested potential collectors and school teachers, libraries and study collections for scholars.

In this regard, César Graña has perceptively distinguished between museums with an orientation to men of leisure based on class membership and scholarly interests and those with a didactic purpose directed to a larger public. In these terms he opposed the patron-oriented model of the Boston Museum of Fine Arts to the public-oriented one of the Metropolitan Museum of Art. According to his analysis the Boston Museum was the creation of a few major collectors and scholars with little concern for the broader public. He argues that it differed fundamentally from a public-oriented museum, such as the Metropolitan Museum of Art, which was committed to a didactic purpose.[17] Supporting his argument, the centennial history of the Boston Museum of Fine Arts reveals that even when support for opening it to a lower-status public came from one of its own board members, the project was controversial and short-lived.[18]

Graña implies that the reasons for the differences between these types of museums lies in the older, established character of Boston society, as opposed to the more democratically oriented, status-striving, newer regional elites. Yet as I show below, a reexamination of these museums' development casts doubts on Graña's typology. I shall argue instead that, in fact, public service was a secondary goal serving instrumental purposes for *all* art museums. Regardless of their rhetoric, much of it persuasive, and the startlingly high attendance figures that they published, their primary goals lay elsewhere.[19]

For the purposes of this analysis it is worthwhile to consider an art museum reputed to be even more public-oriented than the Metropolitan Museum of Art and located in an even newer region, the Art Institute of Chicago. Founded nearly a decade later than the two eastern museums, in contrast to Boston the Art Institute leadership deliberately adopted policies that would increase the number of visitors, both casual and committed. Unlike the Boston Museum, which located itself at the outskirts of the city, its leaders purposefully chose a location in the center of public activity, even if it meant paying high rent. The Art Institute kept long hours virtually every day and an evening each week to enhance its convenience; published general, informative documents and periodicals; scheduled frequently changing exhibitions of all types, ranging from high art to interior decorating; established a library and art school; held concerts and receptions; provided space for clubs and artists, architects, and craftsmen; and sponsored public lectures. All this activity led one trustee to say, "We have everything but a dog fight here," a statement which is cited with pride by later Institute personnel.[20]

The most visible evidence of a public commitment that they offered was

Table 8.1 Visits to Leading Public Art Museums: 1900

City	Museum Visits	Population	No. of Visits as Percentage of City's Population
Chicago	(AIC) 861,000	1,698,575	51%
New York	(Met) 703,000	3,437,202	20
Boston	(MFA) 224,000	560,892	40

SOURCES: Lawrence Vail Coleman, *The Museum in America: A Critical Study,* 3 vols. (Washington, D.C.: American Association of Museums, 1939); Richard B. Morris, ed., *Encyclopedia of American History, Bicentennial Edition.* (New York: Harper & Row, 1976), p. 659; Eugenia R. Whitridge, "*Art in Chicago: The Structure of the Art World in a Metropolitan Community*" (Chicago, Ill.: University of Chicago, 1946).

attendance figures. Compared to other museums these were indeed impressive. In the late 1880s the Art Institute could already boast of nearly half a million visitors, and by the turn of the century, 861,000. The Metropolitan had only 703,000, and even the American Museum of Natural History, a popular didactic institution that had over a half million visitors in 1907, could not compete with the Art Institute, then approaching one million. In contrast, the Boston Museum attracted only 224,000 in 1900.[21]

Yet these claims notwithstanding, the differences between Boston's "patron-oriented" museum and other cities' "public-oriented" ones become questionable once we place them in the context of the population base of each city, as Table 8.1 indicates. Clearly, by comparison with the Art Institute of Chicago, Boston's Museum was as exclusive as Graña contends. On the other hand, it would appear, paradoxically, that it is the Metropolitan Museum of Art that failed in its public mission, whereas Boston lived up to it far more than its leaders may have intended. Such a conclusion, however, would be premature for several reasons. First, the administrative boundaries of these cities hamper our ability to make direct comparisons. Whereas New York had recently incorporated culturally well-endowed Brooklyn, Boston was, and remains, administratively distinct from Cambridge, with its lively cultural life. Second, the numbers of visits on which these figures are based are not broken down by "repeat" as opposed to "one-time" visitors, so that their significance is unclear. Third, we cannot judge the social level of visitors from numbers alone. Most important, the quality of attendance data in general is highly suspect, since they are generated by the museums themselves, rather than by an external, objective body.

Despite the shortage of objective measures, Graña's typology is not entirely without foundation. Quite clearly there are differences among these museums that stem from the conditions under which they were founded and which affected them long afterward. The most salient of these conditions, I would argue, are the size and quality of their initial collection, the density of the existing cultural matrix in their city, and the degree to which they were dependent on the public coffers. In this regard, Boston's museum, the patron-oriented institution *par excellence,* started with fairly substantial holdings, having had the use of existing collections of the Boston Athenaeum and of a large number of established collectors, whereas both the Metropolitan and the Art Institute began with sparse art resources, combined in the latter case with very few established cultural institutions. One consequence of these differences is that Boston's elite was able to establish and enlarge their museum without counting on funds solicited from their city to the same degree that both the Metropolitan Museum and the Art Institute did. Thus even though Boston's museum founders made the mayor of the city a board member, a practice common in most museums, it was of far greater importance to them to reinforce ties with Harvard University, whose alumni provided their most important personnel, both trustees and curators, than with the despised political machine that was gaining power. The Metropolitan Museum of Art and the Art Institute of Chicago were obliged to use every means possible in order to obtain municipal support. Citing their commitment to educational aims, the Metropolitan's founders did not disdain to deal even with Boss Tweed to gain his support for building and supplying part of the Museum's operating expenses. Attendance figures were an important device to gain this support. Once the city's commitment was assured, and as the collection increased, however, their enthusiasm for the public waned.[22]

Despite the vastly increased attendance at all these museums today, when we examine the internal stratification of museum personnel, as we shall now see, the relative importance assigned to public education has changed less than their numbers suggest.

HIERARCHY OF MUSEUM FUNCTIONS

An art museum's priorities are revealed not only by its constitution and attendance figures—which are, in any case, indicative of over-use by higher status groups and extreme under-use by lower—but also by the changing internal stratification in its division of labor. At their founding, trustees were at the top as providers of funds and facilitators of contacts with important external actors who could create a political and budgetary environment favorable to their survival. In general, unless the curatorial functions were performed by trustees themselves (not uncommon in many museums), curators were clearly their employees, often learning their craft on the job. Moreover, as DiMaggio has shown, a substantial cadre of curators were "exotic" in origin, coming from Europe and even as far afield as Japan, with no base of support except for their esoteric knowledge and their patron, generally a trustee.[23] For practical purposes, therefore, trustees could treat museums as their private fiefs and personal monuments, paying lip service to a public mission without committing much effort to its accomplishment.

Trustee dominance began to weaken somewhat in the twentieth century as the university discipline of art history and professional organizations connected with museum work gained authority. In the process, museum workers became somewhat autonomous of trustees. Alert to new opportunities emerging from changes in tax laws, and with the advent of some public funding under New Deal programs, as well as the growing sophistication of trustees themselves, dynamic museum directors could reorient their institutions in more serious directions, transforming collections from merely fashionable gifts to scholarly purposes,[24] replacing at retirement the dilettantish curators with academically certified experts. The newer curators, themselves better educated, often solidly tenured, became freer to parlay their expertise to their own advantage because of the growing number of job opportunities as new museums were founded and as the art market expanded. By developing external support systems, such as professional associations, they were able to gain more control over purchase funds with fewer strings attached and could more effectively manipulate the choices of art-collecting trustees.[25]

As far as public education was concerned, however, scholarly curators were no more interested than men of wealth had been, and perhaps even less. In fact, on the whole, despite Graña's notion, there was not a great deal more concern among public-oriented museums to initiate any but highly motivated visitors into the intricacies of connoisseurship. This becomes clear if we consider that a genuine concern with educational outreach should be accompanied by a commitment of a substantial part of its budget, and the assignment of professional personnel to those pursuits. Instead we find that educational functions were the least likely to be supported with internally generated funds, specialized personnel, and, until very recently, great effort.

Museum education is held by some to be an important curatorial function, one which should be taken seriously and not, as Joshua Taylor, late Director of the National Collection of Fine Arts of the Smithsonian Institution, argued, be "fobbed off"on an underpaid educational staff. Yet just as "the university has not bridged the gap between top professors and the community," the museum does even less well with respect to curators, whose proper goal should be the breakdown of insularity between university scholars and museum staff in order to provide an "elite experience for everyone."[26] But the fact is that the bulk of educational programs is carried out by a few staff members with the aid of volunteers almost everywhere.

Although as students future curators and educators often start out together, usually in art history, their career lines diverge when the successful Ph.D. (earlier, the M.A.) aspires to a curatorship or university appointment, whereas the Master's (earlier, Bachelor's) "drop-out" becomes a recruit for museum education. Whereas curators are expected to be "object-oriented," museum educators are characterized as "people-oriented," with the chief function of being "popularizers."[27] But they are rarely given the means, support, or rewards that would validate the importance of their work for the museums. They are paid less than curators, and their major activity is organizing volunteers who do much of the educational work, especially for children. That curators have gradually excluded volunteers, except from clerical tasks, is a sign of their strong professional standing, whereas the continuing presence of volunteers in museum education shows what a long way educators must go before they approach that level of prestige. It is not surprising, therefore, that educators are frequently frustrated and consider their position as a temporary stop on the road to something else, perhaps to becoming director of a small museum.[28]

In looking at what educators actually do, we find that aside from their preferred tasks of preparing educational exhibits and written materials, they have little enthusiasm for their other activities. In most museums they provide little more than a perfunctory orientation for volunteers. At best, even at the Art Institute, with its strong commitment to public instruction, and a department headed by a highly qualified person, most education staff members are still trained on the job, in turn training the volunteers. At the Art Institute, unlike many others, this is done with care, the educational staff exercising close supervision over them. Yet although educational staff care a great deal about providing "quality" service, they despair of doing so effectively for the groups that might benefit the most. In fact, in Chicago, the inner-city schools, whose children need the most preparation, are the least organized. Though geographically more proximate to the museum, they have fewer lines of communication to educational services than the prosperous suburban schools. It is not surprising, therefore, that education people come to view their task as mere "public relations." As one staff member put it, "the problem is that, unlike the Symphony Orchestra which claims to provide public service, the museum must actually *do* it." The Orchestra, she pointed out, has the "unique advantage of being able to limit admissions to the audiences which can buy tickets, and the limits of seating in the hall." Her conclusion was that much of the instruction is wasted on people "who are uninterested unless their family background prepares them to receive it." Thus the public service of the art museum reflects precisely the status inequalities of the society in which it is embedded.[29]

The reasons for this stem from the fact that museums subdivide their public, measuring what each segment receives in both quantity and quality of instruction according to what each is likely to offer in return. For prospective donors, curators and even the director engage in pure courtship and intensive connoisseur training on a one-to-one basis or through collectors' clubs, in hope of influencing their taste, and to persuade them to donate works and money to the institution. At the other extreme is prepackaged "mass" education for large groups of children, at best superficial and often amounting to no more than a day off from school.

The low status of the art education profession, the prevalence of unpaid volunteers, a largely female staff, a predominantly child client and, as we see below, a small financial outlay testify to the low priority assigned to this activity. Nevertheless, it cannot be lightly dismissed, since for large parts of the community who are not in touch with museum culture through school or other organizational ties, the art museum may seem an esoteric and unappealing place.[30] Since they are aware of no compelling vocational reason, they are not likely to come into the museum's range voluntarily. The average museum-goer, after all, receives no observable benefits comparable to those for a major donor. Unlike educational institutions that provide their clientele with a certificate, a symbol that they consider useful in their search for employment, the symbolic rewards of museum education are too subtle to be perceived by most of nonelite public.[31] It is nonetheless in the interest of museums to brandish and even exaggerate the numbers of visitors they attract as they lobby for governmental support.[32]

THE INCENTIVE OF PUBLIC FUNDING

Before the 1930s museum instruction was limited for the most part to small groups, mostly of adults, or to lectures requiring payment of admission fees. It took federal funding under New Deal programs to pay unemployed artists who provided instruction for both visiting teachers and school children, and to create "outreach" programs in poor neighborhoods in some cities.[33] More recently, under the federal poverty program, outreach efforts to culturally deprived groups were revived. When it comes to allocating their own funds, however, museums are niggardly, devoting only 13 percent of budget to museum instruction.[34] Even the Art Institute of Chicago, in setting $46 million as the goal for its Centennial Fund, earmarked at the most only 8 percent of the total for instructional purposes, the bulk of which involved construction costs.[35] It is not surprising, therefore, that populists have regularly denounced the leading art museums for failing to "establish contact with the general community," for allowing the "upper layer of cultured residents" to monopolize educational services and arrogate to themselves the right to appreciate the arts, for becoming "hypnotized by the charms of collecting and scholarship."[36]

Yet not all museum personnel see eye to eye on this question. The cleavage among professional "museum people" was posed in startlingly clear terms in the early 1970s, when in the course of a public symposium, two museum directors debated the "crisis" of the museum before a lay audience. The director of a university-connected (public) museum asserted,

> I find it very difficult to be a populist . . . I slightly freeze up. The real crises of what face us are not museums at all, but education. More and more are being worse and worse educated . . . Processes of education shouldn't go on in the museum; in fact, the entry of people could be done best after written or oral general examination.

This statement met with applause and cheers from the audience. In response, the director of a major New York Museum of contemporary art (private) asked, "But *after* they'd paid their admission?"[37]

The question of who pays for the museum is no minor matter, because as we have seen, it is largely as a result of governmental support and prodding that art museums have come to reach out to new publics. They benefit not only from direct governmental subsidies but indirectly from tax incentives for donations and real estate exemptions, justified by their nonprofit, public-service status. Despite their penchant for allocating the fewest possible of their own resources to public education, their increasing reliance on direct public funding and their concern with maintaining an environment hospitable both to their altruistic goals of supplying a "merit good"[38] for society and to the pecuniary enhancement of their trustees' art dealings impel museums to use many techniques for reaching a far larger segment of the population than in the past. Among these techniques the oldest is the "blockbuster" show, providing spectacular though often superficial entertainment, with the disadvantage of creating disruption and crowding. In order to overcome these problems other devices to disseminate museum culture yet insulate the already committed sectors of the public are being used. Among these is the sporadic revival of the satellite museum, in the form of branches set up in neighborhoods away from the main premises. Another means is television programs for a scattershot approach to museum instruction with a potentially wide audience. Televising art has the further appeal of high visibility which attracts corporate sponsorship as well as government subsidy.

Whether these mass approaches succeed in providing an "elite experience for everyone," as Joshua Taylor hoped, or merely represent a stopgap measure against criticism, the more successful they are in raising public interest in the arts, the greater the likelihood that future museum-goers will be better prepared to enter the institutions without having to pass an examination.

CONCLUSIONS

The ambiguities inherent in art museum educational policies are embedded in the character of the institution, the diverse motives of the groups that created and maintained museums, and the demands of outsiders who have a stake in the institution's policies. As with educational institutions, so art museums are victims of their own success. Even though their past efforts to gain a large public indicate less commitment to democratization than they claimed, they managed to enlarge it to a degree that strains their facilities. The expansion of their public, both *in situ* and at a distance as "appreciators," belies the criticisms by education-oriented observers. At the same time that this outcome suggests the growth of a shared cultural consensus, however, since in a modern society their public is not homogeneous but disposes of diverse levels of ability to manipulate the symbols of high aesthetic culture, the status claims of groups composing it may be reinforced. Thus the growing sophistication of nonelite publics requires a better quality of display, more scholarly selection of works, and a higher standard of public education. This public decries the amateurishness of the inheritors of wealth and their sycophants as much as they do the obstreperousness of a mass public. In this perspective, the sophisticated public is claiming legitimacy for its own distinction as a status group in relation on the one hand to dominant elites and on the other to the unsophisticated public, new to the museum world.

At the same time, however, we must remember that aesthetic culture itself is not reducible to reified categories but is constantly being redefined. Art now may include academic, craft, folk, pop, or mass cultural products. The redefinition of these products as *art* involves status groups composed of collectors, patrons, donors, and intermediaries such as dealers, experts, and critics, as well as creators, such as painters or composers. And art museums and their personnel, no less than other cultural institutions, are involved in the process of changing the definitions. One of the consequences is that even the curatorial goals have become more democratic as the museums welcome into their halls works that were not considered *art* until they were granted entry: African "primitive" works, folk art, comic strips, and even industrial artifacts. The outcomes are a change in the nature of the experience they provide, as well as a change in the characteristics and expectations of their public.

Thus the real world of art museums is characterized by the ongoing interplay of forces, both internal and external, that resist reductive conclusions, whether based on functional systemics or hegemonic analysis. As with other organizations, empirical reality suggests that the dilemmas created by the competing goals built into their very structure promote modifications with consequences unforeseen by their initiators.

NOTES

1. This is an outlook that pervades most of the structural-functional analysis of Talcott Parsons, as indicated, for example, in his *Structure and Process in Modern Societies* (Glencoe, Ill.: The Free Press, 1960).

2. Howard S. Becker, *Art Worlds* (Berkeley, Calif.: University of California Press, 1982).

3. Pierre Bourdieu, *La Distinction: Critique Sociale du Jugement* (Paris: Editions de Minuit, 1979). [An English language edition is available as *Distinction* (Cambridge, Mass.: Harvard University Press, 1984).]

4. Implicit in Bourdieu's outlook is the idea of hegemonic control over dominated status groups in society. See, for example, his *L'Amour de l'Art: Les Musées d'Art Européens et leur Public* (Paris: Editions de Minuit, 1966). For a far more radical and heavy-handed analysis, see Nicos Hadjinicolaou, *Art History and Class Struggle* (London: Pluto Press, 1978).

5. The analysis of the aura of art and the ambiguities of its potential loss in the world of modern technology are discussed in Walter Benjamin's famous essay, "The Work of Art in

the Age of Mechanical Reproduction," published in *Illuminations* (New York: Schocken, 1969). The subject is further probed in Bourdieu, 1966, op. cit.

6. Frederick Antal, *Florentine Painting and Its Social Background* (London: Routledge & Kegan Paul, 1948); Benjamin, op. cit.; Bourdieu, 1966, op. cit.; Herbert J. Gans, *Popular Culture and High Culture* (New York: Basic Books, 1974); Arnold Hauser, *The Social History of Art*, 2 vols. (New York: Alfred A. Knopf, 1951); Pitirim Sorokin, *Social and Cultural Dynamics* (New York: American Book Company, 1937); Thorstein Veblen, *The Theory of the Leisure Class* (New York: Modern Library, 1931); Max Weber, *The Rational and Social Foundations of Music*, trans. Don Martindale et al. (Carbondale, Ill.: Southern Illinois University Press, 1958).

7. These themes are treated by the present author in "The Art Institute of Chicago: The Sociology of a Cultural Organization" (Ph.D. diss., University of Chicago, 1974), and more centrally in "Conflicting Visions in American Art Museums," *Theory and Society* 10 (1981): 103–125.

8. Peter M. Blau and W. Richard Scott, *Formal Organizations: A Comparative Approach* (San Francisco, Calif.: Chandler Publishing Company, 1962), 222.

9. Museums, as the analysis reveals, are a prime example for the paradigm suggested by Charles Perrow in his article, "The Analysis of Goals in Complex Organizations," *American Sociological Review* 26 (1961): 854–866.

10. For a fascinating and detailed social history of this phenomenon, see Richard A. Altick, *The Shows of London* (Cambridge, Mass.: Harvard University Press, 1978).

11. See Zolberg, 1981, op. cit., and Magali Sarfatti Larson, *The Rise of Professionalism: A Sociological Analysis* (Berkeley, Calif.: University of California Press, 1977).

12. An early but neglected work dealing with this conflict is Hugh D. Duncan's *Culture and Democracy* (New York: Bedminster Press, 1955).

13. On the impact of the French Academy on the cultural policies of a number of European countries, see André Corvisier's *Arts et Sociétés dans l'Europe du XVIIe Siècle* (Paris: Presses Universitaires de France, 1978). For the commercial side, see Altick, op. cit.

14. Karl E. Meyer, *The Art Museum: Power, Money, Ethics* (A Twentieth Century Fund Report) (New York: William Morrow, 1979); Janet Minihan, *The Nationalization of Culture: The Development of State Subsidies to the Arts in Great Britain* (New York: New York University Press, 1977).

15. Neil Harris, *The Artist in American Society: The Formative Years, 1770–1860* (New York: Braziller, 1966); Lillian B. Miller, *Patrons and Patriotism: The Encouragement of the Fine Arts in the United States, 1790–1860* (Chicago, Ill.: University of Chicago Press, 1966).

16. This ambiguity is brought out both in Zolberg, 1974, op. cit., and with particular cogency by Paul DiMaggio in "Elitists and Populists: Politics for Art's Sake," *Working Papers for a New Society* (September–October 1978); "Cultural Entrepreneurship in Nineteenth-Century Boston (Chapter 2, this volume); and "Cultural Entrepreneurship in Nineteenth-Century Boston, Part II: The Classification and Framing of American Art," in *Media, Culture, and Society* 4 (1982): 303–322.

17. César Graña, "The Private Lives of Public Museums: Can Art Be Democratic?" in *Fact and Symbol: Essays in the Sociology of Art and Literature* (New York: Oxford University Press, 1971).

18. Walter Muir Whitehill, *Museum of Fine Arts, Boston: A Centennial History*, 2 vols. (Cambridge, Mass.: Harvard University Press, 1970), Vol. 1, 298–299.

19. Calvin Tomkins, *Merchants and Masterpieces: The Story of the Metropolitan Museum of Art* (New York: E. P. Dutton, 1973).

20. Eugenia R. Whitridge, "Art in Chicago: The Structure of the Art World in a Metropolitan Community" (Chicago, Ill.: Ph.D. diss., University of Chicago, 1946), 121; and John Maxon, *The Art Institute of Chicago* (New York: Harry N. Abrams, 1970).

21. Whitridge, op. cit., 113 and 121.

22. This is apparent whether viewed from the outside (Zolberg, 1974, op. cit.; Graña, op. cit.) or as inadvertently revealed by one of its own high officials (Maxon, op. cit.).

23. DiMaggio, 1982, op. cit.

24. This was the case not only in art museums (Zolberg, 1974, op. cit.) but in other types of museums as well, as shown by Geoffrey Hellman, *Bankers, Bones and Beetles: The First Century of the American Museum of Natural History* (New York: The Natural History Press, 1968).

25. Zolberg, 1981, op. cit.

26. Joshua Taylor, speaking at a meeting of the College Art Association in 1973, illustrated the built-in conflict between democratic goals and the concern of traditional publics for museum artworks.

27. Zolberg, 1974, op. cit. Bourdieu goes beyond the museum and fine arts alone to analyze the creation of valued meaning with respect to other forms of culture. See, for example, his "La Production de la Croyance: Contribution à une Economie des Biens Symboliques," in *Actes de la Recherche en Sciences Sociales* 13 (1977): 3–43.

28. Richard Muhlberger reported these results of a survey to the College Art Association meeting in New York in 1973. A detailed account of the debate on this subject is found in Zolberg, 1974, op. cit.

29. Zolberg, 1974, op. cit., p. 169.

30. Robert Coles provides poignant evidence on this subject in his contribution, "The Art Museum and the Pressures of Society," in Sherman Lee, ed., *On Understanding Art Museums* (Englewood Cliffs, N.J.: Prentice-Hall, 1974).

31. Bourdieu, 1977, op. cit.

32. This is a recurrent concern, as shown in publications of the American Association of Museums, especially in *The Belmont Report* (Washington, D.C., 1965) and their *Directory of the United States and Canada* (Washington, D.C., 1965). Not surprisingly, these issues were even more strongly emphasized in the years when the government was launching programs to subsidize museums. That public agencies are aware of the necessity for objective assessments is equally clear from the support by the National Endowment for the Arts of the indispensable study by Paul DiMaggio, Michael Useem, and Paula Brown, *Audience Studies of the Performing Arts and Museums: A Critical Review* (Washington, D.C.: National Endowment for the Arts, 1978).

33. Lawrence Vail Coleman, *The Museum in America: A Critical Study*, 3 vols. (Washington, D.C.: American Association of Museums, 1939).

34. This is the estimate provided by Muhlberger, op. cit.

35. Zolberg, 1974, op. cit., 169.

36. Theodore Low, *The Museum as a Social Instrument* (New York: Metropolitan Museum of Art, 1942), is the source of these quotations. As recently as 1979, Karl Meyer, (op. cit.) found similar outlooks to be common.

37. Zolberg, 1974, op. cit., Chapter 6.

38. Dick Netzer, *The Subsidized Muse: Public Support for the Arts in the United States* (New York: Cambridge University Press, 1978).

9

The Elusive Promise of Management Cooperation in the Performing Arts

MARC R. FREEDMAN

Management cooperation among nonprofit performing-arts organizations is an intuitively attractive notion capable of eliciting wide rhetorical support from these organizations and their funders. This is not surprising: Nonprofit arts organizations are unfettered by antitrust regulations, are dedicated by charter to the public interest, and often labor under severe financial constraints. Compared to the for-profit sector, then, the barriers to effective cooperation among nonprofits seem quite low, and the potential payoffs high.

The surprise is that despite such strong attractiveness in theory, few successful instances of cooperation by performing-arts organizations can be found. A wide disparity exists between cooperative rhetoric and cooperation's record.

This chapter seeks to illuminate this disparity, and to do so through focusing on one of the most prominent, and most representative, incarnations of cooperation: the attempt by performing-arts centers to provide central management services to their resident groups.[1] The legacy of this examination is a robust appreciation of the strategic, economic, and political factors that impede, and commonly cripple, well-intentioned cooperative initiatives.

The chapter proceeds in three parts. The initial section chronicles past and present attempts at centralized management. It is followed by an analysis of this experience. The concluding section looks at some lessons distilled

For encouragement, ideas and commentary, I am indebted to Paul DiMaggio and Patricia J. Doyle. I would also like to thank Michael Hoffmann, Carol Thomson, Michael Bailin, Natalie Jaffe, Alex Hoffinger, and Lisa Mannelia for their valuable assistance. Research and institutional support from Yale University's Program on Non-Profit Organizations, the Cleveland Foundation, and the Yale School of Organization and Management is gratefully acknowledged.

from centralized management, applying them more broadly to suggest alternative avenues for future collaboration and to advance an assessment of cooperation's prospects as a strategy for improved management in the performing arts.

THE ORDEAL OF CENTRALIZED MANAGEMENT

Attempts at centralization of basic management functions in the performing arts have proven difficult to implement and sustain. At the outset, however, this outcome is well masked by the seemingly good sense of cooperation. The candidates for centralized services—symphonies, dance companies, theatre groups, and other nonprofit arts organization—generally share a performing-arts center and are required to execute the same basic administrative functions. These tasks, such as bookkeeping and accounting, marketing, box office operations, scheduling, and purchasing, require staff time and attention. Pooling responsibility for such tasks is, in theory at least, a means of saving money through achieving economies of scale.

Performing-arts centers have been the most common vehicle for management cooperation. These centers are usually the sole point of intersection among the resident groups. Centers must perform the same management functions as their constituents. And they often appear unentangled with the competitive ambitions of these groups. Consequently, performing-arts centers have seemed the logical choice to provide combined services to their member organizations.

Yet despite these apparent advantages, efforts at centralization have almost invariably resulted in frustration. Asked about appropriate instruments for encouraging collaboration between performing-arts centers and resident groups, William Severns, recently retired administrator of the Music Center of Los Angeles County, suggested that "a long, black, buggy whip and chair" should be mandatory equipment.[2] His cynicism reflects the viewpoint of many performing-arts center directors who, after identifying common ground with their constituents, have frequently found themselves thwarted in efforts to provide centralized services.

Severns' Music Center, currently home to the Los Angeles Philharmonic, the Mark Taper Forum, the Los Angeles Master Chorale, and the Joffrey Ballet, opened its doors in 1964, offering a range of cooperative services, including accounting, advertising, and box office operations. The resident groups participated briefly, but the arrangement soon crumbled as these groups withdrew.

More recently, the Music Center attempted to persuade residents to agree on a single unit to handle all television contracts for performances at the facility. The idea received initial endorsement, but when negotiations got underway, disagreement among the parties made it impossible to close a single contract. The effort was soon jettisoned.

Another attempt at centralized management was mounted at the Milwaukee Performing Arts Center, where, in the mid-1970s, Managing Director Archie Sarazin created the Performing Arts Advisory Service to manage nonprofit resident groups. The Service managed the Milwaukee Ballet briefly, and then disbanded.

Other, less ambitious efforts have fared no better. In Syracuse, New York, for example, the Civic Center of Onondaga County has been unable to institute even joint purchasing arrangements among constituents. This should not be taken to mean that joint purchasing cannot work; however, the Syracuse example does reveal how difficult even the most simple forms of collaboration can be to introduce.

For every case in which collaborative management efforts have been tried and failed, there are several in which cooperation has not left the ground. New York's Lincoln Center is instructive in this regard. Powerful and established performing-arts companies, instrumental in establishing the Center, shaped its management structure and carefully restricted it from intervening in member group operations. The Metropolitan Opera, the New York Philharmonic, and the New York City Ballet have retained their independence, even managing their own performing spaces within Lincoln Center. Like the major residents of Los Angeles' Music Center, each of these groups handles its own box office.

In contrast to the quick demise of cooperation in Los Angeles or the congenital abstention of Lincoln Center, San Francisco's performing-arts groups have pursued a course of evolutionary withdrawal from management sharing. The three major constituents of the San Francisco War Memorial complex were once thoroughly intertwined. The San Francisco Opera and the San Francisco Symphony shared a manager in the 1950s, and the San Francisco Ballet was a division of the Opera. The arrangements proved poorly suited to the growth and transformation of the companies in the 1960s and 1970s and eventually dissolved. During the summer of 1983, the last vestige of cooperation was shed when the Opera and Ballet decided to discontinue shared computer services. Both organizations had achieved a level of activity, complexity, and specialization that justified ownership of their own computer, and they moved to take advantage of this opportunity for independence.

As the preceding overview suggests, the record of performing-arts centers in providing unified administrative services for their member organizations has been consistently bleak despite variation among centers in the nature of their constituencies, the quality of their management, and the historical trajectories of their local performing-arts worlds. The ubiquity of failure in such varied sites suggests that the usual practice of blaming the manager or local idiosyncracies when cooperative efforts founder is misleading. Instead it is necessary to look for common elements in the organizational and political environment of collaborative management plans. For this purpose, two reasonably well-managed, but only partially effective, attempts to institute extensive administrative centralization, the Atlanta Arts Alliance and the Kentucky Center for the Arts, warrant close examination.

The Atlanta Arts Alliance represents the most durable and comprehensive attempt at centralized management in the performing arts. Because of its age, the Alliance is often upheld as a model for collaboration of this type. It was the product of a disaster, a tragic 1962 plane crash in Paris that killed 122 prominent members of Atlanta's arts and cultural community. The principal purpose of the Alliance was to preserve the Atlanta Symphony, the Atlanta College of Art, the High Museum, and the Alliance Theatre through the difficult period following the crash. These organizations relinquished their status as independent nonprofit corporations and joined together under the umbrella of the new Alliance.

The Alliance manages an arts center created as a memorial to the victims of the crash, operates a united arts fund-raising campaign, and provides accounting, payroll, recordkeeping, subscription, and box office services for its member organizations, called "divisions." Alliance management approves all budgets for these divisions to ensure that they are balanced.

Measured against the backdrop of most collaborative management efforts, the Alliance is a shining success: It has certainly passed the test of time, surviving for more than two full decades. Its history has not been an entirely happy one for the divisions, however. In fact, the Alliance's durability may reflect, more than anything else, division managers' fears about alienating private funders in a region where noncorporate private and public funds for the arts are scarce. Robert Woodruff, the Coca-Cola magnate who has given over $30 million to the Alliance since its inception, is reputed to have made his sponsorship contingent upon the continuation of merger among the member organizations. According to Alliance Executive Vice President Beauchamp Carr, funders "who do not understand the arts, and who believe them to be badly managed because they lose money each year," have pressured the Alliance for continued centralization of management.[3]

The Alliance has performed credibly in raising funds and administering the performing-arts center. But it has stumbled in providing central management services to the divisions. Charles Yates, who resigned as the Alliance's top administrator in 1984 after serving through the 1970s, was a skillful fund-raiser who focused on development. At the same time, the divisions—and their management requirements—were growing rapidly. Between 1981 and 1984, for example, the total annual Alliance budget grew from $12 to $20 million, a tribute to Yates' fund-raising success and an indication of the divisions' increased size, complexity, and growing management needs.

According to Thomas Bacchetti, vice president of the Alliance and managing director of the Atlanta Symphony, accounting services have been "woefully inadequate . . . we don't get the information we need and we pay a lot for it."[4] Andrew Witt, Managing Director for the Alliance Theatre Company, agreed, complaining about the time lag involved in obtaining "simple" budgetary information.[5] Such difficulties are perhaps inherent in the attempt to manage organizations as diverse as a symphony and a museum with 52-week-a-year schedules, a theatre company organized around seasons, and an educational institution operating on the semester plan. But they are consequential nonetheless. Of necessity, the residents have formed shadow administrative structures that perform many of the same functions as the Alliance. The strain in the Alliance, at least until recently, has been considerable. In July 1983, Bacchetti predicted that the Alliance would "spin apart due to the centrifugal motion of its members."[6]

In 1984, Don Gareis, a career Sears executive, was appointed president of the Alliance. He began to address the organization's management difficulties, commissioning a long-range plan for the Alliance and convening a management group consisting of managers from the four divisions. He has also supplied each division with two personal computers to handle specialized information and to supplement the services provided through the Alliance's mainframe.

The Alliance affords a study of centralized management imposed and perpetuated from the outside and reveals the complexity of serving four very different organizations at the same time. Although new leadership is likely to alleviate some of the tensions emerging out of this arrangement, it remains to be seen whether the complex and growing configuration of arts organizations can continue to be managed effectively by a central unit.

If Atlanta's member organizations were forced together by necessity, the Kentucky Center for the Arts has elected to exhort and entice its constituents to experiment with cooperative management. When the Center opened in November 1983, it offered expertise in accounting, box office management, and program printing to its resident groups: the Louisville Orchestra, the Louisville Ballet, the Kentucky Opera Association, and the Louisville Children's Theater. It has been the Center's intention, as it matures, to enlarge this menu of services, all of which are provided on a voluntary, fee-paying basis. The Center's director, Marlow Burt, has attempted to create strong incentives for members to participate, hiring expert financial and computer personnel and implementing a sophisticated computer system.

Burt's program has had several factors operating in its favor. The Center opened with a management team that for four years had been working as a unit with participating groups in designing the center and its operating systems. Louisville arts organizations have a long history of collaboration in fund-raising, as evidenced by the Greater Louisville Fund for the Arts, founded in the late 1940s. Perhaps most important, Burt, as director, has earned the respect of the resident group managers and crafted an intelligent and flexible approach to cooperation.

Despite these advantages, only box office services have been voluntarily accepted by the resident members, and implementation of these services has been plagued with difficulties. Burt has been forced to pressure residents to use the program printed by the center, departing from the original intention of offering services exclusively on a voluntary basis.

The Kentucky Center's experience underscores the difficulty of inspiring resident groups to participate in centralizing their management functions, as the Atlanta case illustrates the difficulty of imposing cooperation. In different ways, both Louisville and Atlanta represent propitious settings for implementing effective cooperative management. The following section attempts to unravel why it is that neither has been, on balance, completely successful.

THE ORGANIZATIONAL DYNAMICS OF CENTRALIZED MANAGEMENT

The key to explaining the ordeal of cooperation is in understanding why it is that performing-arts groups resist, refuse, and impede implementation and continuation of centralization. This question is rendered more perplexing by the rhetorical enthusiasm for cooperation, not only among expected proponents like performing-arts center directors and private funders but among managers of performing-arts group as well. Andrew Witt, managing director of the Atlanta Ballet, asserts that "groups could realize tremendous benefits through working together."[7] His counterpart at the Atlanta Symphony, Thomas Bacchetti, acknowledges that "some joint activities would undoubtedly be useful."[8] Although Mark Light of the Louisville Ballet rejected the Kentucky Center's accounting services and holds strong reservations about the Center's ticketing and program printing efforts, he joined forces with the Louisville Orchestra to purchase a computer. According to Light, performing-arts groups can cooperate effectively when "they have considerably sympathy of interests and knowledge of each other's needs."[9]

In order to address the reasons this enthusiasm does not translate well into practice, it is necessary to undertake a larger examination of the impetus for and objectives of cooperation. After setting this context, the position of performing-arts groups can be better viewed.

Impetus and Objectives

Centralization of management functions is rarely an evolutionary development. Rather, it is overwhelmingly the product of some major event that provides an opportunity for reorganization. The two most prominent forms of impetus are the opening of a performing-arts center (as in Louisville) or the occurrence of a debilitating crisis (as in Atlanta).

The creation of a performing-arts center militates toward collaboration in several ways. It places constituents together, often for the first time, bringing into sharp relief the promise of cooperation in such operational functions as scheduling, purchasing, and box office services. Furthermore, performing-arts centers often purchase computers and management software that participating groups would like to use but cannot afford independently, creating another obvious area for joint endeavor. Attempts to introduce centralized management systems have followed closely the opening of performing-arts centers in Louisville, Los Angeles, Denver, Cleveland, and many other locations.

Crisis is the other common impetus to centralization. The Atlanta plane crash that produced the merger of four major arts organizations is an unusually dramatic example. A less tragic and more recent occurrence in Hartford likewise illustrates the power of crisis to produce centralization.

In 1982, the floundering Hartford Ballet, poised on the rim of bankruptcy, with loan repayments in jeopardy, received corporate and public support on the condition that it enter into a de facto merger with the Connecticut Opera and Hartford Chamber Orchestra. A special committee drawn from the boards of the organizations involved established a contractual union for three years, with George Osborne, formerly the Opera's manager, serving as general director in charge of all managerial functions for the three participating groups.

If efforts at centralization are usually occasioned by dramatic events, their proponents tend to share certain objectives. The primary goal of centralization is efficiency: in the management of groups, in the management of the arts center, and in the distribution of philanthropic dollars. A secondary goal, almost as common, is the desire of arts funders and performing-arts centers for greater control over the operations of resident organizations.

The underlying argument for consolidation of management is the promise of enhanced efficiency through economies of scale and administrative rationalization. In theory, it should be less expensive for a central unit to produce services for several users than for each of those users to produce the same services on its own. The cost per unit should drop as fixed costs are spread and duplication and inefficiency are banished.

For funders, economies of scale represent an opportunity to stretch philanthropic dollars further and to promote better operations, especially if, as is often the case, they perceive rampant waste and mismanagement. In the words of Atlanta Arts Alliance president Dan Gareis, corporate and other private funders will not happily "tolerate duplication and inefficiency."[10]

For the performing-arts center, centralization offers the prospect of reducing fixed cost, particularly for administrative staff and special equipment, and for expanding the center's role in the arts community. Louisville's Marlow Burt states this view succinctly: "Millions of public dollars have been spent on the Center. Its responsibility transcends simply operating a building. Simultaneously, resources are scarce and can be conserved by centralizing several management services through the Center."[11]

A less prominently discussed objective of centralization is control, especially when confidence of donors in the management of arts organizations is weak. In Hartford, the merger placed control over all operations in the hands of an administrator who had inspired confidence in funders and board members, and it removed authority from the previous managers. From the standpoint of funders, centralization allows easier monitoring of management performance, because formerly diffuse responsibilities and systems are lodged in a single place and executed through a single set of procedures.

Similarly, managers of performing-arts centers seek to increase the dependence of their member organizations because they are concerned about establishing the importance and indispensability of their own institutions and because they prefer to have control over organizations with whom their centers occasionally compete. And providing such services, especially financial services, gives the center administration access to information about the member organizations that may be useful in negotiations.

For their part, performing-arts groups have been almost invariable suspicious of plans for managerial consolidation and have stiffly resisted attempts to implement them. Their suspicions are often discounted by arts-center managers and the funding community. For example, many performing-arts center directors attribute general resistance from resident groups to what Milwaukee's Archie Sarazin identifies as the "egos" of arts managers.[12] Marlow Burt suggests that cooperation would be easier if arts managers had "more confidence in their own ability and the Center's ability."[13] Atlanta's Don Gareis calls for more "trust" by participating groups in the Alliance's intentions and capacity.[14]

These statements reflect the service providers' response to the puzzling failure of potential clients to rally around what appears, from the providers' perspective, to be a technically irrefutable proposition for enhanced operating efficiency. Like most such explanations, they focus on the attributes of persons—suspiciousness, egotism, or incompetence—rather than on structural factors. However, the core problems the arts-center managers face are universal and unlikely to be explained on grounds of personality. Without a doubt, some egotism exists in the performing arts, and group managers are not impervious to its touch; certainly, more confidence and trust on the part of these managers would advance the prospects of cooperation. But to understand the surprising failure of coordination in the delivery of administrative services to performing-arts organizations, it is necessary to move away from *ad hominem* explanations and focus on the strategic, political, and organizational context in which such efforts occur.

Contrary to the conventional wisdom within the arts community, especially among arts funders and performing-arts center directors, resistance on the part of performing-arts organizations to cooperative administrative services is based on sound, if not particularly systematic, management thinking. The managers of participating groups question not only centralization's unanticipated strategic and political consequences but its basic operational advantages. This response occurs on two levels. It originates in general concerns about cooperation and its potential impact on competitive position, autonomy, and managerial effectiveness. And it focuses on the objectives and organization of centralization, as one specific incarnation of cooperation. These layers of resistance will be examined in turn.

Resistance to Cooperation

It is difficult to overestimate the intensity with which many performing-arts organizations view themselves to be in competition with other companies, for audiences and, more fiercely, for contributed income. This competition has a visceral feel to it and can be traced in large measure to survival instincts and the constant, gnawing sense of not having enough money to continue operating in a viable manner. Under these circumstances, most groups perceive a frustrating dynamic in which the gains by one organization in grants or audiences must come at the expense of the others. Whether or not this widely held view (the opposite of which is invariably expressed at public convocations of arts supporters) is accurate—and the evidence on this point is far from clear—even the perception of competition is a substantial impediment to the sharing of management services.

There are two reasons for this. First, centralized services make it impossible for a participating organization to employ innovations that will give it a competitive edge. Second, centralization creates at least the possibility that some participants will receive better services than others, thus placing competitors at a disadvantage. (That these somewhat contradictory worries coexist in the minds of many arts managers is evidence less of irrationality than of the tension surrounding the issue of competition.)

The threat of reduced autonomy also figures prominently in resistance to cooperation and is related to the reality of competition. Organizations are wary of cooperative arrangements that may constrain their ambitions for the future or endanger their control over public image or the confidentiality of financial data. Groups are extremely wary of having their image diluted, even in subtle ways.

Finally, many administrators have legitimate concerns about the actual (as opposed to theoretical) efficiency of coordination. Coordination of services creates direct costs in the form of fees to the service-providing arts center; indirect costs in staff time devoted to negotiations with the arts center and other members and to monitoring of center services; and, in the worst case, direct costs involved in duplicating unsatisfactory services in-house. Managers also worry about the quality of service, especially if they believe that extricating their organizations from a cooperative arrangement may incur the wrath of corporate or public funders.

The prospects of lost competitiveness, reduced autonomy, and managerial inefficiency loom over any cooperative initiative. In order for the constructive participation of performing-arts organizations to be secured, these concerns must be either defused by careful attention and effective handling or overcome by the potential benefits of the collaborative project. As the upcoming section contends, centralization is not able to succeed on either count; its allure for performing-arts groups is limited and its manner of delivery exacerbates the inherent reservations of these groups.

Resistance to Centralization

Participating performing-arts organizations question the efficiency of centralization and the reality of its apparent economies of scale. This is not simple quibbling, because the primary objective of centralization is enhanced efficiency in the execution of basic management services. The centerpiece of the managers' position is that proposed basic functions cannot be easily standardized, especially when participating groups are diverse, structurally different, or growing. The specialized needs of diverse groups, they argue, will either be ignored, at the expense of participants, or will clog the system, rendering it cumbersome and expensive to maintain. Allen Cowen, president of the Greater Louisville Fund for the Arts, a united arts fund, suggested that coordinated management systems may actually cultivate "diseconomies of scale."[15]

The Atlanta Arts Alliance's troubled efforts to accommodate the needs of the Symphony, Alliance Theatre, High Museum, and College of Art illustrate this problem. Division managers have not been satisfied with the quality or timeliness of services, despite the Alliance's impressive financial staff and powerful computer system.

Another example of the difficulties of standardization can be located in the Louisville Orchestra's participation in the Kentucky Center's single-ticket box office services. All of the groups involved in the service have had technical complaints; however, the Orchestra's dissatisfaction has ranged further. According to its General Director Karen Dobbs, the Orchestra has "had problems with the Center's box office services because our patrons were not able to receive preferred seating through the service. Furthermore, we felt the tickets needed to look better, and did not reflect the image we are trying to maintain."[16]

This case is particularly striking because box office services can be classified—along with scheduling and purchasing—as a relatively simple form of centralization, unencumbered by many of the complicating factors that afflict marketing and financial management and, as such, are technically somewhat more susceptible to standardization. In fact, single-ticket services are the only form of centralization that has taken hold in the performing arts; they are currently in effect at Playhouse Square (Cleveland), Heinz Hall (Pittsburgh), Kennedy Center (Washington, D.C.), the Brooklyn Academy of Music, the Denver Center for the Performing Arts, and the Tulsa Performing Arts Center, as well as the Kentucky Center.

Negotiating contracts, contending with dissatisfaction, and attempting to bring about change consume substantial amounts of staff time for both the arts center and its member organizations. What is more, the participating organizations must allocate staff time to monitor the arts center's performance of routine services on a daily basis. Once sacrifices in flexibility, response time, and coordination costs are factored in, the efficiency of centralized management is less than obvious.

Consolidated management systems also threaten to incur long-range costs for participating organizations that eventually withdraw from the system. Member organizations are reluctant to have expertise in basic administrative functions lodged in the performing-arts center, outside their own four walls. The externalization of expertise increases their dependence on the center since withdrawal would require an investment of start-up costs to regain competence in the functions that the arts center had performed.

Furthermore, even if centralization does increase efficiency, this advantage is not in itself likely to galvanize performing-arts managers into action. Most arts administrators focus on entrepreneurship and growth. They recognize the value of cutting costs, but when reducing expenses incurs risks and increases uncertainty, they are more inclined to pursue possibilities for new revenue.

The vehicle for administering cooperation is as important as the kinds of services that are provided. Efforts to centralize management have usually cast performing-arts centers as central service providers. However, resident groups have been dubious about the suitability of performing-arts centers for this role.

Competition exists not only among member organizations but between performing-arts groups and the arts center as well. Performing-arts centers play many roles, and some of these impinge upon the role of service-provider. Centers are landlords and producers. They often promote events that compete with the programs of their resident groups, such as concerts by visiting symphonies or dance companies; and they negotiate with member groups over rent and service charges. In many cities the arts center seeks contributed funds from the same corporations, foundations, and public agencies as does it constituents. Consequently, performing-arts managers worry about systems of management sharing that could leave them beholden to a competitor for basic services.

Managers of member organizations also express concern over the arts center's management capacity. Many centers propose centralizing services when they are themselves brand new, with little experience in managing even their own operations. Participating groups also wonder whether a management system established to administer a building is suited to an organization that must act swiftly and in an entrepreneurial manner. This point is probably not a strong argument against the center's capacity to undertake joint purchasing, for example, but it is more compelling in areas like financial management and marketing.

THE PROSPECTS OF COOPERATION

The principle lesson of centralization is that cooperation is not easily accomplished. Performing-arts groups are steadfastly inclined toward independence, wary of cooperation's unanticipated consequences and dubious about its hidden costs. Although it is not easy to convince groups to abandon their independent orientation and concerns about cooperation, the frustrating experience of centralization should not be taken to preclude other forms of cooperation. No clear model or body of knowledge about successful cooperation exists, but interest in cooperation is alive in all quarters, and there are cooperative initiatives arguably more successful than centralization. United arts funding, for one, has been far more durable and widespread. The joint purchase of equipment, in particular computer technology, has inspired numerous ad hoc arrangements, as well as an ambitious automation consortium currently being mounted in Hartford. These other cooperative endeavors temper, somewhat, the cynicism that unfolds from an examination of centralized management's record.

As previously stated, for any form of cooperation to succeed in securing the active interest and sustained participation of arts organizations, it must overcome the tests of competition, autonomy, and efficiency. By keeping these impediments in view, and by employing the shortcomings of centralization as points of departure, it may be possible to chart some more promising avenues for future cooperation.

Objectives

The primary objectives of centralization—efficiency and control through consolidation of basic management services—are not sufficiently important to performing-arts groups to galvanize them into cooperation. If anything, these objectives are inclined to sharpen resistance.

Cooperation is more likely to work when its basic objectives are to provide access to new markets or opportunities where all participants stand to gain, yet none can penetrate independently. Corporate and workplace giving campaigns by united arts funds are one actual example of this approach; another possibility resides in regional marketing.

United arts funds are mechanisms for raising operating support for collections of arts organizations, usually through an annual fund-raising campaign. Many funds target corporate giving and are able to deliver support that would be arduous, if not impossible, for groups to tap independently. Access to corporate officials is limited, and corporations are so numerous that approaching them is a labor-intensive exercise. Corporate funders respond well to a coordinated appeal rescuing them from hours of agonizing deliberation over many proposals. Another activity of many united arts funds, workplace giving campaigns, illustrates how access to potential contributors can be far more likely for a consortium operating under a broad banner, "The Arts," than for a single organization.

Regional marketing also falls into this category. It is difficult for a single performing-arts organization to institute effective marketing designed to draw visitors from outside its metropolitan area because the expense of advertising beyond the local community is likely to exceed additional revenues received. Furthermore, a visitor who comes to see the ballet, for example, may spend the weekend, attending the theatre and visiting the museum as well. When this happens, a free-rider problem develops: Other groups benefit from the ballet's regional advertising without having to bear any of its cost. A regional marketing consortium can avoid this dilemma by distributing costs across all the organizations that stand to benefit.

Organization

The prospects of centralization have not been advanced by the performing-arts center's role as service provider and coordinating agency. The centers are poorly suited strategically, politically, and technically for the task.

The organization of any form of collaboration will have an important impact on its chances of success. The two basic criteria for an effective arrangement are functional capability of accomplishing the substantive goals of the project and political acceptability to participants.

A carefully crafted organizational model for cooperation, designed to address both of these criteria, can be found in the governance structure of Hartford's Arts Automation Consortium (AAC). The AAC is a network developed by the Greater Hartford Arts Council to provide computer equipment and expertise to six participating organizations.

The governance plan provides for three levels of management. Policy is determined for the AAC by an autonomous six-member governing board, composed of one member from the board of each of the six major users. Operational oversight is provided by a six-member management committee, composed of the general manager of each user. Daily administration is the province of a full-time computer-systems specialist. This arrangement, which is too new to evaluate, is structured to allow regular input and monitoring from participants.

Catalysts

Centralization has suffered from both too much impetus and not enough impetus as illustrated by the counterpart cases of Atlanta and Louisville. Atlanta reveals that funders can enforce cooperation if they are so disposed, but that they cannot mandate its success. Louisville shows that a voluntary appeal based on quality of services will not move groups to join forces.

Funders have a key, but delicate, role in aiding effective cooperation. They can bring organizations to the table in order to initiate discussions about common ground and the prospects of cooperative projects. They can underwrite these early explorations with grants to hire consultants and perform feasibility studies. Finally, they can commit support for ventures that meet their specific criteria. Initiative and leadership throughout, however, will have to reside with the participants. Otherwise, no cooperative initiative will take root.

CONCLUSION

While all of these alternative approaches to cooperation merit further experimentation and study, optimism should be guarded. First, most of them are untested. And second, even if the cooperative project has been well conceived, based on appealing objectives, built on a sturdy institutional arrangement, propelled by funding support, and led by a diplomatic partisan from one of the participating performing-arts groups, the project's success will still depend on a number of factors; for example, whether potential participants have a history of good relations and whether the relative size and power of these participants is conducive to a compatible combination.

Moving from the critical perspective of analyzing centralization to the more prescriptive outlook of the last section only serves to underscore a basic point threaded throughout this chapter: Despite the wide rhetorical appeal of cooperation, this organizational strategy is, in reality, only viable under fairly narrow circumstances. It appears that the banner of cooperation, if waved high enough, will elicit universal applause; as specific plans come into focus, however, a bewildering set of complications are revealed. These complications call into question cooperation's essential promise as an vehicle for improving management and expanding resources in the performing arts.

NOTES

1. This study is based on three rounds of telephone interviews with arts managers and performing-arts center directors in Atlanta, Louisville, Hartford, Milwaukee, Los Angeles, Denver, New York, Syracuse, Washington, D.C., San Francisco, Cleveland, and Pittsburgh. These interviews were conducted between July 1983 and May 1984 and during two-day site visits to Atlanta, Louisville, and Hartford in April and May 1984. In addition, audited financial statements, public relations materials, and newspaper articles were examined in the course of this study.
2. William Severns, former administrator, Los Angeles Music Center Operating Company, telephone interview, July 1983.
3. Beauchamp C. Carr, vice president, Atlanta Arts Alliance, interview in Atlanta, Georgia, May 1984.
4. J. Thomas Bacchetti, executive vice president, Atlanta Symphony, telephone interview, May 1984.
5. Andrew M. Witt, managing director, Alliance Theatre Company/Alliance Children's Theatre, interview in Atlanta, Georgia, May 1984.
6. Bacchetti, op. cit., telephone interview, July 1983.
7. Witt, op. cit.
8. Bacchetti, May 1984, op. cit.
9. Mark Light, managing director, Louisville Ballet, interview in Louisville, Kentucky, May 1984.
10. Don Gareis, president, Atlanta Arts Alliance, interview in Atlanta, Georgia, May 1984.
11. Marlow Burt, executive director, Kentucky Center for the Arts, interview in Louisville, Kentucky, May 1984.

12. Archie A. Sarazin, managing director, Milwaukee County War Memorial Performing-Arts Center, telephone interview, July 1983.

13. Burt, op. cit.

14. Gareis, op. cit.

15. Allen H. Cowen, president, Greater Louisville Fund for the Arts, interview in Louisville, Kentucky, May 1984.

16. Karen Dobbs, general director, Louisville Orchestra, interview in Louisville, Kentucky, May 1984.

10

Financially Troubled Museums and the Law

NANCY L. THOMPSON

The financial problems of art museums are ubiquitous. "Escalating costs," writes Philippe de Montebello, director of the Metropolitan Museum of Art, "constitute the most acute problem facing museums today."[1] Stephen E. Weil, deputy director of the Smithsonian Institution's Hirschhorn Museum, states the problem even more baldly: "In terms of operating funds," American museums "are—for the most part—broke."[2] Museums' financial woes are also timeless. In his classic study, *The Museum in America* (1939), Laurence Vail Coleman, then director of the American Association of Museums, complained, "Museum income is never adequate. The necessity for making it as large as possible rests upon every institution without mercy."[3]

Although, in recent years, no major U.S. museum has been forced to shut its doors because of inability to pay debts, there is nonetheless a widespread fear among museum professionals that the economic crisis is worsening. A comprehensive national study of museums, undertaken in 1979 by the National Institute for Museum Services, disclosed that 1 in 10 museums, and almost 1 in 5 art museums, suffered operating deficits in its last fiscal year. More than one-third reported that over a quarter of their collections were in serious need of upkeep. During the previous year, one-third of these museums had reduced their level of activity because revenues had not kept up with inflation.[4]

Most large museums rely on income generated by invested endowment to balance their budgets. Traditional views of fiduciary responsibility have counseled a high degree of conservatism in the investment of such funds. Moreover, museum directors or trustees must heed restrictions that donors have placed on the types of investment that can be made, despite the fact

This chapter represents an extensive revision of a paper written while the author was a student at the Yale Law School.

that many such restrictions reflect a preinflationary era of stable investment returns and price levels.[5]

The inflation of the 1970s forced modern investment managers to seek more productive investments in order to maintain revenues in times of inflation. Several museums have adopted creative strategies for using endowment funds. In the early 1970s, the Museum of Modern Art began to appropriate a fixed percentage of the average market value of its funds (usually based upon an average long-term yield) as income for use in payment of expenses, regardless of the actual dividends and interest received. The Metropolitan Museum has adopted the fixed rate of return method as well, despite the fact that when the investment portfolio does poorly, the museum must advance funds from endowment principal in order to finance expenditures, a practice that has engendered some criticism.[6]

For some museums, however, efforts to institute more advanced financial practices, to implement creative approaches to enhancing earned income, or to find new sources of contributed revenues simply do not work. Such museums, for a time at least, may enter into a financial crisis and resort to severe measures. Each of these strategies may bring directors or trustees into contact with the judiciary, and with a body of statutory and case law that is both confusing and inconclusive. Directors and trustees whose institutions face severe financial constraint may discover that the law limits their options in unexpected ways. The purpose of this chapter is to summarize the legal environment that museums face, suggest some ways in which museums may respond to extreme financial exigency, and offer some solutions to the disputes that have vexed jurists and legislators in their treatment of charitable trusts and nonprofit corporations.

The timeliness of the topic is reflected in the many museums that have closed galleries, shortened their hours, or reduced spending on upkeep and art conservation, and in frequent news accounts of museum financial difficulties. It is reflected, as well, in the substantial number of cases in which state attorneys general have entered litigation against museum trustees or directors, charging them with wasting or mismanaging assets, or misusing their discretion. In almost every such case, such allegations rest in part on the fact that the museum in question had been operated at a consistent deficit, allegedly to the detriment of undermaintained collections and an underserved public.[7]

Such cases raise important legal questions about the fiduciary responsibilities of museum trustees and directors to the public and to the donors from whose lifetime and testamentary gifts the endowment funds originated. The answers to such questions affect the flexibility with which museum trustees and directors can meet the challenges of operating under financial constraints. The pages that follow explore the legal implications of three strategies, in order of increasing stringency, that museums in severe financial straits may find themselves exploring: reduction of services and the invasion of capital to cover operating costs; invocation of the legal doctrines of deviation and *cy pres* to alter the terms of the trusts from which museums benefit; and dissolution of the organization, through merger with another museum, dispersion of collections, or bankruptcy. Before addressing these strategies directly, however, we must look briefly at the broad legal context within which these nonprofit institutions operate.

THE AMBIGUOUS LEGAL CONTEXT OF MUSEUM GOVERNANCE

The legal situation of museums is complicated by the fact that there are both public and private museums. Although this chapter is concerned primarily with the latter, even here diversity creates complexity; for some private museums are charitable trusts, whereas others are nonprofit corporations.[8]

Charitable trusts are created by an individual donor for the benefit of the public. Property given in trust is managed by trustees, who have traditionally been held to the strict standards of care, skill, and loyalty imposed upon trustees of private trusts. Trustees are expected to observe conservative standards of investment, have not been permitted to delegate management authority to others, and have been held strictly accountable for their actions. Such trustees are permitted to depart from the ordained purposes and uses of the trust only with judicial authorization.[9]

Nonprofit corporations are chartered by the state and must report periodically to state officials on their financial status. They are in many ways a hybrid between charitable trusts and for-profit corporations. For example, they may hold some assets in trust, others outright. It is estimated that nearly 70 percent of art museums are set up as charitable trusts governed by private nonprofit foundations.[10]

To complicate matters even further, consensus over the treatment of nonprofit corporations has eluded judges and legal scholars. As Henry Hansmann has argued, "The basic corporate law applicable to non-profit corporations is at a remarkably immature state of development, and remains startlingly uninformed by either principle or policy."[11] Nonprofit corporation law is currently a muddled hybrid of inconsistent principles borrowed, respectively, from trust and corporate law.

To What Fiduciary Standards Are Museum Trustees Held?

There is no unanimity as to whether the standard of fiduciary duty to which the directors of a charitable corporation are to be held is that applied to trustees of private or charitable trusts or rather that observed by the directors of for-profit corporations. This distinction is significant because traditionally the former have been held to higher standards of fiduciary duty than have the latter.

In general, however, the trend in recent years has been for courts and legislatures to hold the directors of charitable or nonprofit corporations to the standards of fiduciary duty that must be observed by the directors of for-profit corporations. This is the so-called business judgment rule, which allows the directors more freedom in investing the assets of the corporation and in delegating management duties to subordinates than had historically been permitted trustees of a charitable trust.[12] The corporate standard of duty has been applied to nonprofit corporate directors by the American Law Institute-American Bar Association (ALI-ABA) model Non-Profit Corporations Act (1964). Under such a standard, trustees are allowed considerable discretion in investment decision making.[13]

The functions of such trustees are, in many cases, indistinguishable from those of their business counterparts, for they supervise their organizations' income-earning activities and, increasingly, are permitted to delegate investment authority, another form of business activity.[14] More generally, courts seem prepared to adhere to the following rule in scrutinizing trustee behavior. "Trustees having the power to exercise discretion will not be interfered with so long as they are acting bona fide. To do so would be to substitute the discretion of the court for that of the trustee."[15]

This liberalization of standards is important, for it gives trustees more flexibility in investing and using endowments. For example, it opens the way to the use as income of realized appreciation on endowment principal, a practice permitted on a limited basis by the Uniform Management of Institutional Funds Act, which has been adopted by several states. (By contrast, conservative opinion still holds that such funds may only be spent with explicit judicial authorization.)

Despite the general trend towards liberalization, a pair of recent cases involving educational institutions may have held trustees to more rigid standards than apply in the corporate sphere, subjecting their decision making to factual scrutiny and repudiation. In the Wilson College case *(Zehner* v. *Alexander)*, for example, the judge found that trustees lacked the authority to close a financially troubled college.[16] He criticized the practices of the board on several specific counts, chiding it for delegating too little managerial authority, developing an ineffective student recruitment strategy, and cutting clerical assistance—all actions that would seem to be within the discretionary exercise of business judgment.[17] Such judicial scrutiny would not be applied to the business judgment of a for-profit corporation's board of directors that had decided to dissolve the corporation, for example.

In a somewhat similar case *(AAUP* v *Bloomfield College)*, a nearly insolvent college laid off several tenured faculty members in order to save money. Ruling in favor of the plaintiff professors, the trial judge discerned bad faith in this action, then went beyond this specific finding to contest the trustees' assertion of financial exigency, noting that the college held a valuable golf club that it could sell to raise funds in lieu of dismissing faculty. The appeals court agreed with the finding of bad faith in the faculty dismissal, but held that the lower judge's statements about the golf club were inappropriate: "The exercise of the business judgment whether to retain or to sell this valuable capital asset was exclusively for the board of trustees of the college and not for the substituted judgment of the court." Indeed, the appeals court held that it was up to the trustees, not to the court, to determine when the college was in a state of financial exigency.[18]

Trustees continue to exercise their best business judgment in managing their institutions; however, the unresolved ambiguity of the laws governing charitable corporations may at least in theory permit courts to intrude at their discretion into the realm of trustee decision making, in their role as protector of the public welfare.

Who May Sue Nonprofit Museums?

The court may not, however, act *sua sponte* (on its own initiative) to supervise philanthropic organizations. It may only adjudicate disputes involving them if these have been brought before it by the attorney general of the relevant state or by persons having special interests in the performance of a charitable trust (for example, a group of trustees). Nearly all states authorize the attorney general to oversee the fulfillment of fiduciary duties by directors of charitable trusts and corporations; only 15 states, however, require charities to report to the attorney general annually on their financial status.[19]

Exemplary of a state attorney general's procedure in enforcing a charitable trust is the litigation involving Chicago's George F. Harding Museum, *Scott* v. *Silverstein*. In that case, the Attorney General successfully alleged that the museum was being mismanaged by its directors in breach of their fiduciary duties, in that

> the directors failed to display museum artifacts to the public, in violation of the museum's corporate charter, mismanaged museum assets by purchasing investment real estate, consistently operated the museum at a deficit, awarded each other excessive salaries, and secretly sold a painting from the museum collection . . . [and that] museum artifacts were deteriorating because of mismanagement.[20]

It is not clear, however, just what degree of trustee mismanagement is necessary to move an attorney general to action. Operating deficits alone have never inspired an attorney general to sue. But annual reporting statements revealing consistent operating deficits may invite the scrutiny of attorneys general and suggest the presence of mismanagement in more tangible ways.

Although attorneys general are permitted not just to monitor nonprofit museums but also to investigate them, the language of state statutes authorizing such investigation generally is permissive rather than obligatory. Actual practice varies from state to state, depending on the attorney general's prosecutory zeal and the resources that his or her office possesses.[21]

In most states, taxpayers lack standing to sue for the enforcement of charitable trusts; the rationale is that frivolous litigation by those without any genuine interest in the institution might harass nonprofit organizations and overload the judicial process.[22] In the case of *Weigand* v. *Barnes*

Foundation, for example, a taxpayer sued a Philadelphia art museum to compel its officers to alter admissions rules which, she claimed, so limited access to the foundation's galleries as to defeat the purposes of the trust that created it. The court ruled that "in the absence of statutory authority, no person whose interest is only that held in common with other members of the public can compel the performance of a duty owed by the corporation to the public."[23]

By contrast, parties deemed to have special interests in the performance of a trust have been granted standing to sue to enforce trust principles. Active trustees, for example, have been granted standing to sue their fellows on behalf of the corporation.[24] Founders of trusts or their heirs, however, are generally empowered to sue only if the founder explicitly restricted the donation so as to maintain a clear interest in its disposition. In such suits, the attorney general must join as a party.

In recent years, several jurisdictions have illustrated a willingness to broaden standing to parties other than the attorney general. In *Jones* v. *Grant,* a state supreme court granted standing to a college's students, staff, and faculty to sue the directors to force them to account for the misuse of federal and church funds.[25] Similarly, in *Stern* v. *Lucy Webb,* the judge granted standing to plaintiffs in a class action suit against a hospital on grounds that they, "purporting to represent a class of users of the hospital's services, have a sufficient special interest to challenge the conduct of the trustees operating this charitable institution on a theory of breach of trust."[26]

By analogy, the *Jones* case suggests that a museum's members and other donors might be able to sue in order to ensure that directors observe requisite fiduciary duties of care, and the *Stern* case suggests that standing might accrue to anyone who used a museum by visiting it.

The single recent case of which the author is aware involving standing to sue a museum for breach of trust, *Rowan* v. *Pasadena Art Museum,* ended inconclusively.[27] Former trustees of the museum sought standing to sue Norton Simon and other current trustees of the museum for allegedly violating their fiduciary duty to uphold the museum's charter by replacing the museum's formerly modernist exhibitions with art works from Simon's own collection. The former trustees sought to sue even though the state attorney general had not granted them relator status, which would permit them to institute a proceeding in the name of the attorney general. The court in this case, however, disposed of the lawsuit on the merits and therefore did not rule expressly on the issue of whether such formerly involved parties had standing.

Henry Hansmann has argued that broadening standing, in accordance with the holdings of the *Stern* and *Jones* cases, to include patrons and clients of charitable organizations would strengthen the rationale for applying business-corporate, rather than private-trust, standards of fiduciary responsibility to nonprofit corporation trustees. (The risk that a more liberal standard of care would generate more lawsuits seems to be minimal, for those states that already have broad standing rules have experienced no torrent of frivolous litigation.) Business boards, after all, are subject to suits from stockholders, which act as a check on director discretion. Because charitable trustees experience no comparable threat of litigation, they are reasonably held to the higher trust standards of fiduciary responsibility.[28]

In sum, then current case law is murky with respect both to the standards under which nonprofit corporate trustees operate and the classes of plaintiffs that possess standing to sue. One happy solution to this ambiguity would be the establishment of business-corporate rather than trust fiduciary standards and the broadening of standing to include nonprofit organizations' clients and patrons. The former would offer trustees sufficient latitude and flexibility to deal creatively with fiduciary adversity, whereas the latter would ensure that they be held accountable for their decisions.

REDUCING COSTS AND CONVERTING ASSETS

In cases of extreme financial exigency, museums have employed at least three strategies that, undesirable as they may be, are deemed to be preferable to seeking a court-sanctioned change in the purposes of the trust or in the charter of the museum or to dissolving the museum altogether. These strategies include cutting costs by reducing services, selling parts of the collection, and using capital for daily operating expenses. Let us consider the legal implications of each of these strategies, one at a time.

Reducing Services: How Many Costs Can a Museum Cut and Still Be a Museum?

Museums may shorten their hours, close their galleries, and curtail the services they offer to the public. At some point, however, the museum that pursues such cost-saving strategies may violate implicit or explicit terms of its charter and thus evoke judicial notice.

The nature of a museum's obligations to its public depends upon the specific charter or trust indenture by which the museum was founded. Apart from the individual requirements of these documents, however, there exists a tacit understanding of what a "museum" must provide in order to be considered a museum.

The Association of Art Museum Directors, for example, defines a museum as "a permanent, nonprofit, institution . . . which acquires objects, cares for them, interprets them, and exhibits them to the public on some regular schedule."[29] The voluntary accreditation program of the American Association of Museums requires that to claim museum status, an institution must exhibit its collection "to the public on some regular schedule, e.g., regular and predictable hours which constitute more than a token opening, so that access is reasonably convenient to the public."[30] Such access is required because "objects in tax-exempt institutions are held in trust for the public . . . they are the cultural property of the public, both present and future."[31] Although neither of these definitions bears the force of law, both of them reflect the current state of professional opinion as to the minimum a museum must offer its public.

In several cases, actions by trustees that severely restricted public access to the museums they managed prompted attorneys general to sue them for breach of trust. In both of the two most notable cases, those involving the Barnes Foundation and the Harding Museum, specific terms of the founder's trust seem to have been violated by the trustees. In both cases, however, judicial language implies that a generalized *public* interest was being violated as well.

In *Commonwealth* v. *Barnes Foundation,* the court found the trustees to be in violation of their trust indenture because they denied the public access to the Barnes Foundation art gallery despite the donor's stipulation that "the plain people . . . shall have free access to the art gallery and the arboretum on those days when the gallery and arboretum are to be open to the public," but at most two days a week.[32] The museum, which contained a valuable collection of Baroque and Impressionist works, claimed tax exemption yet made access to the collection almost impossible. In addition to finding a specific violation of the trust indenture, the court went on to note that because the Barnes Foundation was granted tax exemption as an institution of public charity, it was obliged to open its doors to the public at least some of the time.

This case suggests that tax exemption could be withdrawn from a museum that had so limited public access that it, in effect, had ceased to function as a public institution. It is unlikely that such sanctions would be taken against any museum whose restrictions on access result from a financial incapacity to remain open. Certainly no judicial enforcement action was contemplated against the Detroit Institute of Arts when a municipal crisis closed it for a month in 1975 and resulted in long-term reductions in gallery hours.

Nonetheless, extreme and open-ended cutbacks of museum services may be grounds for judicial action. In his complaint against the board of trustees of Chicago's George F. Harding Museum, the Illinois attorney general charged that the museum violated both the terms of the founding donor's trust and the public's implicit right of access to the museum because it had placed most of the collection in a warehouse, permitting the public to see only a small portion of it, and that by appointment only. The attorney general contended, "the Museum's artifacts and assets have not been fully utilized for public appreciation."[33] The museum directors, argued that the Harding was a "teaching museum" and that the collection was being used for teaching purposes.[34] The articles of incorporation of the Harding Museum, however, stated its purpose as "the accumulation and perpetuation of knowledge of ancient arts and sciences, for the improvement of the mind by the collection, preservation and exhibition of ancient and authentic objects," thus supporting the interpretation of the attorney general.[35]

In a somewhat similar case, a perceptible decline in the public services offered by Long Island's Vanderbilt Museum prompted the New York attorney general to scrutinize trustee management of that institution. The investigation disclosed some evidence of possible impropriety on the part of the trustees, who were political appointees. But the genesis of the investigation was the museum's decreasing ability to render to the public the services to be expected from a museum. The American Association of Museums had recently voted to suspend the Vanderbilt's accreditation because of "inadequate care of facilities and collections," which were uncatalogued, unprotected from heat and humidity, and, consequently, deteriorating. (The Museum's executive director attributed this plethora of problems to inadequate funding.) Apparently this museum had fallen beneath the functional level deemed adequate to serve the public trust.[36]

A state legislature, too, may enforce a minimal definition of the word "museum." A recent addition to the California Tax Code, for example, exempts museums from a use tax on the purchase of art objects if they open their galleries for a certain number of hours and welcome the public free of charge on a regular basis.[37]

Deaccessioning

Museums may also seek to channel fixed assets, be they endowment monies, physical property, or artworks, into forms and functions in which they can be immediately useful in paying operating expenses. In particular, art museums often become repositories for more than art works of quality. Well-meaning but tasteless benefactors may donate works of art of less than exhibition quality. Or the museum may have upgraded its collection so that mediocre works that once formed its core are no longer needed. Because collections demand space, protection, and maintenance, it seems sensible for the museum with precarious finances to "deaccession" (the museum profession's euphemism for "sell") artworks that are unexhibitable and unwanted.

Whether a museum may sell undesirable artworks in order to raise operating funds depends on the terms under which the art was acquired. The Hirschhorn's Stephen Weil argues that any artwork that a museum purchases out of unrestricted funds should be available for deaccessioning for any purpose as the trustees deem necessary.[38] In contrast, the College Art Association's 1973 "Resolution Concerning the Sale and Exchange of Works of Art by Museums," issued in the wake of controversy over the New York Metropolitan Museum's deaccessioning of portions of its DeGroot Collection, warned that "works of art should be considered for sale or exchange only for the purpose of expanding or increasing the value of the collection, not for operating expenses or building funds."[39] Indeed, most formal deaccessioning policies provide that proceeds from sold works of art may be used only to purchase other works.[40]

Such policies serve as a bulwark against allegations that museum are wasting assets, since, in effect, the artworks are simply being traded. And when applied to artworks donated without restriction, such conservative policies reassure donors and their heirs that the donative intent to make art available to the public will be perpetuated, even if the art itself has changed. Nonetheless, maintenance of an overly large collection may operate to the detriment of public access if, for example, funds from selling artworks are used solely to buy others rather than to build quarters large enough to exhibit all of the art or to pay operating costs for the facility. Under such circumstances, more flexible policies may be in order.

If trustees supervise deaccessioning and observe corporate standards of care and discretion, it is unlikely that an attorney general would investigate a good-faith decision to sell artworks from unrestricted sources and to channel the proceeds into operating funds.[41] It is possible, however, that a court might conclude that past trustees, by earmarking general funds for specific uses, have created a binding charitable trust that precludes later sale of assets in order to turn the proceeds to another use. In *Authors Club v. Kirtland,* for example, a literary club had received a bequest from Andrew Carnegie and with it established a general fund to aid indigent writers.[42] When club members resolved to use the fund to defray ordinary operating expenditures, later donors, who had contributed to the fund in reliance upon the apparent restriction of the purpose for which it would be used, sued. The court supported the plaintiffs, holding that a restricted charitable trust had been created and could not be used for other purposes. To forestall such interpretations, boards employing general funds to purchase fixed assets should explicitly reserve the right to use them for different purposes at a later date.[43]

Deaccessioning of unrestricted artworks may raise other legal issues, however. If an artwork, originally purchased out of general funds, is sold, only subsequently to soar in value, could trustees be charged with wastage of assets? Presumably if the transaction were made in good faith, following a business judgment standard of care, the museum directors would not be liable for such a decision.[44]

Some critics of deaccessioning have predicted that if museums adopt the practice of selling art to meet operating deficits, the government might make future financial aid contingent upon the museum's willingness to take such a drastic measure. For example, public agencies might demand that museums sell art from their collections as a self-help measure before becoming eligible to receive matching public funds.[45] Another observer fears that publicly owned collections supported by public and private funds might be pirated by politicians, who could force the routine sale of art to meet operating expenses.[46] It seems probable, however, that existing safeguards are adequate to forestall such occurrences, for such abuses would trigger both public outcry and the scrutiny of the state attorney general, acting in the public interest.

Up to now, we have considered deaccessioning only those works of art that the museum purchased out of general funds or received without restriction. The deaccessioning of artworks that have been donated with specific restrictions is another matter. The complaint filed by the Illinois attorney general in the Harding Museum case, for example, alleged that the defendants "intentionally and in disregard for the corporate charter have sold a valuable original painting from the museum collection for the purpose of raising monies to offset the wrongful and recklessly incurred annual deficits."[47] The attorney general made special note of the fact that the revenues were earmarked for operating funds, arguing that "a fundamental rule of museum management is that the proceeds of the sale of artifacts donated to the collection should be used for new acquisitions and not for the general support of the museum."[48] Similarly, when the Metrolitan Museum of Art sold off much of the collection of Adelaide Milton De Groot, the sales provoked an investigation by the New York attorney general. Although the De Groot bequest was precatory rather than binding in its stipulation that the Metropolitan donate to other museums such works as it did not wish to keep, the museum ultimately agreed to make its future sales of artwork public.[49]

How can museum trustees best manage necessary deaccessioning without running afoul of the law? In general, museum trustees planning to deaccession unrestricted artworks should establish priority lists based on the manner in which the artworks were acquired (e.g., from unrestricted funds, directed, bequest, or other means) and based on the quality of the works themselves. Perhaps, in addition, art historians could be consulted as experts to assess, to the extent possible, the relative quality of artworks proposed for deaccessioning so that only the most mediocre works would be removed from the collection. Artwork donated under restrictions on future use should be sold only in the event of the gravest exigency and then, whenever possible, only after securing approval from the donors or their heirs. Out of deference to the donors' original intent, every effort should be made to use proceeds from the sale of artworks directly for the benefit of the remaining collection, for example, for better climate controls, lighting, or conservation facilities, all of which directly support the preservation of art for the public's enjoyment and appreciation.

Trustees may also attempt to sell works to institutions within their own community, so that the local public may continue to enjoy it. However, such a strategy might interfere with the trustees' concomitant obligation to use the museum's assets as efficiently as possible and thus to receive the highest possible price the work could command on the open market. If the highest bidder should be a private purchaser, could the trustees be held liable for injuring the local public interest in being able to see the art? Presumably, this is a matter for trustee discretion. Existing cases suggest a judicial interest in keeping art that is to leave one institution within the same geographic area whenever possible.[50] But there is no indication that trustees would be liable if they failed to do so.

Using Endowment Principal to Pay Operating Expenses

Under certain circumstances, trustees may apply endowment fund principal to museum operating costs without soliciting prior court approval. In general, such use is permissible when funds are unrestricted, although the strategy is regarded as appropriate only when operating deficits are severe. For example, in 1979, the Brooklyn Museum incurred a substantial deficit when promised contributions for a special exhibition failed to materialize. In order to pay off the debt, the museum dipped into over $400,000 of principal from two unrestricted endowment funds at a sacrifice of over $20,000 in interest. Although there was adverse public comment, other evidence of the museum's financial plight (such as major cuts in department budgets) existed, and the attorney general did not initiate an investigation.[51] Indeed some museums invade endowment principal regularly: In one recent 13-year period, for example, the Museum of Modern Art spent $3 million of its endowment to meet current obligations.[52]

Several states have statutes governing the management of institutional funds which permit museums to utilize even restricted endowment funds by using realized appreciation for operating expenses. Nonetheless, "conservative opinion still holds that capital gains cannot be spent from restricted endowment funds without some sort of court proceeding."[53]

One observer has suggested that in those states that observe a business judgment standard of trustee responsibility, trustees may borrow principal from restricted endowment funds and transfer proceeds from its sale to the general purpose endowment in order to meet operating deficits. As long as the transaction is treated as an internal loan, at an appropriate rate of interest, and is likely to be repaid, such arrangements may pass corporate standards of scrutiny.[54]

It is not clear how widely such strategies for manipulating restricted endowment funds are employed, nor is it evident how courts would regard such nonconservative practices. Such uses of restricted funds would probably not be feasible in jurisdictions that still observe trust standards of fiduciary responsibility for directors of charitable corporations.

Moreover, it is obvious that the availability of such strategies as deaccessioning and use of endowment capital for operating expenses is dramatically limited by trust restrictions. It has been argued that gifts given with trust restrictions are detrimental to the public interest.[55] Museum directors agree, in principle. But it has also been estimated that over 90 percent of artworks in museums were donated with restrictions; monetary gifts are often similarly hindered.[56] To deal with such assets, then, museums must seek the aid of the courts. They cannot escape the strictures of long-dead donors at their own discretion. It is to this problem that we now turn.

USE OF DEVIATION AND *CY PRES*

There are two methods by which charitable trustees may deviate from the stated purposes of a trust in order better to effectuate the specific goals of a settlor or the needs of the trust or institution as a whole. A "deviation" permits trustees to alter the *administration* of a trust, for example, selling a certain piece of land held by the trust to raise income, even if the trust instrument has not provided for the sale of that piece of land. The use of *cy pres* permits trustees to alter the trust's *purposes* in order to serve a related or broader set of charitable ends if the original purpose for which the trust was established has become impossible to obtain.

The doctrines of both deviation and *cy pres* are premised upon the theory that "the testator would have desired that the property be so applied if he had realized that it would be impossible to carry out the particular purpose."[57] Trustees of a financially troubled museum may under some circumstances petition the courts to invoke one of these doctrines in order to free assets from restricted uses and apply them toward the more general benefit of the institution and the public.

Deviation

Restatement (Second) of Trusts § 381 provides that the court will direct or permit the trustee of a charitable trust to deviate from an administrative provision of the trust if it appears to the court that compliance is impossible or illegal, or if it appears that owing to circumstances not known to or anticipated by the settlor at the time the trust was established, compliance would defeat or substantially impair the accomplishment of the purposes of the trust.

Deviation is generally invoked to permit the sale or increased use of property to fulfill a specific goal of the donor. Under circumstances of fiscal exigency, the court may authorize a sale or mortgage of trust property in order to raise funds, or it may authorize use of principal to make up for diminished value of trust income.[58] Vermont law, for example, permits educational corporations to petition the court to use the principal of restricted endowments if they become unable to pay their expenses from current receipts.[59]

Courts will not authorize such sales or endowment invasion if they are not necessary for trust purposes; deviation demands that the petitioning trustee demonstrate that unless the court approves a liberalized use of funds the original purposes of the settlor in establishing the trust will be frustrated.[60] Numerous commentators, however, have urged liberalization of the doctrine in order to allow change from specific terms of a trust if the continued restriction of a fund would simply be inefficient or impractical for the institution.[61] Courts have, on occasion, so construed the doctrine.[62] Extension of such usage would permit art museums to free ample but restricted funds, given in trust for specified purposes, for application to purposes in greater need of resources.

Nonetheless, most courts have tended to hold to a conservative standard in permitting deviation. In two cases in the early 1960s, for example, courts held that changed economic conditions and general inflation were factors insufficient to warrant a change in the usage of museum funds.[63] These cases, however, predated the acute contemporary consciousness, cultivated by the inflation of the late 1970s, of the financial plight of charitable institutions with conservative or limited investment portfolios.

Harris v. *Attorney General* exemplifies the contemporary treatment of deviation in the courts.[64] Trustees of the financially strapped Hill-Stead Museum petitioned the court for permission to sell an auxiliary building in order to generate additional income for the trust. The court construed the donor's language regarding the use of the building as merely precatory; however, the court went on to conclude on its own initiative that the building was impractical as a museum, costly to maintain, and capable of providing needed income to the trust if sold. It concluded that change in the trust's financial circumstances justified the building's sale.

The court furthermore reinforced an earlier deviation that allowed trustees to spend trust principal as required to replace essential property. Finally, on a motion by counterclaimants that the trustees' financial inability to provide insurance had so impaired accomplishment of the testator's goals as to cause the trust to fail, the court concluded, somewhat circuitously, that because the donor perceived her art as unique and irreplaceable money could not adequately substitute for it; thus provision of insurance was held to be a matter for the prudent judgment of trustees. Throughout its opinion, this court expressed a strong interest in preserving the museum, which counterclaimants sought to close on grounds that the trust had failed. The court permitted deviations as necessary to ensure the institution's survival. The court did state, however, that principal was not to be used to maintain the property.

In another recent opinion, *In re Petition of Trustees of Hyde Collection,* the court concluded that keeping an art collection intact was more important than providing insurance, given the apparent terms of the donor's trust indenture.[65] The court suggested that the donor did not specifically require insurance but had instead relied on trustee prudence to care for the collection in the most practical way. Because endowment income was adequate to fund improved building security but not to carry insurance, the court permitted a diversion of funds to the former end.[66]

In a similar case, *Parkinson* v. *Murdoch,* a court permitted trustees to deviate from the terms of their trust by using principal to provide a curator for an art collection, reasoning that

> As a necessary incident to the carrying out of the expressed intention [of the donor] to provide an art collection which would last throughout the years, the trustees

also have a duty to see that the objects of art purchased are properly housed and cared for so as not to deteriorate. . . .[67]

In each of these cases, then, a court permitted a deviation from specific trust restrictions in order better to effect the testator's purpose of making the art available to the public in perpetuity.

Courts may also authorize curtailment of part of an art collection in order to protect the collection as a whole. In *Final Judgment in the Matter of the Application of the New York Historical Society for Modifications of the Thomas J. Bryan Indenture,* the court accepted the trustees' contention that external circumstances had so changed as to make literal compliance with the trust impossible (although they failed to describe those changed circumstances), and it permitted them to display only some artworks in a collection and to sell or exchange the rest, investing the proceeds in a fund for maintenance of the remainder and for acquisition of additional items.[68]

Deviation is often sought to permit the directors of a charitable trust to sell its site and move to another location because of insufficient funds for maintenance of the present building.[69] In *Watkinson Library* v. *Attorney General,* the court permitted a library to sell its decaying building because the funds left for its preservation generated insufficient income to maintain it.[70]

Many courts blur the doctrines of deviation and *cy pres* together in practice, failing to distinguish between administrative variations and substantive changes in purpose. In some jurisdictions, courts have rejected the *cy pres* doctrine only to use the doctrine of deviation in certain cases to the same end.[71]

In the early 1950s, for example, the Cleveland Museum had acquired more art than it had room to display and sought a declaratory judgment authorizing it to divert certain trust funds from their original purpose, the purchase of artworks, to the construction of a new wing to display the art. In its decision, the court strained nobly to give the trust funds a general purpose, writing

> The purpose of the settlors was a broad one . . . they aimed at helping to create and maintain an Art Museum which would endure indefinitely . . . In their day the most practical way for accomplishing their expansive purpose was to set aside funds for the acquiring of objects of art . . . today the museum's problem is quite different . . . now it is for an additional building. . . .[72]

The court thus concluded that although the settlors' purpose had not failed—the museum was thriving—a deviation of trust income to a building fund would reflect the donors' own inclinations given the changes in circumstance that they had not foreseen.

This liberal judicial view that restricted funds may be used to respond to changing needs would, if more generally held, be an invaluable asset to financially constrained museums. For example, such an application of the deviation doctrine might allow museums to deaccession and sell restricted artworks (with judicial approval) for a range of purposes. Museums that request court approval before deviating from restrictions on the use of their property also forestall subsequent investigation by enforcement agencies.

There appear to be no reported cases in which a museum has petitioned a court to sell restricted artworks in order to use the proceeds for operating expenses. Because rechanneling of investments, sale of physical plant, and redirection of restricted funds have all been approved as equitable strategies, however, sale of artworks would presumably fall under the same permissive rule. Given the public interest in the perpetuation of charities, courts would appear ready to permit some truncation of the museum's goals to ensure its survival. Presumably donors' intents would suffer more if a museum closed altogether than if it continued to display its art in a different way. As the court commented in *Scott* v. *Silverstein,* "the charitably minded would be discouraged by the sight of charitable institutions gradually closing.[73]

The *Cy Pres* Doctrine

If a simple change in administration of specific terms of a trust cannot suffice to salvage a financially troubled institution, its trustees may petition the court for application of the broader *cy pres* doctrine. Restatement (Second) of Trusts § 399 defines *cy pres* as follows:

> If property is given in trust to be applied to a particular charitable purpose, and it is or becomes impossible or impracticable or illegal to carry out the particular purpose, and if the settlor manifested a more general intention to devote the property to charitable purposes, the trust will not fail but the court will direct the application of the property to some charitable purpose which falls within the general charitable intention of the settlor.

Thus an application of *cy pres* could permit a museum to apply restricted funds to more practical uses. *Cy pres* is also invoked to distribute the assets of defunct charitable institutions in a manner that carries out the donor's intent as closely as possible.

Three conditions must exist before a court may invoke *cy pres* for a charitable trust: a valid charitable trust must exist, the settlor's particular purpose must have become impossible or impracticable of performance, and the settlor must be shown to have had a general charitable intent.

It is not always clear that a gift to a charitable corporation has created a charitable trust. Generally, if the property is restricted to a particular charitable purpose, a valid trust exists.[74] However, the general equitable interest in sustaining charities wherever possible requires that "if it is reasonably certain that the testator intended that the bequest be devoted to purposes of charity, even though there is no formal trust, a gift in trust will be implied."[75]

Impracticability of performance is also difficult to establish. In recent years, there has been some judicial tendency towards leniency in defining what is impracticable. Thus according to Restatement (Second) of Trusts § 399 (Comment q), *cy pres* may be applied when to carry out a specific purpose would fail to accomplish the general charitable intent of the settlor, particularly when there has been a change of circumstance after the creation of the trust.[76] Nonetheless, when the court finds the execution of the testator's stated purpose practical, it will generally fail to apply *cy pres,* even if the purpose is undesirable.[77]

Courts have usually been adept in liberally construing trust language to find a general charitable intent beyond the specific purpose for which property was given. "Equity is always more ready, in the case of a gift to a charitable institution which is no longer functioning, to infer a general charitable intention than to infer the contrary."[78]

Many of the cases of deviation previously described involved changes of sufficient magnitude as to fall plausibly under the *cy pres* doctrine. In practice, the line between the two doctrines is a thin one.

In *Application of Arms in re Louis Comfort Tiffany Foundation,* for example, a trust fund established to support an educational art institute and museum produced declining income, which proved increasingly inadequate to support the aging, deteriorating trust property. Upon petition, the court permitted the trustees to sell the physical plant and transfer the proceeds to the trust fund, with the income to be applied to the creation of fellowships for artists. It also authorized the trustees to create a permanent physical memorial to the founder as they saw fit, either by maintaining the art museum upon the property or by selecting art objects at their discretion to be given to other museums for display. The court treated its action as deviation, but it spoke of the donor's purposes as being "increasingly impossible," and by changing the purposes for which the trust fund and the art works were used, in fact, applied *cy pres* principles.[79]

In general, courts are becoming more flexible in their use of deviation and *cy pres,* especially when the survival of a charitable institution is at stake. Moreover, as jurisdictions increasingly accept use of the business-judgment standard of investment and management skill for trustees of charitable corporations, they may be less willing to interfere with trustee decisions about the rechanneling of restricted assets, and more willing to approve trustee petitions for *cy pres* upon lesser showings of need.

At the same time, continued judicial oversight is necessary to ensure that trustees do not depart too widely from trust restrictions in the use of assets. Ultimately, less formal instruments, such as court-appointed referees or administrative tribunals, might reduce the burden on the judiciary by entertaining petitions for equitable relief from obsolete trust restrictions.[80] For the present, museums should not neglect to use deviation and *cy pres* as devices for reallocating restricted assets to the greater benefit of the museum and its public.

CLOSING A MUSEUM'S DOORS

As we have seen, courts place a high value on the survival of charitable institutions and permit substantial alterations in the terms of trusts to that end. Nonetheless, museums' deficits may grow so large as to prevent continued operation, triggering the trustees to seek the termination of the trust or disgruntled creditors to bring dissolution proceedings against the museum. In recent years, several museums have quietly ceased to exist because they lacked adequate funds to pay operating expenses.[81]

Dissolution and the Law

Almost every state has codified statutory procedures for the voluntary or involuntary dissolution of nonprofit organizations.[82] Forty-eight states require that the attorney general approve the dissolution plan of a nonprofit organization, which includes its scheme for the distribution of assets remaining after payment of debts.[83] In most states, a *cy pres* distribution of remaining trust assets is required upon dissolution.

In 47 states, the attorney general may institute involuntary dissolution proceedings against a charitable organization upon grounds that vary from state to state and include insolvency, public injury, failure to report, and failure of purpose due to impracticability. Although extensive supervisory authority exists, however, it is exercised actively by attorneys general in only a few states, most notably Ohio, New York, California, and Illinois.[84]

New York's statutes, although more elaborate than those of most states, provide a useful illustration of legislative and judicial concerns. The Non-Profit Corporation Law generally allows either the director or the board members of a nonprofit corporation to petition for judicial relief if the corporation's assets are insufficient to discharge its liabilities. The supervising court may, at its discretion, appoint a referee to hear the matter or a receiver to manage the trust property. As necessary, the court may issue injunctions to restrain the corporation from disposing of its assets or to restrain creditors from harassing the insolvent nonprofit corporation. The attorney general is a necessary party to any judicial dissolution proceeding.[85]

If a museum chooses to dissolve or is compelled by proceedings undertaken against it to do so, it must dispose of its assets. In such cases, there is a natural tension between the rights of creditors to payment and the rights of donors to see the purposes of their gifts in trust fulfilled. State statutes usually rank the order in which assets are to be disposed. In New York, for example, N-PCL § 1005 of the Not-for Profit Corporation Laws provides that "after paying or adequately providing for the payment of its liabilities, the remaining assets of the corporation shall be distributed" in a manner consistent with the purposes of specific trusts that the organization holds. Such statutory language might seem to indicate that creditors are to be paid off first, even out of restricted assets if necessary. But no cases support such a conclusion, and general trust law principles protect property held under restricted trust from creditors.[86]

New York museums are chartered under the Education Law, which addresses the issue of museum dissolution more explicitly than does the more general New York statute governing nonprofit corporations. Section 220 of the Education Law provides that when assets are ready for disposal, art objects

> as far as possible shall not be sold but shall be tranferred to libraries, museums. . . . If there be any surplus moneys after payments of debts and expenses of liquidation, the court may direct that same be devoted and applied to any such . . . charitable or other objects or purposes as trustees may indicate by their petition. . . .

This statute suggests that artworks are protected from use to pay off creditors to a greater extent than restricted trust funds might be.

Such statutes for *cy pres*-like distribution of assets of charitable corporations often do not consider the intent of donors in making a distribution, instead simply attempting to transfer assets to a charity with a similar purpose. In *In re Will Goehringer,* for example, the court expressly distinguished between *cy pres,* which it characterized as preeminently concerned with perpetuating the intent of the creator of the trust, and the dissolution statutes of the Education and Not-for-Profit Corporation Laws, which seek to transfer assets to another charitable corporation with similar purposes.[87]

This approach to distribution of assets is not limited to New York. Internal Revenue Service regulations (§ 1.501(c)(3)-1(b)(4)), for example, require as a condition for tax exemption that should a charitable foundation dissolve, its assets are to be distributed to another exempt purpose or revert to federal, state, or local government for use in the public interest. Similarly, § 46 of the ALI-ABA Model Non-Profit Corporation Act requires that, upon dissolution, assets "held . . . subject to limitations permitting their use only for charitable . . . educational or similar purposes . . . be transferred or conveyed to one or more . . . organizations engaged in activities substantially similar to those of the dissolving corporation."

Hansmann has criticized the vagueness of the Model Act and its many statutory imitators. It is unclear, for example, whether "limitations" refers only to those imposed explicitly by donors or, more broadly, to the implicit expectations of donors of nonrestricted gifts that their donations will be devoted to charitable ends. Indeed, Hansmann argues, "the restriction might be read to apply to all assets held by a nonprofit corporation . . . however acquired . . . [on the] theory that any organization that holds itself out as serving charitable purposes is impressed with a constructive trust, and therefore holds its assets 'subject to limitations.' "[88]

Read most broadly, then, the law would seem to protect even artworks purchased with unrestricted funds from being sold to satisfy creditors. Despite its high valuation of charitable purposes, however, the law is also concerned with proper payment of debts; it is thus unlikely that such an extreme view would prevail.

In voluntary dissolutions, distribution of assets is planned by trustees (with the attorney general's oversight) and submitted for approval to the court. If dissolution is undertaken at the behest of creditors or the attorney general, a receiver often designs the distribution plan.[89] Even when the trustees or the receivers act in good faith, the court is under no obligation to accept the plan submitted, even if the attorney general has approved it.[90] The attorney general may challenge the details of any divestiture plan proposed by trustees. Potential beneficiaries of the distribution do not have standing to challenge such plans, however.[91]

Judicial Prohibition of Dissolution

In several cases, courts have overruled trustees' use of discretion and refused to permit the voluntary dissolution of a nonprofit corporation, concluding that the public interest is better served by keeping the institution open. In *Zehner* v. *Alexander* (the Wilson College case), the court concluded, first, that the trustees' decision to close the college represented an alteration of the fundamental purposes of the institution, thus requiring judicial scrutiny under the *cy pres* doctrine;[92] and, second, ruled, as a matter of fact, that the college's purpose had not failed and that consequently the trustees could not shut it down.[93] Similarly, in *Application of New York Law School,* the court denied the trustees' application for dissolution of the institution, finding that the law school had "done its work well" and that there were too few other law schools in the area to accommodate all prospective students.[94]

In *Conway* v. *Emeny* (earlier litigation involving the Hill-Stead), the court found that trustees had acted in bad faith in seeking to dissolve a landmark historic house museum, the Hill-Stead Museum.[95] Although the donor had provided that trustees should have "absolute discretion" to terminate the museum and transfer the assets to another charity if public interest in the museum flagged, the court found that the trustees, in so deciding, were tainted by their interest in the other charity. Because the court felt that there was a strong public interest in the institution and that it "enjoys a wide reputation and is highly regarded by experts," it construed testamentary language to confer upon itself the right to restrict the trustees' decision, and hence to refuse to dissolve the institution.

The court also overruled the wishes of trustees in a more recent, and more complex case, *In re Estate of Hermann.*[96] Here a testator had established a museum trust and a separate testamentary trust to provide for the museum's maintenance. After several years of operation, the museum's trustees petitioned for termination of the museum trust on grounds that the physical plant was decaying, funds were insufficient for renovation, and only one person a month was visiting the museum. The first court to consider the matter ordered the sale of the museum's physical plant and transfer of the artworks to a local library for exhibition, but it refused to terminate the museum trust. Several years later, the testamentary trustees contended that the museum was no longer an "operating foundation." The court handling this matter went beyond the request made by the trustees and ruled that the museum trust had failed. It based this decision in part on the fact that it was alleged that the museum and its art had "been almost totally ignored by the public during the past five years" because the art was mediocre. The appeals court found that the trial judge had abused his discretion because he had

> terminated this trust for the sole reason that the art it is designated to support 'does not warrant the maintenance of a building' and that the public continues to ignore the display. . . . [I]t is difficult to conceive of a subject less appropriate for judicial review than the quality of an artistic work. . . .

Consequently, the appeals court held that the museum trust still existed. It stated that "It is apparent that the *objets d'art* exist, that adequate funds are now on hand to acquire land and to construct a building." It ordered the testamentary trust to continue to pay over its income to the museum trustees. In so doing, it sought to perpetuate the interests of the testator rather than to serve an expressed public interest.

These cases indicate that in deciding which interests should be protected and to what end, courts often exercise personal judgment. The judge in the Wilson College case, for example, upheld what he perceived as the public interest in keeping the college open, even at the cost of turning a small liberal arts women's college into a vocational community college. In *Hermann,* on the other hand, the appeals court perpetuated a donor's wish to display his art collection even though the public found it distasteful.

In some of these cases judicial involvement was generated by allegations of trustee misconduct. In cases where trustees' actions clearly constituted an abuse of their discretion, the court could properly intervene. In others, however, there were no clear indications of trustee misconduct, rendering questionable the court's substitution of its judgment for that of the trustees, for the court is authorized to reverse the decisions of trustees only if there is evidence that they acted in bad faith or arbitrarily and capriciously in an abuse of their discretion.

Distribution of Assets According to *Cy Pres* Principles

In some states, no statutes provide for the distribution of the assets of dissolving nonprofit corporations. In these states, courts may order the transfer of assets according to *cy pres* principles. Even when charitable corporations are deemed by state law to own the assets given to them absolutely (rather than holding them in trust), *cy pres* will apply for purposes of distribution.[97]

Case law indicates several judicial trends in the application of *cy pres* to the distribution of assets of dissolved institutions. First, the assets should be transferred to the site and setting most similar to that of the failed trust. In determining similarity, geographic proximity and similarity of purpose are equally valued.[98]

Second, if art is transferred, any trust funds out of which it has been maintained should be transferred as well. In *City Bank Farmers Trust Co.* v. *Arnold,* an art collection was transferred to Yale University by means of *cy pres* and the building that housed it was sold.[99] The court ruled that Yale should also receive the trust fund that the testator had established for the care of the art.

Not infrequently, a financially troubled museum's physical plant so decays that it can no longer properly house the art.[100] Courts seem quite willing at this point to authorize transfer of collections *en masse* to another museum. In some cases such a transfer is dealt with under the doctrine of deviation, as a change in the administration of a trust. When the art institution that formerly housed the collection is dissolved, however, it would seem that a change of purpose has occurred and that *cy pres* would thus be the appropriate instrument.

Courts have exhibited a strong interest in keeping transferred assets of dissolved art museums together; but the reported cases that reflect this tendency all deal with charitable trusts, formed by one person. The assets are thus arguably more coherent, or at least historically more linked together, than the vast collections of large generalist museums, which tend to be charitable corporations.[101]

The transfer of an entire collection to an analogous institution, however, may not necessarily keep it intact. In *Gordon* v. *City of Baltimore,* for example, the court applied the equivalent of *cy pres* to transfer the books from an insolvent library to another library nearby.[102] The court upheld the discretion of trustees in selling a large part of the collection which duplicated holdings in the new host library.

When nonprofit institutions dissolve, voluntarily or involuntarily, courts possess much potential supervisory authority. They can determine whether the organization should be permitted to dissolve and, if the museum does dissolve, how its assets should be distributed. Existing cases indicate that courts have not been reluctant to exercise this power, and in some cases have overridden trustee decisions in order to effectuate their visions of the public good.

Some states have enacted statutes that obviate the need to demonstrate a general charitable intent by donors in order for trust assets to be distributed to like institutions. Such statutes may help to streamline the distribution process and to remove that factual inquiry into donative intent that may bog courts down or afford them untoward discretion in reversing the decisions of trustees.

THE BANKRUPT MUSEUM

Up to now, we have been using the term "insolvency" to refer to severe financial exigency such that an organization cannot meet debts incurred in the ordinary course of business. The law also recognizes a second form of insolvency, "bankruptcy insolvency." An organization experiences bankruptcy insolvency when its aggregated property is not sufficient to pay its debts. This condition calls for a formal bankruptcy proceeding involving the marshalling of assets, their liquidation, and the distribution of proceeds pro rata among the creditors.

Because nonprofit organizations hold assets in trust, the simple framework of bankruptcy law cannot directly be applied to them.[103] Indeed, the federal bankruptcy bode (11 U.S.C. § 303(a)) exempts nonprofit organizations from involuntary bankruptcy proceedings.[104] Creditors who wish to sue for the assets of nonprofit corporations must therefore proceed under the applicable state insolvency laws.[105] Such reported cases of bankrupt nonprofit organizations as exist, for the most part, date from the Depression.[106]

Nonetheless, there are a few points of bankruptcy law that may be relevant to charitable corporations. First, mere organization under a nonprofit charter may not in itself exempt an institution from involuntary bankruptcy proceedings if the court finds that the volume of unrelated for-profit business activities pursued by the nonprofit corporation is sufficient to warrant loss of exemption.[107] There is no consensus on how dominant the for-profit activity need be to result in loss of exemption. If the institution is primarily eleemosynary and pursues profitable activities that are "substantially related" to its charitable purposes rather than representing in themselves its dominant pursuit, it ought to be exempt.[108]

According to 11 U.S.C. § 301, nonprofit corporations may enter voluntary bankruptcy proceedings. Very little case law exists regarding nonprofit bankruptcy, however.[109] As in other kinds of insolvency proceedings, the major questions have to do with the rights of creditors in relation to property held in trust. Can the community's interest in preserving art for public viewing, for example, be overridden by the interest of creditors in having their debts paid?

The law has placed a high priority on preserving charitable property.[110] If all assets of charitable corporations were protected from creditors, however, nonprofit organizations would effectively be immune from voluntary as well as involuntary bankruptcy, to the detriment of creditors and probably of nonprofit organizations as well, since few creditors might offer credit if they lacked the means to collect on debts. At the same time, naked exposure of museum assets to creditors could lead to dispersal of art works to the highest bidders, potentially from other countries or from private homes, in order to satisfy the creditorial appetite.

The 1978 Bankruptcy Code 11 U.S.C. § 541(b), provides that trust property may not be levied against by creditors.[111] Where assets were given with specific purposes, such restrictions protect them from the creditor's reach just as they would protect them from discretionary shifts in use by trustees. The issue again becomes one of breadth of definition: Should all art in a museum be regarded as tacitly held in trust for the public and thus protected from creditors? Will trusts be implied from any gift, or must the gift of artworks be made expressly in trust for the public?

Existing case law suggests that the unrestricted assets of charitable corporations are subject to the claims of creditors.[112] Outright gifts, too, seem to be subject to proper bankruptcy proceedings. In one case, for example, the court determined that income from a trust estate was itself being given outright, was not by trust terms held for restricted purposes, and thus could be levied against.[113] Generally, when trust income is to be applied for the use and benefit of an organization, courts of equity may direct the application of such income to the payment of debts. Courts have also permitted creditors to levy against physical assets held by charitable trusts or corporations if they are held without restrictions.[114]

What, then, of art which the museum has itself bought from unrestricted funds? Can it be levied against, or is it held pursuant to a binding public trust? To protect the public interest, it might seem that any art held by a museum should be protected from liquidation. But, as in deaccessioning, pragmatism would suggest that legitimate creditors of the museum deserve to be paid off as fully as possible. If all art were protected, any museum might with its last bit of cash buy artworks which would then be judgment-proof.

The case law holds that assets given with specific restrictions and purposes will be protected from creditors in bankruptcy. In *Hobbs* v. *Board of Education,* the leading case in this regard, the court found that the endowment funds of an insolvent college were charitable trusts and thus safe from creditors, because, in effect, they were not owned by the college. Such property was crucially different than property that the corporation could use freely for its own general purposes: "Where donations are made for the general purpose of carrying on a business of any kind, though in the form of a trust, the absolute control of the *res* being bestowed upon the donee, the property is liable for debts incurred for the purpose intended. . . ."[115]

Despite this protection, an insolvent museum could presumably petition the appropriate court for *cy pres* relief, which would free it from onerous trust restrictions so that it might more fully satisfy its creditors. Indeed, at least one commentator has advocated recognition of the authority of bankruptcy courts to exercise equitable *cy pres* power.[116] According to this line of argument, invocation of *cy pres* would be most useful in cases of reorganization of the bankrupt entity.

Certainly, in bankruptcy proceedings the interests of the public must be balanced against those of creditors. Perhaps the same experts who analyze the quality of artwork to be culled for deaccessioning purposes could be called in to evaluate the art holdings of bankrupt institutions. Those considered to be most important (by standards of excellence, popularity, or art-historical significance) could be transferred by deviation or *cy pres* to other museums and thus preserved for public enjoyment. The rest could be sold to satisfy creditors; wherever possible, they should be sold to other museums rather than to private collections, so as to preserve them to the greatest extent possible for the public.

CONCLUSION

> A museum does not "own" but, rather, is the steward of the art it possesses. . . . No charitable corporation may "own" corporate property . . . in a museum, it is the public that are the shareholders and museum trustees are legally accountable.[117]

Such trustee status is a mixed blessing for the museum. On the one hand, trusteeship protects the artworks that have been given in trust from being sold to satisfy creditors. On the other hand, by blocking the most efficient use and allocation of available resources, trust restrictions may seriously hinder the attempt of museum trustees to keep the institution solvent.

The financial problems that currently plague museums require clarification of the legal standards that govern museum affairs. Because of their necessary and increasing involvement in business activities, museum trustees should be held to the business-judgment standard of care and skill that applies to corporations that are run for profit. This standard—less burdensome that the one traditionally attached to private trusts—grants trustees a freedom of investment and management that could greatly facilitate efficient museum administration. At the same time, this standard prevents unwarranted judicial intervention into the good-faith exercise of reasonable business discretion.

Courts should extend acceptance of reasonable trustee business judgments into the provision of the equitable doctrines of *cy pres* and deviation. If trustees believe that restrictions on a fund or other asset harm the welfare of the museum, courts should be willing to consider applying these doctrines in order to free the assets for more efficient use, without requiring the trustees to show that the original purposes are impossible to fulfill. An expansion of standing to enable members and patrons to sue museum trustees for breach of fiduciary duties would adequately ensure that trustees would not abuse their power and would seek permission to change the use of restricted assets only when and insofar as necessary.

When museums must close, courts should continue to supervise the distribution of artworks to similar institutions for continued enjoyment by the public. To protect both the public and museum creditors, courts should ensure that expert professionals evaluate works of art so that only the most expendable artworks are sold. Artworks remaining after dissolution, even dissolution by bankruptcy, should be transferred to similar institutions according to *cy pres* doctrines.

Ultimately, such a liberalized application of *cy pres* and deviation doctrines to allow museum trustees to use existing restricted funds and assets where they are most needed is not in conflict with the continuing public interest in seeing art, nor with the interest of donors in making art available to the public. Similarly, applying corporate standards to the management of museums will allow museum directors and trustees to act with maximum efficiency for the continued preservation of the museum trust.

NOTES

1. Philippe de Montebello, "The High Cost of Quality," *Museum News* 62 (1984): 46–49.
2. Stephen E. Weil, *Beauty and the Beasts: On Museums, Art, the Law, and the Market* (Washington: Smithsonian Institution Press, 1983), 48.
3. Lawrence Vail Coleman, *The Museum in America: A Critical Study* (Washington: American Association of Museums, 1935), 177.
4. National Center for Educational Statistics, *Contractor Report: Museum Program Survey* (Washington, D.C., 1979), 53, 67, 69.
5. W. Cary and C. Bright, *The Developing Law of Endowment Funds* (New York: The Ford Foundation, 1974), p 8.
6. See, e.g., *The New York Times,* March 5, 1978, sec. III, p. 3, col. 1.
7. See, e.g., Complaint in the Harding Museum litigation, *Scott* v. *Silverstein,* filed Nov. 1, 1978, Cook Co. Chancery Division, Illinois.
8. J. Merryman and A. Elsen, *Law, Ethics and the Visual Arts,* 2 vols. (New York: Matthew Bender, 1979), Chapter 7.
9. National Endowment for the Arts, *Museums USA* (Washington, National Endowment for the Arts, 1974), 139.
10. Henry Hansmann, "Reforming Non-Profit Corporations Law," *University of Pennsylvania Law Review* 129 (1981): 500.
11. Marion Fremont-Smith, *Foundations and Government* (New York: Russell Sage Foundation, 1965), 84.
12. Fremont-Smith, op. cit.
13. See, e.g., *Stein* v. *Lucy Webb Training School for Deaconesses and Mistresses,* 381 F. Supp. 1003 (D.D.C. 1974).
14. Fremont-Smith, op. cit., 154–155.
15. Hansmann, op. cit.
16. See *Zehner* v. *Alexander,* Adjudication and Decree Nisi (Franklin Co. Orphans Ct., Pa.), May 25, 1979.
17. Judicial Fact-Finding, *Zehner,* No. 229.
18. *AAUP* v. *Bloomfield* College, 129 N.J. Super. 249, 322 A.2d 846 (N.J. 1974); and appeal, 136 N.J. Super. 442, 346 A2d 615 (N.J. 1975).
19. Office of Ohio Attorney General, Status of State Regulation of Charitable Trusts, 5 Comm. on Private Philanthropy and Public Needs, 2705, 2710–25 (1977).
20. See Complaint, *Scott* v. *Silverstein,* filed Nov. 1, 1978, Cook Co., Chancery Division, Illinois.
21. J. Abbott and R. Kornblum, "Jurisdiction of Attorney General over Corporate Fiduciaries under the New California Non-Profit Corporations Law," *University of San Francisco Law Review* 13 (1979): 753.
22. Merryman and Elsen, op. cit.
23. *Weigand* v. *Barnes Foundation,* 97 A2d 81, 82 (S. Ct. Pa. 1953).
24. Fremont-Smith, op. cit., p 87.
25. *Jones* v. *Grant,* 344 So. 2d 1210 (Ala. 1977).

26. *Stern* v. *Lucy Webb,* 381 F. Supp. 1003 (D.D.C. 1974).
27. *Rowan* v. *Pasadena Art Museum,* Case No. C 322817; Sup. Ct. Cal. 1981.
28. Hansmann, op. cit. 568–569, 610.
29. Report of American Association of Museum Directors, 1971.
30. Resolution of the American Association of Museums, November 3, 1973.
31. Ibid.
32. *Commonwealth* v. *Barnes Foundation,* 398 Pa. 458, 159 A.2d 500 (S. Ct. Pa. 1960).
33. Complaint, *Scott* v. *Silverstein,* Count I, No.s 6, 9.
34. *Scott* v. *Silverstein,* Plaintiff's Draft Pre-Trial Order, 36.
35. *Scott* v. *Silverstein,* 374 N.E.2d 756 at 758.
36. *The New York Times,* October 30, 1980, sec. II, p. 1, col. 2.
37. California Revenue and Tax Code, § 6365: "The museum must be open not less than 20 hours/week, not less than 35 weeks/year, and be open without charge not less than 6 hours/month."
38. ALI-ABA Course of Study, *Legal Problems of Museum Administration* (Philadelphia, Penn.: ALI-ABA, 1974), 274.
39. The College Art Association, Resolution Concerning the Sale and Exchange of Works of Art by Museums, 1973, No. 7.
40. The reader should refer to individual policies of museums, such as those set forth in Merryman and Elsen, op. cit., Part 7.
41. J. Michael Montias, "Are Museums Betraying the Public's Trust?" *Museum News* 51 (1973): 25–31.
42. *Authors Club* v. *Kirtland,* 248 App. Div. 82, 288 N.Y.S. 916 (N.Y. 1936).
43. ALI-ABA Course of Study, op. cit., 276.
44. Ibid., 256ff.
45. Ibid., 275–276.
46. Kenneth Hudson, *Museums for the 80s: A Study of World Trends* (London: UNESCO, 1977), 84.
47. Complaint, *Scott* v. *Silverstein,* Count I, No.s 12(e), 15, 18.
48. *Scott* v. *Silverstein,* Plaintiff's Pre-Trial Order, 36.
49. Karl E. Meyer, *The Art Museum: Power, Money, Ethics* (New York: William Morrow 1979), 118.
50. *Watkinson Library* v. *Attorney General,* 16 Conn. Supp. 448 (Sup. Ct. 1950).
51. The New York Times, July 9, 1979, sec. III, p. 13, col. 1.
52. Ibid.
53. J. Wheeler, "Fiduciary Responsibilities of Trustees in Financing of Private Institutions of Higher Education," *Journal of College and University Law* 2 (1975): 210.
54. Ibid.
55. Montias, op. cit. 25–31.
56. ALI-ABA Course of Study, op. cit., 272.
57. 4 *Scott on Trusts* (2d), § 399 (Boston: Little, Brown, 1967).
58. Fremont-Smith, op. cit., 84.
59. V. Stat. Ann., tit. 16, §§ 3681–84.
60. 4 *Scott on Trusts* (2d), § 381.
61. See K. Karst, "The Efficiency of the Charitable Dollar: An Unfulfilled State Responsibility," *Harvard Law Review* 73 (1960): 433.
62. See discussion in E. Fisch, *The* Cy Pres *Doctrine in the United States* (New York: Matthew Bender, 1950).
63. *Cocke* v. *Duke University,* 260 N.C.1, 131 S.E.2d 909 (1963); *Toledo Trust Co.* v. *Toledo Hosp.,* 174 Ohio St. 124, 187 N.E.2d 36 (1962).
64. *Harris* v. *Attorney General,* 31 Conn. Supp. 93, 324 A.2d 279 (Conn. 1974).
65. *In re Petition of Trustees of Hyde Collection,* Warren Co. Sup. Ct. (N.Y. 1974).
66. Art insurance premiums have soared in recent years, especially for special exhibitions showing loaned objects. Up to 55 percent of the Guggenheim's exhibition costs are for insur-

ance, for example. See Irving Pfeffer, "Insuring Museum Exhibitions," *Hastings Law Journal* 27 (1976): 1123.

67. *Parkinson* v. *Murdoch*, 332 p.2d 273 (Kansas 1958), p. 277.

68. *Final Judgment in the Matter of the Application of the New York Historical Society for Modifications of the Thomas J. Bryan Indenture*, S. Ct. (N.Y. 1967).

69. Fisch, op. cit. § 6.04.

70. *Watkinson Library* v. *Attorney General*, 16 Conn. Supp. 448(1950).

71. Fremont-Smith, op. cit., 79.

72. *Cleveland Museum* v. *O'Neill*, 129 N.E.2d 669, 1955.

73. *Scott* v. *Silverstein*.

74. 4 *Scott on Trusts* (2d), § 348.1.

75. Fisch, op. cit., 130–131.

76. Ibid., 143.

77. See discussion in 4 *Scott on Trusts* (2d), op. cit., § 299.4.

78. 14 C.J.S., § 52.

79. *Application of Arms in re Louis Comfort Tiffany Foundation*, 64 N.Y.S.2d 693 (N.Y. 1946).

80. Karst, op. cit., 469–472.

81. Conversation with Leonard Easter, Volunteer Lawyers for the Arts, November 1981.

82. H. Oleck, *Non-Profit Corporations, Organizations and Associations*, 14th ed. (Englewood Cliffs, N.J.: Prentice-Hall, 1980), 376.

83. Fremont-Smith, op. cit., 127.

84. See, e.g., E. Taylor, *Public Accountability of Foundations and Charitable Trust* (New York: Russell Sage Foundation, 1953).

85. See N.Y. Non-Profit Corporation Law, §§ 1101 et seq.

86. See, e.g., Fisch, op. cit.

87. *In re Will of Goehringer*, 329 N.Y.S.2d 516 (N.Y. Surr. Ct. 1972).

88. Hansmann, op. cit., 576.

89. Oleck, op. cit., 376.

90. H. King, "The Voluntary Closing of a Private College: A Decision for the Board of Trustees?" *South Carolina Law Review* 32 (1981): 547.

91. *Veterans Industries of Long Beach* v. *Lynch*, 8 Cal. 3d 902, 88 Cal Rptr. 303 (Cal. 1967).

92. Fact-Findings, *Zehner* v. *Alexander*.

93. Decree Nisi, *Zehner* v. *Alexander*, 83.

94. *Application of New York Law School*, 68 N.Y.S.2d 838 (Sup. Ct. N.Y. 1946).

95. *Conway* v. *Emery*, 139 Conn. 612, 96 A.2d 221 (Conn. 1953).

96. *In re Estate of Hermann*, 454 Pa. 292, 312 A.2d 16 (S. Ct. Pa. 1973).

97. Cary and Bright, op. cit., 76–77.

98. See, e.g., *Olds* v. *Rollins College*, 173 F.2d 639 (D.C.C.R. 1949).

99. *City Bank Farmers Trust Co.* v. *Arnold*, 283 N.Y. 184, 27 N.E. 2d 984 (N.Y. Ct. App. 1940).

100. See, e.g.: *Watkinson Library* v. *Attorney General*, 16 Conn. Supp. 448 (Sup. Ct. 1950); *Application of Arms in re Louis Comfort Tiffany Foundation*, 64 N.Y.S.2d 693 (Sup. Ct. 1946).

101. See, e.g., *Trevathan* v. *Ringgold-Noland Foundation, Inc.*, 410 S.W.2d 132 (S. Ct. Ark. 1967).

102. *Gordon* v. *City of Baltimore*, 237 A.2d 98 (Md. 1970).

103. See discussion in Oleck, op. cit., 365 et seq.

104. See also 9 *Am. Jur.* 2d § 227.

105. Oleck, op. cit., 370.

106. See *In re Elsford Country Club*, 50 F.2d 238 (S.D.N.Y. 1931).

107. Michael Sovern, "Section 4 of the Bankruptcy Act: The Excluded Corporations," *Minnesota Law Review* 42 (1957): 203–204.

108. Ibid., 235.

109. Oleck, op. cit., 373.

110. Cary and Bright, op. cit., 76–77.

111. Collier's 14th ed., ¶¶ 70.25, 70.26.

112. See, e.g., *Ward* v. *St. Vincent's Hospital,* 39 App. Div. 624, 57 N.Y.S. 784 (S. Ct. 1st Dept. 1899).

113. See, e.g., *Bradshaw* v. *American Advent Christian Home and Orphanage,* 199 So. 329, 145 Fla. 270 (Fla. 1940).

114. See *Arkansas Baptist College* v. *Wilson,* 138 S.W.2d 376 (S. Ct. Ark. 1940).

115. *Hobbs* v. *Board of Education,* 126 Neb. 416, 253 N.W. 627 (S. Ct. Neb. 1934).

116. M. Reese, "*Cy Pres* Powers of the Federal Bankruptcy Courts," *Fordham Urban Law Journal* 5 (1977), 435, 443.

117. Meyer, op. cit.

IV

NONPROFIT ENTERPRISE IN COMMERCIAL CULTURAL INDUSTRIES

11

Politics and Programs: *Organizational Factors in Public Television Decision Making*

WALTER W. POWELL and REBECCA JO FRIEDKIN

The standard criticisms of commercial television are by now familiar: It is an extremely profitable, oligopolistic industry that promotes throwaway commodities and conspicuous consumption; it is a "wasteland" offering bland, homogenous fare; and the combination of industry concentration and a limited range of programming results in little that is innovative, as well as a failure to present a diversity of views.[1]

Public television, one of the few widely accessible alternatives to commercial television, is sometimes held up as a more worthy enterprise; its stated mission is to strive for both excellence and diversity. The extent to which public television meets that challenge is an important question.

Commercial television operates according to a simple set of rules: Programming decisions are responsive to a market system based on ratings. In contrast, participants in public television do not have clear criteria to guide them in making decisions and evaluating the results. Lacking objective tests of efficiency or effectiveness, public television is insulated from the benefits and penalties of a market-based price system. Public television must cope with diverse and uncertain funding sources and respond to multiple, and sometimes incompatible, goals. The history of public broadcasting reveals a basic lack of agreement as to what it is and what its mandate should be.[2] The stated mission, in effect, is to offer all things to all people: programs that meet the needs of minority and specialized taste groups and organization that achieves the Federal Communication Commission's goal

An earlier version of this chapter was published as "Political and Organizational Influences on Public Television Programming" by Walter W. Powell and Rebecca Friedkin in *Mass Communication Review Yearbook,* Vol. 4 (1983), pp. 413–438. Research support was generously provided by the Program on Non-Profit Organizations, Yale University. We wish to thank Paul DiMaggio and John Simon for many helpful comments on an earlier draft.

of localism, or community control. Recent events have brought to the fore basic questions about the legitimacy of public television: Are the costs justified given the size of the audience reached? Our research was conducted at a time (1980–82) when public television confronted fundamental questions about its mission and purpose, as well as faced sharp reductions in operating revenues as a result of federal budgetary cutbacks.

In this chapter we examine how external political forces and internal organizational features influence which programs are shown on public television. Drawing upon interviews and field work conducted from 1980 to 1982 at WNET-TV (New York City, New York, and Newark, New Jersey) and CPTV (Connecticut), a consortium of five small stations with a central office in Hartford,[3] we begin with an analysis of the environment of public television and the processes involved in financing and distributing programs. We then turn to an examination of the organizational structure of the two television stations and show how departmental arrangements, staff politics, and program characteristics shape decision making.

The public television system operates on two levels. At the local level there are some 300 public stations. These stations can be roughly divided into two types. A few large stations regularly produce programs for national broadcast. WNET is the largest station in the country, often touted as the system's "flagship" station. The vast majority of stations, however, are small and produce only a few hours of local programming each week. These "consuming" stations purchase virtually all of their programming. CPTV falls in this category.

At the national level, the Corporation for Public Broadcasting (CPB), the Public Broadcasting Service (PBS), the National Association of Public Television Stations (NAPTS), and National Public Radio (NPR) are the organizational entities that manage and link the public broadcast system together. The Corporation for Public Broadcasting is a private nonprofit organization, financed by the federal government, and governed by trustees appointed by the President. The main conduit through which federal monies flow to public television, CPB distributes money directly to stations, finances program development and production, and provides funds for PBS and NPR. The Public Broadcasting Service operates the satellite interconnection, distributes programming to member stations, and makes long range plans for public television. The National Association of Public Television Stations is the station membership organization and represents the local stations in Washington. National Public Radio fulfills all of these functions for public radio stations. Although public radio and television are separate operations, NPR receives 20 percent of its financing from CPB, thus setting the stage for disputes with public television over the allocation of funds.

The public broadcasting system is both administratively complex and loosely organized. "Turf battles" are not uncommon. Conflicts over the relationship between CPB and PBS, between radio and television, and between larger producing stations and small consuming stations are frequent and acrimonious. Power struggles are ongoing, as each element in the system jockeys to use the rapid changes taking place in public broadcasting to its own advantage. We will not review these disputes here, but we do examine the influence these various national organizations exert over decision making at the local level.

In addition to the various organizations that constitute public broadcasting, public television stations turn to many other constituencies for resources and support. These relationships are crucial for a station's financial health, and differences in the structure and program output of stations can be explained by variations in the flow and allocation of the resources they receive.[4]

Public television stations represent a peculiar hybrid of nonprofit, public, and proprietary organizational forms. Public television operates like a public agency because as much as 70 percent of the budget of a small station comes from federal, state, and municipal governments. A typical public station also receives approximately 25 percent of its financial support from members and expends considerable effort on membership and fund-raising drives and auctions. In this manner, public television resembles many voluntary associations. Along with a great many other nonprofit organizations, public television solicits financial support from private foundations and corporations. In addition, public television competes with commercial television for the attention of viewers and vies with network and cable television, as well as many of the newer forms of video entertainment, for artists, producers, and programs.

SOURCES OF FUNDING

A major source of uncertainty for public television is the precarious and turbulent nature of its funding environment. Not only is money scarce, but external funding relationships are unpredictable.[5] Station executives spend a great deal of time and energy developing, maintaining, and smoothing relationships with key funders. The yearly funding cycle requires much staff time, makes long-range planning difficult, and increases the possibility that funding decisions shape program content. We briefly describe each of the five major sources of funding for public television, its importance, and the unique contingencies and problems it poses.

Federal Funding

The federal government, although not the largest funder in absolute terms, has been the most important continuous source of money for public television. In fiscal year 1983 the federal government supplied 17.1 percent of the income for public television.[6] The federal government is the only funder that directly affects the entire public television system, through its appropriation to CPB. More than 40 percent of CPB's budget must be "passed through" directly to the stations, in proportion to their ability to raise matching, nonfederal funds. Known as Community Service Grants (CSGs), these federal matches are one of the few "no-strings-attached" grants to public television stations.[7]

The degree to which funding is uncertain is well illustrated by the history of federal support for public television. Long-standing concerns that public broadcasting be financially insulated from political interference, through a self-sustaining and long-term funding mechanism that could allow the planning necessary to produce quality television, have often been enunciated but never implemented. The current administrative and funding arrangements were established by the Public Broadcasting Act of 1967, based partly on the recommendations of the Carnegie Commission on Educational Television. The Commission suggested that the financing of public television be accomplished through a tax on television sets (as in England). Intensive lobbying by television manufacturers killed this proposal, and no alternative was found; instead CPB is funded from general revenues on a year-to-year basis. Although these appropriations increased substantially from $5 million for fiscal year 1969 to a peak of $172 million in fiscal year 1982, neither long-term security nor insulation from political pressure has been achieved.

The most dramatic case of political interference occurred in 1972 when President Nixon vetoed a two-year, $155 million authorization for CPB. Although he justified the veto on the grounds that local stations needed a greater voice in public television,[8] it was widely known that the administration was displeased with the content of many programs, especially such public affairs series as *The Great American Dream Machine* (a political cabaret with a strong antiwar bent), *Washington Week in Review*, and *Black Journal*. The Nixon veto led to a reduction in funding (to $110 million), and demonstrated the political vulnerability of public broadcasting.[9]

In response to the Nixon veto, Congress began appropriating funds for CPB up to three years in advance, beginning in 1975 for fiscal years 1976–78. This mechanism was intended to provide more stable and unobtrusive federal support and to allow public broadcasting to engage in more effective long-term planning. The principle of advance funding, however, has not operated consistently. Although funds have generally been appropriated at least two years in advance, the Reagan administration's budget cuts have proved to be the most serious shock to the system since the 1972 veto. The original Reagan budget proposals recommended the rescission of appropriations already made for fiscal years 1982 and 1983. Congress rejected budget reductions for 1982, but cut the 1983 CPB appropriation by 20 percent. The anticipated stability of advance funding was destroyed, and federal budget battles have plagued public television throughout the Reagan years.

The budget reductions created obvious financial problems, and the protracted political bargaining has intensified an already high level of uncertainty. For example, in a four-month period in 1981, the budget for fiscal year 1984 was reduced from $172 million to $137 million, then to $130 million, next to $105.6 million. The administration then recommended a further cut to $95.5 million. Eventually $130 million was settled on. In an unanticipated manner, the advance funding mechanism has exacerbated public television's budget problems by making it harder to receive financial commitments. For the past several years, the federal government has been operating under continuing resolutions rather than formal budgets. This has meant that no budgetary allocations are actually fixed, for they can be changed every time Congress extends the continuing funding resolution. Under such a process, the fact that public television funds are set in advance only means that there is more opportunity to change them.

Additional federal support for public television comes from the National Endowments for the Arts and the Humanities, the National Science Foundation, the National Institutes of Health, and other government agencies. These grants are typically for development and production of specific programs, rather than for general purpose funds. Program-specific funds are also available through CPB.

Two important points about program-specific funding from federal agencies are worth noting. First, the process of obtaining funding is labor-intensive and lengthy, often taking several years. Proposals for funding must be reviewed by a panel of experts, who must reach a consensus before granting final approval. Second, federal funding of this sort is commonly used as "seed money" and usually requires matching funds from nonfederal sources. Partial funding from the government lends legitimacy and prestige to a proposal that is then submitted to foundations for additional support.[10] Thus, even small reductions in federal spending have a far-reaching impact on public television programming. Moreover, budget cuts may lead public television stations to avoid risk in order not to jeopardize future funding from the government or private underwriters.

State and Local Funding

State and local governments, along with state colleges and universities, represent the largest portion (34.3 percent in fiscal year 1983) of financial support for public television. It is at the state level that direct political pressures, or fear of such pressures, most clearly affect stations, particularly small consuming stations. Through both overt and implied means, state governments place constraints on public affairs programming. According to a former WNET executive, the restrictions are greatest at state-operated stations.[11] "Most of them simply can't do public affairs shows that look critically at their own state government because of the funding constraint. There is a terrible baggage that comes with state money." Even community-run stations, such as WNET and CPTV, feel pressures to deal favorably with state officials. The WNET executive just quoted noted that despite WNET's diverse sources of support, "We have to ask the majority leader of the State Assembly to come on the air and answer questions. We do this stroking because we want the money from Albany." CPTV executives were proud of their coverage of the state legislature, noting that it was a service not provided by commercial stations, but they also acknowledged the value of such coverage in obtaining state funds.

Foundations

Private foundations were once the single largest source of contributions to public television. Most notably, the Ford Foundation provided $292 million,[12] including construction grants, from the early 1950s to the mid-1970s. During public television's early years, Ford grants literally kept the system alive. Ford Foundation support was phased out, however, ending in fiscal year 1977, and foundation grants now constitute less than 3 percent of public television's revenues.

As a rule, foundation grants are available for the support of specific programs or artists. Foundation support has been crucial to bringing innovative, "risky" programming to public television. A notable project is the TV Laboratory at WNET, established in 1972 with grants from the Rockefeller Foundation and the New York State Council on the Arts. Additional money has come from the Ford Foundation and the National Endowment for the Arts (NEA). The TV Lab was created to explore the artistic and technological potential of television through research, experimentation, and the creation of innovative projects for broadcast, and it serves as a major link between public television and independent filmmakers. The Lab has run an artists-in-residence program and has produced or funded such diverse programs as *Making Television Dance,* with Twyla Tharp; *Lathe of Heaven,* a speculative fiction program; programs exploring abstract video graphics; and numerous powerful documentaries such as *Vietnam: Picking Up the Pieces,* and *Health Care: Your Money or Your Life.* More recently, the TV Lab coordinated a series by independent producers titled *Non-Fiction Television.* The series included hard-hitting documentaries on the CIA and US foreign policy and on the use of deadly force by the police.

Corporations

In the early 1970s, as foundation support declined and federal support became politically contentious, public broadcasting turned to major corporations for program underwriting. It was not a role that corporations actively sought for themselves. The corporate share of public television revenues has grown from 4 percent in 1973 to almost 15 percent in 1983. But a much larger percentage of the budgets of producing stations comes from corporations. For the period from 1977 to 1982, corporate underwriting accounted for 22 to 25 percent of WNET's total revenues. More important, almost half of the national programming on public television is financed in part or in full by corporate donations. Corporations generally fund the production and presentation of such continuing series as *Great Performances* or *Masterpiece Theatre,* rather than contributing discretionary or development money or financing individual programs. The logic behind this policy is clear: A major series has high visibility, which corporate public relations departments can use to their advantage.

Corporate underwriting grew dramatically during the 1974 oil crisis, a time when U.S. oil companies were under heavy public criticism. Support of public television provided the oil companies, who remain the primary corporate contributors to public television, with one answer to their apparently declining legitimacy.[13] Yet continued increases in corporate support for public television are not guaranteed. More nonprofit organizations now compete for corporate dollars, and pay and cable television offer alternatives for corporations that wish to use the television medium to develop their corporate image or deliver a message to upscale audiences.

Some researchers suggest that corporate giving is motivated more by the desire to influence public opinion than by a sense of social responsibility. Ermann argues that the operative goal for corporate philanthropy is "milieu control," or image management. Burt found that corporations in industries dependent on individual consumption are most involved in philanthropy. Corporate philanthropy is also positively associated with general advertising expenditures, a more direct form of image building.[14]

The underwriting of public television shows can be seen as a form of specialized advertising. Audiences for the shows supported by corporations tend to be well educated and well-to-do.[15] Barnouw argues persuasively, and our research substantiates, that most corporations interested in image enhancement want their names associated with non-controversial, high-quality shows—shows that he calls "safely splendid."[16] The director of public affairs programming at WNET said that the biggest difference between public affairs and cultural programs involves problems with underwriters. He noted ironically that "Exxon had the right idea doing *Live from Lincoln Center.* Mobil Oil had the best idea when they funded *Upstairs, Downstairs.* These are benign shows. They are not offensive, they are not going to get anyone angry. Public affairs shows get underwriters angry."

Nothing quite comparable to this direct relationship between program content and corporate sponsorship currently exists in commercial television. Corporate underwriting of public television resembles the early days of network television, the so-called golden age when advertisers were commonly sole sponsors of programs.[17] The advertisers were very much concerned with the image of their products, hence they routinely read scripts in advance of filming and sought to approve or reject actors, writers, and directors. As the television audience grew, however, advertising costs rose dramatically. Advertisers could no longer afford to sponsor an entire show. Today network television is a seller's market, with companies standing in line to purchase time. Advertisers no longer screen scripts in advance; instead they view completed shows and if they disapprove, they arrange to purchase time on different episodes or shows. Although advertisers on commercial television will on occasion cancel their ads because they disapprove of a program's content, thus influencing the program's chances for renewal, such actions are atypical.[18] In contrast, corporate underwriting of public television is highly concentrated among a handful of firms. There is no queue of firms anxiously waiting to underwrite shows. Hence the few companies who contribute have considerable leverage, if they choose to exercise it, over program content. Given these constraints, station personnel assume that most corporations will fund only certain types of programs: prestigious cultural fare, well-balanced public affairs shows like *The MacNeil/Lehrer Newshour,* or shows that appeal directly to corporate–executive viewers, such as *Wall Street Week* or *Firing Line.* Proposals for other kinds of shows are rarely submitted to large corporations for consideration.

Individuals

Member contributions are another primary source of funding. They have increased in recent years, primarily because of more strenuous and sophisticated solicitation by the stations. In 1979, members accounted for 11.8 percent of total income; by 1983, individuals contributed 23 percent of the budget for public television.[19] Nevertheless, only 1 in 10 people claim ever to have contributed to their local public television station; among frequent viewers, only 27 percent report ever having given money to public television.[20] Generating subscription dollars requires considerable expenditure of time, money, and volunteer effort. Stations are plagued by an ongoing tension between the need for on-air promotional events, such as pledge drives and auctions, and the possibility of irritating or even disaffecting viewers with extended interruptions. Connecticut Public Television recently conducted a pledge week with a "soft sell" campaign, for which they received much praise, but little money. The vice president for development commented that "compliments mean trouble. It means you're not getting money, you're getting compliments."

The mix of funding sources, their respective contingencies, and the political tensions within the system combine to shape programming decisions, a point we underscore in our analysis of the program selection and distribution system.

PROGRAM SELECTION AND DISTRIBUTION: ADMINISTRATIVE CONSTRAINTS

How does a program come to be shown on public television? Although public television does not operate as a centralized network as CBS, NBC, or ABC do, a core of programs are aired by most member stations. These programs are obtained by stations via two mechanisms, the Station Program Cooperative (SPC) and free distribution by PBS to member stations.

The Station Program Cooperative, administered by PBS, was established in 1974 to decentralize decision making in public television and give more voice to many small consuming stations. Producers, including public stations and independent producers, submit several hundred program proposals on a wide variety of topics at an annual program fair. The stations go through several rounds of bidding to narrow the number of selections to 30 or 40 proposed programs. The final cost of a program to a station is based on the number of other stations purchasing the show and the size of the station's Community Service Grant. Producers modify their proposals during the early rounds to try to accommodate stations' needs and to garner support. Stations are not committed to the purchase of a program until the final round of bidding, and only those stations that purchase a program may air it. The entire proposal and selection process takes about six months.

Program selection mechanisms, including the SPC, are a major source of conflict between large and small stations. The SPC is dominated by large producing stations that are reputedly unresponsive to the needs of smaller stations. The SPC buyer at CPTV complained about the purchasing power of the large stations: "because of their size, and the pricing formula, they can out-vote others because they have so much money." Large stations include administrative overhead costs in their program budgets and then pass these costs on to other stations through the SPC. This makes station-produced shows more expensive than programs produced by independent filmmakers, a fact resented by small stations with limited budgets. Small stations also complain that they are not fairly credited for their role in supporting the productions of large stations. The station manager at CPTV stated that "the system is collectively financed by everyone, but WNET and WGBH [Boston] get all the credit." However, the SPC buyer for CPTV pointed out that there is a strong incentive to buy programs through the SPC rather than through individual acquisition because satellite transmission of core shows by PBS eliminates many technical problems.

The SPC was intended to alleviate the powerlessness of small stations and institute a more democratic choice process for nationwide programming. Although generally recognized as an improvement over previously more centralized decision processes, the SPC has not lived up to expectations, and it has been widely criticized.[21] Despite its free market intentions, for example, the SPC is slow, administratively cumbersome, and very conservative. Katzman and Wirt found that purchased programs tended to have "at least one or two and often all three of the following characteristics: (1) prior national or multi-station exposure, (2) a low price and/or an exceptionally good value per unit time, and (3) a bandwagon effect."[22] The result, they point out, does not necessarily reflect the desires of the stations. Conservative choices can be artifacts of the selection process. "If 15 new programs are each supported in the voting by 10 stations, none of the new programs would be purchased even through the 150 stations all wanted something new."[23] The SPC is not the only reason why few new programs are shown on public television—established programming is easier to obtain underwriting for and helps retain audiences—but it does exacerbate the situation.

Free distribution by PBS is a second mechanism by which programs come to be shown, one that delivers a mixed bag of goods. Fully underwritten programs do not go through the SPC but are made available to all stations free of charge. Individual stations decide whether or not to air such programs, but there is clearly a strong financial incentive to broadcast free material. Because these programs are not subject to a bidding process, underwriters have substantial control over program content. The popular series *Masterpiece Theatre,* funded by Mobil Oil, is an example of a core prime-time program provided in this manner. Interestingly, WGBH, the producing station, did not originally want to acquire the highly successful series, *Upstairs, Downstairs,* for *Masterpiece Theatre,* but was urged to do so by Mobil.[24]

Free program offerings, in spite of their seemingly benign nature, can also generate tensions between large and small stations. For example, several major corporations sponsored *Free to Choose,* a series based on the writings of conservative economist Milton Friedman that extolled the virtues of laissez-faire capitalism and was produced by the Erie, Pennsylvania public station. By making the program freely available, the Erie station received much national exposure. With a program such as this one, there is pressure on large stations to carry the free program. The director of broadcasting at WNET noted that the producing station "may not care whether Cleveland picks it up, or Portland. But they most definitely want it to be seen in New York, and if WNET turns down these shows, especially those that are free, we are seen as being unresponsive to the system."

The programs purchased through the SPC or provided free by PBS are generally the "tried and true" of public television. They are usually of high quality, and they receive the great majority of corporate underwriting funds and program-specific government grants. But there are two other major sources of programming, ones that provide more varied and less expensive choices for the stations. The Inter-regional Program Service (IPS), run by the Eastern Educational Television Network, operates as a minimarket for programs, somewhat like the SPC, but different in several respects. First, IPS makes programs available that have already been produced, whereas the SPC offers program proposals and occasional pilots. A program buyer at WNET jokingly described the difference between the SPC and the IPS as:

> At the IPS you can watch what it is you are going to buy. At the SPC you read a proposal and try to guess if the station can really deliver it. They might promise Liza Minelli in a song series, but then they'll get someone off the streets and say "well, actually she's the same size as Liza." So, at IPS it's an easier choice.[25]

Second, programs acquired through IPS are generally less expensive because the primary production costs have already been paid. Third, the IPS is more flexible than the SPC because it meets frequently, has fewer participants, and uses a simpler bidding process that links the stations and producers directly. Inter-Regional Program Service programs constitute a small portion of a station's prime-time schedule, so there is less urgency and the bargaining is less complex than at the SPC.

Finally, IPS and regional networks provide programs that are more suited to a local market than the programs nationally broadcast by PBS, for which PBS requires clearance for broadcast in all public television markets. Stations in large metropolitan areas, such as WNET, often purchase programs from IPS that would be considered too risqué, because of language or nudity, for a PBS national feed.

Stations also acquire programs directly from such sources as foreign television producers and networks, independent producers, and other public stations, which sometimes sell programs on a station-by-station basis. The documentary *Police Tapes,* for example, was shot on location in the South Bronx by WNET. The show won numerous awards, had extensive international distribution, and garnered exceptional ratings in New York. It was eventually purchased by ABC for network broadcast, but only after first being rejected by the SPC because it was considered too controversial. Rather than making it freely available, WNET sold *Police Tapes* to about 20 public stations directly.

Small stations depend almost exclusively on the SPC and free PBS distribution for their programming, partly because they cannot afford the operating costs of long broadcast days, and partly because they lack the discretionary funds for independent acquisitions. As a result, the conservatism and bandwagon effects of the SPC and the financial incentive to air free programs leave consuming stations little discretion over their prime-time schedules. In contrast, large stations have considerably more program options. Longer broadcast days provide more time slots for special acquisitions, which can be funded from larger discretionary budgets.

Large stations have greater influence on program content for the whole system because of their direct involvement in program production. The major producing stations, such as WNET and WGBH, are responsible for most national programs. In contrast, consuming stations produce a few hours a week of local programming, usually public affairs or news shows. These local programs are often strongly shaped by local political realities. Moreover, locally produced programs are generally difficult to underwrite because of their small viewing audience. During the budgetary crisis of the 1980s, many stations have had to cancel or drastically reduce their local programming. Nevertheless, these shows are perceived to carry out an important component of public television's mandate. The station manager of CPTV noted that local programming is necessary to maintain a good staff, and thus a strong station. "Cutting local programming kills the station. It kills us in terms of what our mission should be, what our staff wants to be doing, and retards our building for a stronger future."

The role of independent producers deserves special comment. Although public television has provided a major forum for independent producers, the relationship between producers and stations has been strained, and access to the public airwaves is limited: Only about 5 percent of public television programs are made by independent producers. The CPB has attempted to improve relations with independent producers by offering them direct program grants. Although direct funding of independents relaxes financial constraints, the lack of sustained contact with stations during the production phase may ultimately mean that the independent's work will not be deemed suitable for broadcast through PBS. This was the case with the final segment of Peter Davis's documentary, *Middletown*, which included teenagers' frank discussions of race, sex, and drugs. PBS required cuts in the segment before approving it for broadcast. The producer refused and withdrew the last show. Disturbed by the ensuing public controversy, PBS attempted to provide "balance" by offering an "objective" commentary on the series as a final replacement show. Despite frequent criticism, independent producers often prefer public television to commercial television because public television is willing to broadcast a documentary in its entirety. Network television, on the other hand, uses only short segments of a documentarian's footage, usually weaving them into the evening news.[26]

These tensions illustrate the widely divergent demands made upon public television by various constituencies who seek to use the system for their own purposes. Programming decisions are influenced by financial conditions at local stations, the amount of underwriting money available for particular shows, the need to placate various supporters, concerns over station morale, and the quality of relations between stations and creative artists.

Given the financial dependence of public television, local stations may appear to have little choice or control over programming. This is often true for smaller stations, as subsequent analysis of CPTV will show. However, larger stations can and do exercise power over programming decisions. An analysis of the internal organization of a large public station, WNET, illustrates how such stations decide which programs to produce for national broadcast.

STATION ORGANIZATION: INTERNAL CULTURES AND CONFLICTS

A large public television station is a loose confederation of various autonomy-seeking groups. Most public stations have multiple, and often conflicting, goals. Various groups, both inside and outside the station, attempt to put public television to their own use. For artists as well as corporate funders, public television is a vehicle for delivering a message, a resource that interest groups seek to appropriate. In this respect, public television is a pluralist entity: many disparate groups seek to "capture" it as a means of serving their own purposes. The managers of public television stations also have their own missions and visions and are, naturally, concerned with the continued existence of their stations.

The most salient internal conflict that affects program choice and content, evident at both WNET and CPTV, is between programming staff, responsible for the development and production or acquisition of programs, and the funding staff, charged with obtaining program-specific grants from corporations, foundations, and federal agencies.[27] Although specific administrative arrangements vary from station to station, this internal conflict is common to stations across the country. (Indeed, some variant of this problem vexes most nonprofit organizations in which product development or service delivery is separated from fund-raising). As a general rule, programming staff are primarily concerned with the quality of program content, and they believe that funding staff should help them finance the programs they choose. Personnel responsible for raising money are more concerned with the ease with which financial support for a program can be secured and the maintenance of long-term funding relationships, and they want programs to be developed with these aims in mind.[28]

Perhaps the clearest example of the programming/development conflict was at CPTV, where, because of the station's small size, the problem was an interpersonal dispute rather than an interdepartmental issue. The director of programming described the conflict as "a power thing. . . . We evaluate our activities differently. Development is concerned with how much money and membership are generated by a program. I am concerned with audience. If 17,000 people watch *Monty Python,* that's good. I'm not as concerned with how many of them give money." The conflict between these two organizational functions is evident in three aspects of the programming process: program content, program scheduling, and program funding strategies.

Program Content

Most decisions about the content of specific programs, as well as ideas for program development, are the purview of the programming department. At WNET, underwriting personnel are frequently displeased with program decisions and want greater influence in these matters. The most common complaint of the underwriting officers at WNET was that Programming does not consult with them sufficiently during the program development stage. One underwriting officer bluntly stated, "Program development is not a two-way street. If it were, funding would be easier to obtain. We know what kinds of programs the corporations and foundations want." Another underwriting officer recalled an instance when a major corporation was interested in supporting a national public affairs show, but he was unable to go to Programming and say, "Look, I have a corporate sponsor, let's produce another show." He was distressed that WNET could not respond to opportunities such as this, but did not consider whether or not WNET should produce another public affairs show, given its current mix of productions and program schedule. Another underwriting staff member's comment, "A lot of the program ideas circulated around the station don't fit well with corporate interests," clearly illustrates the divergent premises on which the two departments operate.

During our field observations, changes were introduced to increase the amount of input that underwriting staff have in program decision making. An executive in charge of underwriting described these changes as follows:

> It used to be that Programming would decide they wanted to do a show on dance. They would develop it and then we would get, through the interoffice mail, a sheet saying, "we're going to do this dance program," and then we would have to go out and sell it. That has changed. Now, from the very outset of serious discussion about a project, someone from my department is involved with Programming in the discussion of the likelihood of funding, the content of the show, what sort of competition there is for the show, and so on.

This executive stressed the collaborative nature of the relationship between Programming and Underwriting. His staff's reaction, however, was mixed. One officer found her role in program decision making enhanced, noting that:

> Someone from Underwriting is there from the start so that major decisions are made in conjunction with us. I would know we couldn't raise $500,000 for a one hour show so I would tell them to cut the production costs in half. Or, I would explain that a particular program should have a host, because you can take a host on a ten city tour to raise money. Or, I might tell them to get the program developed by October since there's a foundation deadline in mid-October.

Another underwriting officer painted a less rosy picture. She described her limited input into program development:

> We have ideas for programs, we send them to Programming, but we don't get anything back until the show has been decided upon. In some cases I'll have some input into marketing. There was a summer musical series that they wanted to do. I told them that if you want to sell this series you need to add four cities to the sites, and that will make the shows much more appealing to underwriters. So, really, my input is catch-as-catch-can.

A member of the publicity department also expressed a need for marketing input into program decisions. "For example, with the *Dick Cavett Show* I'll tell the producer that the ratings sweeps are coming up and Cavett should schedule the best possible guests. The production units simply aren't aware of the importance of ratings. They're only starting to accommodate these requests."

These comments illustrate the widely held view among nonprogramming employees that program development decisions should take into account potential audience size and the chances for obtaining underwriting support. Some underwriting officers evinced little concern for program content. One stated that she found "no moral imperative in public TV." Other staff were more inclined to balance financial and marketing concerns with respect and pride in high-quality programming. One marketing employee commented that "at a commercial station, program content would never be separated from marketing issues, as they are at WNET." In public TV, she said, "programming is more important than sales, whereas in commercial TV programming is a slave to sales." One underwriting officer spoke of the need, in theory, for a balance. "I care about the substance—and, of course, the goal for all of us is good programming—but right now, money's really my main concern."

Programming employees, by contrast, feel that program development and content are their prerogative. A programming director at WNET, commenting on the high quality of public television programming and on his disdain for concern over ratings, lamented, "People in public broadcasting used to think they were doing God's work. They felt they were doing good, worthwhile shows, and that audience size was not something that was relevant to a decision about program content."

Program Scheduling

The interests of programming and underwriting or development departments often conflict during quarterly fund-raising drives. Public television has devoted a great deal of market research to the analysis of what types of programs generate the most membership dollars. Based on this information, the director of development at CPTV feels he "should be able to determine what gets on the air—particularly during the fund-raising weeks." Local programming is usually dropped during pledge weeks because it has been shown to attract few new members. This practice, of course, runs counter to the programming department's priorities. In explaining a pledge-week schedule, the programming director pointed out that "at 7 P.M. we will not drop local programs. They are usually bumped during membership weeks, but I am concerned with keeping my staff happy, and I want those programs on the air."

The major determinant of program scheduling is the mix of programs purchased by a station through the SPC. These programs are scheduled by PBS, but some flexibility is retained at the station level. Most nationally distributed programs are "fed" by the PBS satellite several times during the week. A station may air a show at one of those times or tape it and air it later. Since it is easier and cheaper to air programs when PBS feeds them, SPC purchases generally set a good portion of a station's schedule. At CPTV, the director of programming entered a recent SPC purchase round with two lists of programs. The "A" list was her first priority and the "B" list was to be purchased with whatever funds remained. In drawing up her lists, she was guided by personal preference and viewer appeal. A show's prospects for obtaining local underwriting did not influence her choices. In fact, she deliberately included some programs that were difficult to underwrite in her "A" list. She noted that the development department was displeased with her plan but said "that's the way I want to do it, and as long as I get support from high enough places, I'll do it this way."

A final example of scheduling considerations involves the decision to counterprogram against commercial stations. A programming executive at WNET noted that, for example, 10:30 P.M. on Sunday is an awkward time slot. "If someone is watching commercial television at 10:00 the chances of them changing the channel to WNET at 10:30 are slim, since no commercial shows end at that time." He complained that he cannot convince other people at the station of the importance of lead-ins and scheduling issues, even though these concerns are commonplace in commercial television. In contrast, another programming executive believed that WNET has a core, loyal audience that is different from the audience that watches commercial TV, and that "trying to schedule against the networks is not a winning game for WNET."

Program Funding Strategies

Programming staff tend to resent pressures to concentrate on "fundable" fare. They feel that only a narrow range of programs appeal to corporate underwriters and do not want to restrict their work to such shows. Programming personnel believe their charge is to create excellent alternative shows that should be supported on the basis of their quality, not marketability. Of particular concern to Programming is the "inordinate" amount of time underwriting officers spend on a small handful of national productions.

A marketing person at WNET expressed a different view when he stated that "underwriters want younger male audiences because they're more influential, which is why *The MacNeil/Lehrer Newshour* is so popular with corporations. Science shows have high marketability for this same reason." Interest in specific target audiences by corporate underwriters means that many programs receive little or no attention from the underwriting department. A WNET proposal for a children's program, partially funded by a CPB matching grant, is a good illustration of the problem. Although half of the money was secured by Programming, Underwriting was very slow to pursue the additional funds. After several months of inactivity, a programming officer began pressuring Underwriting. However, he was all too aware of the realities of the situation, noting that "kids' shows are hard to fund, since kids don't go running to their parents telling them to buy Exxon."

Local programming also receives little attention from underwriting departments. Virtually all corporate support goes for nationally broadcast programs. Underwriting maintains that local programs are not comparable in quality, have smaller audiences, and thus are difficult to fund. Programming people counter that Underwriting does not even *try* to finance local shows. This problem is particularly acute at CPTV and, on occasion, Programming secures financing for local productions on its own, much to the displeasure of the development department. In one instance, a programming employee learned from a friend at an insurance firm that the company had considered underwriting a program and would be interested in a musical variety show with appeal to minority audiences. The company's interest was well suited to a weekly music program produced by the station that featured local ethnic musicians. The development department, preferring to approach a company for a larger sum to help underwrite the costs of purchasing an expensive national show, complained that a major company's support was "wasted" on a "small potatoes show."

There is also conflict over what types of business firms are appropriate underwriters and worth the efforts of the development department. At CPTV, *Monty Python's Flying Circus* was underwritten by Nimbus Waterbeds, an atypical business supporter. Although Programming welcomes such an arrangement and wants more support from small businesses, Development prefers to devote its time to courting large corporations that can provide more money.

Decisions about the allocation of underwriting officers' time also determine the prospects of special programs. Such programs are seldom underwritten. One underwriting officer at WNET stated:

> It's simply not worth my time to go to a corporation to ask for money for a small, one-shot show. I only go to corporate underwriters if I have a particularly attractive package and I can give them good service so they can see how public TV works, and potentially they might become a big underwriter.

Underwriting officers at WNET were very concerned that good relations be maintained between the station and corporate supporters. One underwriting officer described her job as "servicing" corporations. She noted:

> The station must have a commitment to their corporate underwriters. We should let them know what the programs are about, and who the guests will be. We should send them reviews and clippings of the shows. Servicing involves stroking them, it involves inviting them to special events, it involves lots of other possibilities for entertaining them. In short, you have to fully execute the contract. I see my job as sales. There is a lot of prejudice here about the mission of public TV and many people here don't want to be bothered with the job of raising money.

The same underwriting officer emphatically stated that corporations do not influence program content, "although clearly you can't find underwriting for programs that are biased in viewpoint or very avant-garde." The extent of her self-censorship was evident in her approach to corporations:

> Some corporations have a negative opinion about public TV. I don't sell programs to these corporations until I know what message they would like to get across . . . If we want corporations to get involved, we have to give them more. A proposal should simply list the priorities for the corporation. What are the things that could be gained from underwriting this show? I am constantly pressuring this station with the idea that corporations have to have something visible in return for underwriting a show.

At WNET the programming staff has a strong commitment to the station's flagship role as a major national production center. The largest station in the public television system, WNET is perceived to have an obligation to set system-wide policy by example. This requires a commitment to both quality and innovation. The director of programming pointed out that the station is also accountable to its local viewers, whom he believes are the "smartest and most stringent in their demands of any public broadcasting audience in the country." He went on to comment that the station's location in New York gives it a dual role: "We have to meet the needs of New York City, a small, self-contained world unto itself, and we must, because it is New York, meet the expectations of other stations, the federal government, and the national audience for public TV." Program producers also believe WNET must take risks in order to lead the way for the entire system. A clear example of this role is the station's airing of controversial documentaries. Even if most public stations refuse to air a controversial program, WNET will usually run it. In 1982, *Blood and Sand,* a program about the Nicaraguan revolution, was shown in New York, although few other stations aired it. Back in May 1980, *Death of a Princess* threatened diplomatic relations with Saudi Arabia. According to a WNET executive, "it was absolutely never, never an issue as to whether or not we would show it."[29] Such commitment is necessary in order for WNET to maintain a strong programming staff. Nevertheless, these same programming strengths create difficulties in obtaining outside funding.

THE INFLUENCE OF FUNDING SOURCES ON PROGRAMMING

The lack of adequate funding for public television creates a situation of dependency for public television stations.[30] It is widely recognized that most sources of money have strings attached. Each funding source has its own biases about what it wants to support and what it expects to receive in return. As former PBS President, Lawrence Grossman, has stated, "Every source of money is tainted. With federal funds we worry about becoming a governmental broadcasting arm. Corporate money makes you steer away from controversy. Membership money means you cater to upper middle class viewers. The saving grace is that we have diversified sources."[31] Indeed, no one would suggest that one single source of funding is preferable to the present complicated mix of support. One WNET executive said that although funding sources and multiple responsibilities create headaches, "it is easier to attempt to partially satisfy a number of different people, than to try to totally please one person." Another executive noted that, "Sure, we try to be all things to all people—that guarantees that sometimes we win and sometimes we lose. I prefer that to an either/or situation."

The mix of funding sources is, however, costly in effort spent on raising money and maintaining the funding relationships. Funders routinely make requests of public television, many of which are reasonable from the funder's point of view but burdensome for the station. In one instance, a corporation funding a public affairs show requested that the host visit the corporate headquarters once a year, and that the corporation be given advance notice of guests so it could circulate the information to its employees and the local community. The host was uncooperative on both counts, and the corporation discontinued its support, tactfully citing an economic downturn as the reason.

Some demands more directly concern program content, as we saw in the case of self-censorship on the part of underwriting staff. We now turn to an analysis of how the interests and demands of funders influenced the development and content of one series. Note, however, that supporters rarely demand *specific* changes in program content. It is difficult to point to cases in which programs were altered because of a funder's direct request. Rather than dictate policy, funding sources set clear boundaries within which program development must proceed if the relationship between funder and station is to last more than a year.

The series *Dance in America* exemplifies the complicated web of relationships necessary to produce a public television program.[32] *Dance in America (DIA)* was part of a larger series, *Great Performances (GP),* a major effort to produce public television programs of comparable quality to programs produced in Great Britain, which because they combine high quality with low acquisition cost, have long been the staple of American public television. *Dance in America* received wide critical acclaim, in large part because WNET producers won the support of an initially dubious dance community. Dance companies found that following their appearances on *DIA,* ticket sales increased.

The *DIA* programs received funds from several sources: Exxon, NEA, CPB, the sale of *DIA* to other public stations through the SPC, and WNET's own discretionary funds. We conducted interviews at WNET during the planning period for the 1981–82 *DIA* season, its sixth year of production.

Dance in America represented a reasonably successful partnership of government, business, dance community, and public television. Each of the funding sources provided generous support. Exxon had given approximately \$0.5 million a year since *DIA*'s inception. (Although this amount made Exxon a major *DIA* sponsor, it was only a portion of the corporation's overall support of around \$3 million a year for public television.) The National Endowment for the Arts contributed a comparable amount; in fact, the Exxon money was a required match to the government funding. The Corporation for Public Broadcasting provided approximately \$250,000 a year for *DIA,* and the sale of the series through the SPC brought more than \$1 million annually.

Dance in America also illustrates the peculiar nature of public television. At the outset of the series, the participants shared a common goal—program success—and the funders adopted the strategy of letting WNET and the dance community make program decisions. However, with *DIA*'s success came lofty expectations on the part of funders. The National Endowment for the Arts felt the time was ripe to show off all kinds of dance—experimental, ethnic, jazz, tap, and so on—on public television. It wanted to include documentaries in the series to help educate the viewing public about new dance forms. In short, NEA was a champion of stylistic pluralism. But Exxon was concerned that *DIA* continue to live up to its own standard of excellence. Its ideal was to showcase Balanchine and Baryshnikov. The Corporation for Public Broadcasting was interested in having more regional dance companies be involved in *DIA*. They urged WNET to consider coproductions with other public stations around the country in order to add regional diversity and, not incidentally, open the door to obtaining money from state arts agencies and local foundations. The New York dance community wanted to present postmodern avant-garde dance works. Other public television stations wanted popular dance segments to increase the size of the viewing audience. In essence, WNET was an access point for a host of groups who sought to use *DIA* to achieve their own ends.

In the early seasons, conflicting demands were met by producing a wide range of shows, matching the range of interests of *DIA*'s diverse constituencies. These were WNET's "bargaining chips," to use the words of one *DIA* producer, and the diversity and generosity of funding sources permitted WNET some discretion. But over *DIA*'s first five years, funding levels remained stable while production costs more than doubled. (Rampant inflation plagued both public and commercial productions during this period.) The challenge for WNET was not simply to produce high-quality shows on an inadequate budget; it was also to cope with the multiple demands of artists, funders, and other public television stations when resources were shrinking, a thornier issue.

It became impossible to meet the conflicting demands of the various participants with declining resources. The number of original productions in the series had to be reduced, and inexpensive acquisitions of foreign-produced shows were substituted as replacements, making it harder to satisfy the creative expectations of funders as well as to present an exciting lineup of new shows each season. As a result, audience ratings remained fixed or declined, and other public stations complained about the high cost of a series that was becoming increasingly narrow and less interesting each year.

As the participants became less satisfied with the end product, they attempted to exert more influence over the programming process. For example, CPB wanted dance productions specifically designed for a television format, and made its contribution contingent on greater regional diversity. Exxon, which had no interest in low-cost regional productions, held back final authorization of funds until it saw the complete roster of productions. But producers at WNET complained that they could not come up with a season of shows without knowing how much money they had to work with. The various participants began offering specific ideas for *DIA*, thus placing the station in a reactive position and further weakening WNET's role as producer. The various proposals were seldom compatible with one another. As one producer said, "Exxon proposed three programs that were their cup of tea—but none was NEA's bag."

To complicate matters further, one of the principal directors for *DIA* left WNET to join CBS Cable in a similar capacity because he was tired of "coping with contingencies in public TV." He noted, "I just wanted to work and not have to worry about finances." (Ironically, CBS Cable soon went bankrupt. Although it produced critically acclaimed programs, it also ran up $30 million in losses in its first year of operation.) Decisions about *DIA* affected the planning and budgeting for other WNET programs, strained the quality of relations between WNET and funding sources, and influenced how much money would be spent by other stations in the annual SPC. Other stations counted on WNET's success in order for them to have programs to broadcast. For the 1981–82 season, the *DIA* segment of *Great Performances* was cut back considerably. Only three programs, each featuring the work of George Balanchine, were broadcast. Exxon and NEA continued to fund this reduced schedule.

With *DIA*'s success came both increased expectations and declining resources. In public television the ultimate measure of success is whether or not participants report satisfaction with the results. (It is worth noting, however, that *DIA* was very successful in bringing dance into the cultural mainstream. Several years ago, CBS broadcast *Baryshnikov on Broadway* during prime time and it was rated one of the top 10 shows of the week. This success was attributable, in part, to the "research and development" work done by WNET with *DIA*.) As funders sought more influence over the content of *DIA*, WNET lost its ability to maintain some autonomy by balancing the funders against one another. To continue with *DIA*, WNET needed NEA money, but the NEA grant was subject to a 50/50 matching funds provision. Thus without the Exxon money, the coffers would have been empty. In addition, CPB was increasingly willing to support independent producers rather than WNET, because independents have lower overhead costs. At the same time, the dance community and WNET's pool of talented producers and directors, as well as corporate underwriters, began to see cable television as an alternative forum. WNET lost its position as the exclusive domain for quality dance programming. Both artists and funders had more choices and, as a result, they exerted more influence over WNET. WNET's reduced attention to dance is a reaction to its limited control over needed resources. The financial complexity and personnel turnover endemic to public television result in, to quote the director of the TV Lab, "the sad fact that nothing that is successful on public television endures."

SUMMARY

Given the financial constraints under which public television operates, it is sometimes surprising that any controversial or innovative programming is produced. In addition to sustaining smooth, ongoing ties with various funding sources, a producing station must maintain contact with many artistic communities. If program development is not continuous, stations risk losing the creative producers and directors on their staffs to commercial competitors. For a station to remain viable, management must also allow program producers and artists some latitude to develop program ideas free of undue financial constraints. Given these tensions, the record of public television in producing a lengthy list of high-quality programs in a working environment that is both heavily politicized and short on resources is no small feat.

In addition, the current financial crisis threatens public television in other ways. Good ideas may go unexploited for lack of resources. The scramble for funds and the time spent on negotiations leave little lead time for thoughtful planning. The opportunities posed by new technologies provide the most talented and marketable employees opportunity for exit. The staff that remains will have to do more with less and they may be less capable of making do with fewer resources.

Compared to commercial television, public television has offered more opportunity for voice both to funding sources, such as major corporations and governmental agencies, and to creative artists, such as members of the dance community and independent producers. In contrast to commercial television executives, public television managers lack the resources, and the power associated with them, to plan and execute the kinds of policies they would like to pursue. A public television station is an assortment of mini-organizations, each composed of staffs with their own priorities and with varying degrees of loyalty to public television. Caught between shrinking budgets and new communications technologies, public television must survive on less federal support. Stations have turned to their members, corporate underwriters, and their own initiatives to make up for lost federal dollars. The case of *Dance in America* suggests that, with declining resources, public television will become even more subject to outside control.

NOTES

1. Douglas Kellner, "Network Television and American Society," *Theory and Society* 10 (1981): 31–62.

2. This lack of agreement is even reflected in the language used: prior to 1967, noncommercial television was referred to as "educational television"; since then the common name has been "public broadcasting."

3. Most of the interviews and some of the field work at the two stations were conducted by Powell. He was assisted at the Hartford, Connecticut public station by Marguerite Schaffer. At WNET-TV, Claire Sokoloff helped with the interviewing and did much of the field work. Friedkin collaborated on the analysis of the data and kept track of numerous reports and statistics on public television finances.

4. Jeffrey Pfeffer and Gerald Salancik, *The External Control of Organizations* (New York: Harper & Row, 1978); and Carl Milofsky, "The Contribution of Nonprofit Organizations to Community," in Walter W. Powell, ed., *The Nonprofit Sector: A Research Handbook* (New Haven, Conn.: Yale University Press, 1986).

5. The recent controversies over public television documentaries—e.g., *Middletown, Mat-*

ters of Life and Death, Blood and Sand—War in the Sahara, and *From the Ashes . . . Nicaragua Today*—point to the way in which financial uncertainty has increased tensions within the public television community. There is friction between CPB and PBS, and concern within the public broadcasting community that PBS has become too eager to rein itself in. Program producers fear that PBS is soft-pedaling controversial material and hoping to survive on safe cultural and scientific shows aired in highly visible time slots. Moreover, critics charge that PBS is using its control over program scheduling to force changes in the content of completed programs. PBS maintains that growing financial constraints require it to concentrate its focus and "plan, develop, coordinate, and deliver the best possible Prime Time national program service" with the capacity to attract nationwide audiences (p. 3 of a PBS release, "Key Program Elements of Four-Year Plan," March 24–25, 1982). Many of the smaller public television member stations heartily support PBS's effort to centralize control, preferring that the hard choices about their future be made by PBS. In other words, their preference is for a network. Both independent producers and large stations, however, are opposed to moves by PBS to increase its control over decision making. The large stations see their influence slipping and fear a loss of support for the programs they produce. Independent producers, as well as production centers at producing stations, worry that a new era of timidity has set in as a consequence of budgetary cuts.

6. Corporation for Public Broadcasting, *Annual Report* (Washington, D.C.: Corporation for Public Broadcasting, 1984).

7. Nearly 50 percent of CPB's budget is passed through to stations; an additional 20 percent goes to grants for programs. The remainder is used to operate CPB, to fund PBS and the Station Program Cooperative, and to fund public radio.

8. Public Papers of the President: Richard Nixon, 1972 (Washington, D.C.: U.S. Government Printing Office, 1972), 718.

9. For a detailed discussion of the Nixon veto, see Robert K. Avery and Robert Pepper, "Interconnection Disconnection: The Evolution of the CPB-PBS Relationship," *Public Telecommunications Review* 4 (1976): 6–17; see also Carnegie Commission on the Future of Public Broadcasting, *A Public Trust: The Report of the Carnegie Commission on the Future of Public Broadcasting* (New York: Bantam Books, 1979).

10. For example, an underwriting officer at WNET spoke of the need for obtaining National Science Foundation support for a series then being developed, *The Brain:*

"Can you imagine how hard it would be to peddle this show to major firms without the imprimatur of NSF? It's not that the federal money is that large, but NSF funding serves as leadership dollars and better enables us to obtain additional funds. Without NSF support, other funders will be suspicious."

11. There are four types of governance structures among public television stations, based on who operates them: a state or municipality, a college or university, a community, or a public school system. The difference is a matter of licensing (a legal grant of a charter from the Federal Communications Commission) as well as governance. Depending on the nature of the legal charter, the composition of a station's board of directors will vary. Both WNET and CPTV are community-run stations.

12. Richard Magat, *The Ford Foundation at Work: Philanthropic Choices, Methods, and Styles* (New York: Plenum Press, 1979).

13. Although on-air advertising by corporate underwriters is restricted by FCC regulation, there are no prohibitions against off-screen advertising. Corporations back up their programming contributions with large promotional budgets. For example, Mobil Oil Company gave $3.5 million for programs in 1978 and allocated another $2 million for advertising. Gulf Oil Company allotted $1.4 million for its sponsorship of *National Geographic Specials* in 1978 and spent $1.8 million in advertising the programs.

14. David S. Ermann, "The Operative Goals of Corporate Philanthropy: Contributions to PBS, 1972–1976," *Social Problems* 25 (1978): 504–514; and Ronald S. Burt, "A Note on Corporate Philanthropy" (University of California, Berkeley, Survey Research Center Working Paper 36, 1980).

15. Ermann, ibid.; and Office of Communication Research, *Review of 1980 CPB Communication Research* (Washington, D.C., 1981).

16. Erik Barnouw, *The Sponsor: Notes on a Modern Potentate* (New York: Oxford University Press, 1978), 68.

17. Todd Gitlin, *Inside Prime Time* (New York: Pantheon, 1983), 252–256.

18. *The Lou Grant Show,* broadcast by CBS in the 1970s, is a recent example. See "Kimberly-Clark Pulls Ads from Ed Asner TV Show," *Wall Street Journal,* May 6, 1982, 46, western edition; and Mark Dow and David Talbot, "Asner: Too Hot for Medium Cool," *Mother Jones,* August 1982, 6–13.

19. The 1979 figures are from S. Young Lee, *Status Report of Public Broadcasting 1980* (Washington, D.C.: Corporation for Public Broadcasting, Planning and Analysis, 1981), 17. The 1983 figures are from Corporation for Public Broadcasting, *Annual Report, 1984* (Washington, D.C.: Corporation for Public Broadcasting, Planning and Analysis, 1984).

20. Ronald E. Frank and Marshall Greenberg, *The Public's Use of Television* (Beverly Hills, Calif.: Sage Publications, 1980), 191.

21. See, among many, Natan Katzman with Ken Wirt, "Program Funding in Public Television and the SPC," in Douglass Cater and Michael J. Nyhan, eds., *The Future of Public Broadcasting* (New York: Praeger Publishers, 1976), 251–274; and Michael G. Reeves and Tom W. Hoffer, "The Safe, Cheap and Known: A Content Analysis of the First (1974) PBS Program Cooperative," *Journal of Broadcasting* 20 (1976): 549–565.

22. Katzman and Wirt, ibid., 255.

23. Ibid.

24. Carnegie Commission on the Future of Public Broadcasting, op. cit., 108.

25. All quotes not attributed to a particular source are from fieldwork and interviews conducted at WNET and CPTV between 1980 and 1982.

26. Bill Moyers, who has had his own public affairs shows on both commercial and public television, captures the comparative costs and benefits of the two in the following statement made in the *New York Times,* April 11, 1978:

> The commitment to quality is high in both places. On CBS there are first class journalists, but they don't get the time on the air. On public broadcasting they have the time on the air, but they don't have the resources. The one has the money, but not the time; the other has the time, but not the money.

27. At WNET a recent reorganization, from a functional structure to a multidivisional structure with three programming divisions (national, local, and educational) and a for-profit enterprises division, was implemented to help reduce conflict and enhance cooperation among programming and fund-raising staff. Each division has its own programming, underwriting, and publicity departments. Furthermore, the separate for-profit division is both an effort to generate profits and an attempt to keep the other divisions "pure." On paper, the reorganized structure should reduce the tension between Programming and Underwriting. In practice, conflict has not been eliminated, but disputes are no longer exacerbated by the fact that personnel are located in different departments and report to different supervisors. Most of our interviews took place prior to the reorganization or shortly after its initial implementation.

28. Fund-raising is handled by the development department at CPTV and by the underwriting department at WNET. Our use of department titles depends on the station under discussion.

29. See *Death of a Princess,* Harvard Business School Case 9-381-106, for a detailed discussion of the controversy created by the showing of this program in both Britain and the United States. In particular, Mobil Oil, a generous sponsor of public television, ran a position statement in the Op-Ed page of the *New York Times* and other major papers criticizing the program. The Acting Secretary of State, Warren Christopher, relayed a letter from the Saudi ambassador to the United States to the president of PBS; Christopher asked that PBS "give appropriate consideration to the sensitive religious and cultural issues involved."

30. Lee, op. cit., 23–24, notes that in 1978, U.S. public broadcasting revenues (radio and

television combined) totalled $552 million, whereas commercial broadcast revenues were over $9.5 billion. The per-person cost differences are also quite large: $10.64 for commercial radio and $0.37 for public radio; $24.09 for commercial television and $2.15 for public television. Public television production costs are, however, much lower, approximately 40 percent to 50 percent of the costs per hour of commercial television production.

31. *Newsweek,* November 20, 1978, 139.

32. The analysis of *Dance in America* is based on fieldwork done at WNET.

12

Should University Presses Compete with Commercial Scholarly Publishers?

WALTER W. POWELL

The history of book publishing is replete with alleged crises and so-called revolutions. Heated debates about the commercialization of writing and the bleak financial status of the book industry are commonplace to almost every period in the industry's history.[1] As just one example, at the turn of the century *Publishers Weekly* ran stories by publishers lamenting that baseball and bicycle-riding would reduce the public's interest in books. In the 1980s, cutbacks in library budgets and in support for higher education have created new problems for scholarly presses. Although financial and marketing difficulties seem to be perennial with scholarly publishers, this sector of the industry has typically managed to survive economic downturns much better than trade publishing.[2] Scholarly publishing is a fairly stable business with less risk and more steady demand than in other sectors of the book industry.

Nevertheless, many university presses now find themselves under pressure from their parent universities to become self-supporting. New sources of financing and new markets are being sought. Increased export sales, increased subsidiary rights income, alumni book clubs, and cooperative promotion and distribution are but a few of the possibilities that university presses are pursuing. New, challenging technologies—microform publication, videodiscs, electronic journals, and computer data bases for on-demand publishing—are also being explored for the more efficient and less costly means of publication they may offer.

In addition, changes in the structure of trade publishing have created new opportunities. University presses and commercial scholarly houses are moving into the territory the larger trade houses have vacated in their

This chapter is based on a keynote address given at the annual meeting of the Association of American University Presses in Spring Lake, New Jersey, June 21, 1982. A shorter version of that talk appeared in the October 1982 issue of *Scholarly Publishing* under the title, "Adapting to Tight Money and New Opportunities." The paper appears here with the permission of the University of Toronto Press.

quest for best sellers. As trade publishers have increased their expectations of the number of copies a book needs to sell in order to be deemed successful, they have become less willing to take on books that are eminently worthwhile but have modest sales potential. The crush of big books has given impetus to scholarly presses. As a consequence, there has been a change in the mix of titles published by many university presses. Their lists now include novels, a few textbooks, and even how-to books. In general, there are more trade-oriented titles and fewer specialized scholarly books. The lists of many university presses are now hard to distinguish from those of for-profit scholarly publishers. These changes have not gone unnoticed by university faculty or by commercial publishers.

In the context of these recent changes, it is instructive to examine the similarities and differences between nonprofit university presses and commercial scholarly houses. Implicit in this examination is the question of whether university presses can compete with commercial firms, as well as whether such competition is appropriate.

In the course of interviews and participant observations I conducted with colleagues at a number of different publishing houses,[3] we encountered a variety of problems that stemmed from the university press strategy of pursuing a larger audience. At one of the university presses we studied, the classification of trade books was a major source of confusion and rancor. The decision to designate a book as a trade title rested with the sales manager. He had a vested interest in classifying at least a few of each session's books as trade titles because, whereas the sale of academic titles by direct mail was the publicity manager's job, the sale of trade books was his exclusive domain. The editors at the press were naturally pleased when one of their books received trade billing. They felt that a trade book was more consequential than a typical academic title because it reached a larger audience. Selling books in general bookstores was also something of a novelty at the press. Outside the editorial department, however, the consensus was that the sales manager was too liberal in his selection of trade books.

The sales manager's classifications created problems for the publicity department. It was responsible for advertising and promoting trade titles, yet it had little input into the choice of trade titles and frequently disagreed with the sales manager's decisions. Since their budget was quite limited, the publicity staff adopted the practice of selecting one of the trade books as the title having the widest general appeal that season. They spent most of their time, energy, and money on this book and more or less ignored the other books designated as trade, treating them as typical academic titles. This practice disturbed the editors of the neglected titles, who frequently made eloquent appeals to the publicity department for more media exposure for their trade books.

In the absence of sufficient money for promotion and marketing, such problems are common. Yet even if adequate funds were available to university presses, the broader issue of whether trade titles are too risky for university presses remains: The commercial trade publisher's operating norms of selling books in large quantity over a short period of time are quite different from the university press strategy of selling books in smaller quantities over long periods of time.

Other nonprofit organizations also currently face financial cutbacks and the challenge of new opportunities posed by new technological ventures. These nonprofit organizations are similar to university presses in that they also actively compete with commercial firms. The fundamental questions that many of these organizations are asking themselves are, How can we maintain our integrity and remain true to our purpose in the face of economic crises? And how do we find new funding sources without jeopardizing ongoing activities?

COMPARISON WITH PUBLIC TELEVISION

There are some interesting parallels between the circumstances found at some university presses and the problems faced by public television,[4] as well as a few lessons that can be drawn from a comparison of the two institutions. By 1980, public television faced sharply rising production costs and competition from new communications technologies such as cable television. In the early 1980s, financial problems were exacerbated by steep reductions in federal support. More than operating funds were involved; programming was and continues to be seriously affected by cutbacks at the National Endowments for the Arts and Humanities and the National Science Foundation. As a consequence of this steep decline in federal support for public television, stations had to join a long queue of nonprofit organizations knocking on the doors of foundations and corporations. It was all too obvious, however, that corporations and foundations could not and would not be able to replace federal support.

The Reagan administration, the Federal Communications Commission, and some members of the public broadcasting community encouraged public television stations to become entrepreneurial and to utilize new communications technologies to expand their financial base. Faced with declining support, public television counted on increased member contributions and new ventures—cable TV, teleconferencing, satellite broadcasting, videocassettes, specialized magazine and book publishing, foreign markets, and subsidiary rights sales—to carry them through this period of austerity.

But initial moves into these new areas brought howls of complaint from commercial firms who resented competition from nonprofit organizations.[5] The Internal Revenue Service moved to examine the tax status of some of the new ventures. As a response, many stations spun off for-profit divisions whose sole purpose would be to pursue money-making ventures. A number of powerful forces, however, constrain public television entrepreneurship:

Political factors: Misperception and/or disapproval of for-profit activities by a station's board of directors, station staff and members, the press, and commercial firms.

Organizational factors: Foremost, the lack of operating capital, and thus the need to incur substantial financial obligations to banks and to raise seed money from foundations; a lack of managerial experience; the difficulties of competing with the wealthier and more powerful commercial rivals.

Regulatory factors: The danger of losing nonprofit tax status; thorny problems of internal contracting and accounting for time spent on for-profit and nonprofit activities.[6]

These new ventures have raised considerable concern over the mission of public television. For example, some stations are producing programs for cable television. If they produce the same type of programs they broadcast on public television, why should those programs be shown on public television only after their commercial broadcast? Or if public television stations produce more standard, popular fare, what effect does this have on their image and their personnel?

A recent experiment with advertising on public television—mandated by Congress—raised similarly vexing questions: Will advertising cause a reduction in membership support? Will corporations continue to underwrite programs if they are also asked to advertise? Will labor contracts have to be renegotiated because lower wage rates and special rights given to nonprofit organizations are no longer warranted? Because ratings are the basis of any advertising rate schedule, will programming have to be changed in an effort to obtain a wider audience? Will advertising trigger serious political and financial opposition from commercial broadcasters?

Some employees feel the new ventures are far too risky and expose the stations to undue financial risks during a lean period. The costs of the new ventures are being reevaluated, and stations are analyzing whether they have overextended themselves. Future entrepreneurial efforts will probably be undertaken with more caution and considerable advance planning. Station executives are asking themselves what criteria for expansion are appropriate to an organization in which legitimacy is a crucial concern and conventional tests of market and ballot do not apply as readily as they do in commercial and governmental organizations.

ASSESSING APPROPRIATE ACTIVITIES

How should such nonprofit organizations as university presses decide what are appropriate new ventures? In my opinion, three closely related concerns must be taken into account. The first is to utilize the organization's comparative advantage by specializing in what it does best. The second is to recognize the important role played by such noneconomic factors as reputation and goodwill. The third, and perhaps the most crucial, is not to forget obligations and responsibilities to the academic community, which is the primary base of support for university presses. Authors and readers are a resource; they must be kept informed and their opinions solicited about current developments. University presses can and should do more to stay in contact with their faculties. It is part of the mission of nonprofit publishers, and it makes very good business sense.

Specialization

The law of comparative advantage was first set out almost two centuries ago by the economist David Ricardo in his studies of patterns of specialization and exchange among nations.[7] It is obvious that if one country is better at producing foodstuffs and another excels at manufacturing goods, both can save resources by trading—each exporting to the other the good it produces at the lower cost. Specialization of this kind permits larger outputs and economies of scale in production. But Ricardo's basic finding was a counterintuitive one: even if one country is more efficient than another in the production of *every* commodity (that is, if it has an absolute advantage in every commodity), both countries will still gain by trading. Even if a country is at an absolute disadvantage in relation to another country in the production of all goods, it is said to have a comparative advantage in producing the goods that it can produce least inefficiently.

Applied to nonprofit organizations, Ricardo's insights suggests that an organization will gain the most by specializing in what it is best at and at finding someone else to do other work. Even if the service that is hired is not as good as one it could provide, an organization is still better off emphasizing its strengths. Take the case of a university press with a good-sized backlist and good distribution capabilities. It is looking for ways to generate additional revenues from the sale of backlist titles. It considers starting an alumni book club, hiring a subsidiary rights person to pursue foreign translations, and launching a major promotional campaign to tout its backlist. But unless it is well endowed, the press should not try to do all three at the same time. It would risk too much financial exposure. The choice should be the alumni book club because it will build on the press's existing strength in distribution. For the other ventures, it should look for other presses with strengths in those areas, who could reduce their costs by taking on added work. If none exist, another possibility might be starting a collaborative arrangement in which many presses could avail themselves of a subsidiary rights service. In difficult economic times, nonprofits should emphasize what they do best and find other firms to provide additional needed services. Nonprofit organizations have more to lose than commercial firms; they may lose not only money but their reputations and nonprofit tax status as well.

Reputation and Goodwill

As part of our research on the book industry, we collected data concerning author-publisher relations from a random sample of over 200 authors. For purposes of comparison we surveyed authors who had recently published books with several large university presses, a major college text house, a variety of different-sized trade publishers, a small commercial scholarly house, and a large professional monograph publisher. University presses were found to have a number of distinctive features. As one might expect, they received the lowest marks for book distribution, speed of decision making, and size of advances. On a positive note, a major concern of the authors in our sample was their publisher's regard for the integrity of their work: university presses received very high marks on this. Their books carried a mark of prestige and were noted for their high quality of design. Commercial houses paid much less attention to these concerns. Moreover, the nonprofit tax status enjoyed by university presses exempts them from the *Thor Power Tool* ruling in the United States,[8] and as a result their books can be kept in print longer and greater emphasis given to the backlist.

Problems with copy editing as well as other aspects of the production process were commonplace for many authors, but not for those published by university presses. Most presses have a staff of manuscript editors or copy editors, unlike many commercial houses, which rely on outside freelancers. In addition, university presses employ a high-quality labor force. In many university towns there is a captive labor pool of faculty spouses. This overqualified staff can be a great boon for authors.

The most pronounced complaint of the authors in our sample was editorial turnover. If an author's editor departed from the house sometime during the publication process or upon the book's release, the author was likely to be unhappy with the publisher. In this respect, university presses turn out to be rather different from for-profit presses. We found that university presses have much greater editorial stability than their commercial counterparts.

All these factors are noneconomic ones. They are not easy to evaluate in financial terms. Nevertheless, they are essential elements in the publishing process and important ingredients in a satisfactory author-publisher relationship.

Obligations

Of the many different sectors of the book publishing industry, scholarly publishing—and here I include commercial houses as well as university presses—is the one most closely tied to both the producers and the consumers of the books. The scholar and the editor are often linked: Careers, reputations, and theories may rise and fall with the fortunes of commercial scholarly houses and university presses. In scholarly publishing, "invisible colleges"—closely tied groups of scholars working in the same general area located on different campuses—play a crucial role as talent scouts and gatekeepers. The would-be author who ignores this system and sends a manuscript to an editor without some imprimatur from a member of the appropriate invisible college does so at his or her own peril.[9]

Yet in some respects, university presses are not as open to the academic community as are commercial scholarly houses. Both university presses and commercial scholarly houses were more receptive to the young writers in our sample (under age 40) than were trade or text houses. Commercial scholarly firms, however, were much more likely than university presses to sign previously unpublished authors. Series editors—well-known senior scholars who have staked a claim to an area of research and who, in return for a small percentage of royalties, are responsible for new books published in their general area—serve as vital links between the commercial monograph houses and new talent. Series editors are knowledgeable about up-and-coming young scholars and about those who are played out. By contrast, such senior scholar brokers are somewhat rare in university press publishing. The advisory board at most presses performs a similar evaluative function, but university presses generally lack comparable talent scouts.

One consequence of this lack of communication between university presses and the academic community—in particular, junior faculty—is that some university press policies are not well understood. Among the more serious problems are:

Multiple submissions: Is this practice permissible or frowned upon?

The slower, more deliberate pace: Why does the review process at university presses take longer? What is gained from this longer time period?

Multiple bidding: On what basis do university presses compete with each other and with commercial houses?

Advance contracts: The practice of offering a contract on the basis of a proposal or incomplete manuscript is confusing. Do these quasi-official documents really mean anything? Are they helpful?

Two- and three-tiered lists: Why do some books receive a great deal of attention while others are handled much more quietly? Are there financial reasons behind this or is it just a consequence of the author's academic status?

These are but a few of the topics about which faculty need to be educated. Presses should also explain why most dissertations, even those from elite universities, are difficult to publish. Many junior faculty do not understand that libraries typically buy only the books of established writers or that promotion seldom creates an audience where one does not already exist. One press director we interviewed was particularly open with his faculty. He stated, "I tell the faculty straight out. If the eminent senior faculty do not publish with us it is impossible for us to do books by promising young faculty and graduate students."

Commercial publishers are not expected to make these efforts. But it should be the responsibility of university presses to do so, and I maintain that it is also a sound organizational practice. One of the most common errors that nonprofit organizations are making in this period of financial crisis is to overlook relatively quiet interest groups. As they scurry about looking for new sources of funding, the problem of balancing the demands of many different stakeholders is greatly increased. And the organization, in responding to one set of pressures, may take actions that will cause other supporters to become disaffected and unhappy.

Our survey of authors demonstrated the value of open communication on the part of publishers. The signing of a book, an act dominated from the publisher's side by the acquiring editor's enthusiasm, is an occasion for great expectations, at least on the author's side. The book is usually something the author has lived with for at least a year or two and which will, the author hopes, repay the time put into it not only in terms of some money but also fame. It is these lofty expectations, we believe, that explain why most of the authors in our survey were disappointed in their publishers. The one striking exception was a group of favorable responses from authors who had recently been published by a large professional monograph house. This firm had the highest percentage of satisfied authors of any house we studied. In general, university presses did fairly well on this survey, while trade and text houses fared quite poorly. What was particularly interesting was that over 70 percent of the authors of this particular monograph house were extremely satisfied with the advertising, promotion, and distribution. The key was the manner in which the house approached its authors. The editors were very direct and open: they told the author what kind of services would be provided, explained that every book receives a features mailing and an ad in a major journal, and solicited the author's suggestions. In short, they were honest about the limited sales prospects, open to ideas, and responsive to the author's concerns.

SUMMARY

In general, our research and our interviews with authors suggest that university presses have higher standards than commercial houses and pay more attention to the quality of the design and production, as well as remain truer to the integrity of an author's work. On the negative side, however, university presses are slower, somewhat less accessible to young authors, and less candid with authors about a book's prospects than are commercial scholarly houses. In light of these differences, the recent moves by university presses to produce more popular and marketable titles raise questions about the extent to which such policies will make university presses even less accessible to junior faculty and newly minted Ph.Ds. At the very least, it should be the responsibility of university presses to keep faculty members informed about the new directions being pursued and the financial circumstances that make such activities necessary. I do not doubt the ability of university presses to compete with commercial firms, nor do I question the motives of the individual presses. But I do worry about the aggregate consequences for the scholarly community if the distinction between nonprofit and for-profit publishers becomes more blurry. The result of such a process could lead to a very different publication system, one in which access is much more limited than is currently the case. And the experience of public television should serve as a reminder that changes in strategy can raise serious questions about purpose and mission, as well as endanger nonprofit tax status.

NOTES

1. For an extended discussion of this cyclical view, see Chapter 1 of Lewis Coser, Charles Kadushin, and Walter W. Powell, *Books: The Culture and Commerce of Publishing* (Chicago: University of Chicago Press, 1985).

2. See the discussion of the financial health of different subsectors of the book industry in Chapter 1 of Walter W. Powell, *Getting into Print: The Decision-Making Process in Scholarly Publishing* (Chicago: University of Chicago Press, 1985).

3. The research is based on interviews and participant observation in a large sample of for-profit and nonprofit publishing houses. For a detailed discussion of the research design, see "Appendix on methods," 375–381 in Coser, et al., op. cit. and the introduction to Powell, *Getting into Print,* op. cit.

4. Walter W. Powell and Rebecca Jo Friedkin, "Politics and Programs: Organizational Factors in Public Television Decision Making, (Chapter 11, this volume).

5. The landscape is dotted with commercial firms, research firms, travel agencies, professional service firms, etc. that are suing or lobbying or just plain screaming about the nonprofit firms that are said to be "unfairly" competing with them with the help of the law—tax exemptions, favorable postal rates and pension laws, and the preferences for nonprofits that are built into all kinds of government grant and contract programs.

John G. Simon, "Research on Philanthropy," (Paper delivered at the 25th Anniversary Conference of the National Council on Philanthropy, Denver, Colorado, November 1979, 9).

6. For a detailed discussion, see James D. Levine, "Public Television Funding: Tax and Policy Implications" (Yale Program on Non-profit Organizations Working Paper, New Haven, Conn., April 1982).

7. David Ricardo, *Principles of Political Economy and Taxation,* 9 vols., ed. P. Sraffa (Cambridge: Cambridge University Press, 1951–52).

8. In January 1979, the U.S. Supreme Court ruled in a case brought by the Thor Power Tool Company against the Internal Revenue Service that, contrary to what the plaintiff claimed, warehouse stocks of tools could not be depreciated for tax purposes unless they had left warehouse inventory. This meant that the tool industry had to discontinue its practice of carrying inventories at reduced prices for tax purposes. Soon thereafter, the Internal Revenue Service ruled that this decision was not only binding on the power tool industry but also applied, *inter alia,* to the publishing industry. To the IRS, books are products, just like tools or toilet paper. As a result of the *Thor* ruling, some publishers have had to change their accounting procedures and the value of their backlist books in stock. Other publishers had already followed these accounting procedures; for still others who publish few backlist titles, the *Thor* decision is of little consequence. University presses, as nonprofit organizations, are tax-exempt and hence not affected. But for many high-quality commercial firms, both scholarly and trade, the backlist has provided the backbone of their operations through thick and thin, and they depended on being able to depreciate the value of their backlist inventory. Now it is no longer as economically feasible to maintain stock on many titles and sell them gradually through backlist orders. A house that formerly kept titles in print may decide to remainder them rather than to bear the cost of maintaining them in print. Such destruction will be especially harmful for research monographs, which are slow to sell.

9. See Chapter 5 of my *Getting into Print,* op. cit.

13

Should the News Be Sold for Profit?

CHRISTOPHER JENCKS

Serious questions have been raised about the way in which the United States gathers and distributes news. Few American journalists are satisfied with existing arrangements, and many have chronic fantasies about starting their own newspaper or magazine (though few, it seems, imagine starting an organization to produce television news). But despite perpetual grousing, American journalists seldom discuss how news ought to be collected and distributed in a democratic society. Unlike their European counterparts, they have made no political effort to improve existing institutional arrangements.

Having begun my career in journalism, I find this reluctance to think about alternatives both puzzling and discouraging. Why, for example, are so few journalists disturbed by the fact that news is collected and distributed for private profit? Other professions, while frequently avaricious, at least recognize that the organizations through which they deliver services—universities, hospitals, courts—run better on a nonprofit basis. Why shouldn't newspapers, news magazines, or television news be run the same way?

Eliminating the profit motive does not imply public ownership or control of the new media. It is quite compatible with the present method of financing the collection and distribution of news, which depends in large part on intermingling news and commercial advertising. Nor does eliminating the profit motive imply dismantling existing news organizations; it would simply mean lending these organizations enough money to buy out their stockholders and then running them on a break-even basis.

Let me begin by conceding what many readers might not concede, namely that the profit motive is the best-known method of making an organization give its customers what they want when they want it. News is no exception to this rule. Profit-oriented news media are concerned with maximizing advertising revenue. To accomplish this they tinker endlessly with both the format and substance of the news in order to attract the largest and most affluent audience they can. Such efforts appear quite successful; if public enlightenment depended simply on getting as many people as possible to read newspapers and watch television news, there would not be much basis for complaint against the existing system.

But what the public wants is not always what it needs. And when a profit-oriented organization has to choose between giving people what they want or giving them what they need, it almost always chooses to gratify wants. The argument that people don't know what is good for them is, of course, hard to reconcile with conventional democratic ideas. Democracy assumes that in the last analysis people are the best—perhaps the only—judges of their own needs. Those who believe in democracy are rightly suspicious of experts who claim to know the public's needs better than the public itself does. But although skepticism is certainly warranted, a closed mind is not. We all know of instances in which people want things that are bad for them. The task of social reform is to deal with such situations without doing more harm than good.

In the case of news, the conflict between what we want and what we need derives from well-known human weaknesses: exhaustion and laziness. Most of us read newspapers and watch television while we are half-awake in the morning or after a tiring day's work. Our appetite for difficult ideas or moral ambiguity is even lower than usual at these times. A news organization seeking to maximize its audience therefore finds that it pays to make the news simple and exciting, not complex or challenging.

Those who manage the news media justify this approach by arguing that the public is divided into two distinct groups: a small number of "intellectuals" who want detailed information, careful analysis, and moral challenge, and a much larger group of "ordinary people" who want quick summaries, simple concepts, and moral reassurance. Defenders of the present system then describe their critics as elitists who don't understand ordinary folks. But this argument is too simple. Eggheads and yahoos certainly exist. For the most part, though, this is a schism *within* the mind of each reader or viewer. "Intellectuals" are hardly immune to the appeal of easy entertainment, as the fascination with Watergate attested; and although "ordinary people" often prefer entertainment, most also have a certain appetite for education—for experiences that literally "lead them out" of the narrow confines of their everyday lives. Furthermore—and this is the crucial point—most people regard their impulse to be educated as more creditable than their impulse to be entertained. We are proud of the moments when we rise to an intellectual or moral challenge. The moments when we ignore or avoid such challenges, although far more numerous, leave us with no comparable sense of satisfaction. Thus, while it is true that most people want the news to be entertaining most of the time, it is also true that most people "want to want" the news to be enlightening.

An organization that collects and distributes the news therefore faces an uncomfortable choice. One alternative is to ask as little as possible of its audience, maximizing its size but losing its respect. Television networks have made this choice and have learned to live with the fact that even the most assiduous viewers have a low opinion of the medium. Newspaper chains, which seldom care about the respect of local readers and usually see each local paper as a "profit center" rather than a community service, tend to make the same choice.

The other alternative is for a news organization to seek the respect of its audience and worry about audience size only insofar as that is essential to solvency. Public television sometimes adopts this stance. But public television has kept itself financially precarious by refusing to accept most forms of advertising. A number of family-controlled papers, such as the *New York Times,* the *Washington Post,* and the *Los Angeles Times,* also seem to value their reputations more than they value maximum profits—though all strive to ensure "adequate" profits. If all newspapers were produced on a nonprofit basis, I think they would place far more emphasis on winning the public's long-term respect and far less on maximizing audience size. The same is probably true of television news. The lure of profit is one of the few motives strong enough to make an organization pursue policies that risk public obloquy. Eliminate this motive and you shift the balance toward respectability.

Eliminating the profit motive would create a crisis of legitimacy in existing news organizations. Instead of letting the shareholders choose their directors, these organizations would have to select trustees in some other way. Furthermore, once they defined their official purpose as "public service" rather than private profit, tremendous controversy would arise about what the public really needed and who should define these needs. The experience of other nonprofit organizations, such as universities and hospitals, suggests that in the long run the professional staff would probably acquire a major role in running the organizations and deciding what was really "news," regardless of how trustees were selected. This would be a drastic change. Today's news organizations treat journalists as hired help, not professionals, and give them very little voice in running the organizations they work for.

What distinguishes a profession is its ability to convince other people that only members of the profession know enough to evaluate practitioners' work. This claim allows the profession to exercise significant control over its members' careers. Doctors or lawyers, for example, can expect those who hire them when they finish school to be doctors or lawyers themselves. This pattern will persist throughout their careers. If they make a serious mistake, those who evaluate its seriousness will again be doctors or lawyers, unless they end up in a malpractice suit. Scholars, too, can expect those who hire and promote them to be mainly fellow-scholars. Journalists, by contrast, must entrust their careers to the judgment of corporate managers. These managers are often called "editors," which makes them sound vaguely like fellow professionals, and are often former journalists. But that is no more relevant than the fact that the managers of universities are called "deans" and are often former scholars. A manager inevitably comes to identify with the organization, not with a former craft. If journalists wanted professional autonomy comparable to scholars, they would have to ensure that their careers depended largely on judgments made by other working journalists, not by editors or other corporate managers.

A journalist's claim to autonomy differs from that of most professions, however, in that it does not rest on strictly technical expertise. A journalist is more like a teacher than a scholar. Like teachers, journalists seek to instruct their audience and must often try to get people to absorb ideas they don't find intrinsically interesting. Unlike teachers, journalists cannot force people to pay attention by giving exams on their material. They are therefore under constant pressure to bring everything down to the level of the least attentive reader or viewer—much as teachers are under pressure to bring everything down to the level of the least attentive student. Some measure of professional autonomy would give journalists the short-run protection they need in order to persuade the public to accept their judgments about what is worth knowing over the long run. If the news media operated on a nonprofit basis, journalists would almost certainly be better protected in this respect.

If one is convinced that the news media should be nonprofit, the next question is how we might get from here to there. In the case of television, the change could be relatively simple. Congress could instruct the Federal Communications Commission to reserve certain hours of the day for national and local news and to restrict broadcasting during these hours to nonprofit organizations, which would lease broadcasting facilities from existing commercial stations. CBS, NBC, and ABC News would presumably separate from their profit-making parents, establish themselves as independent nonprofits, and apply for the right to broadcast national news. Under the FCC's present, rather arbitrary, licensing procedures, these new nonprofits would probably get their licenses and continue to enjoy oligopolistic privileges. Local television news organizations would presumably follow the same pattern. The main change would be in the internal operation of these groups.

The transition to nonprofit status would be somewhat more complicated in the case of newspapers and newsmagazines. In the print media the division between news and entertainment is not so clear-cut, and separating the two functions is probably impractical. An entire publication would therefore have to be converted to nonprofit status. The most politically promising way to do this would be to allow shareholders to convert their stock to government-guaranteed bonds on favorable terms. Such conversion might be made mandatory when shareholders died or wanted to transfer the shares.

Such changes are hardly imminent. The question, however, is not whether they are imminent but whether they would be desirable. If a consensus were to emerge among journalists that news ought not to be sold for profit like shoes or deodorants, I suspect journalists could alter other people's views rather quickly. At the moment, journalists are not even thinking about such questions.

V
EUROPEAN PERSPECTIVES

14

Public Support for the Performing Arts in Europe and the United States

JOHN MICHAEL MONTIAS

In Western Europe, a broad variety of organizations offer plays, operas, classical music, and ballet. Some, like the Dutch orchestra foundations, are akin to American nonprofit organizations; others, especially in Germany and France, are public agencies subordinate to central, regional, or municipal organs of government. In the European capitals, and in some of the largest provincial cities, private proprietary theaters play an important role. Most European performing-arts organizations—including many private ones—receive subsidies, although only those that are not strictly private and proprietary are dependent for the bulk of their incomes on public support. Generally speaking, government subsidies are on a lavish scale, while the donations of individuals, businesses, and foundations, in contrast with the United States, are modest or minimal.

Ideally, I would have wanted to link each major organizational form to a pattern of behavior. Lacking information sufficiently detailed to do this, I have had to confine the analytical portions of this paper to a single organizational distinction: between "private proprietary organizations" and "all other organizations" in the performing arts. The latter group comprises nonprofit organizations of the American type and quasi-governmental organizations of the French or German type. I call all companies, enterprises, associations, foundations, or firms belonging to this group "nonprofit organizations" (NPOs), although the reader should keep in mind that some of them may differ substantially from organizations that are

From *Comparative Development Perspectives,* ed. Gustav Ranis and Robert L. West, published by Westview Press, copyright © 1983. Reprinted by permission. The author is grateful to Avner Ben-Ner, Henry Hansmann, Daniel Levy, Paul DiMaggio, Richard R. Nelson, Susan Rose-Ackerman, and John Simon for their very helpful comments (empirical, theoretical, or of both kinds) on an earlier draft of this chapter.

legally classified as nonprofits in the United States. However different they may be, most NPOs in Europe and the United States share one characteristic: they are recognized by virtue of having been created by an organ of government or by an explicit act of a specialized government agency such as the Conseil d'Etat in France or the Internal Revenue Service in the United States as being of public interest or utility (in German *gemeinnützig*, in French *d'utilité publique*). This public-utility attribute legitimates the direct aid (subsidies) or indirect support (tax exemptions) that they receive from government agencies.

The paper is divided into several parts. I begin by summarizing the divergent histories of public support for the performing arts in continental Western Europe and the United States; next I assemble statistics on the organization and the financing of theatre, opera, concert, and ballet organizations in the 1970s in both parts of the world; finally I analyze the theoretical behavior of nonprofit organization producing "elite" and "popular" shows in competition with a private-proprietary sector producing only "popular" shows. The chief purpose of the modeling exercise employed in this part is to show the consequences of increased levels of subsidies on the choices made by the manager of this hypothetical NPO between the two types of shows.

HISTORICAL SURVEY

France

In Europe, partronage of the performing arts by ecclesiastic and secular authorities goes back to the Middle Ages. In the fifteenth century it was already common practice for the aldermen of northern French towns to allot funds for the staging of mystery plays which were generally put on by members of church groups ("confraternities"). In some instances all the expenses of a play—chiefly for costumes and staging—were paid from the town treasury.[1] From the late sixteenth century on, as European kings and princes acquired absolute power, they took over the twin roles of policing and subsidizing the stage. Monopolies and privileges were granted to royal companies that catered to elite tastes. In seventeenth-century Paris, companies that did not secure royal or aristocratic patronage and sought to play for a broader public were harassed by the police; if they were not banned altogether, they had to restrict their entertainment to pantomime, puppetry, and other exhibitions that were not in direct competition with the established companies.[2] In France and Sweden, theatre companies and musical groups in the capital or at the seat of the court enhanced the prestige of the royal house. This was reason enough to merit support.

After the French Revolution of 1789, which proclaimed the freedom of founding new theatres, centralized controls were reimposed, first under Napoleon, then under the restoration. The modern pattern emerged in mid-nineteenth century: in the capital, a handful of subsidized theatres and opera houses coexisting with more numerous commercial establishments (42 private theatres in 1878); in the provinces, each municipality of any consequence financing the erection and the operation of a theatre building for the free or low-cost use of theatrical and operatic companies (resident in the larger cities, itinerant in the smaller), which frequently also received an operating subsidy from the city. Controls on the repertory and even on the staff of theatrical companies were exercised by the departmental prefects and by the Ministry of the Interior until the 1870s.

Germany and Austria

From the late seventeenth century on, German and Austrian princes set about creating theatres and opera houses, frequently providing a permanent home and financial support for companies, many of which had been regional touring groups in the past. During the Enlightenment, the notion gained currency among German-speaking intellectuals that the theatre was capable of providing an essential part of a good citizen's education and that public funds deserved to be given out to advance this end, just as they were given for the purpose of educating the young.[3] A *Kulturtheater* was needed to uphold higher moral aesthetic, and even patriotic standards. In the absence of political centralization, the emperors of Austria, the kings of Prussia, the princes, margraves, and electors of the German-speaking world created their own court theatres. Emperor Joseph II of Austria founded a national theatre in 1776 "for the development of good taste and the improvement of morals."[4] From 1791 on, Goethe directed the court theatre of Weimar which became a showplace for German Enlightenment. Some municipalities, in emulation of the high nobility, also began to found and support their own theatres and operas about this time.

The eighteenth century debate on the value and purpose of the theatre began to affect the administration of theatrical establishments in the first half of the nineteenth century. In 1808 Freiherr von Stein proposed that the Prussian theatre be detached from police control and placed under the supervision of the Ministry of Cults and Education. "The theatre," he pleaded, "is an educational establishment *(Bildungsanstalt).*" *Bildung,* a word with no precise equivalent in English connoting education and cultivation, was the intellectual foundation upon which later advocates of public support for the arts were to build.

Emancipation of the theatre from police authority was only accomplished in the wake of the Revolution of 1848. Shortly after that event, Edward Devrient, a leading theatre man of his time who was largely responsible for drawing up a plan for reform of the Prussian theatre, wrote a widely disseminated manifesto in favor of a subsidized *Bildungstheater.* "All that is capable of edifying and refining mankind," he argued.

should be protected by the state and be made independent of naked gain; this applies to art as well as to school and church. Competition . . . must be excluded once and for all. Private industry, whether in the form of rental concessions or of autonomous enterprises, under the present circumstances can bring no higher benefit to the theatre; without the backstop of monetary support which will guarantee the independence of the stage from the crowds that bring money, the theatre cannot be conducted on pure principles.[5]

Prussian nationalism was surely not absent from Devrient's proposals. But his ideas were also influential in cities and smaller states where the desire to base art on high principles (mixed with local pride) motivated the adoption of his policies.

Already in 1818, the general assembly of one of the German kingdoms (Württemberg) resolved to subsidize its national theatre and opera house in Stuttgart from the regular budget. This lasted only two years, however, after which the assembly refused to meet this "wasteful expense" and the king was forced to meet the deficit of the former Court Theatre from his own pocket.[6] About the same time the municipality of Mannheim began to share in the burden of maintaining the National Theatre created in 1774 by the Duke of Gotha. In 1839 the city placed the theatre under *régie* (direct management) and undertook to guarantee all its losses. The city of Freiburg followed Mannheim's example in 1868. The same policy was adopted by Strasbourg in 1886, Mülhausen in 1903 (both of these presently French cities then under German suzerainty), Kiel in 1907, Essen, Hagen, and Leipzig in 1912, Breslau, Dortmund, and Eberfeld in 1913.[7]

In the case of symphonic music, wealthy patrons and "free associations" *(freie Genossenschaften)* created and financed large new ensembles. Private and cooperative support provided the bridge between the patronage of princes and other potentates of the eighteenth and early nineteenth centuries and the state-subsidized activities of the post–World War I era.[8]

The rise of publicly and cooperatively supported organizations in the second half of the nineteenth century coincided with a growing gap between bourgeois-popular and elite culture. Elite groups were able to mobilize public support for "serious" theatre and music at a time when—and perhaps because—commercial enterprises were increasingly pandering to the "bad taste" of the dominant bourgeois public.[9]

By the 1920s, theatre, opera, and orchestral music were dominated by *gemeinnützig* (public-interest) organizations supported by local and state organs. In 1929 these NPOs employed 89 percent of the singers, two-thirds of the actors and actresses, and over 80 percent of the musicians engaged in professional activities.[10]

Many of the NPOs were *régie* enterprises, owned by and directly subordinate to municipal and state organs which covered their financial deficits. The financial guarantees against unforeseen losses, in an industry where such losses frequently occurred due to the vagaries of an uncertain demand, placed a substantial contingent burden on the budgets of the cities and states (later *Länder*) that had committed themselves to this *Kulturpolitik*. Nevertheless, by the 1920s these included virtually all the cities and states that had any theatre or opera whatsoever. Data for theatre-and-opera subsidies, as initially estimated or forecast *(Voränschlage)* and as they were actually realized in the 1920s and early 1930s, were published

Table 14.1 Percentage Breakdown of the Earned Income and Subsidies of the Nonprofit German Theatres (1911, 1926/27, 1934/35, 1973/74) (percent)

	1911	1926/27	1934/35	1973/74
Subscriptions and tickets[a]	63.2	60.1	44.5	12.0
Radio and TV income	—	0.1	2.3	0.2
Other earned income[b]	5.7	8.2	6.2	5.4
Private Support	3.9	1.0	—	0.1
Government subsidies	27.2	32.3	40.7	81.9
Total Income	100.0	101.7	93.7	99.6

NOTE: The percentages do not add up to 100.0 in 1926/27 and 1934/35 because they have been computed from sector-wide averages in each income category, some of which, for lack of detailed data, were based on an incomplete coverage of all theaters in the sector (note in the source). The data for 1911 cover only eight theaters, those for 1934/35 only municipal theaters.
[a] Including sales to theater groups, associations, students, etc.
[b] Programs, cloakroom receipts, guest appearances, tours.

SOURCE: Fritz Herterich, *Theater und Volkswirtschaft* (Leipzig: Duncken and Humbolt, 1937) 281, 187; Deutscher Bühnenverein, *Theater-statistik 1973/74* (Köln, 1974), 56.

shortly before World War II—the only ones of the kind that I have come across for any country. They show wide disparities for München (DM 2.3 million compared to an estimated DM 0.8 million), Berlin (4.4 million versus DM 2 million), Wiesbaden (DM 1.5 versus DM 0.75 million), and Weimar (DM 1.6 versus DM 1.1 million). On average, losses in the 1926-27 season exceeded estimates by 43.3 percent for state theatres and 35.2 percent for municipal theatres.[11]

The same statistical source provides a valuable glimpse of the long-term structure of receipts of the German nonprofit theatre and opera in 1911, 1926/27, and 1934/35. This structure is compared to data for 1973/74 in Table 14.1.

Imperfect as the data in Table 14.1 may be, the trends they reveal are too pronounced to be fortuitous. The share of subscriptions and tickets in total income fell drastically over the years covered, from over 60 percent in the pre-World War I period to 44.5 percent under Nazi rule (for municipal theatres only), down to 12 percent in 1973/74. Private support accounted for a small but significant part of total income in 1911; it has been negligible in recent years. Government support—the obverse of the above phenomena—has had to fill an ever-widening gap. As in the pre–World War I period, this gap has been filled by municipal and state (later *Länder*) subsidies, not by the central or federal government, which, for the most part, has relegated cultural policy to regional and local organs of power.

Sweden

In Sweden, as in France, the history of patronage in early modern times coincides with the largesse of the reigning monarchs. During the period of Enlightenment, especially in the second half of the eighteenth century, the kings of Sweden emulated their fellow autocrats in France, Austria, Prussia, and Russia by founding academies of letters, royal theatres, and opera houses.[12] After 1809, the Riksdag, or Parliament, which now ruled over the constitutional monarchy, voted the national budget, a modest part of which was given over to support of the arts. The civil officials of the nobility wished to continue the royal patronage of the arts on an eighteenth-century scale or beyond, but their pro-art policy was resisted by the economy-minded representatives of the peasantry in the Riksdag. The influence of the latter was especially strong in the last forty years of the century. It was not until late in the nineteenth century that representatives of the industrial bourgeoisie and labor members of the Riksdag were able to muster the votes for a more generous arts policy.[13] But the sluices only became wide open a decade after World War II, once the social democratic governments had met the most pressing social welfare needs of the nation: the arts were now ready for the benefactions that government officials, intent on recreating the brilliant patronage of the enlightened monarchy of the eighteenth century, could at last lavish on them.

The Netherlands

The Dutch national government launched a serious program of support for the performing arts later than the other European countries so far considered; but its commitment, once made, went very deep. The watershed here was World War II, shortly after which a dramatic increase in subsidies to all cultural and welfare activities took place.[14] Symptomatic of the government's enhanced commitment was the decision taken in 1948 to help symphony orchestras break their dependence on the box office by guaranteeing the full salaries of all accredited orchestra players.[15] Since that time the salaries of actors employed by national theatres have also been guaranteed. Thus, when the *Nieuw Rotterdamse Toneel* and the *Nederlandse Comedie* closed "under popular pressure" during the course of the 1970/71 season, for reasons discussed below, the government saved very little money because it continued to pay the two theatres' salaries.[16]

The Dutch experience with the large-scale subsidization of music and theatre in the 1960s and 1970s is so interesting and instructive that it deserves separate consideration. In the late 1960s, as part of the European youth revolt which culminated in the French university riots of 1968, Dutch students and intellectuals assailed the repertoire of subsidized orchestras and theatres. The *Notenkraker* (Nutcracker) group raised an outcry against the performance of esoteric music. The "Tomato Action Group" castigated and forced the closing of *De Nieuw Rotterdamse Toneel* and the *Nederlandse Comedie* for their failure to stage serious plays relevant to their social concerns. Soon thereafter, in the early 1970s, new companies *(Werk Theatre, Satyr, Baal, de Appel)* were created that specialized in tragedies and serious social plays. The old, established state and municipal theatres adapted their repertoire to this "activist" demand. Light and middle-brow plays and operettas which had helped to stretch out subsidies and sustain socially redeeming works in the past were thrust aside.

This virtual seizure of the subsidized theatres by activist minorities was, from the viewpoint of attendance, a disaster. Attendance at all professional subsidized theatres, which had been hovering around 1.4 to 1.5 million from 1965 to 1969, fell to 1.1 million in the 1972/73 season and 907,000 in the 1974/75 season.[17] What is more, the professional private theatre, which had been gradually edged out of the market by the mid-1960s, underwent a brilliant revival in the 1970s. Attendance at private theatres which had fluctuated between 150,000 and 250,000 in the period from 1965–69 rose to 750,000 in the 1974/75 season. As the director of the Association of the Netherlandish Theatre companies put the matter in an interview, the subsidized theatre, by specializing in tragedies and serious plays, had left a gap in the market which was soon filled by the private theatre. In the last section of this chapter, a stylized version of this development is analyzed theoretically.

United States

The lack of a tradition of royal patronage combined with a strong Puritan tradition helps to explain the almost total absence of government support for the performing arts in eighteenth- and early nineteenth-century America.

New England and Dutch Calvinists, the Quakers, and other religious groups strongly disapproved of the theatre, which, according to a widely shared view, encouraged "shiftlessness, idleness, and immorality."[18] As late as 1774, the Continental Congress issued a resolution calling for the suspension of "horseracing, gambling, cockfighting, exhibition of shows, plays, and other expensive diversions and entertainments."[19] In the last one or two decades of the eighteenth century, religious prejudice against theatre was still so strong that plays had to be advertised as "moral lectures."[20] In a cultural climate of this sort, when cities were still small and most taxpayers were farmers who had not the time, the money, or the inclination to attend performances, the expenditure of government revenue to subsidize the theatre was unthinkable.

In the first half of the nineteenth century, British touring companies supplied most of the better theatrical fare. Native companies—including the popular minstrel shows—appealed to an uneducated public, which also patronized the circus, the exhibition of freaks, and other outlandish curiosities. The great P. T. Barnum offered both "high" and "low" art. In his autobiography, he explained his policy as follows: "Show business has all phases and grades of dignity, from the exhibition of a monkey to the exposition of that highest art in music or the drama, which entrances empires and secures for the gifted artist a worldwide fame."[21] To be sure, he made more money exhibiting curious animals and freaks than presenting high art, with the exception of singer Jenny Lind's prodigiously successful tours. Barnum expressed views on the business of art that were widely held at the time. "Art," he argued,

> is merchantable, and so with the whole range of amusements, from the highest to the lowest. . . . People cannot live on gravity alone; they need something to satisfy

their gayer, lighter moods and hours, and he who ministers to this want is in a business established by the Author of our nature.[22]

If God Himself smiled on such enterprises, why should government tamper with them?

Not all Americans conceived of art as an ordinary consumption activity that private enterprise could satisfy just as any other. Already in the 1830s the painter William Dunlap had called for government support of the fine arts, including especially the theatre, on the model of France and Germany where the theatre was flourishing under government auspices.[23] He proposed that the states establish their own theatres "in order to eliminate the profit motive from theatrical enterprises and thus improve the quality of both the plays and the performances themselves."[24] But his plan found no political support and withered on the vine.

Another painter, Rubens Peale, sought to introduce high culture to Baltimore in the 1820s and 1830s by mounting an operation with the aid of civic-minded patrons that combined business and art. His was a farraginous mixture of high and low art and of natural science, typical of his time. The "Baltimore Museum" that he dedicated to the "improvement of public taste and the diffusion of science" exhibited contemporary paintings, copies of old masters, and natural-history specimens; it also staged theatrical performances "in order to meet the annual deficits of the institution."[25] When the enterprise began to fail, Peale attributed his difficulties to "the sordid calculations of shortsighted commercial avarice"—by which he meant his patrons' unwillingness to put up the funds that were necessary to turn it into a success. The subsequent fate of the institution, according to cultural historian Lillian Miller, "is a story of gradual deterioration from a museum devoted to art and science to a theatrical 'saloon' and finally to a P. T. Barnum showcase."[26] The city of Baltimore itself, as far as I can make out, never contributed a penny to bail out the failing enterprise.

At the federal level, if there was any serious consideration of subsidizing the arts at all in pre–Civil War days, it was directed toward the plastic arts—chiefly to the decoration of public buildings. But the government's participation was limited by the apathy of a Congress engrossed in the controversies between North and South, free and slave interests, and national power and states' rights.[27]

The alternative to commercial theatre and opera in the eighteenth and nineteenth centuries was not the state-subsidized quasi-governmental enterprise but the amateur, religious, or other noncommercial group. Church music and college theatricals flourished already in the eighteenth century.[28] "Thespian" and "Aeolian" musical societies began to mushroom in colleges and cities. The New York Philharmonic Society was founded in 1842 as a cooperative venture, almost exclusively with foreign-born musicians, who paid the expenses and divided the profits. New York's Concordian and Euterpian Societies, Boston's Handel and Haydn Society, and Philadelphia's Musical Fund Society began to cater to the tastes of city elites. After the Civil War, conservatories were founded in all the larger cities. In the late 1870s and early 1880s, wealthy patrons banded together to launch new orchestras and build opera houses. The Metropolitan Opera, founded in 1883, was one such enterprise. Paul DiMaggio has recently shown how in Boston, the traditional "Brahmin" elite, after yielding its dominant position in city politics to a new class of immigrants and parvenus around the time of the Civil War, founded "a system of nonprofit organizations that permitted them to maintain some control over the community even as they lost their command of its political institutions."[29] The Boston Symphony Orchestra, together with the Museum of Fine Arts, were the kingpins of these NPOs in the arts. These organizations drew their sustenance from a tightly knit group of rich, civic-minded patrons, not from the city treasury. The growing gulf between cultural and political elites of nineteenth-century America, which had no evident counterpart in Europe, made it much more difficult to transfer the responsibility for supporting cultural activities from private to public patronage when the old Maecenates could (or would) no longer carry the burden.

The rise of a professional theatre "for art rather than for profit" lagged behind the parallel development in music. It was not until shortly before World War I that the first attempts were made to found professional theatres dedicated to high-minded artistic ideals.[30] The deficits incurred by these avant-garde theatres were met—if they were met—by private backers and members' contributions. With the exception of the well-endowed New Theatre founded in New York in 1909, which folded after two seasons of heavy losses, the art theatres were small and economically run. Actors who were not yet unionized were paid very small salaries when they were paid at all. In the 1920s the "noncommercial movement" developed rapidly—from 50 groups in 1917 to over 1000 by 1929, including college and university theatres.[31] The first municipal theatres were founded in this period, including one supported by the town of Northampton in Massachusetts. Large cities, however, did not begin to subsidize the theatre until the 1930s, and very few are doing so systematically to this day.

A handful of states, spearheaded by New York, made their initial moves toward a policy of regular support of the performing arts in the late 1960s and early 1970s. The federal government, with the exception of the generously funded Federal Theatre (1935–39), did not, so to speak, get into the act until Congress passed a bill establishing the National Foundation on the Arts and Humanities in 1965 and money was appropriated for its component organization, the National Endowment for the Arts, in the following year.[32] Federal government subsidies in the 1970s in part supplemented, in part supplanted, the help given by the major foundations (Ford, Rockefeller) in the 1960s.

To sum up, government at all levels in the United States came to subsidize the arts at least a century after such support had become a regular practice in Western Europe. The lack of a tradition of princely patronage, lingering puritanical attitudes, the dominance of a mercantile spirit, a widespread ideology of self-reliance, the generosity and enterprise of wealthy patrons cooperating to found "societies" to supply the cultural activities they desired, all help to explain the distinct American pattern of development.[33]

We should also take into consideration the more democratic way of running cities and state government in this country that did not give music- and theatre-loving elites as much opportunity to impose their tastes on the public as in Europe.[34] The idea, fostered by European elites, that theatre and music should be part of a good citizen's *Bildung* never took root in America. Finally, as we shall see in the next section, the more generous provisions for deducting donations to the arts in the U.S. Internal Revenue code stimulated private patronage in the United States and staved off the necessity of government help to keep arts institutions on an even keel.

A STATISTICAL OVERVIEW OF THE CONTEMPORARY ORGANIZATION AND FINANCING OF THE PERFORMING ARTS

Organizations

Official European statistics cover the heavily subsidized nonprofit sector fairly well; data for the private proprietary sector, however, are scarce, and when available, frequently of mediocre quality. What is called "private" may be an amalgam of proprietary organizations and struggling theatres and ballet companies that are too small or too recently founded to be recognized as worthy objects of subsidization by the state. Table 14.2 illustrates the multiplicity of organizational forms in the theatre and opera of the German Federal Republic. The registered associations in Table 14.2, like the French *associations reconnues d'utilité publique,* are those judged by a government agency to be of public benefit. In my analysis of public subsidies in the tables that follow I have taken the registered associations out of the private sector and included them in the nonprofit sector.

"*Régie* management" refers to direct management by agents appointed by a state *(Land)* or municipality *(Gemeinde)* for the account of that agency. The expenditures of theatres and operas under *régie* management are comprised in the budget of the founding agency. Limited liability companies, by contrast, are responsible for covering their expenditures from their receipts and such subsidies as they may receive from one or more government agencies. Some of these companies were private, others public. The shareholders of the public ones may be states, municipalities, or a mixture of both. Private individuals, as far as I am aware, do not hold shares in these public companies.

Of the 45 German "culture orchestras"—essentially, orchestras playing "classical music"—14 were organized under *Länder* and 21 under municipalities, 8 were associations, 1 was a limited-purpose association, and 1 a corporation under public law *(Körperschaft des öffentliches Rechts).*[35]

Table 14.2 Organizational Forms of Theatres and Operas in the German Federal Republic, 1973/74 (number of organizations)

			"Public" Theatres or Operas Organized Under:			
	Grand Total	"Private"	Total	States (Länder)	Municipal-ities	Mixed Sponsorship
Individually owned	38	38	—	—	—	—
Registered associations	24	17	7	—	—	7
Régie management	49	—	49	13	36	—
Limited liability companies[a]	40	24	16	3	6	7
Others[b]	17	4	13	—	2	11
Total	168	83	85	16	44	25

[a]Gesellschaften mit beschrankten Haftung.
[b]Civil law corporations (Gesellschaften bürgerliches Rechts), limited purpose associations (Zwechverbanden), companies in which liability of one partner is limited (Kommand Gesellschaften) and private firms (Offene Handelsgesellschaften).

SOURCE: Deutscher Bühnenverein, *Theater-statistik* 1973/74, (Köhn, 1975), 12–14, 52.

The organizational status of French theatres and orchestras is as variegated as the German. The *Comédie Française,* although legally an association (the full-fledged sociétaires still draw part of their income in the form of shares), is in reality a national theatre receiving a large part of its income from the central government budget, as do other national theatres *(Chaillot, l'Odéon, L'Est Parisien, Strasbourg).*[36] Major subsidized theatres in the provinces—chiefly founded by municipalities—are linked to the central government by "conventions" or contracts that specify the number of new plays and the total number of performances they must "produce" in a three-year period to earn a fixed amount of subsidies for that period.

In 1979, there were 27 major regional theatres linked to the central government by such "conventions." Most of these theatres were originally founded by municipalities and operated as concessions; they have of late been placed under the direct management *(régie)* of their municipal governments because of the difficulty of finding "concessionaires" willing to take on substantial risks of incurring unforeseen losses.[37] These provincial theatres make up what the Ministry of Culture and Communications calls "la décentralisation dramatique." More authentically decentralized are the 300-odd "independent companies," most of which apply for central-government aid; of these only about a tenth are successful in the national competition for subsidies. The legal status of some of the small, financially weak companies is often ill-suited to their operation. For if they are organized as associations, the law of July 1901 which regulates such organizations does not allow them to engage in commercial activities and hence to obtain a theatre license.[38] Some theatres, nevertheless, are organized as informal associations and even receive subsidies from the central government. A few have opted for the status of *Societé Ouvrière de Production* (workers' cooperative), created "by workers or employees desirous of exercising their profession in common."[39] A few theatres have no juridical status to speak of: they are classified as "de facto companies" (societés de fait) and are not eligible for subsidies at all.[40] All these small "decentralized" companies are essentially nonprofits. But even individually owned theatres and theatres organized as limited-liability companies—representing the so-called private sector—may receive subsidies if they produce new plays by French authors or stage old plays in substantially new ways.

In Holland, most subsidized theatres, orchestras, and ballet companies are organized as foundations. The Nederlandse Opera of Amsterdam, for instance, is a foundation covering 75 percent of its expenditures from state subsidies and a part of the rest from hosting provincial municipalities when the opera goes on tour.[41] Such foundations are administered by boards on which representatives of subsidizing government agencies are assured a seat and a measure of influence. In Sweden, national theatres are typically administered by five-member boards, two of which are appointed by the government. The directors of municipal theatres are appointed by the town council which covers the theatres' financial deficits.

The Financing of the Performing Arts

The statistics of receipts and expenditures of performing arts organizations in Tables 14.3 and 14.4 cover exclusively autonomous professional organizations. They exclude orchestras that are part of a radio network, military bands (because they are not professional), and school theatres (because they are neither autonomous nor professional).[42] In accord with the basic principle of classification set forth in my introductory remarks, nonprofit organizations comprise public institutions, associations, foundations, and joint-stock companies whose shares are held by public institutions. "Private" organizations are strictly proprietary (although they may also receive public subsidies).

In Austria and France, as shown in Table 14.3, the total receipts including subsidies—which approximately equal the expenditures or factor costs—of nonprofit performing-arts organizations vastly exceed those of private organizations. No precise statistics are available for the other countries, but a comparison of the size of audience in the two types of German and Dutch theatres indicates that the predominance of the nonprofit sector holds for these two countries as well.[43]

Table 14.4, showing the percentage distribution of the total incomes of performing-arts organizations, throws into relief the enormous difference between Western Europe and the United States in financing the arts. In the dominant nonprofit sector, earned income in the five European countries listed represented between one-tenth and one-third of total income (approximately equal to total expenditures). The Swedes have gone farthest down that route: ticket income accounted for only 10.5 percent of total income in the 1974/75 season (3 percent of the Royal Opera's and 7 per-

Table 14.3 Financing of the Performing Arts, Western Europe and the United States in the Early 1970s* (millions of national currency units)

			Direct Subsidies				
	Date	Earned Income	National or Federal	State and Local	Private or Foundation	Other Income	Total
Austria							
Nonprofit opera and theater	1973	282.2	680.3	253.5	2.1[a]	—	1218.1
Private theatre[b]	1973	43.0	31.7	21.5	0.5[a]	—	96.7
France							
Public/nonprofit	1973	136.0	178.0	113.0	—	—	427.0
Private	1973	80.0	1.0	—	—	—	81.0
Germany							
Nonprofit[c]	1973/74	195.3	2.9	883.4	5.0	10.6[d]	1097.2
Private	1973/74	n.a.	—	14.3	—	—	n.a.
Netherlands							
Nonprofit							
Theatre	1972/73	6.5	12.1	10.8	1.9[e]	—	31.3
Other[f]	1972	3.6	16.5	7.6	—	—	27.7
Sweden							
Nonprofit	1974/75	29.4	181.7	69.7	—	—	280.8
United States							
Nonprofit[g]	1970/71	90.4	3.4	4.9	58.2	10.5[h]	167.4
Private theatre[i]	1970/71	105.1	—	—	—	—	105.1

NOTES: * Operational budgets only, excludes capital expenditures.
[a]Proceeds from lotteries.
[b]Three large private theaters in Vienna.
[c]Theater, opera, and symphony orchestras, only.
[d]Subsidies from public radio-television stations, public lotteries ("lotto") and "other public sources."
[e]Financial aid from Omroep Foundation.
[f]Nederlandse Opera, Het Nationale Ballet, and Concert Gebouw Orchestra, only.
[g]These estimates, based on the Ford Foundation survey of 166 performing arts organizations, may seriously underestimate the contribution of state and local subsidies, due to underrepresentation in the Ford sample of small companies which were more dependent on state support. State legislative appropriations to all the arts were $25.2 million, of which at least 40 percent, or $10.8 million, were allotted to professional performing arts agencies (see DiMaggio 1981, 4–9).
[h]Corpus earnings used for operations plus certain transfers from endowments.
[i]Broadway and commercial touring, only (23.5 million audience in 1977); excludes small summer stock (4.9 million estimated audience), large musical arenas and hard tops (6.6 million), and summer theater (11.1 million).
SOURCES AND METHODS: Austria and Germany: Deutscher Bühnenverein, "*Theater statistik 1973/74*," Köln, 1975.
France: For Paris-based private and public nonprofit theaters and orchestras, Ministère de la Culture et de l'Environnement, *Annuaire statistique de la Culture, Données de 1970 à 1974,* La Documentation Française 1977, vol. 2; for provincial theaters, orchestras, and opera houses, data were extrapolated from fragmentary statistics for 1970–71 in annex 1 to the unpublished report prepared for the Ford Foundation, *Theater and Music in Western and Northern Europe 1960–1972,* by Ruby d'Arschot.
The Netherlands: Ministerie van Cultuur, Recreatie en Maatschappelijk Werk, *Toneel ter Zake,* The Hague, 1978, 5, 57; data for other nonprofit, annex 3 of the Ford Foundation report by Ruby d'Arschot.
Sweden: Statistika Centralbyran, *Statistik Arsbök for Sverige 1976* (Stockholm), 330–336.
United States: The Ford Foundation, *The Financing of the Performing Arts: A Survey of 166 Professional Non-profit Resident Theaters, Operas, Symphony, Ballet, and Modern Dance Companies* (New York: The Ford Foundation, 1974).

Table 14.4 Financing of the Performing Arts, Western Europe and the United States in the Early 1970s (Percent of Total Income)

	Date	Earned Income	Direct Subsidies: National or Federal	Direct Subsidies: State and Local	Private or Foundation	Other Income	Total
Austria							
Nonprofit opera and theatre	1973	23.2	55.8	20.8	0.2	—	100.0
Private theatre	1973	44.5	32.8	22.2	0.5	—	100.0
France							
Public/nonprofit	1973	31.9	41.7	26.5	—	—	100.0
Private	1973	98.8	1.2	—	—	—	100.0
Germany							
Nonprofit	1973/74	17.8	0.3	80.5	0.5	1.0	100.0
Netherlands							
Nonprofit							
Theatre	1972/73	20.8	38.7	34.5	6.1	—	100.0
Other	1972	13.0	59.6	29.4	—	—	100.0
Sweden							
Nonprofit	1974/75	10.5	64.7	24.8	—	—	100.0
United States							
Nonprofit	1970/71	54.0	2.0	2.9	34.8	6.3	100.0
Private theatre	1970/71	100.0	—	—	—	—	100.0

SOURCES: Same as for Tables 14.3.

cent of the symphony orchestras' total incomes in that season).[44] Comparable figures for the Paris *Opéra* and the *Comédie Française* were 20 and 21 percent, respectively, in 1974.[45] In Austria, earned income came to 23.2 percent of total income in the subsidized sector. In contrast, in the United States even the nonprofit sector in the Ford Foundation survey of 166 NPOs covered 55 percent of its expenditures from ticket incomes. In the aggregate, the earned income of the 32 U.S. operas covered 65 percent of their total income.[46] Even the private theatre received generous state and local subsidies in Austria and Germany, amounting to over 50 percent in the former and to roughly a quarter of total income in the latter.

Although the financing of the performing arts in the English-speaking countries other than the United States is not systematically examined in the present study, it may nevertheless be observed that the patterns of public and private support in the United Kingdom, Australia, Canada, and New Zealand more closely resemble those prevailing in the United States than they do those in continental Europe. The share of earned income in the total receipts of NPOs in the United Kingdom, Australia, and New Zealand in the early 1970s may not have been quite so high as in the United States and Canada (32 to 49 percent in the first group, 55 to 60 percent in the second), but it was still appreciably higher than in Austria

(23.2 percent), Germany (17.8 percent), the Netherlands (20.8 percent), and Sweden (10.5 percent). France, with 31.9 percent, representing the highest share of earned-to-total income in my sample of European countries, was on a par with New Zealand's 32 percent.[47]

In the United Kingdom, Australia, and New Zealand, there was a marked disparity between theatre and opera on the one hand, and orchestral music on the other, in the extent to which NPOs covered their expenditures from their own receipts. The share of earned income exceeded 50 percent in theatre and opera companies, but it was only 16 to 21 percent for orchestral groups.[48] This difference was not nearly as marked in the United States and Canada. In fact, when orchestras are removed from our list of performing-arts organizations, the overall averages are remarkably similar in all the English-speaking countries. On the continent, no clear pattern of privileged public support for music or any of the other arts emerges from the statistics: all forms of "high art" were, and are, heavily subsidized.[49]

Among the sources of support ("nonearned income"), the national government provided a major share in Austria, France, Holland, and Sweden. In the federated system of West Germany, support for the arts is the near-exclusive responsibility of the states *(Länder)* and the municipalities. In no country of Western Europe did private, business, and foundation support contribute more than a few percent of total income. The United States again marks a sharp departure from the European pattern of finance. Here, private and foundation support made up about 76 percent of the unearned income of the NPOs in the Ford Foundation sample and perhaps 55 to 60 percent for all NPOs.[50] Even in the English-speaking countries other than the United States, which in this as in other respects represented an intermediate position between the United States and continental Europe, the share of private, business, and foundation support was relatively modest, namely, 8 percent in Australia, 13 percent in the United Kingdom, 6 percent in New Zealand, and 15 percent in Canada.[51]

The relatively low federal subsidies listed for the United States in Tables 14.3 and 14.4 are now, of course, antiquated. Total subventions from the National Endowment for the Arts, expressed in 1972 prices, went up from $10 million in 1972 to $90 million in 1980.[52] Appropriations by State Art Councils rose from $28 million in 1971 to about $40 million in 1980, also in constant prices. Unfortunately, we do not have financial statistics for performing-arts organizations, such as the Ford Foundation collected for the early 1970s, to assess the impact of the increase in government subsidies on the "income gaps" of these organizations. The data available for symphony orchestras alone—major regional and metropolitan organizations—do not point to a radical increase in the percentage of total incomes accounted for by government subsidies. Tax-supported grants (federal, state, and local) represented 14.5 percent of the total income of 160 orchestras in 1973/74 and 14.7 percent in 1978/79.[53] When the data are in for the entire decade of the 1970s they are likely to show some widening of the "income gap"—government subsidies accounting for a larger share of total incomes—but nothing like the preponderance of such subsidies in the budgets of comparable organizations in Western European countries.

So far we have looked only at current government support for the performing arts—essentially at the operating subsidies of theatres, opera houses, symphony orchestras, and ballet companies. But the total contribution of government to the arts is a good deal larger than just operating subsidies: it includes capital expenditures, which in domains other than the performing arts typically exceed current expenditures, and specialized arts education (music schools and so forth). In France, where the accounts of central government carefully distinguish current and capital expenditures, the capital expenditures in 1973 amounted to about half the level of current government expenditures on the theatre and music in 1973, compared to nearly three-quarters of such expenditures in the plastic arts (chiefly for art museums).[54] The statistics of Table 14.5, wherever possible, comprise both current and capital expenditures as well as specialized arts education (chiefly music and art schools).

Of the data in Table 14.5 only those for the Netherlands have been published by the government in the desired format. They include both current and capital expenditures and cover central, provincial, and municipal support for the performing and for the plastic arts; they segregate subsidies to special schools, training young people and adults in the various arts; and they are net of any receipts received directly by government organs in each sector. France's data for support of the arts at the central government level are also excellent, but those for local support are at best fragmentary. The British data assembled by Peacock and Godfrey exclude capital expenditures and professional training in the arts as well, in the case of "total government support," as subventions to historic homes.[55] The United States data are poor at all levels and represent only an approximation to the desired statistics.[56] Nevertheless, the disparity between the level of government support of the performing arts between Austria, Germany, the Netherlands, and Sweden (seven to thirteen dollars per capita), and Great Britain and the United States (less than half a dollar per capita) is so large it cannot possibly be bridged by more comprehensive coverage of expenditures in the Anglo-Saxon countries. Indeed, the inclusion of capital expenditures and specialized arts education in Germany and Austria would in all likelihood widen their lead over the United States and Britain in their level of government support for the performing arts. I doubt whether more complete statistics for French expenditures on the arts at the municipal level would alter France's overall record, about midway between the high-expenditure and the low-expenditure countries.

Indirect Support

The data in Tables 14.2 through 14.4 refer to direct government support only. They do not reflect the indirect expenditures in the form of tax exemptions, tax deductions, and free rent of government-owned facilities.

Table 14.5 Total Government Support for the Performing Arts in Western Europe and the United States

	Percentage Share of the Performing Arts in:				Government Support for Performing Arts as Percent of National Income	Per capita Government Support	
	Federal or National Support for the Arts	Total Government Support for the Arts	Federal or National Budget	All Government Budgets		In National Currencies	In U.S. Dollars
Austria (1973)[a]	n.a.	n.a.	0.6	0.51	0.19	166.0	8.30
France (1973)	27.2	n.a.	0.13	n.a.	0.04[b]	8.5	2.10[b]
German Fed. Rep. (1976)[a]	12.0	53.1	0.005	0.30	0.13	17.9	7.00
Great Britain (1970/71)[a]	39.0[c]	35.4	0.05	0.04[d]	0.023	0.18	0.44
Netherlands (1975)	38.3	54.5	0.24	0.50	0.23	32.6	13.40
Sweden (1970/71)	63.4	67.0	0.37	0.33	0.19	36.4	6.90
United States (1974)	40.0	47.0[b]	0.014	0.02[b]	0.008[b]	0.44	0.44

NOTE: Total government support for the arts includes specialized arts education, museums, and conservation of monuments. It excludes television and radio, archives, literature, cinema, and libraries. Current and capital expenditures as well as transfers are covered, except as otherwise indicated.

[a]Current expenditures, only.

[b]Based on a very rough estimation of municipal and other local expenditures.

[c]Includes central government subsidy to the BBC for music and ballet.

[d]Exclusive of professional training in the arts.

SOURCES: Austria and France: Sources to Table 14.3.

Germany: Deutscher Bühnenverband, *Theater-statistik 1978/79* (Köln, 1979).

Great Britain: Alan T. Peacock and C. Godfrey, "Cultural Accounting," in M. Blaug, ed., *The Economics of the Arts* (London: Mark Robertson, 1976), 91.

Netherlands: Central Bureau voor de statistiek, *Statistiek inkomsten en uitgaven van de overheid voor cultur en recreatie 1975* (The Hague, 1979), 8, 24.

Sweden: Claude Fabrizio, Le Projet Suédois de Démocratie Culturelle: Essai de Comparaison avec la Situation Française" in *Notes et Etudes Documentaires*, July 22, 1975 (no. 4205–4206).

United States: Dick Netzer, *The Subsidized Muse: Public Support for the Arts in the United States* (Cambridge: Cambridge University Press, 1978), 46, 79, 90, 93, 95.

National and local budgets and national income data for all countries listed are from the official statistical yearbooks of the respective countries.

Tax exemptions are especially important in Western Europe, tax deductions in the United States. In France, the normal rate of the value added tax (VAT) was 17.6 percent in the period covered in the tables. For the arts the tax is legally reduced to 6 percent. But in fact the actual rate, paid by both nonprofit and profit theatres, is still lower. The tax base *(base imposable)* for the first 140 performances of "dramatic, lyrical, musical or choreographic works newly created in France or of new productions of classical works" *(oeuvres classiques faisant l'objet d'une nouvelle mise en scène)* is only 30 percent of the ticket price (which is itself, in the case of subsidized works, only a fraction of value added). As a result, a VAT of 2.1 percent of receipts "has almost become the rule in the theatre."[57] Supposing the full 17.6 percent rate had applied to an estimated 80 percent share of value added in the total expenditures of all professional performing-arts organizations,[58] the tax bill would then have come to FF 72 million in 1973 instead of FF 5.4 million that were actually paid (on the assumption that all performing-arts organizations remitted 2.1 percent of their earned income to the Treasury in the form of VAT). If these numbers are correct, the national government's contribution should be raised from 179 million FF to 246 million, or 42.7 percent of the total income of performing-arts organizations. For the nonprofit sector alone, the national government share would then rise from 41.7 percent to 48.5 percent of total income.

In Germany, performing-arts organizations are totally exempt from the VAT (and as far as I can make out pay no other taxes of any significance). If the normal rate of 12 percent of VAT were applied to 80 percent of the expenditures of nonprofit organizations in the sector, they would have to remit DM 106 million to the treasury. However approximate this figure may be, it clearly shows that the indirect contribution of the federal government is many times greater than its direct contribution (of the order of 9 percent of all expenditures including VAT taxes at the 12 percent rate).

Free or subsidized rent of opera houses, theatres, and concert halls make an important "hidden" contribution to nonprofit performing arts organizations all over Europe but one that is difficult to capture statistically. In the Federal Republic of Germany, rental expenses account for only 0.7 percent of the total expenses of all nonprofit theatres and opera houses.[59] According to a French author's analysis of the expenditures of a "typical" private theatre in Paris, rent and rental expenses came to 4.5 percent of total yearly expenditures.[60] If we assume comparability of real expenditures in Germany and France, the implicit subsidies stemming from free or concessionary rentals may amount to 3 to 5 percent of the total expenditures of German nonprofit theatres and opera houses.

If indirect aid in the form of rental subsidies and tax exemptions is counted, total government support for the performing arts in the Federal Republic rises above the figures in the last column of Table 14.5 by about 28 percent, to at least $9.00 per capita.

In the Netherlands, municipalities run their own (subsidized) theatres which sign contracts with theatre groups and opera and ballet companies for performances. They may pay outright for a performance, share in the ticket receipts, or charge rent for the hall placed at the disposal of the performers. A governmental study of seven major Dutch theatres *(Schouwburgen)* shows that, in the season 1972/73, precisely two-thirds of their total expenditures were covered by subsidies (Ft 5.6 million) and only one-third from their rental and other receipts (Ft 2.8 million).[61] The subsidies of municipalities to all 54 theatres in activity in the season was Ft 16.7 million (but it should be kept in mind that the theatres held opera and ballet performances as well as theatricals). In the same season, the 11 subsidized theatre groups covered in the data for Table 14.3 received subsidies equal to Ft 14.8 million, amounting to 79.2 percent of their total expenditures.[62] When subsidies to theatre groups and to theatres are consolidated, they rise up to Ft 39.6 million: Ft 24.6 million (62.2 percent) from the municipalities, Ft 12.1 million from the central government (30.5 percent), and Ft 2.9 million from the provincial authorities (7.3 percent). The data in Table 14.5, however, are not affected by these adjustments, since they already comprise both subsidies to theatres and to theatre groups.

In France, most of the larger nonprofit theatres and opera houses in the provinces are owned by either a municipality or one of the 21 *Maisons de la Culture*, which themselves are jointly owned by the central government and one or more municipalities. I have not found statistics that would enable me to compute the subsidies associated with the operation of these theatre and opera houses as distinguished from the costs of the performances that took place in them.[63]

Indirect government expenditures on the arts in the United States are a different nature altogether. The bulk of these expenditures are in the taxes forgone by the federal government whenever individuals make deductible contributions to the performing arts. Mark Schuster, in his doctoral dissertation *Income Taxes and the Arts: Tax Expenditures as Cultural Policy*,[64] estimated that cultural institutions of all kinds received contributions amounting to $530 million in 1973, of which $310 million, or 58 percent, was in the form of tax expenditures. If this percentage is applied to the estimated $58.2 million donated to the performing arts in 1970/71, we obtain a figure for indirect support of $34 million. This rough estimate is of course intended to cover *all* NPOs, not just those included in the Ford Foundation sample, which tallied only $8.3 million in the way of direct subsidies from all governmental services. If this sum of $34 million is added to the $94 million in direct support at all levels of government estimated for 1974, we obtain a figure for total per capita government support of almost $0.60. This is of course still way below the level of government support in the Western European countries in our sample.

The tax legislation of European Countries also encourages donations to the arts, but it is generally less permissive in the provisions it makes for deductions than in the United States. In Germany, individuals may deduct up to 5 percent of their taxable income, and enterprises up to 2 percent of their gross income, for donations aimed at promoting the public interest. In France, individuals may deduct only 0.5 percent of their net income for donations to *organismes d'intérêt general* (an additional 0.5 percent is permitted in case the donation is made out to the Fondation de France). Enterprises may deduct up to 1 per 1000 of their gross income for such purposes. In most instances, aggregate donations came to far less than the permissible limit obtained by applying the maximum percentage to estimated total incomes. Thus, in France, a study made in 1965 showed that donations in a sample of 300 enterprises only amounted to 0.22 per 1000 of their gross income as against the 1 per 1000 permitted.[65] Private philanthropic activity in Europe may well be more inhibited by a lack of tradition of giving and by high levels of government support of welfare, educational, and arts institutions. In France especially the patronage of private individuals and firms is regarded with suspicion, for fear of money-minded interference. The tendency is to "demand more state intervention because it offers better guarantees of liberty and equality."[66]

Conclusion

No matter how the financial statistics of the performing arts are put together—whether or not, for instance, they include capital outlays and indirect government expenditures—the inference is inescapable that total per capita government support is many times greater in continental Western Europe than in the English-speaking countries.

This conclusion applies to the arts in general. I have already speculated about the origins of these differences in the historical section of the chapter. A subsidiary question that I have not addressed is this. What accounts for the differing shares of the performing arts in total government support for the arts in various countries? I have no conclusive answer to this question, but I am struck by the influence on these shares of the historically conditioned burden that the federal or central government must bear for conserving the monuments inherited from past generations. In France and Holland, where about a third of all central-government expenditures for the arts are normally earmarked for conservation, this onerous responsibility exerts an adverse influence on the size and share of the budget for the performing arts. In Sweden, conservation expenditures amount to a much smaller share of the total government support—less than 10 percent. Here, the performing arts represent a larger share of total support than in the other countries. In this country, which is less encumbered (and embellished) by vestiges of the past, there should be more leeway, given the total amounts budgeted for the arts at all levels of government, to finance the performing arts. I am not confident enough of the data in Table 14.5, which show that less than 50 percent of total support to the arts went to the performing arts, to assert that this proportion was abnormally low by European standards. In any case, we should recall that the tradition of government aid to museums and to the adornment of public monuments is older here, and perhaps better entrenched, than that of government aid to theatres, opera societies, and orchestra groups. It may be that the proportion will gradually change in favor of the performing arts as U.S. levels and patterns of public support for the arts come to resemble European precedents.

A RETROSPECTIVE ANALYSIS

The story of the European financing of the performing arts may be summarized in the following points.

1. Government support has deep historical roots but has grown especially rapidly in the period after World War II. It now represents the bulk of receipts of professional organizations.
2. The level of private donations, which were never a preeminent source of support (if we except princely patronage which may be likened to government support), has declined over time. They are now a very minor source of receipts in all countries surveyed.
3. Nonprofit organizations (as defined in this paper to include quasi-governmental organizations) have gradually acquired a dominant place in music and theatre. In the last 10 years, however, the private (commercial) theatre in the Netherlands, for reasons that will be explored, has regained some of the ground it lost to the nonprofit theatre in the 1960s.

In this analytical section I outline a model, fully fleshed out in a mathematical note which is available from the author. The model can be made to yield a pattern of behavior consistent with the historical evolution just listed.[67] The model is, of course, a stark simplification of this complex history. It abstracts from reality, in particular, by assuming that the costs of producing shows and the preferences of consumers of the performing arts remain constant as government support increases. This approach assumes away the possibility that the widening gap between the expenditures and receipts of performing-arts organizations was actually due to rising wage costs unmatched by increased consumer expenditures on the products of the industry. Such a rise in wage costs, according to William Baumol's well-known diagnosis of the deteriorating financial conditions of the performing arts, might be ascribed to the fact that performing-arts organizations must pay their personnel wages and salaries that are more or less competitive with those paid in rising labor-productivity sectors (such as manufacturing), despite their failure to match the productivity gains of these sectors. The model also ignores the inroads of the motion pictures, television, and phonograph records on consumer demand for the performing arts, which have historically contributed to the gap between box-office receipts and expenses. As we shall see below, the model can accommodate rising production costs or declining consumer demand, but it focuses exclusively on the effects of a change in a single variable—government support—all others being held constant.

The model analyzes the behavior of a single nonprofit organization assumed to be representative of all the NPOs in the performing-arts sector. This NPO is engaged in competition with a private (profit-oriented) sector, but only the first-round effects of this competition are tracked in this analysis. When the NPO, for example, reduces the price of a popular type of show that is competitive with shows produced in the private sector, it necessarily encroaches on the sales of the latter. No consideration is given to the possibility that private enterprises might lower their prices to regain at least some of their customers.

Suppose the NPO were offering a single type of show for a uniform price per attendant. It faces a demand schedule for tickets showing what the audience for the show would be at every price. There will normally be a capacity limitation for the size of the audience attending any one performance. Provided customers are indifferent between attending sooner or later, the total audience at any given price may be defined as the capacity attendance multiplied by the number of days during which the show is put on. For an NPO constrained from incurring losses or earning profits, the total audience at which price equals average total cost per attendant determines the number of days during which the show will be performed. If there are two audience levels for which this equality holds—the first where average cost per attendant is falling, the second where it is rising—the NPO will presumably choose the higher level of total audience. The only limit that needs to be taken into consideration is the number of days in the season during which shows are normally staged. In the absence of a binding constraint on the limited run of the production, it is evident that, when total costs are reduced, the demand schedule will intersect with average total cost at a point corresponding to a lower price and a larger audience. This will also be the result if the NPO receives government subsidies or private donations which will, in effect, offset its fixed costs.

This one-product model has been subjected to econometric tests. Burkhauser and Getz have estimated the impact of subsidies on the output, measured by the number of performances, and on the employment of nonprofit symphony orchestras. They found that, because the price elasticity of demand for tickets was small (from -0.128 to -0.132), subsidies caused only very moderate increases in output and that their main impact was in reducing ticket prices.[68]

Consider now an NPO producing two kinds of shows—elite and popular—where only popular shows compete for the audience of the private profit-oriented sector. Let v and w represent the size of the audience (number of tickets sold) attending elite and popular shows respectively. Normally the demand for each type of show is represented as a function of its price. But we can also regard prices as inverse functions of audience size. Since the two types of shows are substitutes in consumption, we also want the price corresponding to a given audience size for each type of show to decline whenever the audience for the other type of show increases. An example of two linear price functions satisfying the conditions might be:

$$\pi = 5 - 2v - .1w$$
$$\psi = 10 - w - .1v$$

where π is the price of elite shows and ψ of popular shows.

In this example, the demand for popular shows is more elastic and greater at any price than that for elite shows. In each equation, own-demand (v in the case of π and w in the case of ψ) has a greater impact on price than the demand for the other type of show. (If this were not so, simultaneous equilibrium in the two markets would not be possible.)

The net revenue of the NPO may be written:

$$NR = \pi v + \psi w + S + D - C$$

where S denotes government subsidies, D private donations, and C total costs, which will normally be an increasing function of v and w.[69] If the organization is neither to make profit nor to suffer a loss, this expression must be set equal to zero.

In contrast to the one-product model discussed above, there will generally be an infinite number of combinations of v and w that will satisfy the net-revenue-equal-zero constraint for given levels of subsidies and donations. In Figure 14.1 each ellipse-like contour is the locus of all such combinations corresponding to a certain level of S and D (both assumed here to be constants, exogenous to the problem). With the smallest S and D, only the innermost contour is attainable. Since it does not intersect either axis, we know that some of both types of shows must be produced if no losses are to be incurred. Points on a given contour located below the straight line marked $d(NR)/dw = 0$ and to the left of the line marked $d(NR)/dv = 0$ are inefficient in the sense that more of both types of shows could be produced without violating the constraint. (They are equivalent to a point equating average cost and average revenue at a low level of output in a one-product model.) A point such as q located inside the contour would generate profits. By definition, it would be shunned by the NPO. A point outside a given contour would be unattainable, given the level of S and D corresponding to this contour, because it would be conducive to losses. As the level of S and D increases, we pass on to successively higher contours. With the second contour, it becomes possible (though inefficient) to meet the no-loss constraint while producing nothing but popular shows. The third contour indicates a level of S and D so large as to make it possible to produce nothing but elite shows, even though there was less demand for them than for popular shows. In this particular case S and D are even large enough to cover all fixed costs so that both shows could be staged at no charge at all to consumers.

This rather laborious introduction is intended to drive home a key point of this paper: the imposition of a no-profit-no-loss constraint leaves the managers of NPOs with considerable scope to choose the mix of popular and elite shows that best suits their preferences or whatever goal they may

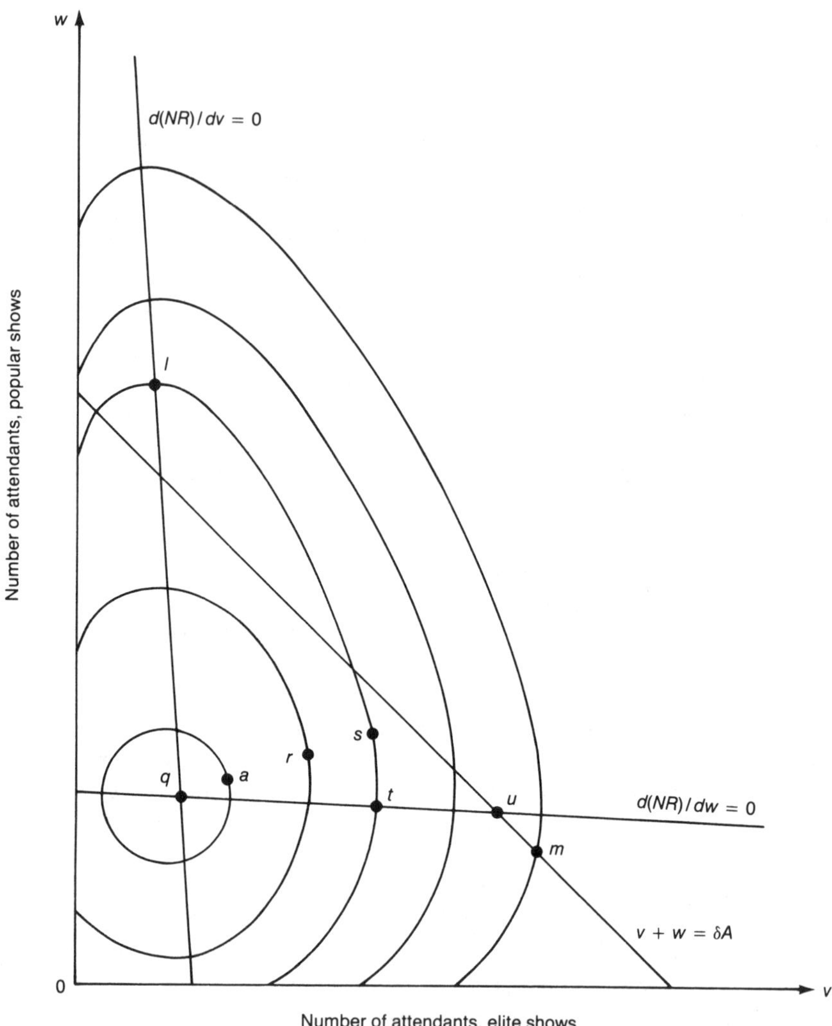

Figure 14.1 Number of Attendants of Popular and Elite Shows Given by a Non-profit Institution

be pursuing (including the satisfaction of their administrative superiors or the support of the constituency that elected them to the job). The mathematical analysis (presented fully in the note, available from the author) may be used to ascertain the choices that managers would make, for various levels of S and D, if they were bent on maximizing their audience for elite shows. It is readily shown that they would set a price for popular shows that would maximize their net revenue from staging such shows and expand the level of output of elite shows to a point where their price π would fall below marginal cost. Indeed, managers, given sufficiently high

S and D, might wish to drive the price of elite shows below zero: they might use the profits made on popular shows to pay audiences to attend their elite shows. This is an example of the well-known phenomenon of cross-subsidization familiar to students of NPOs.[70] Less immediately obvious is the conclusion of the model that an increase in subsidies will normally cause managers to increase v at the expense of w, the audience for popular shows. This point is illustrated in Figure 14.1 by the negative slope of the line marked $\mathrm{d}(NR)/\mathrm{d}w=0$, the locus of all combinations of v and w selected by a manager maximizing v, given increasing levels of S and D. (It is easily verified that this line will be straight if the price and cost equations are all linear in v and w.)[71] The reason why w must diminish as subsidies and donations increase is that these outside sources of finance obviate the need for cross-subsidizing elite shows from the profits of the more popular shows.

A second aim of the model is to predict the impact of higher levels of S and D on the prices of the two types of shows. Now it is immediately obvious that as v increases in response to higher levels of S and D, the price of v must fall (since the decline in w is only moderate compared to the increase in v, which has a stronger impact on π than does w). But what happens to the price of popular shows, competitive with the shows put on in the private sector, as the level of S and D rises? We have seen that the level of w will undergo a moderate decline. This should, other things equal, cause a rise in ψ. But there is also the larger increase in v to take into account, which should have a depressing effect on ψ. It is shown in the mathematical note that if the cross-effects of v on ψ and of w on π are about the same size, the net impact of the two tendencies will be to leave ψ unchanged.

The capacity limitation mentioned earlier stems from the limited length of the season. The constraint will only bind if the total demand for both types of shows is high enough for the NPO to run a number of performances in excess of the days available in the season. Such situations—possible for various combinations of v and w—are represented in the figure by the straight line with a unit negative slope marked $v+w=\delta A$, where δ is the number of days in the season and A is the daily capacity of the theatre or hall available to the NPO. Starting from a demand-constrained regime, an increase in subsidies may eventually cause the NPO to run up against its capacity constraint. If it is expanding along the line $\mathrm{d}(NR)/\mathrm{d}w=0$ (consistent with the manager's maximization of v), it will hit the constraint at point u. Any further increase of S and D would involve a sharper tradeoff between v and w than before. Moving along the capacity constraint from u to m, for instance, would require the NPO to reduce w at the same rate as it is increasing v, which implies in effect that every extra day during which it stages an elite show must be compensated by a one-day reduction in the run of the popular shows. This will necessarily cause an increase in ψ (since ψ is necessarily more sensitive to a decrease in w than to an increase in v of the same magnitude).[72]

The model is more flexible than this stripped-down version might indicate. The analysis in the mathematical note introduces separate quality variables for elite and popular shows. As the quality variable increases (e.g., as the number of different productions of a given type of show is raised), the demand for this type of show rises, but at a diminishing rate. It turns out that, under reasonable assumptions about cross-effects (of v on ψ and w on π), the same results hold as in the simpler model in the case where it was assumed the manager was maximizing the audience of elite shows: an increase in subsidies and donations will cause w to decline at a moderate rate as v rises.[73]

The consequences of growing government support for the performing arts, culminating in the experience of the Netherlands' theatres in the period from 1965 to 1975, may be traced heuristically with the help of the model. We may begin by assuming that in the 1960s the managers of Dutch theatres had only a moderate preference for elite shows. They were perhaps maximizing their total audience at a point such as a in Figure 14.1. As subsidies rose they moved from a to r and then to s, still using popular shows to subsidize elite shows. Along this path, prices of popular as well as of elite shows were declining.[74] The NPO sector must have been encroaching on the market of the commercial theatre. In the late 1960s, under pressure of Tomato Action Group and of other student groups, the managers of NPO theatres changed their policy: henceforth, they chose their mix as if they were maximizing the audience of elite shows. With a constant level of subsidies, they moved from a mix indicated by point s to one on the same contour indicated by point t. The drastic decline in w concomitant with this move would have been associated with an increase in ψ, thus reducing the NPO's competitiveness with the commercial sector.[75] With an increase in subsidies, a manager still pursuing the maximization of v would have traveled along the line from t to u until he encountered a capacity limit. Along this path ψ would have remained approximately constant. Any further increase in subsidies would have compelled the NPO to give up one unit of w for every unit increase in v, as it moved from point u to point m in Figure 14.1 along the capacity constraint. This, as I have already explained, would have caused another round of increase in ψ, tantamount to a further loss in the NPO's competitive position vis-à-vis the commercial sector in the market for w. If enough NPOs behaved in this manner, as I believe Dutch theatres did in the early 1970s, the joint effect of their output decisions would be tantamount to a withdrawal of the nonprofit sector from the market for popular shows. This behavior would be sufficient to explain the extraordinary revival of the commercial theatre during the first half of the 1970s, which regained much of the ground lost to the NPOs during the 1960s.

In the Dutch story government subsidies played a predominant role, private donations a negligible role. Still, if the model is to have wider application, it may be useful to dwell on the factors determining the level of donations (so far considered exogenous like subsidies). Henry Hansmann, in his model of the performing arts, which inspired my own attempt at modeling the impact of outside financial support on the output of art services, assumes that donations in a one-product NPO will be a constant fraction of the surplus enjoyed by consumers of the product.[76] This consumers' surplus is approximated by the area under the conventionally drawn demand curve. It is easily shown that the effect of a marginal increase in subsidies on this surplus must be positive. In my view this is an unrealistic treatment of donations, at least in Europe where foundations do not give matching grants contingent on government support. In particular, the positive effect of government subsidies on donations postulated by Hansmann is hard to reconcile with the negative association between donations and subsidies revealed by the European experience. In any event, as far as strictly private donations are concerned, I would argue that patrons of the performing arts are more likely to donate money to their favorite organizations if they fear that, in the absence of their donations, the show will not go on. Granted that the size of their potential donation will be partly determined by their consumers' surplus—a measure of how much they would be willing to give rather than do without the service altogether—the fraction of that surplus they will be willing to give may well be inversely correlated with their expectations of the level of output of the NPO (as long as they consider that level to be beyond their own individual influence). If so, the fraction of consumers' surplus donated will be a number from zero to one, diminishing with v. As is explained in greater detail in the mathematical note, the effect of an increase in government subsidies will be to increase donations at a diminishing rate until some critical value of v is attained. From that point on, further increases in subsidies will cause donations to decline and eventually cause them to go down to zero. When donations are on a rising trajectory, their effect is to reinforce the impact of increasing subsidies on v. Conversely, on a falling trajectory, they will diminish the impact of increasing S on v. (Needless to say, if government subsidies are tied to matching funds from private sources, donations will be more strongly correlated with subsidies than this model would lead one to expect.)

We are now ready to explore the consequences for consumer welfare of increasing the level of government subsidies proferred to NPOs. We have found so far that NPO managers were able to exercise discretion in their output mix in meeting the no-profit-no-loss constraint and that subsidies, by relieving them of the financial necessity of producing popular shows that they had no personal interest in staging, could reinforce their personal inclination to put on mainly elite shows. If "consumers' welfare," as experienced by consumers at each point in time, is our criterion, then it is pretty obvious that a manager concerned only with putting on elite shows will act in such a way as to reduce welfare if he receives larger subsidies. This is so almost by definition since shows are only "popular" if they please consumers, and any reduction in the number of popular productions and/or tickets sold to such shows must reduce their welfare. A more analytical way of looking at the matter is to argue that since profits are being made on w and losses on v, the marginal rate of substitution of consumers, equated to the ratio of market-clearing prices π and ψ, cannot be equal to the relative marginal costs of the two types of shows. As long as marginal rates of transformation (ratios of marginal costs) are not equal to marginal rates of substitution for consumers, Pareto-optimality cannot be achieved.[77] Operating the model in reverse gear, we can readily see that a cut in subsidies, by inducing an increase in w and a reduction in v, is likely to enhance welfare. All this of course only applies if and when managers, by imposing their own tastes, pursue a policy at odds with their customers' preferences. A manager maximizing a function of v and w with reasonable weights attached to both may well promote welfare when subsidies are increased by putting on more of both kinds of shows.

The introduction of quality variables, specifically identified in the analysis in the mathematical note with the number of productions of v and w, does not substantially affect our conclusions about the welfare implications of massive subsidies. Under the "normal conditions" defined in the note, some of the subsidies will be used by the NPO maximizing the audience size for, or the quality of, elite shows to increase quality, and some to lower π and widen the audience attending these shows. But as long as the increase in subsidies is associated with a reduction either in the size of audiences attending popular plays or in the number of productions of popular plays, consumers' welfare will be adversely affected.

To these pessimistic arguments, we may counterpose the idea that elite productions have a positive long-run impact on welfare. That is, as consumers are exposed to more difficult works—more complex patterns of symbols in terms of Scitovsky's conception of art[78]—they gradually get to understand and appreciate them.[79] Their relative demand for v-type productions increases. Post hoc, these changes in taste validate the manager's choices. Strictly speaking, this infant-industry argument for subsidies tending to promote elite productions requires that the increase in demand be sufficient not only to bring about a state of affairs where the (v, w) combination chosen by the manager in each period maximizes intertemporal consumer utility but where the increase in consumers' surplus eventually generated is sufficient to compensate for the temporary losses in welfare incurred before the change in taste took place. The argument, in any case, is of doubtful empirical validity. If culture consumers were so malleable, there would be no need to increase subsidies through time as the Netherlands, Germany, and Sweden have done on such a wide scale.

The remaining arguments in favor of massive subsidies to NPOs promoting nonpopular, money-losing cultural ends turn on *Bildung*. These arguments do not necessarily imply that an elitist minority need impose its tastes by social compulsion on a recalcitrant majority, for example, by milking subsidies through manipulation of the political process. Consumers may not enjoy "serious" music or theatre, now or after prolonged exposure. Yet, they may be willing to vote to subsidize music and theatre, or to elect representatives who will promise to subsidize them, because they regard high-culture offerings as being, in one way or another, important to their community or to the nation as a whole. I leave to political scientists and sociologists the task of ascertaining how widespread such an attitude toward merit goods may be. But even if the voter should favor art as *Bildung,* I am not sure that the NPO is the right conduit for large-scale subsidies to achieve this cultural end. There is no guarantee that managers of NPOs, whose policies may be influenced by career and professional considerations having nothing in common with the *Bildung* aims accepted by voters, may, if given too much leeway, move away from optimality, whether welfare if defined in terms of consumers' sovereignty or according to some other, broader notion.

In conclusion, the performing-arts organizations in Western Europe are the recipients of generous government subsidies, which have undoubtedly given much satisfaction to at least a minority of the population, contributed to the cultural education of another segment of the public (partly overlapping with the first), and added to the luster of the states and cities that spent their tax monies on these activities. The United States has only recently begun to emulate the European pattern in this regard, but it has not gone nearly as far in the direction of public support for the arts as European governments have done. The European experience occurred in a sociopolitical environment that differs in essential respects from the one prevailing here. European organs of government are less responsive to popular—not to speak of populist—pressures than ours. Class cleavages, which are more profound than they are in this country, make Europe's common citizens more ready to accept the cultural leadership of its elites. Any policy that would use tax monies to subsidize high culture to the point of virtually giving it away free for the benefit mainly of better-off citizens (as in the case of Swedish opera) would be considered profligate and inequitable by the wide U.S. public. In a highly culturally heterogeneous country such as the United States, the claims for public support are too many to address, let alone satisfy, all of them. At the same time, a policy lavishing subsidies on a few activities, especially of an elite sort, is likely to be resented both by the public at large and by unsuccessful claimants. Arts organizations risk losing the sympathy of the broad U.S. public if they press their demands for government support beyond the point of compatibility with its basic values.

NOTES

1. For details see Jules Magnin, *Les Théatres Municipaux de la Province* (Le Mans: C. Blanchet, 1909), 7–12; and Michele Versillier, *La Crise du Théatre Privé* (Paris: Presses Universitaires de France, 1973), 23–41.

2. Jules Bourassies, *Les Spectacles Forains et la Comédie Française* (Paris: E. Dentu, 1875), 4–5.

3. No author, "Le Théatre en République Fédérale d'Allemagne," *Notes et Etudes Documentaires,* September 15, 1964, no. 3119, p. 1776.

4. Fritz Herterich, *Theatre und Volkswirtschaft* (Munich and Leipzig: Verlage Duncker and Humbolt, 1937), 59–60.

5. Herterich, ibid., 60.

6. No author, op. cit., 6.

7. Herterich, op. cit., 9.

8. In the United States, also, private patronage and associations or cooperatives played a key role in supplying orchestral music in the second half of the nineteenth century. But, in contrast with the German experience, state and municipal organs of government in the United States did not take over the responsibility for financing orchestral music in the first quarter of the twentieth century.

9. On this point see Erika Wahl-Ziegler, *Theatre und Orchestra Zwischen Markthaften und Marktkorrektur; Existenzprobleme und Uberlebenschancen eines Sektors an Wirtschaftstheoretischer Licht* (Göttingen: 1978), 34–35.

10. Herterich, op. cit., 20.

11. Ibid., 290–292.

12. Department of Cultural Affairs, Swedish Ministry of Education and Cultural Affairs, *The State and Culture in Sweden* (Stockholm: The Swedish Institute, 1970), 7.

13. Ibid., 8.

14. The arts may have benefited from the gradual dismantling of the historical *Verzuiling* system whereby each major social group, including especially the Protestant and Roman Catholic communities, had received, and was left to administer, a portion of government support. Since there had been no organized constituency concerned primarily with the arts, there had been little support for arts activities. On *Verzuiling* and its decline, see Ralph M. Kramer, "Governmental-Voluntary-Agency Relationships in the Netherlands," *The Netherlands Journal of Sociology* 25 (1979): 155–173.

15. States General of the Netherlands, Tweede Kamer, 1976–1977 session, "Nota Orkestenbestel" (The Hague, 1977), 12.

16. Interview with Bernt Langenberg, director of the Verenigung van Nederlandse Toneelgeselschapen (Association of Netherlandish Theater Societies), June 1980.

17. Data supplied by the Verenigung van Nederlandse Toneelgeselschapen. Attendance at other performing arts, including symphonic music, where repertory was not nearly to the same extent influenced by the demands of the activists, also fell, but much less drastically.

18. Cited in Russell B. Nye, *The Cultural Life of the New Nation, 1776–1830* (New York: Harper & Row, 1960), 262.

19. Ibid., 263.

20. Ibid., 264.

21. P. T. Barnum, *Struggles and Triumphs: Forty Years' Recollections, Written by Himself* (New York: American News Company, 1871), 71.

22. Ibid., 72.

23. Lillian B. Miller, *Patrons and Patriotism: The Encouragement of Fine Arts in the United States, 1790–1860* (Chicago: University of Chicago Press, 1966), 36.

24. Ibid., 37.

25. Ibid., 132.

26. Ibid., 234.

27. Ibid., 36.

28. In the second half of the eighteenth century, an observer complained that theatricals at Yale "had turned the College into Drury Lane" to the detriment of "the more solid parts of learning" (cited in Miller, ibid., 263).

29. Paul DiMaggio, "Cultural Entrepreneurship in Nineteenth-Century Boston" (Chapter 2, this volume).

30. Except for a few short-lived ventures in the 1890s. For details, see Jack Poggi, *Theater in America: The Impact of Economic Forces* (Ithaca: Cornell University Press, 1966), 102.

31. Ibid., 107.

32. Dick Netzer, *The Subsidized Muse: Public Support for the Arts in the United States* (New York: Cambridge University Press, 1978), 59.

33. In the United States and especially in Canada, there is evidence to show that government and private support for the performing arts are substitutes. See Steven Globerman, "An Explanatory Analysis of the Effects of Public Funding of the Performing Arts," in W. S. Hendon et al., eds., *Economic Policy for the Arts* (Cambridge, Mass.: Abt Books, 1980), 73.

34. It is interesting in this connection to recall the examples of Wurttemberg in the period from 1818 to 1820 and Sweden in the late 1860s, when democratically elected representatives balked at the lavish expenditures on royal establishments.

35. Deutscher Bühnenverein, *Theater-statistik 1973/74* (Köln: 1975), pp. 12–14, 52.

36. The Strasbourg national theatre, unlike the other national theatres, is organized as a "public corporation of an industrial and commercial character."

37. Jean-Pierre Hue, *L'Etat et les Nouvelles Formes du Théatre depuis 1968* (Doctoral Thesis, Université de Rouen, Faculté de Droit et de Sciences Economiques, 1979), 19.

38. An ordinance of October 14, 1945 deemed all "theatrical activity" to be "commercial in nature" but excluded national theatres from this definition. (See ibid., 30.) Several Parisian orchestras (Concerts Colonne, Lamoureux, and Pasdeloup) are also organized as associations but, for some unfathomable reason, they are not denied the opportunity of engaging in regular commercial activity. (I assume that a concert is neither more nor less commercial from a legal viewpoint than a theatrical performance for which tickets are sold.)

39. Hue, op. cit., 234.

40. Ibid., 128.

41. Ruby D'Arschot, *Theatre and Music in Western and Northern Europe, 1960–1972* (Report prepared for the Ford Foundation, New York, mimeographed n.d.), 472–485.

42. At the Yale Institution for Social and Policy Studies meeting where the findings in this paper were first presented, one participant commented that the level of public support for the performing arts in Europe and the United States would look very different if military bands and high school theatricals and orchestras were included in the statistics of public support. In support of this view, Richard Magat brought to my attention a news release by U.S. representative Fred Richmond, who pointed out that, in the recommended federal appropriations for 1982, $89.7 million was earmarked for military bands as against $88 million for the National Endowment for the Arts as a whole. In France, FF 84 million was spent in 1979 for all the musical activities of the Ministry of Defense (chiefly military bands), a sum equal to just over 20% of the Ministry of Culture's budget for music and dance subsidies of all sorts and 5.6 percent of estimated government support for music at all levels (data supplied by France's Conseil Economique et Social, cited by Xavier Dupuy in an unpublished doctoral dissertation at Université de Paris). Since this paper concentrates on the behavior of nonprofit organizations competing with privately owned organizations in the marketplace, the narrower definition used here may be more appropriate than one that would include government support for the arts in the military and the schools. In any event, the more comprehensive data are not available on a comparative basis.

43. In Germany, the "public" theatres had an audience of 17.3 million people in 1973/74, and the private theatres, including cooperatives, of 4.7 million people. In Holland, the audience of "subsidized theatres" was 1.4 million in 1969–70, of private and other unsubsidized theatres about 180,000. In 1974/75, for reasons that will be discussed, the audience of subsidized theatres shrank to 907,000, while the audience of private and other nonsubsidized theatres rose to an estimated 750,000. (Information obtained from the Association of Netherlandish Theatre Societies in Amsterdam.) Because Dutch orchestras and ballet companies are all subsidized foundations or associations, the balance of the entire sector clearly favors "nonprofits."

44. Statistika Centralbyran, *Statistik Arsbök for Sverige 1976* (Stockholm), 330–336.

45. Ministère de la Culture, *Annuaire Statistique de la Culture: Données de 1970 à 1974* (Paris: 1978).

46. The Ford Foundation, *The Financing of the Performing Arts: A Survey of 166 Profes-*

sional Non-Profit Resident Theatres, Operas, Symphony, Ballet and Modern Dance Companies (New York: The Ford Foundation, 1974).

47. C. D. Throsby and G. A. Withers, *The Economics of the Performing Arts* (New York: St. Martin's Press, 1979).

48. Ibid.

49. Holland is probably exceptional in the degree to which nontraditional art forms such as the puppet theatre and pantomime are publicly subsidized. But even in Holland, the line is drawn between modern dance, which is deemed worthy of support, and exhibition ballroom dancing or figure skating, which are not. As far as I can make out, jazz and pop music are not regularly subsidized in any Western European country.

50. *The Economist* (London) published an estimate of this share, which it set at 59 percent for 1975, without supplying details on how the figure was calculated (cited in Throsby and Withers, op. cit., 146).

51. Throsby and Withers, op. cit., 146.

52. Hilda and William Baumol, "On Finances of the Performing Arts During Stagflation: Some Recent Data," *Journal of Cultural Economics* 4 (1980): 12.

53. Ibid., 3.

54. Expenditures on the newly constructed Centre Beaubourg in Paris are kept separately. In 1973, capital expenses for the Centre came to FF 126 million compared to 95.6 million spent on total current and capital support for the theatre and FF 93.7 million for the opera. Data are from Ministère de la Culture, op. cit., 23, 34.

55. Alan T. Peacock and C. Godfrey, "Cultural Accounting," in Mark Blaug, ed., *The Economics of the Arts* (London: Mark Robertson, 1976).

56. On the basis of data published by Netzer (op. cit., 64, 88, 93, 95), I estimated 1974 federal support for the performing arts (as defined in Table 14.5) at roughly \$39 million, and local (municipal and county) support at \$25 million. Total support for the arts (performing arts plus visual arts) in that year amounted approximately to \$79 million at the federal level, \$60 million at the state level, and \$60 million at the local level.

57. Versillier, op. cit., 90–91.

58. In the French national theatres, personnel expenses range from two-thirds to four-fifths of total expenditures. In the Paris Opera, salaries came to over three-quarters of total expenditures in 1974. Purchases of goods and services amounted to 17 percent of total expenses (Ministère de la Culture, op. cit., 176, 227).

59. Deutscher Bühnenverein, op. cit., p. 57.

60. Versillier, op. cit., p. 76.

61. Some theatres, such as De Twentse Schouwburg, are owned jointly by the municipality and a local foundation. In Amsterdam De Brakke Grond Theatre is part of a building complex owned by the (private) AMO-Bank, which, via a management firm, rents the facility for Ft 65,000 a year to a foundation called Theater Unie. Property relations between and among municipalities, foundations, private firms, and theatre associations are too tangled to be described in detail here. (They are summarized in *Toneel ter Zake; Een Onderzoek Naar de Exploitatie—Uitkomsten van Gesubsideerde Toneel Voorstellingen* [The Hague: Ministerie van Cultuur, Recreatie en Maatschappelijk Werk, 1978], 26–27.)

62. Ibid., 18.

63. About 33 percent of all performances in Maisons de la Culture in 1977/78 consisted of music, theatre, opera, and dance; movies represented 53 percent of the total. Data are from Ministère de la Culture et de la Communication, *Données Statistiques d'Ensemble sur les Maisons de la Culture* (Paris: February, 1980), 10.

64. Mark Schuster, *Income Taxes and the Arts: Tax Expenditures as Cultural Policy* (Ph.D. dissertation, Department of Urban Studies, Massachusetts Institute of Technology, 1972), 55.

65. Interview material (Ministère de la Culture et de la Communication). On the other hand, it is said that the 0.5 percent deduction on personal income is automatically taken by most French taxpayers whether they donate to charities or not, so that it has no real effect on giving.

66. Hughes de Varine, "Le Soutien Privé à l'Action Culturelle dans le Cadre Local et

Régional," Ministère de la Culture et Communication, Service des Etudes et de Recherches (Paris, August 1977).

67. The model has the same basic structure as the one first developed by Henry Hansmann in his "Nonprofit Enterprise in the Performing Arts" (Chapter 1, this volume). The differences between my model and his are the following: (1) popular and elite productions are explicitly segregated; (2) a capacity constraint is introduced limiting the total number of tickets sold per day; (3) private donations are treated differently; and (4) the influence of the NPO's output decisions on its competitive position vis-à-vis the commercial sector is examined.

68. Richard V. Burkhauser and Malcolm Getz, "What Federal Subsidies Will Buy: The Case of Symphony Orchestras," Department of Economics and Business Administration (Vanderbilt University, Working Paper 81-W18), 9–10.

69. Costs, in particular, will vary with the number of days during which each type of show is staged.

70. Estelle James, "Cross-Subsidization by Non-Profit Organizations: Theory, Evidence, and Evaluation" (Yale Program on Non-Profit Organizations Working Paper 30, 1982).

71. The line marked $d(NR)/dw = 0$ is the locus of combinations of v and v that would be selected by a manager maximizing v as S and D increased.

72. That is, the own-effect of w on ψ is always absolutely greater than the cross-effect of v on ψ.

73. It may also be noted that the contours will shrink not only when subsidies and donations decline but when production costs increase faster than the sale of tickets, a symptom of "Baumol's disease." The erosion of demand due to competition from movies, television, and phonograph records, if it were not matched by a reduction in costs, would also have that effect.

74. The inverse demands functions for π and ψ in terms of v and w were assumed to be such that a simultaneous increase in both arguments must reduce price.

75. The reason ψ must rise as the output-mix is shifted from point s to point t is this: The shape of any contour is elongated in the vertical direction because, by assumption, w is more popular than v, hence with a given level of subsidies, the audience level w at point l that could be attracted if w were maximized is greater than the level of v at point t where v is maximized. Hence, for any mix of v and w such as the one at point s, which would be chosen if v and w were equally preferred (or at least if w were not strongly preferred), the contour must have a slope with an absolute value smaller than unity. This implies that any gain in v from point s to point t must be associated with at least as large a loss in w. But, since the impact of w on ψ (the "own-price effect") must be greater than that of v (the "cross-effect"), the price-raising effect of the decrease in w must be greater than the price-reducing effect of the smaller increase in v.

76. Hansmann, op. cit.

77. This is not to deny that a subsidy given to a one-product enterprise might increase welfare by reducing the gap between price and marginal cost (a point stressed by Hansmann). What is going on here, however, is that the subsidies make it possible for the manager to alter the NPO's output-mix in a way that is increasingly inimical to consumers' interests.

78. Tibor Scitovsky, *The Joyless Economy* (New York: Oxford University Press, 1975), Chapters 1 and 2.

79. This type of consumer behavior has been modeled by Roger McCain, "Reflections on the Cultivation of Taste," *Journal of Cultural Economics* 3 (1979): 30–52.

15

Tax Incentives as Arts Policy in Western Europe

J. MARK DAVIDSON SCHUSTER

In studying government policies vis-à-vis the arts it is all too tempting to focus on direct government aid to the arts; our attention is focused on direct aid because this segment of the arts support system is the easiest to quantify—the numbers can often be obtained from public budgets—and the easiest to trace. In this sense, arts researchers have been like the person who looks under the streetlamp for the missing wallet, not because that is where it was lost, but because that is where the illumination is the best.

Recent research has begun to call our attention to the fact that we have drawn the boundary of our analysis of arts policies too narrowly.[1] Tax policies, copyright laws, zoning, unemployment and employment programs, urban redevelopment programs, and social security legislation are among the ways that governments can affect the flow of money to the arts and the mix of artistic activities ultimately available to the public. Taken together, these policies—all forms of indirect aid to the arts—provide ways for governments to support the arts without directly writing a check.

One of the distinguishing characteristics of U.S. arts policy is its heavy reliance on tax-based mechanisms to provide indirect aid to the arts. In the United States, taxes forgone through various arts-related tax incentives provide three times the amount of direct aid to the arts from all levels of government.[2] In no other Western country is tax-based indirect aid as important to the arts. But, for the most part, this difference is not due to differences in national legislation. Most Western European countries, for example, provide tax incentives for charitable contributions by individuals and corporations, and many of these countries go further than the United States in tailoring their tax laws to achieve other very specific cultural objectives. The real difference lies in historical patterns of patronage and the modern importance of the public sector in support of artistic activities.

This chapter is based on research supported with funds from a general-purpose grant to the Program on Non-Profit Organizations from the Rockefeller Brothers Fund.

Tax incentives affecting the arts take a number of different forms in Western countries, including—but not limited to—exemptions from capital gains taxes, exemptions from estate and gift (capital transfer) taxes, exemptions from wealth (permanent capital) taxes, charitable contribution deductions from income in calculating income taxes, credits against and exemptions from income taxes, exemptions from local real property taxes, and preferential rates for value added taxes. Each country, in selecting and implementing a variety of the tax incentives from this menu, creates a de facto policy of indirect aid to its arts and culture. Whether or not the government has considered these tax incentives as an explicit policy is unimportant; the result is an implicit policy that has important financial and aesthetic effects on the arts.

In this chapter I discuss some of the more interesting examples of tax incentives as arts policy in Western Europe and compare them, where possible, to similar examples in other countries. Generally, my focus is on the nonprofit arts or on arts goods narrowly defined, but in the last section I show how European countries have used the value added tax to provide incentives and implicit subsidy to the profit-making cultural industries through the market for cultural goods. All these examples make the case that an analysis of governmental arts policy must be expanded to include a consideration of indirect aid mechanisms, and they illustrate well the many issues inherent in determining the appropriate mix between direct and indirect aid mechanisms.

A complete analysis of these tax incentives would evaluate them from two perspectives: with respect to their economic effects and with respect to their cultural and aesthetic effects. Not only do tax incentives affect the relative cost of artistic goods and services, they also affect the relative mix of artistic activities that public and private arts institutions, artists, and entrepreneurs ultimately choose to provide. Unfortunately, with currently available data it is only possible to hint at the likely economic effects of most of these tax provisions, and it is virtually impossible to infer the cultural consequences. Therefore, my primary focus is on describing each of the tax provisions, emphasizing how each can be understood as a form of indirect aid to the arts.

INCOME TAX INCENTIVES FOR CHARITABLE CONTRIBUTIONS

The charitable deduction is widely recognized as the cornerstone of charitable giving in the United States, and the taxes forgone as a result of the charitable contribution deduction are the most important source of indirect government aid to all types of nonprofit charitable institutions. In the view of the *Boston Globe,* "there is something very appealing—one is tempted to say very American—about this system of the individual personally directing the flow of some 'government' dollars."[3] The popular view seems to be that the United States is the only country with such a tax

Table 15.1 Tax Incentives for Charitable Donations in Selected Countries

Country	Type of Incentive	Limitations
Belgium	Deduction	Minimum: Bfrs 1000 per donation Maximum: Lesser of 10% of total net revenues or Bfrs 10 million
France	Deduction	
	Corporations	Maximum: 1 per mille of turnover 2 per mille for groups listed by Ministry of Culture 3 per mille for groups listed by Ministry of Finance
	Individuals	Maximum: 1% of taxable income 5% for groups "in the public interest"
Greece	Deduction	Unlimited
Italy	Deduction	
	Corporations	Maximum: 2% of company income or 5% of salaries
	Individuals	Currently limited to financial support of exhibitions sponsored by gov't approved institutions or gifts to gov't or nonprofit institutions for acquisition and restoration of goods of artistic interest Proposal to expand this to gifts to performing arts organizations
Luxembourg	Deduction	Minimum: Lfrs 5000 Maximum: Lesser of 5% of total net income of Lfrs 5 million Beneficiaries very limited
Netherlands	Deduction	
	Corporations	Minimum: Fl 500 Maximum: 6% of taxable profits after carryover of losses
	Individuals	Minimum: Higher of Fl 200 or 1% of gross income Maximum: 10% of gross income
Switzerland	Deduction	
	Corporations	Unlimited federal
	Individuals	10% of cantonal income tax
West Germany	Deduction	
	Corporations	Maximum: 10% of profit for political parties, social affairs, science, and culture; 5% of profit for other charity; or 2 per mille of turnover
	Individuals	Maximum: 10% or 5% of income (as above)

Country	Type of Incentive	Limitations
Canada	Deduction	Maximum: 20% of net income
United States	Deduction	
	Corporations	Maximum: 10% of taxable income
	Individuals	Maximum: 50% of adjusted gross income
		30% gifts of certain property
		20% to private charities
Denmark	Covenant and	At least 10 years
	Deduction	Minimum: Annual total > Dkr 100
		Each donation > Dkr 50
		Maximum: Annual total of Dkr 1000
Ireland	Covenant	At least 3 years
		Very limited number of beneficiaries
Great Britain	Covenant	Unlimited amount
		At least 4 years
		Higher rate relief up to 5000 pounds
		Some differences in Scotland and Wales
Sweden	None	

NOTES: For France, Italy, the Netherlands, West Germany, Canada, the United States, Great Britain, and Sweden the information in this table is accurate through 1984. Because these laws are not changed frequently, much of the information on the other countries, which is generally accurate through 1978, is undoubtedly still accurate, though there may have been changes in upper limits for contributions.

SOURCES: J. Mark Davidson Schuster, *Supporting the Arts: An International Comparative Study,* report for the Policy and Planning Division, National Endowment for the Arts, Washington, D.C., April 1985. [Canada, France, Italy, Great Britain, Netherlands, Sweden, United States, West Germany]

Ignatius Claeys Bouuaert, *Taxation of Cultural Foundations and of Patronage of the Arts in the Member States of the European Economic Community,* Commission of the European Communities, XII/670/75-E, 1975, 74–104.

Arthur Andersen & Co., "Overview of Governmental Support and Financial Regulation of Philanthropic Organizations in Selected Nations," in *Research Papers Sponsored by the Commission on Private Philanthropy and Public Needs* (Washington, D.C.: U.S. Department of the Treasury, 1977), Vol. V, 2976.

"Ce que l'on peut deduire de sa declaration de revenus pour versement à une fondation," *30 Jours d'Europe,* no. 237, April 1978, p. 19.

Colin Brough, *As You Like It: Private Support for the Arts* (London: The Bow Group, October 1977), 15. [Greece and Switzerland]

Hamish R. Sandison and Jennifer Williams, eds., *Tax Policy and Private Support for the Arts in the United States, Canada and Great Britain* (Washington, D.C.: British American Arts Association, 1981), 8–29. [Canada, Great Britain, and the United States]

"Dons et Subventions Verses à des Ouvres ou Organismes d'Intérêt General," *Notes Bleues,* Bulletin d'Actualité du Ministère de l'Economie et des Finances, no. 96, 8–14 November 1982, Paris, France, and Service des Etudes et Recherches, Ministère de la Culture, Paris, France, "Regles Actuelles de Deductions Fiscales Autorisées en cas de Versements à des Organismes Culturels," January 1984. [France]

J. Mark Davidson Schuster, "Tax Incentives for Charitable Donations: Deeds of Covenant and Charitable Contribution Deductions," Working Paper #71 (New Haven: Yale University, Institution for Social and Policy Studies, Program on Non-profit Organizations, December 1983, forthcoming in the *University of San Francisco Law Review*). [Great Britain]

Alan Feld, Michael O'Hare, and J. Mark Davidson Schuster, *Patrons Despite Themselves: Taxpayers and Arts Policy,* A Twentieth Century Fund Report (New York: New York University Press, 1983), 31, 48. [United States] incentive; Daniel Boorstin, the Librarian of Congress, in discussing arts support in the United States has said, "there are hidden subsidies. There's no other country in the world where people and business are encouraged to support cultural institutions by being given tax benefits."[4]

But the charitable deduction is no longer an exclusively American phenomenon; Canada, West Germany, France, Belgium, Luxembourg, the Netherlands, Italy, Switzerland, and Greece are among the countries that now have clearly recognizable charitable deduction provisions in their income tax laws.[5] Nor is a charitable deduction the only way to provide tax-based incentives for charitable giving. The *Research Papers* of the Commission on Private Philanthropy and Public Needs, for example, were filled with suggestions for alternative mechanisms including, for example, the tax credit, the direct matching grant, the sliding matching grant, and the percentage contribution bonus.[6] Yet, with the exception of the deed of covenant in Great Britain, Ireland, and Denmark, none of these proposals has ever been implemented, so we have little actual experience with which to study their actual effects on charitable giving.

The tax incentives for charitable contributions that are currently in use are summarized for selected countries in Table 15.1. Most of these countries have implemented deductions through which charitable contributions can be deducted from the taxpayer's income before calculating the taxpayer's income tax liability. A donor with a given marginal tax rate in each of these countries would have the same financial incentive for making a contribution; in each case the price of giving one unit of the national currency would be 1.00 minus the donor's marginal tax rate.[7]

These deduction provisions differ in two important ways: limits on the total amount of allowed deductions and constraints on the list of eligible beneficiaries.[8] Some countries, most notably the United States, have very generous upper limits on deductibility; lower limits elsewhere may be deceptive because the donor may be allowed to carry over excess deductions to the following year. Other countries, such as Denmark, have genuinely low upper limits, presumably to place a cap on tax revenues lost through this incentive. Several countries have placed floors on deductibility, insisting that the donor contribute at least a certain minimum amount before receiving a tax benefit.

The policies concerning the range of institutions eligible to receive tax-assisted charitable contributions also vary widely among these countries. In Italy, individual charitable contributions can currently be made to government agencies or to institutions approved in advance by the government in support of exhibitions or for acquisition and restoration of goods of artistic interest. In Luxembourg, beneficiaries are more limited, with the arts represented only by state and municipal museums. In Ireland, the list is extremely limited and apparently includes no arts institutions. In most cases the national government takes a much more active role in determining eligibility than has been the case in the United States. This involvement comes from a desire to target the tax incentive as effectively as possible without spreading it out too broadly and from a fear of encouraging tax evasion.

Whatever the configuration of a particular country's charitable deduction legislation, it is clear that in no other country is the charitable deduction used as much by potential donors and as effectively by potential recipients as it is in the United States. This phenomenon has often been explained by pointing to the low upper limits in force in most countries, but this explanation is unsatisfactory when it is realized that donors are not contributing enough to be constrained by the current limits. The difference in practice surely must be more the result of the relative importance of the public sector in each of these countries and of the relative lack of private initiative and support for the arts in the presence of such heavy public support.

But as Table 15.1 indicates, there is another system currently providing tax incentives for charitable donations in Great Britain, Ireland, and Denmark: the "deed of covenant." Though the deed of covenant is more the exception than the rule for tax-induced donations, it is an intriguing system whose structure and implementation provide a fascinating and instructive counterpoint to the charitable contribution deduction. A comparison of the two helps illustrate a number of the issues inherent in tax-based indirect aid for the arts.

The British Deed of Covenant

The British deed of covenant, unlike the charitable deduction in U.S. law,[9] was not originally created as an incentive for charitable giving.[10] The British income tax originated in Addington's Act of 1803, in which it was established that transfers of income from one taxpayer to another would, for income tax purposes, be treated as the income of the recipient, to be taxed at the recipient's tax rate, and not as the income of the transferor.[11] To guarantee that such transfers could not easily be used to dodge income taxation, they were required to be made under a contract—the "covenant"—on an annual basis for a period of at least seven years. The importance of covenants to charities is clear when coupled with the fact that charities themselves are exempt from income tax; the transferred income is treated as the nontaxable income of the tax-exempt charity.[12] In principle, then, the donor should be able to transfer any amount of pretax income to a charity through a covenant without paying any taxes.

The actual transfer of income under the British deed of covenant is a bit more complicated than this underlying principle of taxation suggests. Because the British tax collection procedure is based primarily upon the Pay-As-You-Earn (PAYE) system, most income tax is withheld at the source so the taxpayer has only after-tax income with which to pay his or her deed of covenant obligations. As a result, the individual donor typically enters into a "net covenant" in which he or she agrees to donate a fixed annual amount of after-tax income to the charity for the duration of the covenant

Figure 15.1 How the Deed of Covenant Works

For purposes of comparison, all of the examples presented assume that the goal of the donor is to channel £100 (or $100) to the charity.

Example 1: Deed of Covenant, Donor Tax Rate = 30% (Basic Rate)

	Donor	Charity
Donor earns:	+ £100	
Donor pays:	– 70 net covenant →	+ £ 70 net covenant
Donor pays:	– 30 income tax (30% × 100)	+ 30 reclaimed by charity
		+ £100 received by charity
	Government	
Gov't receives:	+ £ 30 income tax	
Gov't pays:	– 30 to charity	

Example 2: Deed of Covenant, Pre–1980, Donor Tax Rate = 50%

	Donor	Charity
Donor earns:	+ £140	
Donor pays:	– 70 net covenant →	+ £ 70 net covenant
Donor pays:	– 70 income tax (50% × 140)	+ 30 reclaimed by charity
		+ £100 received by charity
	Government	
Gov't receives:	+ £ 70 income tax	
Gov't pays:	– 30 to charity	
Gov't retains:	+ £ 40 net taxes	

Example 3: Deed of Covenant, Post–1980, Donor Tax Rate = 50%

	Donor	Charity
Donor earns:	+ £100	
Donor pays:	– 70 net covenant →	+ £ 70 net covenant
Donor pays:	– 50 income tax (50% × 100)	+ 30 reclaimed by charity
	– £ 20	+ £100 received by charity
Donor gets:	+ £ 20 higher-rate relief [(50% – 30%) × 100]	
	Government	
Gov't receives:	+ £ 50 income tax	
Gov't pays:	– 30 to charity	
Gov't rebates:	– 20 to donor as higher–rate relief	

Example 4: Charitable Contribution Deduction, Donor Tax Rate = 50%

	Donor	Charity
Donor earns:	+ $100	
Donor pays:	– 100 deductible contribution →	+ $100 received by charity
Donor pays:	– 50 withheld taxes (50% × 100)	
	– $ 50	
Donor gets:	+ $ 50 reduction in annual income tax (50% × 100)	
	Government	
Gov't receives:	+ $ 50 withheld taxes	
Gov't rebates:	– 50 reduction in donor's income tax	

Note: Unlike the deed of covenant, the government is not directly involved in the financial transfer to the charity in the charitable deduction transaction.

agreement.[13] In theory, the charity can recoup all of the taxes paid by the taxpayer on that income by reclaiming them from the government, and that is exactly what happens in the simplest case. (See Figure 15.1, Example 1.)

In practice, the application of deeds of covenant to charitable donations violates this general principle. Charities are only allowed to reclaim taxes at the basic rate of tax in force at a particular time (the lowest tax rate applicable to any individual's income), whether or not the donor actually paid a higher rate of tax, as is shown in Example 2. Until recently, this meant that the higher-rate paying taxpayer/donor actually paid more in taxes on the income involved in the charitable transfer than the charity was able to reclaim, so the difference was retained by the government as part of its general tax revenue. Thus, the deed of covenant in its pure form is essentially a tax credit, with the credit percentage determined by the lowest current tax rate.

Unlike the charitable deduction, by which the donor channels the entire donation to the charity in one payment—including the taxes that would otherwise be due and the donor's private (net of tax) contribution—the deed of covenant separates the flow of money into two streams: the donor's private contribution, flowing directly from the donor to the charity, and the forgone taxes, flowing first to the government and then reclaimed by the charity. From the charity's perspective, it is absolutely clear what the various origins of its funds are: private contributions from private donors and taxes forgone as a result of governmental legislation.

At first glance, this distinction may seem to be without any practical significance—the charity still gets the money—but it becomes absolutely critical when considered with the degree to which public policy deems it appropriate for donors to place conditions on their donations. It is eminently reasonable to allow the donor to have complete control over the private contribution portion of the donation, but to the extent that public policy has encouraged and helped support donations through taxes forgone, it might be argued that the more general interest of the taxpaying public ought to outweigh the voice of the individual donor in determining its dispersal. The charity is free to spend the taxes it reclaims from the government for charitable purposes unrestrained by donor stipulations. In this regard, the deed of covenant stakes out a middle ground between direct governmental aid to charities, in which individuals have no control over the expenditure, and the charitable deduction, in which individuals have complete control.

From Inland Revenue's perspective, this separation of financial flows has other desirable characteristics. It offers an easy way to monitor and affect the distribution of funds by charities.[14] Inland Revenue spot-checks charities to make sure that they are spending their income on charitable purposes. If a violation is found, Inland Revenue simply denies reclamation of taxes on deeds of covenant. Because the system gives Inland Revenue some teeth in carrying out this monitoring, it is unwilling to give up this control.

A related argument in favor of separation of financial flows has to do with taxpayer fraud. Under the charitable contribution deduction, taxpayers do claim deductions for charitable contributions that were never made; the deed of covenant system would seem nearly to eliminate this type of fraud.

Many British charities have long argued that another desirable characteristic of the deed of covenant is the multiyear nature of the contract.[15] The perceived advantage is that it introduces an important element of security into the charity's income flow, making it easier to budget from year to year and minimizing the cost of fund-raising. Whether or not this is true is difficult to ascertain empirically, but it is widely believed.

When the Conservative party returned to power in Great Britain in 1979, its fiscal policies were designed to deemphasize the income tax and to exploit other sources of taxation further, particularly the value added tax (VAT). The Finance Act of 1980 was a watershed for British charities because, in translating these Tory policies into law, it included four provisions that have had a direct financial impact on charities.

The major reform was a reduction of tax rates. Of most immediate concern to charities was the fact that the basic rate of tax was lowered from 33 to 30 percent, representing a cost to charities whose outstanding net deeds of covenant would be supplemented by taxes reclaimed at a lower rate than had been in effect when they were first written. Though the government has, at times, provided transitional relief for charities when such changes in the basic rate were implemented, such relief was not offered in 1980.

The second policy that had an immediate and substantial effect on charities was an increase in the rate of VAT from 8 to 15 percent. Charities are not exempt from VAT and, like all consumers in the economic chain, are expected to pay their share of VAT.

On the positive side, the Finance Act of 1980 provided for "higher rate relief" on covenanted contributions, an additional tax incentive for donors who pay more than the basic rate of tax.[16] This provision was designed to offset partially the cost to charity of the two reforms just discussed.[17] With higher-rate relief, donors can now subtract the gross value of the covenanted donation from their income, thereby avoiding the payment of higher-rate taxes on the donation and lowering its net cost to the donor. (The donor still "pays" the basic rate because it is that portion that is reclaimed by the charity. For an example of the effect of higher rate relief, see Example 3.)

One interesting result of higher rate relief is that the increased fiscal incentives for charitable donations under a deed of covenant are now virtually identical to the incentives offered under the charitable deduction. Compare Examples 3 and 4. These incentives should lead to increased giving, and because they are directly proportional to the donor's marginal tax rate, can be expected to interact with donor preferences to benefit particularly those charities who draw their support from higher income donors. (Indeed, because of this latter point the National Council for Voluntary Organizations has argued for a composite system that would incorporate the administrative advantages of the deed of covenant with an equal increase in the financial incentives for all donors, without offering undue advantages to the charities favored by wealthier donors.)[18]

The success of higher rate relief, from the charity's perspective, will ultimately rest on the ability of charities to explain the new tax provisions to their potential donors and to justify increased charitable contributions for the services they provide. In the first instance, higher rate relief passes the new tax savings back to donors, and because of this, the burden is placed on the charities to convince their donors to pass these savings along to charity in the form of increased covenants. In the words of Prime Minister Thatcher, "the onus is on charities to make these provisions work to their advantage."[19]

The Finance Act of 1980 also lowered, from seven to four years, the required minimum length for a charitable deed of covenant, and it is hoped that this, too, will provide additional encouragement for charitable contributions by making the contractual agreement less onerous. Because of the multiyear nature of covenants, it is still too early to tell just what the combined net effect of higher rate relief and the shortening of the required time period has been.

For someone who is accustomed to the charitable contribution deduction, the most lasting impression of the deed of covenant must be its administrative complexity. British charities struggle with this problem constantly as they try to explain the tax implications of charitable giving to potential donors. The system is not an immediately transparent one, and it requires quite a bit of donor sophistication to be used effectively. Inland Revenue is moving toward a system of self-assessment of taxes, and it is perhaps this change more than any other that will result in a clearer donor understanding of the covenant system.[20] Donors will come to see much more clearly what the tax advantages of their deeds of covenant are, in much the same way that U.S. taxpayers are aware of how charitable contributions reduce their tax liability when they are deducted from income.

Another by-product of the complexity of the system has been the growth of a wide range of administrative arrangements that legally circumvent the deed of covenant system, greatly increasing its flexibility.[21] Through the use of such administrative arrangements, knowledgeable donors can come very close to replicating the wide-open flexibility of a charitable deduction within the more rigid structure of the deed of covenant.

Corporations can also make their charitable contributions through deeds of covenant in order to take advantage of the tax incentive, though the actual procedure is slightly different than the one outlined for individual donors.[22]

The reforms of the deed of covenant in the Finance Act of 1980 have moved the deed of covenant closer to the charitable contribution deduction in two respects: For taxpayers with the same marginal tax rates, the financial incentives for charitable giving are now identical in both systems, and with higher rate relief donors have been given the opportunity to restrict the expenditure of a portion of the taxes foregone via the deed of covenant. While increasing the financial incentives for charitable giving, the changes have abandoned two aspects of the pure covenant system that might have been desirable to retain in a public policy vis-à-vis charity: the principle of weighing each donor's gift equally with tax incentives and the principle of clearly dividing the charitable contribution into two financial streams, separating all the taxes forgone under the tax incentive from the donor's private net-of-tax contribution. At the same time, the deed of covenant is a system that sacrifices some flexibility in favor of the revenue authority's ability to monitor a charity's expenditure of its income, and in favor of the predictability of income flows that may be embodied in the multiyear requirement.

Despite the economic incentives for contributions in the deed of covenant, the financial effect, particularly for the arts, has been quite small. (In fiscal 1982, for example, the government rebated £77 million to charities as a result of deeds of covenant. No records are kept that would allow an easy identification of the portion of these repayments that went to the arts.[23]) Undoubtedly, this is partially because of the complexity of the covenant system, but even the simpler charitable deduction, when incorporated into a system where there is a tradition of large-scale public support, would prove insufficient in and of itself to initiate a strong trend toward private support. In addition, the arts have had some difficulty in staking their claim for additional charitable contributions in an economic period when other, more pressing social needs have been making increased demands on private support.[24]

Private donors are unlikely to find many British museums attractive beneficiaries because they are already receiving substantial subsidy directly from tax revenues. The recent move of the Science Museum and the Victoria and Albert Museum to trustee status was undertaken to bring them in line with the other national museums, which have been trustee museums for some time, and with the hope that it would make these museums more attractive to private donors, thereby easing the pressure on public support. Many arts institutions have "Friends of" organizations associated with them, and these organizations have been successful at attracting covenanted donations, particularly for collection purchase funds. Because these organizations are formed through private initiatives, they do not give the impression of being already heavily subsidized by the taxpayer.

The picture is not very dissimilar for the performing- and other arts organizations that are the traditional clients of the Arts Council of Great Britain. Though most of these institutions are registered as non-profit-distributing companies under the Charities Act and therefore eligible recipients for covenanted contributions, they have not been overwhelmingly successful at attracting private donations either. The Arts Council estimates that only 3 percent of its clients' income comes from private support, and most of that comes from corporate sponsorship, which would be deductible in any event as a business expenditure for publicity. Most covenanted income comes from private individuals who tend to give toward bricks and mortar or other capital projects that have a local attraction.[25]

A charitable deduction or a deed of covenant alone is not sufficient to ensure a healthy stream of private support for the arts, even if the financial incentives are generous and the field of application broad. The tax incentive interacts with donor preferences and with historic patterns of private and public support. Although technical adjustments may be of primary interest in establishing a fair and efficient system of tax incentives, these adjustments will have little effect in a system with little precedent for private support. Many of the Western European countries are currently struggling with the problem of how to increase private support for the arts. Most of them are turning first to the corporate sector in much the same way that President Reagan has recently turned to the private sector for support of human services in the United States. For them, the key does not lie in the implementation of tax incentives; most of them already have tax incentives for charitable contributions in their national tax laws. The key lies ultimately in a changing view of the relative roles of the private and public sectors, a much more difficult problem to address.

CAPITAL TRANSFER TAXES

Tax rules that govern the transfer of artworks are clearly of concern to arts institutions. Formerly part of estate and gift taxes and now, in most countries, in newly unified capital transfer taxes, these are some of the most interesting examples of tax incentives as artistic and cultural policy.

Capital Taxation and the National Heritage in Great Britain

An unusually complete set of tax incentives affecting the transfer of artworks can be found in British tax law, where a series of provisions concerning "Capital Taxation and the National Heritage" are in effect.[26] These provisions are all designed to preserve and provide access to the best examples of the nation's artistic and cultural heritage while providing tax advantages for the owner and, at the same time, limiting the actual cost to the exchequer. Included are "historic properties, land of historic, scenic or scientific interest, and objects and collections of national, artistic, historic or scientific interest [that] form an integral and major part of the cultural life of the country."[27]

The available tax reliefs are consciously designed to take account of the fact that the international price for an artwork is often greater than the price within Great Britain. Thus, the reliefs are quite clearly designed to counteract the incentive for selling the property on the open market and, perhaps, losing it to another country or to private hands. At the same time, an important premise underlying the British tax law is that it is not necessarily desirable for these artworks to come into the possession of public institutions, which have limited funds for conservation, maintenance, and security and limited space for storage and display.

[I]t has been the policy of successive Governments that this national heritage should be conserved and protected for the benefit of the community. . . . so far as possible property of this kind should remain in private hands and . . . where this is no longer possible the owners should dispose of it to those bodies in this country which have been set up specifically to hold such property in trust for the community.[28]

At first glance, the choice to allow tax relief for the transfer of property that remains in private hands seems to be an indefensible one. Two propositions form the foundation of this policy. First, the government believes it is important to exhibit objects of importance to the cultural heritage in an appropriate context, as part of the fabric of society, exploiting any historical associations of the object. In this view, the display of the object out of context, in the relatively sterile environment of a museum, for example, is to be avoided. Second, the private owner may be more interested in and more able to provide for the care and maintenance of the property. This may be particularly true for the security of objects retained in an owner-occupied stately home. Though it would be tempting to conclude that a policy of this sort is a reflection of the current Conservative government's emphasis on privatization, these tax provisions have been in existence in one form or another for a number of years, through a variety of governments.[29]

Three different types of tax relief are available under these provisions: "conditional exemption" the "private treaty sale," and "acceptance in lieu." In the discussion that follows, I generally limit myself to a discussion of the implications of these provisions for the transfer of artworks, but they apply equally to heritage properties of all types.

Conditional Exemption

An individual who acquires a work of art by inheritance or gift may be eligible for "conditional exemption" from capital transfer tax. The work of art must be of national, scientific, historic, or artistic interest and be of sufficient quality to be displayed in a public collection. Thus, the object must be determined by the government to be "museum worthy." The transfer of such an object is exempt from capital transfer tax if the new owner applies for conditional exemption and agrees to (1) keep the object permanently in the United Kingdom (unless the Treasury agrees to allow it to travel abroad temporarily for special exhibition purposes), (2) take reasonable steps to preserve it, and (3) take reasonable steps to ensure public access. These three undertakings are the quid pro quo for tax relief and ultimately define the limits of the public interest in these works. (A similar set of exemptions from transfer duties in exchange for public access exists in France, where the law has consciously been extended to exemptions for artworks in corporate collections.[30])

The public access requirement is the keystone of the public interest in this tax incentive. Owners of conditionally exempt artworks can ensure public access in one of several ways. The object may be exhibited in a room that is open to the public for a reasonable number of days each year (including appropriate publicity and assurances that the object will actually be on display). Free access is not required; the owner may charge a reasonable entry fee. This is the most desirable option when the owner is also the proprietor of an historic home to which the object has an integral connection. Alternatively, the owner can loan the object on a long-term basis for purpose of display to a public collection or to a museum, gallery or historic house run by a charitable trust and open to the public. It is assumed that the custodian institution will display the object and not simply store it, thus serving the public's interest. This option places the burden of preservation and security on the displaying museum while preserving the donor's options for the ultimate disposition of the object (at which point the conditional exemption may or may not be continued, depending on the nature of that transfer).

Finally, the owner can choose to enter the object in a list, maintained at the Victoria and Albert Museum, of conditionally exempt objects. In so doing, the owner agrees to allow members of the public to view the object by appointment and to lend it on request to public collections for temporary exhibition. The list contains precise information on the object itself, on arrangements for public access, and on the general location of the object. It need not identify the owner or the precise location of the object. The object does not have to be viewed in the owner's home and it may be loaned anonymously. These provisions are all designed to protect the security of the object and the owner, but effectively limit public access to the most knowledgeable art scholars, who are most likely to use the system effectively.

The Capital Taxes Office (CTO), which administers the capital transfer tax legislation, has made some estimates of the extent of conditional exemption.[31] The number of claims for conditional exemption has grown gradually over the last few years:

1980–81	67 claims (land and chattels)
1981–82	77 claims (land and chattels)
1982–83	89 claims (38 land claims and 51 chattels)

Claims were not necessarily processed in the year they were initially made, and approximately 5 percent were rejected or withdrawn. The CTO has estimated that for the last two years listed above the value of the exempted claims—either the uncorroborated value claimed by the owner or CTO's "guesstimate"—was £7.3 million and £5.5 million respectively. The proportionate number of claims for land exemption has been increasing, presumably because the bite of capital transfer taxes would be the worst there. It is impossible to estimate from these figures how many works of fine art have come under conditional exemption because other types of objects are included in the exemption and because one claim can include collections with numerous objects.

The owner of a conditionally exempt object can transfer the object to a new owner without tax liability by giving or bequeathing it to someone who renews the conditional exemption; by giving or bequeathing it to a public collection, to a university, or to certain heritage trusts or charities; or by taking advantage of one of the two other reliefs from capital transfer tax. In specifying a limited list of possible recipients for exempt donations of property, British law differs in a significant way from U.S. law, which grants such exemption for donations to any nonprofit tax-exempt organization so long as the property will be used for the tax-exempt purposes of the charitable institution. Thus, British law goes further in determining which institutions are the most appropriate to receive these objects.

An owner who decides to sell a conditionally exempt object loses the exemption on the previously exempted transfer and taxes are due. In addition, the owner is requested to give the public collections three months' notice of the intent to sell. Though such notice is not required, if it is not given the government can withhold an export license indefinitely for an object of national importance.[32] In this way, the British government recently delayed the export of three drawings purchased at auction by the Getty Museum.[33]

The Private Treaty Sale

If the owner should decide to sell a conditionally exempt object, the government is able to participate at an advantage in the bidding for the object through a second capital transfer tax incentive, the "private treaty sale." The government has authorized museums and certain other public—though not necessarily governmental—bodies to offer to pay the owner the net after-tax market value of the work of art *plus* a percentage of the taxes forgone if the object ends up in public hands. For works of art and other objects, public bodies are generally advised to "offer the seller an amount equal to 25 percent of the benefit of the tax exemption, subject to negotiations above or below this figure where flexibility is appropriate."[34] This administrative arrangement is known as the "douceur," literally, the "sweetener." Through the use of the douceur to sweeten the purchase price, the seller and the acquiring institution share, in a sense, the value of the tax exemption. An example makes this clear:

	Open Market Sale	Private Treaty Sale
Current Market Value	£100,000 pounds (paid by buyer)	£100,000 (amount unpaid)
– Capital Transfer Tax (example of 60%)	– 60,000 (collected by gov't)	– 60,000 (forgone by gov't)
Received by Seller Net of CTT	40,000	40,000 (paid by public museum)
+ 25% of Tax Liability (25% × 60,000)		+ 15,000 (paid by public museum)
Total Received by Seller	£ 40,000	£ 55,000

NOTE: For simplicity, this example assumes that no capital gains taxes were due on the sale. If capital gains taxes were due, the douceur would be applied to the sum of the forgone capital transfer taxes plus the forgone capital gains taxes.

The benefit to the seller is clear; he or she nets £15,000 more than would have been possible in the open market (assuming that the negotiated market value of £100,000 is the maximum that could be realized in the international market and not just in the national market). The benefit to the public is not quite as obvious. The public collections obtain a work of art that is worth £100,000 for a direct outlay of £55,000, a net public benefit of £45,000, but a benefit that is only realizable in artistic terms, embodied in the artwork and unable to be translated into support for any other government program. In so doing, the exchequer has forgone £60,000 in taxes, which could have been used to support any public program deemed appropriate. The "true" cost to the government is, therefore, £115,000—£60,000 in forgone taxes and £55,000 in actual expenditure—for a £100,000 work of art. The bottom line in this calculation is ultimately the incalculable benefit of bringing the work permanently into the public collections and avoiding exportation.

In theory, the private treaty sale is self-regulating, based on an agreement negotiated between the potential seller and the public institution. In practice, though, it is not as straightforward as a simple example might suggest. First, it requires the determination of a "market" value as the basis on which all of the calculations will be made. The owner and the institution negotiate an agreed value, but there is little guarantee of how well it will actually represent what the artwork could command on the open market, because the test will never be made. Thus, the value agreed on will depend on the relative bargaining positions and abilities of these two parties alone and not of all the parties who might be involved were the work to be offered on the open market. If the institution is particularly eager to have the object, the seller may be able to negotiate a more advantageous price than the market would afford. This seems to be compounded in the case of artworks for which an auction house or an independent member of the art trade acting on behalf of the owner determines a value for the object.

Second, the parties may negotiate the level of the douceur itself. The 25 percent figure is a general guideline and is not mandated by law.[35] The government recognizes that for low-value objects 25 percent might not provide a sufficient inducement, and that for very high-value items it may not be necessary to offer as much as 25 percent. For artworks, the Office of Arts and Libraries has stated that the douceur is typically between 20 and 25 percent and that they could think of no recent case in which the douceur exceeded 25 percent. The level of the douceur and whether or not it should be fixed by law are two constant points of contention.[36] The auction houses that negotiate on behalf of private owners are particularly resistant to decreases in the douceur, as their fee is pegged to the final sale price. In the case of donations of land and buildings, the douceur is set lower, at 10 percent of the forgone taxes, because there is no danger of these properties being exported if they are not purchased by public bodies.

Finally, the private treaty sale requires that the institution be able to obtain specific information about the seller's potential tax liability. Thus, the Capital Taxes Office is asked to disclose the potential tax liability and confirm the exemption. In providing tax incentives for the transfer of cash or property, either by donation or sale, governments have generally been unwilling to implement schemes that would reveal the donor's tax position to the recipient institution. The tax implications of the tax incentives in U.S. law, for example, are only seen by the donor when annual tax calculations are made. In Great Britain itself, an unwillingness to reveal this information to the recipient institution was given as one of the reasons that higher rate relief on deeds of covenant was rebated back to the donor rather than forward to the charity, though this case certainly would have been considerably more complex than for private treaty sales, as it would have involved making countless potential tax liability determinations.[37]

Survey data indicate that, from 1978 through 1980, English museums and galleries acquired between 50 and 60 items by private treaty sale.[38] Most items were valued at less than £500,000, only 2 at more than £1 million. Scottish arts institutions acquired 26 items. Private treaty sales could not be separated from total acquisitions of Welsh institutions. The Capital Taxes Office has released data on more recent private treaty sales of all types of heritage property to all of the eligible institutions:[39]

1980–81	63 private treaty sales (land and chattels)
1981–82	46 private treaty sales (land and chattels)
1982–83	51 private treaty sales (4 land claims, 47 chattels)

Although they certainly constitute only a small portion of all acquisitions by these public bodies, private treaty sales may represent particularly key objects and properties that would otherwise pass into private hands for another generation or out of the country altogether.

It is interesting to compare the private treaty sale to the "right of preemption" *(droit de preemption)* in French law. The French state has the right to preempt the purchase of an artwork at a public sale by buying it from the highest bidder at his or her bid. The right may be exercised only for works of "great interest to the national patrimony."[40] Critics of this state intervention in the art market point out that when it is known that the work is desired by the public museums, it dampens the interest of private individuals in bidding and may injure the seller by lowering the price ultimately realized at auction (whether or not the government actually exercises its right of preemption). When coupled with the right of retention *(droit de retenue)*, by which the state can prohibit exportation of certain art works, it may also lower the price by dissuading foreign purchasers.[41] On the other hand, it may reduce the seller's uncertainty sufficiently to raise the reserve price.

Acceptance in Lieu

The final tax relief provision, "acceptance in lieu," is linked to the preservation of the national cultural heritage. If capital transfer taxes are due on any assets, certain works of art may be accepted as payment for that liability. Whereas works receiving conditional exemption or eligible for private treaty sales must be "museum worthy," in order to be accepted in lieu of tax payments works must be "preeminent," a stricter standard.

When accepting an artwork as payment for capital transfer tax, the government calculates the value in the same way it calculates the offering price for a private treaty sale: the net value the donor would have realized if he or she had sold the work and paid the taxes due plus 25 percent of the taxes forgone by exempting the transfer from capital transfer tax. (In this case the douceur is fixed at 25 percent, but this restriction may be meaningless given the flexibility inherent in determining an actual market price.) This amount is offset against the tax liability of other property in the estate.

Continuing the example begun earlier, suppose the artwork with a market value of £100,000 had been offered in lieu of taxes rather than sold via a private treaty sale. On the artwork itself £60,000 of capital transfer tax are due. Assume that on the remainder of the estate the additional tax liability is £600,000. Offering the painting in lieu of taxes results in a tax benefit of £55,000 that is offset against the tax liability of the remainder of the estate. Thus, the donor pays £545,000 in capital transfer tax in addition to the transfer of the painting itself. If the donor had simply paid capital transfer tax up front, the total tax liability would have been £660,000 (£600,000 + £60,000). The tax benefit implicit in this particular form of acceptance in lieu reduces the total tax liability by £15,000; the donor ends up "paying" £645,000 in taxes, the £100,000 painting plus £545,000 on the remainder of the estate. £15,000 of tax are forgone (and £100,000 of tax are allowed to be paid in kind rather than in cash) to provide an incentive to channel this artwork into the public domain.

Another possible advantage to the donor using the acceptance in lieu procedure is that the donor can make the offer with the condition that the item should pass to a particular institution or that it should be allowed to remain *in situ*. If the object passes to a private institution or remains *in situ*, formal ownership is vested in an appropriate public body, which "loans" the object and ensures that any conditions are being complied with. Thus, an individual can pay capital transfer taxes with an artwork and still retain physical possession. Once again, the desirability of having the work remain in an appropriate setting is the primary consideration, subject to acceptable arrangements for reasonable public access, security, and conservation.

Most tax incentives, once implemented, can be used by institutions or individuals without limit. The interaction between the financial benefits and the tastes of individual donors, on one hand, and the plans of cultural institutions, on the other, determines the extent to which the incentive is used and the amount of taxes forgone. Acceptance in lieu is unlike other tax incentives in this regard. It is subject to a strict upper limit specified in advance by Parliament. An annual amount is actually budgeted and divided in half between the Office of Arts and Libraries and the Department of the Environment, the two major government agencies charged with the preservation of the national heritage. When an item is accepted in lieu of taxes each pays one-half of the value to Inland Revenue. In recent years acceptances in lieu of taxes have been limited to £2 million.

This unusual attempt to make a tax expenditure explicit through an actual budgetary transfer—the only such example I have come across in investigating tax expenditures for the arts in a number of different countries—has drawn criticism from the Education, Science and Arts Committee of the House of Commons:

> [T]he Committee deplore the practice whereby every time tax is paid in kind in this way rather than in cash, the Treasury insists that the transfer has involved public expenditure. There should be no attempt to inhibit the already limited purchasing powers of Secretaries of State, or of the National Heritage Memorial Fund by notional transfers of this kind made simply for accounting purposes. It is quite obvious that there can be no open-ended commitment on the part of any government to accept objects in lieu of money, but this does not mean that the practice of allowing certain taxes to be paid in kind, where the objects in question are of great importance, should not be unequivocally recognised in law.[42]

Whether or not one agrees with the policy of placing an upper limit on a tax incentive of this sort, making explicit the forgone taxes does help to keep in mind the fact that such incentives do have costs associated with them.

Each year from 12 to 20 cases requesting acceptance in lieu are initiated. In the last two years only 1 or 2 claims have been rejected, probably due more to discouragement given to claimants early in the process than to any looseness of government standards. The fiscal year ending April 1983 was the first time that the whole acceptance in lieu fund was spent. No doubt, this will lead to pressure on the government to increase the limits on acceptance in lieu. No one can be sure what the government's response would be if an extremely valuable heritage item were offered in lieu, posing an unusually high charge against that limit.

Other British Incentives

What have been described here are specific tax provisions that provide incentives so that transfers of properties deemed part of the national heritage will be conducted in ways that reflect the public's interest in those items. It has been the policy of successive governments to encourage such property to remain in private hands, if possible, and for their owners to care for them and ensure public access. These tax provisions are in addition to other, more general, provisions that affect the transfer of all sorts of property to public or charitable purposes. In Great Britain, as in many countries, gifts and bequests of any property to charities are exempt from capital transfer tax and capital gains tax. But such gifts are not deductible from income for purposes of income taxation. Thus, these gifts do not receive the generous twofold tax incentive that U.S. donors receive.[43]

In Great Britain, gifts and bequests to public and quasi-public institutions are also exempt, as are gifts or bequests of certain types of property with public benefit to appropriate non-profit-making bodies (as distinguished from charities in British law). In the latter case, the exemption is granted when the Treasury determines that a goal of the organization is the preservation of such property for the public benefit, that it has the financial capacity to maintain the property, that it will ensure public access and accept restrictions on the use, disposal and preservation of the property, and that the donor will not retain any personal interest in the property. Once again, the public interest is carefully established before the granting of an exemption.

The French "Dation"

One of the most widely known tax provisions in European cultural policy is the French *dation*. Under this provision all heirs, donees, or legatees may pay estate taxes with works of art, books, or collections of objects or of documents of high artistic or historic value. Like the British acceptance in lieu provision, the *dation* was an integral part of a 1968 legislative program to "promote the conservation of the national artistic patrimony."[44] Any such payment is subject to the recommendation of a government-appointed commission, which determines whether or not the works are of sufficient quality to meet this definition, and to a government decision as to whether or not it wishes to accept payment in this way.

Since the recognition of the *dation* as a means of tax payment, the government has received works of Lippi, Fragonard, Rubens, Cezanne, Manet, Renoir, Goya, Ernst, Calder, Pissarro, Monet, and Picasso, among others.[45] But the most extraordinary *dation* has been the "*Dation Picasso,*" which formed the bulk of the collection of the new Picasso Museum in Paris. This *dation* included:

229	paintings
149	sculptures
85	ceramics
1496	pastels, collages, designs
33	notebooks of sketches
1622	prints
35	illustrated books
many	documents
30	works of friends

The estimated value of the estate was FF 1.154 billion. Because Picasso's brother died shortly thereafter, a second estate was involved, and the total estate tax liability was approximately FF 290 million. In other, less extraordinary years the value of works given by *dation* was FF 1.7 million

(1973) and FF 7.7 million (1974). One commentator has concluded that the *dation* has been much more successful than either the right of preemption or the right of retention in enriching the national collections.[46]

Unlike the British acceptance in lieu, the *dation* does not appear to present a financial incentive for paying estate taxes with artworks. If the value of the artworks is simply credited against the estate taxes for the entire estate, the donor ends up paying the same amount of estate taxes (including the agreed on value of the artwork). Whatever advantages there are probably lie in the fact that the estate tax liability may be paid relatively simply, by surrendering artworks rather than having to liquidate them on the open market. An individual who has just inherited an estate and is considering donating an artwork in the estate to the state—such a donation is, in its own right, exempt from transfer taxes—is well-advised to use the artwork as a *dation* instead, because the difference between the market value of the work and the estate taxes that would be due on it alone can then be offset against the taxes due on the remainder of the estate.

What incentive does the government have to turn down a proposed *dation?* The financial implications of the forgone taxes are easy for bureaucrats to ignore when confronted with the opportunity to obtain an important artwork for the national museums for "free." On occasion, the commission has turned down proposed artworks, in one case because the artist owed back income taxes and in another because the artist was already well represented in the national museums. In both these cases, however, the decision was overturned when a new president of the commission was named, presumably because of the negative publicity generated by the former commission president's decisions, which made the government appear ungrateful.[47] Unlimited use of such a tax provision can prove costly, but putting a workable fair limit on its use may be politically impossible.

ARTISTS' INCOME TAXES

All Western countries struggle with problems inherent in the income taxation of artists. What constitutes professional activity as opposed to a hobby? What are deductible business expenses? Where is the boundary between ordinary income and capital gain income? How should donations of the artist's own work be treated? How are income streams that vary considerably from year to year to be handled? How should commissions, grants, or awards be taxed? Though the debates on each of the questions are very real, their solution is more a technical matter depending on the legal framework of each country than a matter of conscious cultural policy.[48]

Into the midst of all the technical provisions dealing with artists' income taxes, one extraordinary provision has crept. In the Irish Budget for 1969–70, the minister for Finance, Mr. Charles Haughey, declared:

> As further encouragement to the creative artists in our midst and to help create a sympathetic environment here in which the arts can flourish, I will provide in the

Finance Bill that painters, sculptors, writers and composers living and working in Ireland will be free of tax on all earnings derived from work of cultural merit.[49]

To be eligible for the exemption the work must, in the opinion of the Irish government, be original, creative, and of cultural or artistic merit. The only other qualification, the residency requirement, is a rather broad one: the artist has to be resident in Ireland for at least six months in the year or own a house permanently ready for his or her occupation, even if for only a day or two in the year. Irish citizenship is not required.

Just as U.S. cities use tax deals to attract new development, Ireland had decided to use tax laws to attract and retain artists, and it was "reported in the international press as the most enlightened fiscal measure ever taken by any Minister for Finance in relation to the arts."[50] This particular tax exemption, though idiosyncratic in the extreme, deserves closer attention as it clearly reveals a number of the pitfalls in using tax incentives as a cultural policy.[51]

By April 1984, the Irish government had approved 1284 applications representing 1116 different individuals, with 134 cases pending.[52] Earlier figures show that approximately 68 percent of those approved have been writers, 23 percent painters, 6 percent sculptors, and 3 percent musicians.[53] Through the first six or seven years, half of those benefiting were non-Irish; the Revenue Commissioners now estimate that a majority are of Irish origin.[54] The best-known artists attracted by this scheme have included a number of international spy writers, such as Len Deighton, Frederick Forsyth, and Leslie Charteris, as well as J. P. Donleavy, Richard Condon, Alun Owen, and Wolf Mankowitz. Irish writers who had emigrated to Britain and returned included playwrights Hugh Leonard and Brian Friel (who simply moved across the border from Northern Ireland to County Donegal).[55]

What was the objective of this exemption? One magazine article concluded:

> By attracting artists who would never have considered taking up residence in the Emerald Isle in view either of the weather or because it is so far from the leading cultural centres, this tax law—which exists nowhere else—has brought about a cultural and literary revival in Ireland, restoring its international prestige.[56]

Yet it seems unlikely that such migration, even in large numbers, would contribute very much to the international artistic prestige of Ireland.

The artists this scheme attracted were those so wealthy that the exemption represented a substantial, but unnecessary, subsidy. It is the wealthy artist who can benefit most but needs it least. One journalist has noted:

> From the point of view of Irish artists, the main disadvantage of the scheme is that very few Irish artists do earn enough to pay income tax and so they gain no benefit from the exemption. Most live "pulling the devil by the tail," and many are of the opinion that a form of subsidy, direct or indirect, to local artists would be more beneficial to the local scene than encouraging a tax-free haven for wealthy foreign artists.[57]

All of this suggests the more general question of why the forgone amount of income tax is the right amount of subsidy in the first place. With indirect aid based in tax incentives it is easy to lose track of the fact that there are real, though difficult to calculate, costs associated with them. The Revenue Commissioners currently estimate that the cost of this relief to the state is approximately £600,000 per year, a figure that seems low.[58]

This scheme is misdirected in another fundamental way. It is directed at the wrong group of artists. While subsidizing creative artists, whose works can be enjoyed anywhere irrespective of the presence of the artist, the exemption offers no financial incentive at all to those artists whose presence is a critical component of the artistic product, the performing artist. A subsidy directed toward the performing artist would seem to be better equipped to have a tangible effect on the cultural life of the country. The practical reason for not extending this benefit to performing artists lay in the difficulty of determining a boundary that clearly defines who is eligible and who is not and that, presumably, would keep the costs of the program within acceptable bounds.[59]

Though the Irish experiment is the most extreme such example, a mythology of sorts has grown up in the United States around the supposed preferential treatment for artists in European tax laws: for example, the widely alleged ability of European artists to pay their taxes with works of art instead of cash. Although this does seem to be true in Italy,[60] it is less clear that this is normally a possibility in any other country. Unfortunately, very little accurate information has been available.

For example, Elias Newman, president of the Artists Equity Association of New York, testifying before the House Ways and Means Committee in 1973, claimed that in the Netherlands artists were not taxed on the first 50 percent of income from works of art and that the tax on the remainder could be paid with paintings or sculpture that were, in turn, given to schools, hospitals, and public institutions.[61] The first has never been true. The second has only a grain of truth: When someone is unable to pay income taxes, the authorities can confiscate the taxpayer's property and hold it pending payment. In the case of artists and many rich people, the property often includes works of art. In the Netherlands, a tremendous stock of such artworks has been seized by the government, particularly in Amsterdam where many artists reside. Some of the artworks are distributed to public buildings for display. In 1979 the government even mounted an exhibition of paintings that were damaged in storage in Amsterdam.[62] Thus, these artworks come into the public domain not because of any special tax incentive for visual artists but because the artists are expected to pay normal income taxes.

Newman went on to testify that France exempts the first 30 percent of an artist's income from tax. This is a bit closer to the truth. French professionals can claim a standard deduction of 10 percent of income for professional expenses. Certain professions, including some cultural workers, are entitled to claim a supplementary deduction. For example, musicians, conductors, and theatre directors are entitled to a supplementary 20 percent (for a total deduction of 30 percent); dramatic artists, cinematographers, and choreographers are entitled to an additional 25 percent.[63] To the extent that these supplements are adequate estimates of actual professional expenses, which could be itemized and deducted if they exceeded the flat deduction, they do not provide subsidy to these artistic professions. If actual expenses are less than the total deduction, the deduction does provide a subsidy, but it is hard to argue that the deduction provides an incentive to become involved in one of these artistic professions. The deduction is better understood as a tax simplification provision, having more to do with ease of tax administration for both the artist and the government.

WEALTH TAXES

Although few countries actually have wealth or permanent capital taxes, where such taxes have been used, their structure often reflects assumptions concerning public policy goals for the arts. A wealth tax may have an impact in the cultural field in one of two ways: by taxing or exempting the property of cultural institutions themselves and by taxing or exempting objects used for cultural activities or of artistic value that are part of otherwise taxable wealth.

Until recently only four members of the EEC had levied a permanent capital tax: Germany, Luxembourg, the Netherlands, and Denmark. Belgium, however, had a special capital tax on the assets of certain organizations.[64] The German permanent tax on capital is broad, encompassing the assets of both natural and legal persons. Organizations whose main aim is to benefit the community are immune in much the same way that U. S. charitable institutions are exempt, say, from local property tax. Only those assets for which rules of valuation exist are liable to the tax, and valuation of artworks in private possession is a tricky matter. Thus, works of art owned by individuals and created by living artists or by artists who have been dead for less than 50 years are not taxed. Other works of art and collections are liable to the tax if their total value exceeds DM 20,000. Property of artistic, historic, or scientific value is only taxed at 40 percent of its value. Such property may be completely exempted if its preservation is of artistic, historic, or scientific value, provided that (1) the general public, or at least researchers, have access to it and (2) it has belonged to the owner or the owner's family for at least 20 years. Incomplete and unsold works of creative and performing artists are not taxed.

The permanent tax on capital in Luxembourg is derived from the German system. Both natural persons and companies are liable to the tax. Recent works of art by Luxembourg artists who are living or who have not been dead for more than 15 years are exempt. Other works of art and collections are taxable only if their total value exceeds Lfrs 500,000. Works that are "of benefit to the community" are taxed at only 20 percent of their value if they are accessible to the public. In some circumstances they may be totally exempt. On the other hand, Luxembourg levies a tax on the assets of nonprofit-making associations and establishments of benefit to the community, thus affecting some cultural activities; the financial impact, however, is minimal. A similar special tax with no specific arts exemptions is levied in Belgium.

In the Netherlands, a capital tax is charged only on the assets of natural persons. Works of art are exempt without limit, except that items of a professional nature are not exempted; unsold art works in the possession of the artist or a collector are therefore liable to tax. Immovable property that comes under the auspices of the nature conservancy law is taxed at two-thirds of its value, a reduction that seems to be offered to give the owner a relatively larger ability to maintain the property in good condition. A further reduction in taxable valuation is available for properties to which the public has access.

Similarly, the Danish wealth tax is levied only on natural persons. Moveable property and household equipment not used by the taxpayer for business purposes are not included in taxable assets, so works of art, books, paintings, sculptures, manuscripts, and other items in private collections are not taxed. The artist's own works are considered to be part of his or her private collection and are not taxed.

From these examples alone one can infer little about the pros and cons of exempting artworks from wealth taxes. To make artworks liable to capital taxes, as several of the countries do at least in part, may encourage owners to dispose of conspicuous objects and to be secretive about the ones they retain. Objects that are sold may come into the public's possession both because they may more readily enter the market and because they may command a lower price, though public purchase funds are limited and international prices likely to remain substantially higher than national prices. Objects that are hidden from view become even less accessible to the public, and that is why public access becomes a quid pro quo for partial or full exemption.

If artworks are to be taxed, valuation is a major problem. Concerning the exemption of artworks from capital tax in the Netherlands, Bouuaert, in his study of taxation and the arts in the EEC, concluded, "While it was initially introduced (in 1892) to *protect* the arts, it has been retained mainly because of the difficulties of assessing the value of property of this kind"[emphasis added].[65] His choice of words is revealing: Just what does it mean to "protect" the arts in the context of capital taxes?

Exempting artworks from capital taxation seems, on its face, to be the more reasonable alternative. Owners will not be provided with an incentive to dispose of their objects, some of which might have close ties to a particular family or building. But this point of view fails to take into account the dynamics of the art market. If artworks are one of the few types of property exempted from capital taxations, then they become a very attractive investment in which an individual can shelter large amounts of personal wealth. The art market should respond with rising prices, fueling speculation and making art an even more attractive way to shield wealth from capital taxation, but making acquisition, either by the public collections or by private individuals, more expensive.

The counterproductive result has been observed whenever the relative tax incentives have been changed to provide greater exemption for artworks:

> English painting of the eighteenth century began to be collected in the United States after the 20 percent duty on classic works of art was repealed in 1909, and . . . modern French paintings began to be collected after the duty on contemporary works was abolished in 1913. . . . (T)he speculation characteristic of . . . art markets has been supported by the absence, in France, of a tax on capital gains and, in the United States, by the tax breaks available to collectors who donate works of art to public museums. Every change in such laws affects the markets for art works and thus the professional lives of everyone involved in the relevant art world.[66]

Whether such an increase in prices in the art market would be desirable from a cultural policy standpoint is problematic, but the possibility that the art market would respond in this way entered passionately into the public debate when the British Labour Government proposed a Wealth Tax in 1974. Hugh Jenkins, in his memoirs of his tenure as Labour Minister for the Arts, has vividly recaptured the intense debate that swirled around his insistence that, in principle, artworks should not be exempted from a wealth tax.[67]

In the context of the Labour Government's program to reduce income inequality in British society, Jenkins regarded denying exemption as a way to "separate fine art from its traditional associations with exclusiveness and personal wealth."[68] For him the public's interest in these art objects lay more in their broad accessibility than in tinkering with and perhaps inadvertently fueling prices in the art market, and he proposed a way to bring more objects of artistic value into public hands while maintaining the intent of the tax. Artworks would not be exempt but the tax would be deferred if the owner agreed to public display of the artwork, to making it available to scholars, or to loaning it to public collections for display. The forgone taxes embodied in the exemption would be exchanged for the public benefit of increased accessibility. Jenkins further suggested that the problem of valuation of those artworks that would be taxed could be solved by the owner making a self-valuation with the stipulation that the government would always have the option of buying the object at that price, providing an incentive to keep the valuation reasonably high. The trade-off was to make possession sufficiently attractive to encourage retention (within Great Britain) but not so attractive as to increase hoarding.

Nearly without exception, the art world, arguing along the general lines that taxation would not be "good for art" and that "art and commerce ought to be kept separated," did not support Jenkins' position. In the end, the debate over exemption for artworks provided the wedge needed by opponents of the wealth tax to bring about its eventual defeat. As a result, most of the interesting public policy questions posed by these events were never addressed directly. Given that many of the artworks that would be liable to the tax were not of British origin, whose heritage would actually be protected through exemption? How much truly valuable artwork still remained in private hands and at what rate would it come onto the market if exemption were not allowed? And, perhaps most important, is protecting art the same thing as protecting the art market?

Denying exemption for artworks can thus be seen as a policy instrument designed to bring more objects of artistic value into public hands or, at the very least, to make them more publicly accessible. It would not be undesirable for objects to come onto the market, if the government could respond adequately with purchase funds augmented with other incentives such as the private treaty sale, and it would not be undesirable for artworks to remain in private hands exempted from wealth taxes in exchange for some form of public access.

In October 1981 the debate surfaced again, this time in France. Laurent Fabius, Budget Minister, introduced the Socialist government's proposed Finance Bill for 1982. The bill included a new wealth tax *(impot sur les grandes fortunes)*, and it specified that paintings, jewelry, and other art objects would be included in the definition of wealth and thus be taxable. To monitor the market and establish the value of these works of art, all sales over ff 5000 would be required to be made by check, and insurance companies would be required to provide information on any individual who had taken out an insurance policy insuring artworks for more than ff 100,000.

The art world was outraged. Collectors, the auction houses, and many major artists united in opposition to the proposal. Daily newspapers and weekly newsmagazines of all political perspectives warned of the death of the Parisian art market: The national art market would go underground, they argued, and the exportation of artworks, already encouraged by higher international prices, would accelerate.[69] Virtually no attention was paid to the likely impact of exemption on the art market; in the popular view, exemption would "obviously" encourage the arts, whereas taxation would discourage them. And no one asked about the effect—if any—on the individual creative artist.

In either case, a wealth tax poses difficulties. If artworks are not exempted, valuation becomes necessary, and it may prove too cumbersome to administer fairly on a large scale. If artworks are exempted, then the state must find a clear definition of what is art and what is not. Of course, this is problematic for any government policy that is designed to treat "art" in special ways.

Finally, President Mitterand intervened personally, deciding that artworks would be exempted from the tax as long as they were not sold for export. In exchange for this concession, a transaction tax on the sale of artworks was increased from 3 to 6 percent for sales in galleries and from 2 to 4 percent for sales at auction. The art world rejoiced. Only a few dissenting voices were heard. One journalist clearly summed up the policy dilemma inherent in such a choice:

> For reasons of equality, the wealth tax was to have been levied on works of art. For reasons of liberty it was lifted. In both cases, the real economic motives were disguised, purely and simply, as moral motives.[70]

Though the battle over exemption of artworks was furious, the irony lay in the fact that the wealth tax would only have applied to the wealthiest of individuals, individuals who, arguably, could afford the tax in any event. Only individuals whose wealth exceeded ff 3 million (5 million in certain cases), roughly 1 percent of French taxpayers, would have been taxed, and the tax rate would have begun at 0.5 percent and increase to a maximum of 1.5 percent. Of course, on the other hand, the revenue forgone by exemption would have been small in comparison to total government revenues to be realized from this tax. This point illustrates a common property of tax exemptions for the arts. While the taxes forgone by any tax incentive for the arts are likely to be small compared to total revenues of the tax in which they are embedded, they nonetheless may have a significant impact on the arts; both impacts must be measured to evaluate the incentive properly.

VALUE-ADDED TAX

All of the member countries of the EEC and a number of other European countries have adopted value-added taxes as important revenue sources. The value-added tax (VAT) is essentially a national sales tax levied on the consumption of all goods and services, and its relationship to the arts poses a number of trickly questions of tax administration and of cultural policy.

The value-added tax is collected through a series of incremental steps. Producers of a good or service pay VAT on the inputs they purchase. They then produce their own output—a good or service that is purchased by another consumer—and VAT is charged on that sale. The amount of VAT paid on inputs is subtracted from the amount realized on the sale of outputs, and the difference is forwarded to the government as tax revenues. Thus, even though the tax is collected incrementally, it is the final consumer who bears the total burden of the tax.

The intent and structure of VAT pose two issues for the arts:

1. To what extent should artistic and cultural "outputs" benefit from lower rates of VAT?
2. To what extent should the arts—particularly nonprofit arts institutions—be exempt from paying upstream VAT on the inputs they purchase?

Both of these issues have been the focus of sustained debate throughout Europe.

In implementing VAT, governments have tried very hard to eliminate possible loopholes. Value-added taxes are levied on all forms of consumption, irrespective of the characteristics of the sector whose outputs are being taxed. They are clearly conceived as a revenue-raising tool and not as a means to encourage or discourage certain activities in accord with government policies.

The theory of value-added tax calls for a single tax rate to be applied to all goods and services, conforming to the actual pattern of consumption by maintaining the relative prices of these goods and services in the marketplace and not distorting competition. In addition, the use of a single tax rate dramatically simplifies tax collection. In practice, however, most European countries actually use two, three, or four different tax rates, and culture is one sector in which VAT rates have deviated from the countries' standard rates. In this regard VAT legislation has been designed to affect rather than to reflect the actual consumption pattern, providing an incentive through lower rates (or a disincentive through higher rates) for certain types of consumption.[71]

Table 15.2 summarizes the VAT rates for selected arts activities in the countries of the EEC. Not only does the general level of VAT vary from country to country, but the actual application of VAT to the arts and culture varies widely within countries, with different cultural sectors liable to different rates of tax. Some of these countries clearly use VAT as a technique to provide indirect subsidies by lowering relative prices for certain artistic activities, while others treat certain cultural goods (e.g., records) as luxuries and tax them at a much higher rate, under the assumption that those who purchase them can well afford higher taxes and that demand for these goods is not highly price elastic.

In considering the actual application of VAT to the arts and culture in Europe, it is useful to distinguish between cultural services and cultural goods. It is clear that in the EEC there is an intent to reduce the rate of VAT on cultural services. The Sixth European Council Directive of 1977, which dealt with questions of harmonization of VAT within the Community, committed the governments eventually to exempt theatre, concerts, and other cultural events, activities that the Community wished to encourage because of their public interest.[72]

In the three EEC countries where the rates have not been reduced for these activities—the United Kingdom, Denmark, and the Netherlands—arts institutions have been lobbying for a reduction based on three arguments: (1) High prices resulting from the imposition of VAT, and particularly VAT at the standard rate, make it more expensive for the public to enjoy these events; (2) VAT is due irrespective of the profit or loss position of the institution, and arts institutions tend to lose money; and (3) it is illogical to tax by one hand activities that may be subsidized by the other. All three of these arguments call for a trade-off between the logic, internal consistency, and relative simplicity of VAT as a tax-collecting mechanism and the use of such a system to provide relative incentives for certain types of activities.[73]

The first argument is one of the traditional justifications for governmen-

Table 15.2 Value-Added Tax: Rates for Cultural Sectors in Selected European Countries

Country	Books	Cinema	Records	Concerts, Theatre, and Events	Other Entertainment	Standard Rate
Belgium	6%	16%	25%[a]	6%	6%	17%
Denmark	20.25	20.25	20.25[b]	22	22[c]	22
France	7[d]	7[d,e]	33.33	7[d,f]	17.6[d,g]	17.6
Great Britain	0	15	15	15	15	15
Ireland	10	10	30–40[h]	15	15	25
Italy	6	14	35[i]	8	8	15
Luxembourg	5	10	10	5	5	10
Netherlands	5	19	19	19	19[j]	19
Sweden	23.46	0	23.46	0	0	23.46
West Germany	7[k]	7	14	0[l]	7	14

NOTES: [a]16% for language teaching and for medical or scientific uses.
[b]20.25% VAT + additional tax on 30% of wholesale price = 41.75% total tax.
[c]Zoos, museums and libraries are exempt.
[d]33.33% for pornographic or violent works.
[e]Nonprofit cine clubs are exempt.
[f]In certain cases the 7% rate is applied only to 70% of taxable value. See text.
[g]7% for music halls, circuses, fairs, and variety shows at which beverages are not served.
[h]30% on records pressed in Ireland, 40% on imported records.
[i]6% for educational uses.
[j]5% for zoos, circuses, and fairs.
[k]13% if considered harmful to young people. (Probably applies to other sectors as well.)
[l]Exemption applies to all public cultural organizations and to other bodies with the same cultural ends; private promoters making use of public organizations such as municipal orchestras are also exempt.

SOURCES: Rates for France, Great Britain, Sweden, Netherlands, and West Germany are accurate as of 1984 (confirmed through personal interviews). Rates for other countries are accurate as of 1980–81. In these cases differences between columns 1–3 and 4–6 may be due to increases in tax rates between 1980 and 1981.

Columns 1–3: "Taux de TVA Appliqués aux Differents Produits de Communication au 15.03.80 dans les Pays de la C.E.E." *Audiovisuels et Communications Digest,* June–July 1980, 9.
Columns 4–6: House of Commons, *Third Report from the Education, Science and Arts Committee,* Session 1981–82, "Public and Private Funding of the Arts: Interim Report on Value Added Tax and the Arts," paper 239 (London: Her Majesty's Stationery Office, March 3, 1982), v.

tal subsidy. If the price of a socially desirable good is kept low, more of it will be consumed. For arts activities this argument raises a serious question concerning the treatment of performances of commercial artistic institutions. Should they receive preferential treatment too, since they are providing services of a cultural nature? Not to extend an exemption to activities sponsored by commercial organizations would give nonprofit institutions an additional unfair competitive advantage, which flies in the face of the theory of VAT as a tax that minimizes distortion of the market. In Great Britain, the House of Commons Education, Science and Arts Committee has argued unsuccessfully that exemption from VAT should be extended not only to nonprofit cultural institutions but to commercial organizations as well, as long as they provide cultural services that are in the "public interest."[74] The government has estimated that such a broad exemption could cost "on the order of 100 million pounds a year."[75]

The second and third arguments also contradict the theory of VAT. Because it is a tax on consumption and not a tax on income or profit, the relative financial position of the institution, and whether or not it is receiving public subsidy, are immaterial as far as the theory of VAT is concerned. Government may well choose to subsidize a nonprofit activity that cannot otherwise balance its books, but to do so through differential VAT rates is to use a policy that is poorly targeted to achieve the desired result. It might be much better to subsidize those deficits through direct governmental aid to particular institutions in need of such support. This appears to be the British government's main objection to VAT exemption for these artistic activities:

> VAT [relief]. . . would apply thinly across the board irrespective of how deserving a body is of support. Grant assistance, on the other hand, can be directed where the effect would be most beneficial—allocations of subsidy to arts bodies are made after an assessment of their total financial circumstances, including the incidence of VAT.[76]

From this perspective the ultimate question becomes, Is direct aid or indirect aid the more efficient and cost-effective mechanism for distributing subsidy? Through tax-based subsidy provisions, a government may avoid the necessity of making difficult decisions as to whom to fund (or not fund), but the level and distribution of that subsidy will be determined by a variety of factors out of the government's control, factors that may ultimately make the subsidy ineffective.

A few attempts have been made to tailor VAT laws to implement very specific cultural policies. In France, for example, whereas most concerts, theatrical performances, and other cultural events are taxed at a reduced VAT rate of 7 percent, there is an additional reduction offered to promote the creation of new French works or productions. For the first 140 performances of dramatic, lyric, musical, or choreographic works newly created in France, or of classic works made the object of a new production, VAT is calculated at the reduced rate on the basis of 30 percent of the price of entry. A work is determined to be "classic" if its author or creator has been dead more than 50 years or if he or she appears on a list that is fixed by agreement between the Ministry of Culture and the Ministry of Economy and Finance.[77] This tax provision promotes French content and perhaps innovation and experimentation in cultural presentations by allowing the incentive to be realized by an entrepreneur (or institution) who chooses to move the mix of cultural activities in this direction.

The most striking differences in VAT rates within countries are found in the treatment of the goods that are outputs of the cultural industries. (See Table 15.2) European cultural ministries are becoming more and more concerned over the economic health of the proprietary cultural industries (the book, film, record, and broadcasting industries), a concern that has not been an important part of U. S. arts policies.[78] These countries often use tax law and regulation to provide protection and incentives for their cultural industries, and VAT has become a frequently used tool for providing such implicit subsidies. In this regard tax-based incentives can be used to provide subsides where direct aid cannot: Western governments generally consider it highly improper, ill-advised, and perhaps illegal to provide direct government aid to profit-making institutions.

The clearest examples of this method of relative subsidy are in the publishing industry. Most European countries tax books and periodicals at rates of VAT below the standard rate, an incentive designed to subsidize the flow of printed information and cultural materials. (In Great Britain, however, the Thatcher government is currently considering making books subject to VAT at the standard rate.) On the other hand, the recording industries tend to be taxed more heavily with the justification that records and cassettes are luxury items and their consumers are better able to pay a higher tax.[79]

But it would be a mistake to think of all lower VAT rates as providing subsidy. Because of the iterative nature of the VAT collection process, there are a number of technical difficulties that arise, particularly in the market for art objects. Most consumer goods travel through the economic chain in an orderly way, incurring VAT incrementally at each step of the production and distribution process until the final tax burden falls on the final consumer. The market for art objects is much less predictable in this way. Artworks move in and out of the hands of private individuals. Each time this happens that individual is treated as a final consumer and has to pay the total of the accrued VAT. When this individual, who is not on the VAT register as a seller of a good or service, sells the work back into the gallery and auction system, he or she cannot reclaim the VAT paid upstream. When the artwork is resold by the gallery or at auction, the work begins accruing VAT at its full price once again. As a result, the tax paid by the previous owner is paid again, in addition to any tax on new increases in the value of the artwork.[80]

Because it is difficult to design a VAT collection system that will avoid this type of double taxation, some governments have tried to accommodate this technical problem either by using a lower base on which to assess the tax or by using a lower tax rate. In France, for example, VAT on artworks is charged at the standard rate on the lesser of 30 percent of the sale price or the difference between the sale price and the price at which the artwork was purchased by the current seller. In the Netherlands, on the other hand, a lower VAT rate of 5 percent is used for artworks.[81] Notice that in the Netherlands the 5 percent VAT rate has two different interpretations: While it is a technical adjustment to the value-added taxation of art works, it is an implicit subsidy to book production.

Some arts institutions may find themselves in the position of offering free services, including admission, to the public rather than charging for them. In these cases there is no VAT due on the institution's output, and the burden of the VAT paid upstream by the institution cannot be passed on to any other final consumer. In a technical sense, the institution is the final consumer. Just as we asked to what extent cultural goods and services should be exempted from VAT taxation, we can ask whether nonprofit institutions should be allowed to recover upstream VAT payments. The finance office of the Arts Council of Great Britain has suggested to arts institutions that to avoid this problem they should charge a nominal fee on which VAT would be due. This collection of a small amount of VAT would allow the institution to recoup all of the VAT payments made upstream.

The European experience with VAT is also useful to illustrate the unintended artistic consequences of tax reform. In the United States we have recently heard calls for a flat-rate income tax, as well as proposals for a value-added tax, both to establish a "fairer" system of federal taxation. The implications for nonprofit charitable organizations of these proposals are difficult to judge because it is not at all clear that it would be possible or desirable to reinstitute the tax exemptions or incentives that these institutions enjoy under the current systems of taxation. Would a charitable income tax deduction also be allowed under a flat-rate income tax? Perhaps, but that undermines the attractive simplicity of the flat-rate proposals. Would the value of sales tax exemptions and property tax exemptions be replaced under a value-added tax? It is unlikely.[82]

The British experience is quite clear in this regard. In Great Britain VAT replaced the selective employment tax and the purchase tax, both of which included exemptions for nonprofit charitable institutions.[83] This switch represented an immediate and substantial jump in the organizations' costs. Nonprofit institutions that did not sell any goods or services of their own had to absorb this cost directly. Institutions that did sell goods or services could, in theory, pass this new cost onto the purchasers of their products, but only through prices increased to reflect the new VAT. Such increases might reduce the consumption of their output. For the art world, this meant less consumption and enjoyment of artistic activities, activities that the government was simultaneously trying to encourage through other policies.

When VAT was instituted in Great Britain in 1973, the chancellor of the exchequer "gave pretty firm assurances that, to the extent that the subsidised theatres and concert halls suffered, additional funds would be made available to the Arts Council to enable the blow to be minimised."[84] But this promise has now been turned on its head. The exchequer has made it clear to the Arts Council of Great Britain that if lobbying for the reduction of the VAT rate for artistic activities were successful, the government would reduce the Arts Council's grant correspondingly, roughly maintaining the overall level of subsidy from all government sources.[85]

The design and implementation of value-added taxes raise two of the most important issues involved in using tax-based provisions to provide subsidy to the arts: What is the appropriate balance between the design of a watertight revenue-collecting instrument and other societal goals? And what should the relationship be between direct aid, which can be used in precisely targeted ways and which makes the evaluation of subsidy more public, and indirect aid, which may be spread thinly across many eligible recipients irrespective of their relative worthiness in a manner that hides the subsidy from public scrutiny? Through the design of their individual VAT systems, each European country has implicitly answered these questions and, despite the intent to harmonize the VAT systems of at least the EEC countries, their answers vary widely.

SUMMARY

Historically, U. S. arts policy has relied heavily on tax-based mechanisms to provide indirect aid to the arts—most notably through the charitable contribution deduction. But now, tax incentives—as well as other forms of indirect aid—are becoming increasingly popular in many countries. As a result, any comprehensive study and evaluation of a government's policies vis-à-vis the arts today must take account of the effects of the various forms of indirect government aid. Futhermore, it is important to recognize that these effects are not only financial; they may also be artistic. The way in which the arts are funded can have a significant impact on the type of art that is ultimately produced and made available to the public.

Tax incentives are the most ubiquitous form of indirect aid to the arts, though to date they have been relatively poorly documented. So that their artistic implications can be fully explored and understood, tax incentives must be studied as cultural policies, not merely as financial conduits. In this chapter, I have discussed some of the more important issues that arise when tax incentives are viewed in this way, issues that must be confronted in designing such incentives for the arts, as well as in the prior decision as to whether the arts should be supported through direct or indirect means.

One issue is the problem of shifting perspectives. The revenue lost through a specific tax exemption or incentive is often significant when viewed on the scale of the revenue-raising instrument in which is it embedded, but when it is viewed from the perspective of the arts its impact might be substantial, for better or for worse. This fact makes it all too easy for government agencies, committees, or legislative bodies making taxation decisions to overlook the impact of a proposed change on a particular sector or to assume that the impact will be small. Often this is exacerbated by the fact that the government bodies concerned with tax policy are not also responsible for arts policy. Each policy may be promulgated without proper regard for the other.

A second issue is disguised behind the rhetoric that surrounds government arts support. It seems to be widely believed that tax exemptions and tax incentives are members of that class of government policies that are, by definition, "good for the arts." But the debate around the exemption of artworks from wealth taxes clearly illustrates that one person's view of what is good for art is not necessarily another's view. That which is good for one type of art may not be good for another, and benefits to one sector may well entail costs to another. A tax incentive, just like any government policy, may ultimately turn out to be counterproductive.

A third issue is the extent to which tax incentives can be usefully targeted to achieve specific policy goals. With a couple of exceptions, the examples in this paper suggest that targeting may be exceedingly difficult because tax incentives operate through the choices of countless individual decision makers who choose whether or not to respond to the incentive. In many circumstances, the flexibility inherent in direct aid programs, where it is possible to make explicit choices about who will receive aid (and who will not), can lead to a more efficient allocation of limited resources. But at the same time, the government might find tax-based subsidy provisions attractive for the very reason that through such provisions it can avoid the necessity of having to make difficult funding decisions.

The recognition that an arts policy is financed out of limited resources points to a related issue. With direct aid programs, budgetary constraints are relatively clear. But it is difficult to predict the true cost of a proposed tax incentive scheme (or even to estimate the true cost of an existing one), and because it may be considerably more difficult to place a meaningful limit on the use of a tax incentive, such incentives may ultimately prove to be particularly costly ways to support the arts. (Even charitable contribution deductions, while limiting the deduction an individual may take, do not limit the number of individuals who may take the deduction other than in the most general sense to taxpayers.) The difficulty of limiting a tax incentive is further complicated by the paradox that many tax incentives work best for those who need them the least: Charitable contribution deductions and the Irish income tax exemption are excellent examples of incentives that increase with the wealth of the concerned individual.

Tax incentives can play an important role in supporting the arts. But they must be seen as cultural policies and debated and evaluated in much the same way that direct aid mechanisms are. Exposing them to the light of public scrutiny, forcing them to answer tough questions concerning their effectiveness, and matching them to the particular circumstances in each country can only improve government's ability to support the arts in a manner that is financially sound and artistically informed.

Update: As this volume goes to press, Britain has introduced charitable deductions for the first time. Since 1 April 1986 corporations have been allowed to deduct charitable contributions from their income up to a limit of 3 percent of dividends paid. As of 1 April 1987 individuals will be allowed to make contributions through payroll deduction plans up to a limit of £100 per year; these contributions will be eligible for a tax credit calculated at the basic rate of tax. Both individual and corporate donors will still be able to take advantage of the deed of covenant provisions.

NOTES

1. Alan L. Feld, Michael O'Hare, and J. Mark Davidson Schuster, *Patrons Despite Themselves: Taxpayers and Arts Policy*, A Twentieth Century Fund Report (New York: New York University Press, 1983).

2. J. Mark Davidson Schuster, "The Interrelationships Between Public and Private Funding of the Arts in the United States," *Journal of Arts Management and Law* 14, 4 (Winter 1985): 77–105.

3. "Getting Credit for Charity," *The Boston Globe* May 30, 1978, 18.

4. "Can the Government Promote Creativity—or Only Artists?" *The New York Times*, April 25, 1982, p 6E.

5. For a summary of the tax incentives for charitable contributions in several European countries, see: Ignatius Claeys Bouuaert, *Taxation of Cultural Foundations and of Patronage of the Arts in the Member States of the European Economic Community*, Commission of the European Communities, XII/670/75-E, 1975; and Arthur Andersen & Co., "Overview of Governmental Support and Financial Regulation of Philanthropic Organizations in Selected Nations," in The Commission on Private Philanthropy and Public Needs, *Research Papers* (Washington, D.C.: U. S. Department of the Treasury, 1977), Vol. V, 2975–2993.

6. The Commission on Private Philanthropy and Public Needs, "Alternatives to Tax Incentives," Vol. IV, Part V, of *Research Papers* (Washington D.C.: U. S. Department of the Treasury, 1977).

7. A particular donor, of course, would not have the same marginal tax rate in each of these countries because of differences in the definition of taxable income and in the determination of tax brackets and tax rates. Yet the similarity in financial incentives in these systems lies in the fact that two donors in different countries with identical marginal tax rates will face identical marginal prices for their charitable contributions.

8. A useful summary of the limitations in each of these countries is contained in Bouuaert, op. cit.

9. For a detailed technical analysis comparing the British deed of covenant with the charitable deduction, see J. Mark Davidson Schuster, "Tax Incentives for Charitable Donations: Deeds of Covenant and Charitable Contribution Deductions," *University of San Francisco Law Review*, 19, 3/4 (Spring/Summer 1985): 329–376.

10. The origins of the charitable contribution deduction and the deed of covenant are discussed in James Douglas and Peter Wright, "English Charities: Part I—Legal Definition, Taxation, and Regulation," Yale. Program on Non-Profit Organizations Working Paper 15 (New Haven, Conn., 1980), 69–70.

11. J. D. Livingston Booth, "Address Given to a Meeting of Charity Representatives at the Middlesex Hospital," July 23, 1980, available from Charities Aid Foundation, Towbridge, Kent, England; and Donald R. Spuehler, "The System for Regulation and Assistance of Charity in England and Wales, With Recommendations on the Establishment of a National Commission on Philanthropy in the United States," in The Commission on Private Philanthropy and Public Needs, *Research Papers*, Vol. IV, 3073–3075.

12. Thus, whereas in U. S. law it is appropriate to think of and analyze the charitable deduction as a tax expenditure, in a system with a deed of covenant that perspective may be less helpful. Ironically, it is the deed of covenant system that separates the taxes forgone into a separate financial stream, which would greatly facilitate the identification and estimation of a tax expenditure.

The careful reader will note that I have not insisted on using the term "tax expenditure" in this paper even though the analysis is clearly within this school of thought. It is less important to reach agreement on whether or not a particular provision of tax law is a tax expenditure than to understand the effects that changes in tax law have on charitable donations. In this regard, Francis Gladstone, Head of Policy Planning for the National Council for Voluntary Organisations, has concluded, "it is quite clear that tax concessions for charities are not a right but a privilege granted by Parliament—a privilege that has to be justified like any other public policy." Francis Gladstone, *Charity, Law and Social Justice* (London: Bedford Square Press, 1982), 143.

The British government, itself, seems to be of two minds on this question. It feels that higher rate relief, for example, "is not a tax expenditure, it's letting people have more of their own money," but it grants this relief to individuals who make a particular type of expenditure, which can only be made to charities. Interview with Anthony Gray, Policy Division, Inland Revenue, July 8, 1983. And the government does now publish an estimate of tax expenditures in which taxes forgone via covenants are estimated: "Britain's Tax Expenditure," *The Economist* (January 27, 1979), 60–61.

Nevertheless, among researchers who have addressed the question of tax incentives for charitable contributions, there is no unanimity as to whether or not it is appropriate to use the tax expenditure concept to study charitable contributions. The tax expenditure concept is most comprehensively discussed in Stanley S. Surrey, *Pathways to Tax Reform* (Cambridge, Mass.: Harvard University Press, 1973). The merits of this concept have been debated in a number of articles: Boris I. Bittker, "Accounting for Federal 'Tax Subsidies' in the National Budget," *National Tax Journal*, 22 (1969): 244–261; Stanley S. Surrey and William F. Hellmuth, "The Tax Expenditure Budget—Response to Professor Bittker," *National Tax Journal*, 22 (1969): 528–537; Boris I. Bittker, "The Tax Expenditure Budget—A Reply to Professors Surrey and Hellmuth," *National Tax Journal*, 22 (1969): 538–542; Alan L. Feld, "Book Review of Surrey, *Pathways to Tax Reform*," *Harvard Law Review*, 88 (March 1975): 1047–1055; and Stanley S. Surrey and Paul R. McDaniel, "The Tax Expenditure Concept: Current Developments and Emerging Issues," *Boston College Law Review*, 20 (January 1979): 225–369. For an argument that the charitable contribution deduction is not a tax expenditure, see William D. Andrews, "Personal Deductions in an Ideal Income Tax," *Harvard Law Review*, 86 (December 1972): 309–385. For a slightly different argument that exemptions from estate taxes for charitable contributions are not tax expenditures, see John G. Simon, "Charity and Dynasty under the Federal Tax System," *The Probate Lawyer* 5 (Summer 1978): 1–92 (also available as Yale Program on Non-Profit Organizations Working Paper 5).

13. For a clear presentation of the differences between net and gross deeds of covenant, see Michael Norton, *Covenants: A Practical Guide to the Tax Advantages of Giving* (London: Directory of Social Change, 1983), Chapter 3.

14. Interviews with Anthony Gray, Policy Division, Inland Revenue, July 8, 1983, and with G. Norman Donaldson, Deputy Director, Charities Aid Foundation, July 11, 1983.

15. Bouuaert, op. cit., 104.

16. An admirably clear description of higher rate relief can be found in Norton, op. cit., 34–46.

17. *Charity Statistics 1982/83* (Tonbridge, Kent, England: Charities Aid Foundation, 1983), 7.

18. National Council for Voluntary Organisations, *Report of the NCVO Working Party—1982* (London: NCVO, 1982), 3, and interview with Francis Gladstone, Head of Policy and Planning, National Council for Voluntary Organisations, July 12, 1983.

19. National Council for Voluntary Organisations, Press Release, "Charities Say: 20 Million Pound Tax Concession Isn't Working," August 13, 1982, 2.

20. For a more detailed discussion of Inland Revenue's perspective on the deed of covenant, see Schuster, "Tax Incentives for Charitable Donations," op. cit., 360–361.

21. All of these schemes for circumventing the deed of covenant system are detailed in Norton, op. cit., Chapters 3–9.

22. For a detailed discussion of corporate deeds of covenant, see Schuster, "Tax Incentives for Charitable Donations," op. cit., 347–350.

23. Correspondence from D. H. Parmee, Inspector of Taxes, Claims Branch, Inland Revenue, June 21, 1983.

24. "Alms and the Man in the Street," *The Guardian*, December 2, 1981.

25. Hamish R. Sandison and Jennifer Williams, eds., *Tax Policy and Private Support for the Arts in the United States, Canada and Great Britain* (Washington, D.C.: British American Arts Association, 1981), 62.

26. For a detailed description of these tax provisions, see Her Majesty's Treasury, "Capital Taxation and the National Heritage" (London: Her Majesty's Stationery Office, July 1983). Information pertaining specifically to works of art can be found in a brochure distributed by the Office of Arts and Libraries, "Works of Art: A Basic Guide to Capital Taxation and the National Heritage" (London: Her Majesty's Stationery Office, 1982).

27. Her Majesty's Treasury, "Capital Taxation and the National Heritage," op. cit., 1.

28. Ibid.

29. Correspondence from David Denton, Policy Division, Inland Revenue, October 4, 1983.

30. Pierre Guerre, "Interest-Motivated Patronage of the Arts and the French Legislation of 1968," in *Support for the Creative Arts: Three Examples (Canada, France, and Spain)* (Paris: UNESCO, 1978), 51–68.

31. Correspondence from David Denton, op. cit.

32. The criteria for determining if an object is of national importance for purposes of granting an export license are in the form of three questions:

> Is the object so closely connected with our history and national life that its departure would be a misfortune?
>
> Is it of outstanding aesthetic importance?
>
> Is it of outstanding significance for the study of some particular branch of art, learning or history?

Office of Arts and Libraries, op. cit., 1982, 1.

33. "Britain Stymies Getty Coup,"*The Boston Globe*, August 9, 1984, 43, and Robert Lenzner, "A Getty Takes on the Getty Museum," *The Boston Globe*, August 16, 1984, 2.

34. Office of Arts and Libraries, op. cit., 1982, 2.

35. For many years the public collections deducted the full amount of the tax exemption in arriving at a price for a private treaty sale. But it was felt that this gave owners no particular incentive to sell to the nation, so the practice developed of offering a higher price, giving the seller the benefit of a part of the exemption. This practice was supported by the Waverley Committee in 1952. In 1957 the policy of offering 25 percent of the forgone taxes was set out in a Treasury Circular, and that practice has been followed ever since.

36. All the arguments concerning level and flexibility of the douceur are nicely summarized in House of Commons, *Minutes of Evidence Taken Before The Education, Science and Arts Committee*, Supplementary Memorandum Submitted by the Department of Education and Science, Office of Arts and Libraries (London: Her Majesty's Stationery Office, February 4, 1981), 78–82.

37. Norton, op. cit., 37.

38. House of Commons, op. cit., p. 78.

39. Correspondence from David Denton, op. cit.

40. "Le Marche de l'Art Moderne en France," *Cahiers du Travailleur Intellectuel*, No. 133, second trimester, 1979.

41. Ibid. The right of retention gives the government control over the exportation of works of art by deceased artists, created more than 20 years before the date of the exportation request. The government can prohibit exit, stopping exportation without changing the ownership of the work, or purchase the work at the value declared by the exporter in the case of a *sortie definitive*. This right has been criticized for having reinforced the differences between national and international prices for artworks and for having driven the international art trade underground.

42. House of Commons, *Third Report from the Education, Science and Arts Committee*, Session 1980–81, "Public and Private Funding of the Arts: Interim Report on Works of Art: Their Retention in Britain and Their Acquisition by Public Bodies," paper 275 (London: Her Majesty's Stationery Office, April 6, 1981).

43. At one time the Conservative Political Center, in a pamphlet, *Government and the Arts*, explicitly went on record as opposing such a twofold incentive:

> We are *not* in favor of this country following the American example of allowing individual

citizens to set against their income tax liabilities (some or all of) the money spent on buying works of art [for eventual donation].

. . . It enables very rich people to buy works of art for their personal enjoyment during their lifetime more or less at the taxpayer's expense. The national collections should be added to by curators, not by business tycoons. Its introduction in America has had the effect of forcing up the market value of works of art throughout the world, and of making it harder for all of our collectors, both public and private, to retain or purchase the world's masterpieces. This is a piece of artistic snobbishness we cannot afford.

Quoted in John E. Booth, *Government Support to the Performing Arts in Western Europe*, Prepared for the Special Studies Project, Rockefeller Brothers Fund, Inc., February 19, 1964.

44. Law Number 68–1251, December 31, 1968, Paris.

45. Pierre Cabanne, "Le Fabuleux Heritage du Fisc," *Matin Magazine*, June 18, 1983.

46. "Le Marche de 1'Art Moderne en France," *Cahiers du Travailleur Intellectuel*, No. 133, second trimester, 1979.

47. Jacques Michel, "La Strategie du Moindre Risque," *Le Monde*, December 31, 1980 and Pierre Cabanne, "Le Fabuleux Heritage du Fisc," *Matin Magazine*, June 18, 1983.

48. For a detailed technical discussion of taxation of artists' income in the EEC see Ignace Claeys Bouuaert, *Fiscal Problems of Cultural Workers in the States of the European Economic Community*, Commission of the European Communities, XII/1039/77-EN, August 1977.

49. Correspondence from M. Dowling, Office of the Revenue Commissioners, Dublin, Ireland, April 10, 1984.

50. Dorothy Walker, "Artists and Irish Taxes," *Art in America*, May-June 1971.

51. It is also interesting to compare the indirect subsidy of the artist in the Irish income tax to a broad direct aid program such as the 'Artists' Scheme" in the Netherlands. See R. Gerritse, *Money for Artists*, Institute for Research into Government Expenditure, Study commissioned for the Dutch Ministry of Culture, Recreation and Social Work, undated, 15–21.

52. Correspondence from M. Dowling, op. cit.

53. *30 Jours d'Europe*, No. 216–217, July–August 1976, 14, quoted in Bouuaert, *Fiscal Problems of Cultural Workers*, op. cit., 30.

54. Correspondence from M. Dowling, op. cit.

55. Dorothy Walker, "Artists and Irish Taxes," and Tom McGurk, "Tax-Free Artists," *Ireland Today*, Bulletin of the Department of Foreign Affairs, No. 902, February 15, 1977, 6–7.

56. *30 Jours d'Europe*, op. cit.

57. Dorothy Walker, op. cit.

58. Correspondence from M. Dowling, op. cit.

59. Ibid.

60. Secretariat d'Etat à la Culture, "Les Aides Publiques à la Création Artistique en Italie," *Notes d'Information*. October 1976, 7.

61. Elias Newman, statement at *Public Hearings on General Tax Reform*, United States House of Representatives, Committee on Ways and Means, 93rd Cong., 1st sess., April 11, 1973.

62. Correspondence from Aadrian Kieboom, Dutch Ministry of Culture, Recreation and Social Work, January 29, 1980.

63. Raymonde Moulin, *Public Aid for Creation in the Plastic Arts* (Oslo: Council of Europe, 1976).

64. For a more complete discussion of permanent capital taxes in the European Economic Community, see Bouuaert, *Taxation of Cultural Foundations*, op. cit., 105–117 and 135–138.

65. Bouuaert, *Taxation of Cultural Foundations*, op. cit., 115.

66. Howard Becker, *Art Worlds* (Berkeley, Calif.: University of California Press, 1982), 172, paraphrasing Raymonde Moulin, *Le Marche de la Peinture en France* (Paris: Les Editions de Minuit, 1967), and Gerald Reitlinger, *The Economics of Taste: The Rise and Fall of Picture Prices 1760–1960* (London: Barrie and Rockliff, 1961).

67. Hugh Jenkins, *The Culture Gap: An Experience of Government and the Arts* (London: Marion Boyars, 1979), 140–162.

68. Ibid. 149.

69. To get a flavor of the debate in the French press on this issue, turn to any of the major newspapers or newsmagazines published during late October and early November 1981. A particularly clearly reasoned article in English is Souren Melikian, "Taxes and Art in France," *The International Herald Tribune*, November 10, 1981.

70. Nadine Descendre, "Les Marchands Exultent: Pour Faire de l'Or en Art," *Nouvelles Litteraires*, November 26, 1981.

71. Gerritse, op. cit., 85.

72. House of Commons, *Third Report from the Education, Science and Arts Committee*, Session 1981–82, "Public and Private Funding of the Arts: Interim Report on Value-Added Taxes and the Arts," paper 239 (London: Her Majesty's Stationery Office, March 3, 1982), iii–iv.

It may be misleading to look only at VAT rates for cultural services for purpose of comparison because various countries have additional taxes that they levy on concert, theatre, or film admissions. Occasionally these are entertainment taxes, which may be discontinued when the VAT rate is raised from a reduced rate to the standard rate, leaving the total level of taxation roughly constant. Other times these are special taxes that are levied for self-financing within a particular cultural sector, e.g., the TSA, a "Special Additional Tax" on admissions to French films, which raises money that is fed directly back into the French film industry.

73. For a brief summary of these arguments, see Ibid. For the government's response to the third point, see "Public and Private Funding of the Arts: Government Response to Interim Report on Value-Added Tax and the Arts (HC Paper 239)" (London: Her Majesty's Stationery Office, June 29, 1982), paragraph 8. See also Harold Baldry, *The Case for the Arts* (London: Secker & Warburg, 1981), 70. A useful summary of this debate is contained in Clive Priestley, *The Financial Affairs and Financial Prospects of the Royal Opera House, Covent Garden Ltd., and the Royal Shakespeare Company*, a report to the Office of Arts and Libraries (London: Her Majesty's Stationery Office, October 1983), 65–66.

74. House of Commons, "Public and Private Funding of the Arts: Interim Report on Value-Added Taxes and the Arts," op. cit., iii–iv.

75. "Public and Private Funding of the Arts: Government Response to Interim Report on Value-Added Tax and the Arts (HC Paper 239)," op. cit.

76. Ibid. The irony of this quote lies in the fact that at the same time both the Conservative Party and the Liberal Party in their election manifestos were calling for reductions in VAT for the arts.

77. "Fiscalité et Culture," Research Note DT/500, Service des Etudes et de la Recherche, Ministère de la Culture et de la Communication, Paris, October 1979, 4.

78. The Council of Europe has sponsored a substantial amount of research on the problems facing the cultural industries. For a discussion of the role played by VAT, see *Cinema and the State*, Report of the Committee on Culture and Education, Document 4306-E (Strasbourg: Council of Europe, 1979), xxiv–xxxi and 33–35, or Committee on Education and Culture, Council for Cultural Cooperation, Cultural Affairs, *The State's Role Vis-à-Vis the Culture Industries* (Strasbourg: Council of Europe, April 1980), 149, 156. See also *Les Industries Culturelles*, Notes et Etudes Documentaires 4535–4536 (Paris: La Documentation Française, Nov. 12, 1979), 157.

79. High rates in certain countries have contributed to piracy of records and tapes. See Gillian Davies, *Piracy of Phonograms*, report XII/235/80-EN, a study for the Commission of the European Communities presented at a conference, *The State's Role Vis-à-vis the Culture Industries*," op. cit. Other information on VAT and the record market can be found in *L'Economie du Disque en France*, Notes et Etudes Documentaires (Paris: La Documentation Francaise), and in "Une Affaire D'Etat: La TVA et le Disque," *Diapason*, 24, January 1978.

80. Sir Anthony Lousada, "Tax and the EEC with Special Reference to VAT," in *Arts and the EEC*, proceedings of a conference of the Institute of Contemporary Art, London, 1979.

For an argument that artworks are not consumer goods and, therefore, should be considered as being outside the field of application of VAT, see Bouuaert, *Taxation of Cultural Foundations*, op. cit., 148–152, and *Fiscal Problems of Cultural Workers,* op. cit., 82–86.

81. Bouuaert, *Taxation of Cultural Foundations*, op. cit., 160–166, and *Fiscal Problems of Cultural Workers*, op. cit., 88–90, "Fiscalité et Culture," op. cit., 5; and Gerritse, op. cit., p. 88.

82. For a more detailed presentation of how this might happen, see Feld, O'Hare, and Schuster, *Patrons Despite Themselves,* op. cit., 207–209.

83. *Charity Law and Voluntary Organisations: Report of the Goodman Committee* (London: Bedford Square Press, 1976), paragraph 128.

84. Baldry, op. cit., 70.

85. Interviews with staff, Arts Council of Great Britain, July 1983.

Index